Praise for *Churning the Earth*

'A masterly, definitive analysis shows the present model of globalization to be a ruthless, job-destroying gamble . . . [The authors'] counsel needs to be heard in South Block and Yojana Bhavan'—*Outlook*

'Provides a comprehensive and rigorous critique of India's path of development'—*Economic & Political Weekly*

'A well-documented, cogently argued and clearly presented people's audit of the Reform Regime'—*The Hindu*

'This book must be read by all those who care not only about India's future but also that of the world, because it is often at the peripheries of empires that successful rebellions are born'—*Himal*

'The critique of India's political economy in *Churning the Earth* has real bite. It is important to ask, as Shrivastava and Kothari do, what kind of world do we want, and what kind of democracy might get us there'—*Oryx*

'[The book gives] a comprehensive framework and [interlinks] a range of issues precisely and cogently . . . It's the best introduction to contemporary India'—*Down to Earth*

'[This is by far the most ambitious attempt] at exposing the toxic side of the India growth story'—*Book Review*

'This book should be made mandatory reading for all gung-ho neo-liberals . . . a searing critique of the country's recent development strategies'—*DNA*

'The authors very purposefully and very passionately convince the reader that India needs a radical change . . . [A] "must-read"'—*Biblio*

'Shrivastava and Kothari have convincingly shown the urgency of countering economic exploitation and environmental devastation'—*Tribune*

'This is a book that everyone involved with public and developmental policy must read'—*Sanctuary Asia*

'[An] incisive analysis of the reforms era . . . The book busts the myth of cities as great levellers of human equity . . . *Churning the Earth* is as much a book of ideas as it is of ethics'—*Sunday Post*

'[It is a must] for every seemingly informed, aware and sentient Indian'—*First City*

PENGUIN BOOKS

CHURNING THE EARTH

Aseem Shrivastava holds a doctorate in environmental economics from the University of Massachusetts, Amherst. He has taught economics for many years in India and the US, and has also taught philosophy at Nordic College, Norway. Since 2005, he has been working independently, researching, writing and lecturing internationally on issues associated with globalization and its impact. He was a speaker at the 2012 World Conservation Congress, in South Korea, and at the 2013 World Social Forum, in Tunisia. He lives in Delhi.

Ashish Kothari is a founder-member of the environmental group Kalpavriksh. He has taught at the Indian Institute of Public Administration, coordinated India's National Biodiversity Strategy and Action Plan process, served on the boards of Greenpeace International and India, and chaired an International Union for Conservation of Nature network dealing with protected areas and communities. He has been active with various peoples' movements and has authored and edited over thirty books.

CHURNING THE EARTH

ASEEM SHRIVASTAVA
ASHISH KOTHARI

PENGUIN BOOKS

PENGUIN BOOKS

USA | Canada | UK | Ireland | Australia
New Zealand | India | South Africa | China

Penguin Books is part of the Penguin Random House group of companies
whose addresses can be found at global.penguinrandomhouse.com

Published by Penguin Random House India Pvt. Ltd
7th Floor, Infinity Tower C, DLF Cyber City,
Gurgaon 122 002, Haryana, India

Penguin
Random House
India

First published in Viking by Penguin Books India 2012
Published in Penguin Books 2014

ISBN 9780143422709

Typeset in AGaramond by SÜRYA, New Delhi

Printed at Repro Knowledgecast Limited, India

www.penguin.co.in

The book is dedicated to the memory of Smitu Kothari, Edward Goldsmith, Ravi Sankaran, Narendranath Gorepati, Rajendra Sadangi, K. Balagopal, Baba Amte and Girish Sant (the last of whom passed away even as we read the final proofs)—all of them dared to imagine a different world and inspired us to dream differently. Above all, the book is dedicated to the many movements for ecological and social justice taking place today, in India and elsewhere. On their ultimate victory rests the future of this country and the world.

'I think that I shall never see
A billboard lovely as a tree.
Perhaps unless the billboards fall,
I'll never see a tree at all.'

—Ogden Nash

CONTENTS

PART II

DAWN: There *Is* an Alternative

ACRONYMS

ADB	Asian Development Bank
APL	above the poverty line
BJP	Bharatiya Janata Party
BPL	below the poverty line
BRICS	Brazil, Russia, India, China, South Africa
CPM/CPI(M)	Communist Party of India (Marxist)
CSO(s)	civil society organization(s)
EIA	Environment Impact Assessment
EU	European Union
FAO	Food and Agricultural Organization
FDI	foreign direct investment
FII	foreign institutional investment
FMCG	fast-moving consumer goods
GDP	gross domestic product
GHI	Global Hunger Index
GM	genetically modified
GoI	Government of India
HDI	Human Development Index
IFI	international financial institution
ILO	International Labour Organization

IMF	International Monetary Fund
IT	information technology
MFI	microfinance institutions
MGNREGA	Mahatma Gandhi National Rural Employment Guarantee Act
MNC	multinational corporation
MoEF	ministry of environment and forests
MPI	multidimensional poverty index
NCEUS	National Commission for Enterprises in the Unorganized Sector
NGO	non-governmental organization
NRI	non-resident Indian
NSS	National Sample Survey
OECD	Organization for Economic Co-operation and Development
PDS	public distribution system
PPP	public–private partnership
RBI	Reserve Bank of India
RED	radical ecological democracy
RTI	Right to Information
SAP	Structural Adjustment Programme
SEZ	Special Economic Zone
TNC	transnational corporation
UN	United Nations
UNDP	United Nations Development Programme
UNEP	United Nations Environment Programme
UPA	United Progressive Alliance
WTO	World Trade Organization

PREFACE

SAMUDRA MANTHAN:
THE GREAT CHURNING

This book takes its title from an ancient Hindu myth in India, which involves the churning of the ocean after the great flood. *Amrit*, the nectar of immortality, was lost in the flood. At the instigation of Vishnu, the devas and the asuras embark on a search for it. Vishnu dives to the bottom of the ocean and takes on the avatar of a tortoise on whose back the churning-pole Mount Mandara arises, the churning-string, the snake Vasuki, coiled around it.

As the devas and the asuras tug at the snake and churn the ocean, a terrible poison (*vish*) rises from the depths. Shiva is approached and he generously drinks the poison, holding it in his throat, which turns his face and neck blue, earning him the epithet Neelkantha. Meanwhile, amrit surfaces as well. The devas and the asuras battle over it. Vishnu takes on the incarnation of the seductress Mohini to tempt the asuras, who are thus led to part with the amrit. Vishnu then hands it to the devas.*

*We have taken recourse to this myth from one of the myriad traditions that the people of the subcontinent share. We could as easily have taken a story from another tradition elsewhere. Readers should

We take this story as a metaphor for the great churning that India is going through. The last couple of decades of globalized 'development', in particular, have brought about far-reaching social, cultural, political, economic and ecological changes. Some of these are a continuation of the past, some entirely new. A considerable amount of 'vish' is emerging, in the form of social disruption, increasing inequalities and environmental damage; simultaneously, a variety of initiatives, struggles and movements are resisting the vish and attempting to find alternative paths to human welfare—the 'amrit' that can bring some semblance of sanity to a country driven by a fierce energy today.

After reading this book, readers can make up their minds as to how they interpret the changes India is going through, in terms of the metaphor—or whether they think a different metaphor might be more appropriate. For us, the purpose would have been served if the book gives some flavour of the great churning and the directions it is taking us in.

The book

Has India ever had it so good? It is today perceived as one of the centres of the world. It is one of the fastest-growing economies. There are real hopes all around that one day we will finally overcome the defeatist legacies of centuries of feudalism and foreign rule and become a fully industrialized, developed country that can hold its head high in the family of world nations, if not

---

not read more into this choice than there is, and certainly not interpret our choice to imply that we favour any one religion or tradition over another. We outrightly condemn communal and fundamentalist beliefs or forces of any sort whatsoever, including attempts by such forces to co-opt environmental or social issues to suit their own motives.

also turn into a formidable superpower. The promise of globalization is immense. The fruit is ripe for plucking and, it appears, India has just a little more to go before it acquires the height and stability to collect big harvests.

This book, however, is written to throw light on the fate of people and communities who are being left behind or being abandoned in India's pursuit of prosperity through globalized development. The disprivileged multitudes of this country—worthy individual citizens and communities of great potential—are suffering on account of the corruption and irresponsibility of successive governments and powerful corporations, and the often misdirected ambitions, follies and excesses of the privileged elite.

The book also addresses those concerned about India's ecological fate, threatened as never before by the predatory impact of growth under globalized competition. It attempts to show that if the warning signs multiplying around us are not heeded very soon, the future of India as a society and a civilization is threatened, thereby implicating every citizen, howsoever privileged he or she may currently be.

'The India story' is easy to misunderstand and overestimate unless placed in the wider context of a rapidly deteriorating environment and a globalized world economy. The context of globalized competition has reshuffled the pack for everyone. Within India it has created more dangers than opportunities as far as the majority of the people are concerned.

Time is not on our side. We are on different coaches of a long, accelerating, burning train. The few air-conditioned coaches in the front are insulated for the time being from the fire that is blazing in the coaches at the back, where the majority of the passengers travel. Some of the coaches have already derailed (think of the 200,000 farmer suicides). However, the wealthy people in the AC coaches want the engine staff to run the train even faster. The latter are fully aware that the flames will be further fed by the wind if the speed is increased, creating many more derailments and casualties. But they are either seduced by the thrill of the ride or appear helpless before the pressure brought upon them by the occupants of the luxury coaches (both Indians and foreigners), no less than by the international station-masters (the International Monetary Fund and the World Bank) who are cheering on each such national train in the ruthless economic race that globalization has unleashed between nations.

There is very little doubt that the reforms which began in the early 1990s (though many of the policy trends date to the 1980s) have brought great material benefits to the richest 10 to 25 per cent of India's population. Not only is this quite palpably true, it is a fact that we underscore in this book, arguing that the same set of policies which have brought such great benefits to the rich have spelt (further) disaster for the poor. As apprehensively acknowledged on occasion by the prime minister himself, the reforms have been socially divisive. The votaries of the reforms, however, argue that they have served not only the interests of the rich, they have answered—or perhaps will eventually answer—the needs of the poor as well. This is what gives the reform process its moral legitimacy.

It is this contention we take issue with. We argue that there are strong empirical grounds for rejecting such a belief. There are also theoretical reasons for doubting that the future will absolve the reformers. Time might reveal that what they have been trying to do—tackle age-old poverty through the deregulation of the market, the withdrawal of the state and further empowerment of the corporate elite—is both politically and ecologically impossible with such a model of economic growth. Further growth along these lines is likely to put terribly destructive strains on both the ecological fabric and human society in this part of the world, as also elsewhere.

Is the prevailing structure of policies serving the needs of the multitudes in whose name the reforms are being carried out? Or is it creating new forms of poverty—through displacement, indebtedness, dispossession, agricultural decline and jobless growth? What is its impact on nature and the availability of resources? Whose interests are *actually* being served by the policies at work?

It should be clear from the outset that both the assumptions as well as the consequences of the growth processes unleashed by the prevailing model of globalized development stretch well beyond the normal purview of economics. They impact the totality of things in earthly existence, in addition to shaping our cognition and perception of these things. Entire ways of life, culture and thought have been and continue to be disrupted, often uprooted, by the forces whose best intellectual defence is modern mainstream economics. Despite accumulating evidence to the contrary, most economists continue to obstinately defend the central role of markets in human affairs. There are, of course, notable exceptions to the orthodox view.

Such an ideological predicament—ultimately made possible by the most powerful technologies (of extraction, production, distribution, consumption and, not to forget, propaganda and surveillance) ever invented—is unprecedented in all of history. Apart from the obvious economic consequences, the forces of globalization today exert a profound influence on values, culture, political organization, inter-community relations and, above all, ecosystems. Their study demands a far-reaching, *holistic* treatment involving practitioners across a wide range of disciplines as much as the millions of citizens engaged in various activities and professions. This book will argue that the specialized, fragmented and compartmentalized way of analysing the impact of globalization that most economists and other 'experts' adopt is itself a serious part of the problem.

The authors of this book cannot pretend to do justice to an intellectual challenge as formidable as the one that confronts the troubled human imagination today. We can only hope to contribute to the creation of the groundwork for fresh public debate on issues which were considered resolved till very recently, particularly in India. Unless such a dialogue is reopened and, additionally, opened up to radically new possibilities, it is a matter of some doubt whether our imperilled species will survive beyond the next few generations. Relying on a wide range of contemporary empirical research and reportage, we feel compelled to suggest, in all humility, and with all due respect to so many people of great ability and character, who have cast their lot with the growth process, that the mistakes made today will profoundly compound difficulties for generations to come.

Structure of the book

The book is written in two unequal parts. The first part (eight chapters) examines the impact of globalization during the reform era, observing both the continuities and the changes from the past, while describing economic, ecological, political and other dimensions. The second part (three chapters) reviews experiments and initiatives being undertaken across the country, which may contribute to the emergence of alternative visions we call 'radical ecological democracy'. Some of the policy alternatives are inevitably fuzzy and imprecise. We have tried to follow the economist John Maynard Keynes's precept in aiming at being 'vaguely right, rather than precisely wrong'.

Chapter 1 provides an overview of contemporary globalization. Chapters 2 and 3 examine the content and socio-economic impact of the reforms. Chapters 4 and 5 scrutinize the ecological consequences, while chapters 6 and 7 take a close look at the old issues of town and country that have resurfaced in the reform era. Chapter 8 takes a critical look at the goal of globalized growth. Chapters 9 and 10 consider alternatives within the overarching framework of radical ecological democracy. Chapter 11 sums up the book.

Readers can read the book selectively, according to their interests and specialization. We have tried to index thoroughly and cross-reference material between the chapters so as to facilitate this. Some repetition and overlap of content across chapters is inevitable in a book like this. We beg the reader's patience for this.

Readership

The book is written for an uninitiated readership, while seeking, at the same time, a reckoning with prevailing policies and some of the edges of critical debates. Thus, while the lay reader may find some sections somewhat challenging (especially in chapters 2, 3 and 4), other readers trained in the social sciences (especially economics) may sometimes find some of the material only too familiar, if not banal. Our hope is that in the space between the gleanings of the interested amateur and the provocations to the experienced professional, the issues become clearer and the urgency for radical policy changes comes through.

Given the scope of the themes that globalization involves, readers abroad should find the book as much of interest as those in India.

A caveat

The manuscript of this book was completed in August 2010. As a result, we have not been able to use data that has appeared since then (such as the preliminary results of the Census of India 2011). While, in general, it is unlikely that the new data would substantially affect the main arguments presented in the text, they may change some of the specific nuances.

Acknowledgements

The primary lesson we have learnt is that a project as challenging as this cannot be undertaken by two individuals! It has benefited so much from the attention and help it has received from a large number of people that it would never have seen the light of day without their support. Some of them are mentioned here.

Thomas Mathew read through most parts of the manuscript, offering unerring editorial and intellectual advice over many conversations. Others who commented on significant portions of the manuscript, helping us correct many a mistake and add interesting insights are Anand Swamy, Sunny Narang, Jean Drèze, Sunanda Sen, Alejandro Nadal, Kavaljit Singh, Rohan D'Souza, Dilip Simeon, Ravi Agarwal, K.J. Joy, Shripad Dharmadhikary, Milind Wani and Tejaswani Apte. Additional inputs, inspiration and support in various forms were provided by the following people: Jaya and Umesh Shrivastava, Sumant Shrivastava, Admiral and Lalita Ramdas, N. Madhusudan, Sagari Ramdas, Maya Joshi, Sudhir Pattnaik, Prafulla Samantara, Bhaskar Goswami, Manali Chakrabarti, Rahul Varman, Rajendra Singh, Priyanka Seshadri, Nancy Sebastian, Arshia Sattar, Sanjay Iyer, Amita Baviskar, Amar Kanwar, Vrinda Grover, Reena Singh, Archana Agarwal, Budhaditya Das,

Late K. Balagopal, V.S. Krishna, Rajendra Kumar, Dibyajyoti Ghosh, Satvir Singh Gulia, Prem P. Verma, Banwari Lal Sharma, Manoj Tyagi, Swapnil Shrivastava, Mike Levien, Manshi Asher, Patrik Oskarsson, Manju Menon, Kanchi Kohli, Lalit Batra, Sunil, Kavitha Kuruganti, Utkarsh Ghate, Avani Mohan Singh, H. Harish Hande, Suresh Kr. Challa, Nandini Oza, Ravindranath, Arshiya Urveeja Bose, Amit Srivastava, Karen Coelho, Shalini Bhutani, P.V. Satheesh, Marie-Hélène Zerah, Lakshmi Narayan, Bablu Ganguly, Dinesh Abrol, Sujatha Padmanabhan, Himanshu Thakkar, Satish Sinha, Ravi Rebbapragada, Sanskriti Menon, Prashant Pastore, Prashant Bhushan, Uzramma, Carine Lundmark, S. Faizi, Neeraj Vagholikar, Suhas Paranjape, Neema Pathak, Vikal Samdariya, Rosemary Viswanath, Aarthi Sridhar, Sebastian Mathew, William Lockhart, Prarthana Banikya, Benny Kuruvilla, Nityanand Jayaraman, Afsar H. Jafri and Mihir Shah. At Penguin Books, R. Sivapriya's and Richa Burman's editorial inputs were invaluable. To all these people, we extend our sincere gratitude. There are many more who were of help to us at different stages of the project whose names are not mentioned here. Our apologies to them.

A special thanks to all those who provided quotes for the book, and apologies that in some cases we had to use excerpts due to constraints of space.

One of us (Aseem Shrivastava) was also supported by the Sangam House Writer's Residency Fellowship during January/ February 2009. Our special thanks to them.

In a book on a theme as contested and topical as the one we have chosen, there are bound to remain many errors, inaccuracies and imperfections. All such shortcomings are due to our own ignorance and limitations, rather than of those whose help and support we sought. We would be grateful if readers could draw our attention to any mistakes they come across, as also to additional information, insights and perspectives that we have not included.

PART I

TWILIGHT

There Is No Alternative

Prologue I

BHARAT ENCOUNTERS GLOBALIZATION

'OF WHAT USE IS MONEY?'

'A market economy,' the economic anthropologist Karl Polanyi wrote in the 1940s,

> can exist only in a market society . . . A market economy must comprise all elements of industry, including labor, land, and money. But labor and land are no other than the human beings themselves of which every society consists and the natural surroundings in which it exists. To include them in the market mechanism means to subordinate the substance of society itself to the laws of the market.[1]

The experience of India's industrialization under market-friendly economic policies confirms Polanyi's disturbing insight. Modern markets work very well for some, not for most. In the process, society as a whole gets subjugated to the requirements of those who control the market.

To meet the ideal of a free-market society hundreds of millions of Indians would need to quit agriculture and traditional occupations, vacate the villages and the forests and make way for modern infrastructure, industries and mines. In such a vision, a mobile phone in every other hand connotes 'development' and 'progress'. But seven out of ten Indians still live in villages. And, not able to see better prospects elsewhere, they are not about to abandon them.

Rural India encounters globalization

We are in a village called Pelpa in the Jhajjar district of Haryana, an hour's drive from New Delhi's international airport. The village falls in an area delineated for a Special Economic Zone (SEZ). It is a PPP, a 'public–private partnership'. The main developer is Reliance Industries, whose share in the project is 90 per cent. The other 10 per cent belongs to the Haryana government. The area they want to acquire is huge: 25,000 acres in all. This threatens to displace twenty-two villages in Jhajjar district and eighteen in Gurgaon. Most of the city of Chandigarh will fit into the SEZ if it ever sees the light of day. The land they want to acquire is almost entirely agricultural. Moreover, while water tables have fallen quite sharply in this Green Revolution region (thanks mainly to the water-intensive inputs required for the cultivation of high-yielding varieties of wheat), most farmers are of the view that the fertility of the land is such that were the government to invest in irrigation even a fraction of what it is doing in the SEZ, productivity would rise dramatically. Almost all of Haryana has fertile arable land. Other than the male youths we spoke to, few wished to quit farming.

At the time of writing, Reliance has not been able to acquire more than a third of the land they had targeted. (The memorandum of understanding was signed in 2005. They were supposed to have acquired all the land in two years, as per the law.) Even a price offer of Rs 22 lakh per acre has not been accepted by most farmers.

To be sure, some farmers (hedging their bets) have sold a part of their land. Others have made distress sales, given the tough economic conditions. But they have not been able to take advantage of the compensation money. We asked a farmer in Pelpa who was attending a meeting of the village elders (known as *tau*s) what he did with the money he had received from Reliance. He responded that he barely got to see the money. We asked whether Reliance had paid him. 'Of course,' he responded, 'but the boys took it away.'

Why did you give them the money, we asked. His response caught us totally off guard.

> My son put a pistol to my head and took the money away. This is becoming quite common here. They [the boys and the young men] are only interested in three things: *gadi*, *daroo*, *bandook* (cars, liquor and guns). Come with me one evening after sundown to the road which bisects the SEZ area. I will be able to show you the line of new jeeps [SUVs] parked along the road. Loud disco music blares out of the vehicles. The boys drink and make merry in them till the early hours of the morning. Our *bahu-beti*s (daughters-in-law and daughters) have stopped stepping out in the evening. It used to be very safe here. Now it isn't. The boys return home in the early hours of the morning, sleep till the afternoon, and in the evening return to their favourite hideaway to repeat the routine. How many months will Rs 22 lakh last if it is being burnt at this rate?

The farmer's wife arrives in the meantime.

> When money is so easy, why would anyone want to work in the fields? The boys drive to Gurgaon and blow up the money

there in no time. None of the young men is interested in agriculture. There is so little money in it. It's difficult to make a living through farming. The government has stopped all support for it, which makes it all the tougher. It is as though the government has decided for us how we are to live our lives. They are willing to give us money as compensation for the land. But do they realize that this is our traditional land, cultivated by our ancestors, our only source of permanent economic security? Of what use is money? How long will it last? The boys are young. They don't know how to handle money.

She goes on:

This is not just the forced takeover of our land and ancestral village, it is also the decimation of our culture and roots. Alcohol was always a problem in our villages. Now, with easy money, alcoholism is a daily nightmare. Men are out of control. Domestic violence is all too common. We do not belong to the city. And our own village seems alien to us now. *Hum toh kaheen ke nahin rahe* (We belong nowhere now) . . .

Rural society in Haryana is in a state of moral breakdown. A certain despair haunts people here. It is the despair of 'traumatized communities that have lost control over their fate', to employ the words of political psychologist Ashis Nandy.[2]

There is a sharp divergence of opinion in these parts of Haryana between the male youths and the older generation (especially women) regarding their future in agriculture. This became clear one morning while we were attending a *mahapanchayat* (meeting of panchayat heads from many different villages) in a village called Badli, close to Jhajjar.

At least a few hundred farmers from about twenty villages were present. There was more than an understandable level of tension in the air. We were informed that we could expect some trouble from local henchmen who had been bribed and instructed in advance to disrupt the meeting.

The meeting began and the *pradhan* (chief) of a neighbouring village began proceedings with a five-minute denunciation of the SEZ policy of the government. In particular, he expressed regret and anger that the government was acting as the *bichaula* (land broker) for a private corporation, tempting farmers here, scaring them elsewhere, to sell their land for industrial development.

Barely had the pradhan finished his speech when a group of about twenty young men from the area, dressed very differently in colourful shirts and trousers, suddenly appeared next to us and started telling us that most farmers were happily willing to part with their lands, that the men who had organized the meeting had already sold theirs and now wanted Reliance to pay a higher compensation. As the next speaker on the podium began to make his speech they stood up, started heckling from the side and ultimately succeeded in shouting him down. They tried to provoke a fist-fight. Fortunately, they did not get the desired response.

The elders wisely decided to suspend the meeting instead of beginning what would surely have turned into an ugly brawl. When we inquired into the identities of the thugs, it turned out that they were boys from the area, many of them from Badli itself. Reliance had turned young and restless villagers into commission agents. It seems they had been given some petty sums of money and liquor the previous night to disrupt the meeting of the elders.

They had also been promised 'jobs' with the company once the SEZ came up. No interviews, no consideration of merit, skill or qualifications. Promises, backed with small change, were enough to buy out the restless youths, eager for urban excitement.

'Reliance agents are getting false affidavits made by farmers, saying that they need money for their children's education, that their land is barren: *banjar zameen*. It's interesting that what they call "banjar zameen" produced 15–20 quintals of wheat per acre last year! You can check the records at the revenue office,' Azad Singh, an aged farmer from Badli, told us. He was also sceptical of what people like him could do with the compensation money:

> What we know best and have done all our lives for generations is farming. How do they expect us to change our occupation at this stage and run some sort of business? In any case, it should be our decision, not theirs. Why should we be condemned to disposability by people willing to shove some money into our pockets? If a hungry man is presented a mound of cash and a plate of food, what will he pick?

'And what will happen to those who do not own any land and work for daily wages on your fields?' we asked Azad Singh. 'Who can say? They are the most disposable of all,' he replied.

A month after the May Day mahapanchayat, news arrived that a young man had been shot dead at point-blank range at the Chaupal quadrangle in Badli village. Old rituals of revenge decide issues when state policies are unsupportive of rural communities.

Like its other big project in Raigad, Maharashtra, Reliance's SEZ project is very far from meeting its land acquisition needs, thanks to the resistance of the farmers. The free market in land is not working for the corporations. Hence, state interventions are being sought.

Meanwhile, social tensions and conflicts proliferate.

Urban poor face globalization

New Delhi has been witness to a tidal wave of slum evictions over the past few decades. Here is a typical testimony, one among tens of thousands, from someone who lost his home to the Commonwealth Games:[3]

> These politicians don't want to remove poverty. They just want to remove the poor . . . Our livelihood, our place of worship and our children's education are all over here. Why are they destroying our lives and sending us to a place that has no scope for livelihood, no education, and no medical facilities? . . . You are just removing the poor from your sight . . . (Sadik Dholakwala)

There are 49,000 slums in India according to the NSS (National Sample Survey Organization) surveys of 2008–09. Many of those who have lost land and/or livelihood in the countryside, or who find conditions in villages oppressive, move to the cities in search of work, and they end up finding accommodation only in the mushrooming slums. These settlements are usually illegal, patronized by political parties and politicians who need the votes of the poor.

Many states in India have official slum clearance boards alongside the development authorities. In the years before the reforms, slum demolitions were occasional events, which caused great public outrage, such as in Delhi during the Emergency years of the 1970s. In recent decades, the drive towards beautification and seizure of urban land for real estate, industrial or retail projects or for building infrastructure (albeit for sports events) has accelerated the pace of evictions.

Indian metros have virtually become financial products, increasingly designed and reshaped to attract not merely international capital but also skilled manpower, like consultants and technical professionals who, in turn, need sanitized, 'global' environments (state-of-the-art infrastructure, hospitals, etc.) for their everyday work. Before such a horizon, the dirt and stink of slums has no place. For the authorities they have become a source of shame and embarrassment and thus their demolition is now quite frequent and routine. Steady and loud political protests have failed to resist the onslaught.

It is impossible to know how many people have been evicted in urban and metropolitan India during the past two decades (for a more detailed discussion, see chapter 3). The state does not keep records. In the paranoid middle-class narrative, slums are dens of crime and squalor which threaten both social peace and public health. The crime is hugely exaggerated. Given the high population densities, there is hardly any, in stark contrast to most big metropolitan centres of the Western world. It is true that the slums are largely illegal, just like some colonies inhabited by the rich. It is also true that they tend to be dirty, there being few public services, if any. There is usually no drinking water source or public sanitation. Ironically, it is the poor who have to shoulder the blame for the rights and opportunities *denied* to them. What drives people to live under such conditions is necessity, not choice. And the necessity (as we will see later in the book) is driven by the same developmental logic which is enriching India's elite and the middle classes. As with rural displacement, the victims are largely from social groups routinely discriminated against—Dalits, adivasis and OBCs (Other Backward Classes).

This, in fact, is not exclusion. It is outright *rejection*—the same fate to which our forest-dwelling adivasi populations are being subjected. It is a process which provokes almost certain dehumanization, especially among the male youth, sometimes giving rise to violence and precisely the crime the slum demolitions are meant to eradicate.

The enormous, undeniable contribution that the people who live in the jhuggis make to the life of the city—from cleaning the streets and watering the parks and gardens of the well-off classes to providing all the domestic help and everyday technical assistance (plumbing, electrical work, carpentry, etc.) to them— is readily forgotten when slums are targeted by the middle-class resident welfare associations. The latter, all too keen to see India build 'world-class' cities through the shortest route, happily use the police or the judiciary to 'clean' and 'beautify' urban centres. In Delhi, slums occupy less than 2 per cent of the land, but are often accused of grabbing land.[4]

As the Jawaharlal Nehru National Urban Renewal Mission (JNNURM) gets under way in sixty-odd cities, there are fears that slum evictions will grow in frequency and brutality. According to housing rights writer Kalyani Menon-Sen, 'The total number of families affected by evictions in the 64 cities where JNNURM is currently being implemented is estimated by activists at well over one million'—a number comparable to that of people already thrown out of their homes during the last decade.[5]

There are countries where the state takes responsibility for the provision of public housing. In a country like Singapore, as much as 85 per cent of the population lives in houses provided by the government, many of them having become part-home-owners over time. In India, public housing for the poor is nearly non-existent in most cities. It is an area where private investment cannot go very far for the obvious reason that there is little profit to be made from the poor. This is why in so many countries (including most countries in the West) housing for the poor has been subsidized by the state.[6]

I

GLOBALIZATION?

'I would define "globalization" as freedom for my company to invest where it wants for as long as it wants, and to produce whatever it wants, by getting its supplies and selling its products wherever it wants, and by having to endure the fewest possible constraints in labour law and collective agreements.'

—Percy Barnevik, president of the
Swiss–Swedish group ABB, 1995[1]

In praise of globalization

Has there ever been a better time to be an Indian? The evidence grows by the hour. Few other places in the world today abound in so many success stories. The future glows with a hope that has eluded us for centuries. We seem to have conquered, once and for all, the worst memories of subjection to centuries of feudal and colonial rule. The 'New India' brims with entrepreneurial energy and youth. Both demographics and visual observation tell us we are the youngest country in the world. At the same time, we are also one of the oldest civilizations. The combination of the two facts places us in a uniquely enviable 'league of one', especially when we remember our sheer size.

The recent expansion of opportunities reflects particularly in the growing confidence and global success of our sportspersons, our artists, actors, writers, scientists and scholars, not to forget the acumen and vision of our entrepreneurs and business leaders. A new breed of young politicians is said to provide the promise that even that most ill-reputed class could be in for a change. For those watching us from around the world, it is more than evident that 'Global India' has arrived, drawing behind it the empowering legacy of centuries of cultural treasures.

If we compare the opportunities that the youth have today with those of even half a generation ago, the difference is so large as to place the young sometimes beyond the reach of the imagination of living elders. Young men and women from our country can today reach out for the best academic institutions and the topmost jobs and opportunities anywhere in the world. Over the last generation both non-resident Indians (NRIs) and resident Indians have made such a big splash abroad—especially in the Anglo-Saxon world—that in many places Indians are at the top of the pile when it comes to shortlisted applications for entry to educational institutions and jobs. From America to Australia, from Africa to East Asia, we can easily find Indians today, many of them doing exceptional work in their respective fields.

However, all this that we have been celebrating is about India. What about Bharat? Has it also been experiencing the same successes and thrills that global Indians are able to enjoy routinely now? And if not, can global India really continue its charmed 'world-class' journey?

India and Bharat

That we have come to live in two countries, India and Bharat, has long been widely recognized. And yet, it is a fact whose full implications remain undigested, even as the schism between the two gets wider due to the policies of the past several decades. While the two countries are joined at the hip—like Siamese twins—they continue to drink at different waterholes. While one grapples with problems of obesity, the other is malnourished. While one shops in dazzling malls, the other finds it every day more difficult to buy what is sold in local bazaars. If one speeds down the new expressways in luxury sedans, the other gets packed into rickety buses headed for very different destinations.

There is also a third country, one that is almost forgotten by those in office: the world of non-human nature. The diversity of wild plants and animals, domesticated crops and livestock of the country is in rapid retreat from a human onslaught that has transformed ecosystems and habitats at a relentless pace. This only threatens to be intensified with climate change. Extinction looms large for thousands of species, and the current phase of economic growth accentuates this threat.

This book questions the sustainability of such a society, ever more divided by economic status, and increasingly at war with the natural environment. It is an exercise in persuasion. What the mass media calls 'the world' accepts and propagates a version of 'reality' which is the primary cause of the enormous dangers that confront humanity. This book is an attempt to challenge such a vision in a country whose enormous biological, economic and cultural diversity and whose very survival as a civilization is today threatened by inappropriate globalized 'development'. We try to show how this process is rapidly foreclosing options for more sensitive and sustainable paths of human welfare.

What's new about globalization?

Certain terms can cause endless confusion. One such term is 'globalization'.

Perhaps the most deceptive mythology surrounding the idea of globalization is that 'the world' sat down one morning, calculated the costs and benefits of globalizing, and found the latter to be far greater. Since such an economic opportunity could not go unheeded, globalization came about as a natural outcome of the operation of 'free markets', inevitable as gravity. But this disarming picture is sharply contradicted by the historical truth.

Let us first clarify what globalization is not. There are many who like to argue that there is nothing fundamentally new about contemporary globalization, especially in India, whose culture and civilization since ancient times have been shaped by a myriad international influences and invasions. India has, in turn, been a great influence on others: during the course of history it has affected the cultures of China, Japan, South-East Asia, the Islamic world, Africa and, not to forget, Europe itself. From Buddhism and philosophy to the fundamentals of arithmetic and algebra, India can take legitimate credit for its contributions to human knowledge and culture. It is this that makes some writers justify present-day globalization retroactively as having always been part of human affairs.[2]

Such a view is profoundly mistaken. In its enthusiasm to celebrate the possibilities of cultural contact between the peoples of the world, it loses sight of the more recent economic and financial integration on terms suitable to the wealthy countries and the elite. Economists like Keynes had warned against such 'entanglement' back in the 1930s, when the world was far less economically integrated. The present global crisis bears out the apprehensions of Keynes.[3]

The partisans of globalization also fail to note the ecological, ideological and geopolitical/military implications of such integration. They thus fail to perceive the unique character of the recent—corporate, state-led—incarnation of globalization which has let loose historic changes, not merely on the subcontinent but on the planet as a whole, jeopardizing the viability of civilization and life on earth as we know it. What we are seeing is a globalization without historical precedent, founded on the most powerful advanced technologies ever known to humanity.

Contemporary globalization is rooted in the world of business, trade, finance, media and technology. It originated in the West and was embraced by Indian and other ruling elites. It has far-reaching consequences for Indian society as much as for those elsewhere. Today's globalization is a definitive prescription not just for a certain arrangement of economic affairs, but for *a way of life*, at the root of which is the thinly concealed, perpetual quest for control and dominance by the elites of the world.

It has nothing to do with the benign mingling of cultures. Its drive comes from the needs of finance capital. Today the volume of international financial flows is in orders of magnitude greater than the volume of international trade and the global GDP (gross domestic product) itself. The tail of finance wags the dog of the real economy. What's more, such financial flows—which of course include debt sold to the Third World—are crucial to what is a growing and massive volume of debt-servicing (repayment of debts and interest) by poor, developing countries. According to one estimate, such countries transferred $550 billion to the affluent world in 2006, on account of such payments. By contrast, the total aid from the rich nations for middle- and low-income countries was only $116 billion in that year, implying a net transfer from the poorer nations to the rich OECD (Organization for Economic Co-operation and Development) countries of $434 billion![4]

The architecture of globalization

The lopsided architecture of current globalization rests on a foundation of powerful ideologies, institutions, policies and interests.

Ideologies

'There is no alternative [TINA],' Margaret Thatcher had pronounced in the 1980s, when she was prime minister of Britain. She was referring to what had by then become the dominant way to run the economy—at the expense of society, the state keeping its hands away from the economy, ostensibly in the interests of individual liberty. (After all, 'there is no such thing as society,' she had added. 'There are individual men and women and there are families.')[5]

The ideology of globalization is called neo-liberalism since it shares with classical liberalism a belief in the steady reduction, if not outright withdrawal, of the state from economic affairs, reposing its faith in 'free markets' as the best route to economic growth and prosperity. The core value of neo-liberalism is competition—among countries and among the individuals within them. (This does not, however, prevent big corporations from cooperating among themselves in various markets to share the spoils.) It is argued that competition brings about efficiency, when it comes to selling something at the lowest possible price (and the best possible quality) to the consumer.

Faith in 'free' markets is the essence of globalized efficiency. Mainstream theory argues that voluntary exchange between autonomous economic agents leads to the most 'efficient' outcomes for each individual. In doing the best for itself, each party to a transaction also ends up benefiting the other—almost as a by-product. Society—which in this view is little more than a collection of individuals—is thus best served by free markets.

The argument for voluntary exchange between individuals easily gets translated into an argument for free trade between nations. The logic for this rests, additionally, on the idea of comparative advantage. In a nutshell, it works like this. If a country is deemed to have a comparative advantage in certain goods, it is *relatively* more efficient at producing them. If nations specialize in exporting those items in which they have comparative advantage, the theory suggests, the production of all goods and services across the globe can be enlarged beyond what could be done without specialization and trade. In this sense there are gains from trade for everyone. This theory lies at the heart of all policy prescriptions stemming from neo-liberalism.

Institutions, policies and interests

For the past several decades neo-liberalism has been led by three powerful institutions. These are the IMF, the World Bank and the WTO. Working in tandem with them is the Manila-based Asian Development Bank (ADB). Since the IMF and the World Bank are headquartered in Washington DC, neo-liberal policies have come to be called the 'Washington Consensus'. These international financial institutions (IFIs) together constitute key pillars of the shadow state which presides over the world economy in the era of corporate globalization, especially the poor countries.[6]

What are the policies prescribed by these institutions? They advise that economies open to trade, capital and investment flows from around the world grow and develop faster and can, therefore, bring about a quicker reduction in poverty, via the famous 'trickle-down effect'. One must not complain too much about rising inequalities in the interim since the wealthy perform an invaluable service to society by investing their wealth and generating jobs in the process, thereby reducing poverty. Growth (resulting from neo-liberal policies) also adds to tax collections and the revenues can be disbursed for social purposes like public health.

Along with the opening up of economies, neo-liberal policies involve privatization of public sector enterprises, including socially critical areas such as water supply, health and education. This is often done under the garb of cutting government spending and balancing the budget. They also normally force a devaluation of the poor, borrowing country's currency, as well as asking for 'flexible labour markets' (which effectively means workers can be hired and fired at will).

Finally, whose interests are being served by globalization? The opening up of markets in industrializing (or 'emerging') economies is driven by the demands of elite consumers and transnational corporations (TNCs), often in partnership with powerful domestic corporations in these countries. They encounter saturated ('mature') markets in the affluent nations and thus cannot meet their growth imperatives unless they expand in the Third World. Privatization of public sector companies and assets gives greater control of a developing economy to the global corporate sector and creates new business for big domestic companies and the TNCs.

Lower state spending also means that important support systems for the poor—such as food subsidies—are withdrawn or curtailed, typically in an inflationary environment. The prescription of lower state participation in the economy also implies, in practice, large tax breaks for wealthy corporations. (If state spending is reduced, why would it need to collect so many taxes?) This is justified on the grounds that such incentives are necessary to invite private investment, generate employment and growth.

Loosening of ownership and tax laws in Third World countries allows First World corporations to not only make more (foreign) direct investment (FDI) in such places. More money is directed by the TNCs towards mergers and acquisitions, and portfolio investments, whereby there is no fresh creation of productive capacity, but only a transfer of ownership of existing real assets. Such investment (called foreign institutional investment or FII) does not lead to employment generation or secure growth. It merely adds to the profits of the TNCs.

Devalued currencies lower the cost of raw materials that are imported by the affluent nations from the developing world. Flexible labour markets, likewise, reduce the cost of labour for the TNCs (and for domestic companies) that relocate to the Third World. In poor countries like India it means the casualization of work, often through outsourcing and subcontracting to the informal economy, where wages are far lower and exploitation runs deep.

Once all these measures are cumulatively able to raise the rate of growth of the real economy, the financial sector of the 'emerging market' starts yielding returns higher than before. Investors in countries both rich and poor—often represented by mutual, pension or hedge funds—are then able to invest in assets in the 'emerging' financial markets which yield returns considerably higher than what they would get in the so-called 'mature' markets.

Most significantly, the debt that borrowing countries incur enable the IFIs to exercise even more policy control on debtor countries to promote the interests of transnational business.

Debt-leveraged imperialism has quietly gained a stranglehold on 'emerging' economies.

A preliminary critique of neo-liberalism

The neo-liberal doctrine must be criticized not only for its effects on trade, investment and finance but also the consequences it has for social welfare, environmental sustainability, control of the economy, labour and the borrowing country's currency. Here we take up only the touchstone of the doctrine—the unqualified prescription of free trade—leaving it to succeeding chapters to tackle the other issues.

The essence of the argument for free trade is that if each country specializes in its area of comparative advantage, overall output in the world economy is maximized. Since tariffs, quotas and duties interfere with the functioning of free markets, ardent laissez-faire (free trade) theorists contend, they ought to be dismantled to allow the gains in efficiency (and thus, growth) to be made under the rules by which competitive markets function. Should serious inequalities emerge (perhaps building on pre-existing inequality in the distribution of wealth), the state can always tax the winners to compensate the losers. In practice, especially in India, this rarely happens—despite ostensibly progressive taxation—because of the huge tax incentives given to investors in the shape of breaks on capital gains, etc. What happens if inequalities emerge *between* countries (as has happened in recent decades)? The question is not even asked most of the time. Or if it is, the misplaced prescription is to increase international aid.

Secondly, most economists take the theory of free trade—from the early-nineteenth-century work of the English economist

David Ricardo—for granted, as though it were everywhere and always true. However, Ricardo's theory rests on one critical assumption: that the factors of production—land, labour and capital—are immobile. Only goods are traded in Ricardo's world.

This assumption is not valid any more. It is true that land is relatively immobile. However, labour mobility is severely restricted due to tough immigration laws. Despite the transport and communications revolution, estimates suggest that migration as a proportion of total world population has been lower in the current phase (since the 1970s) compared to the first era of globalization (1870–1914; see next section).[7] Capital, on the other hand, is all too mobile in the globalized world. Large firms are able to relocate their plants and factories around the world at great speed nowadays.

What is true of physical capital is even truer of financial capital. According to data available from the Bank for International Settlements, the mobility of purely financial capital has reached such astronomical proportions that, in 2007, private trade in foreign exchange exceeded $3.2 trillion *a day* (or $1171 trillion over the whole year, when the world GDP was a mere $66 trillion, almost twenty times less!). Private trading in foreign exchange markets holds such power today that it can wipe out the collective reserves of the entire world's central banks in a few days of hostile private trade.[8]

Global capital mobility also means that some countries and TNCs often gain not just comparative, but absolute, advantage. Jobs begin to vanish on a large scale from countries where wages are high, as capital flies away. As per the theory of free trade, this may increase world production. But there are also losers in the bargain, such as workers laid off in countries from where the capital has disappeared. Moreover, the benefits to the country which gets the capital may be transient. India may be attractive to TNCs up to the point that state policies—towards markets, resources, labour, environment, taxes—are relatively favourable to the big firms. However, if these enticements are reduced, corporations can easily shift to countries that give them better concessions, usually by violating labour and environmental standards.

Finally, Ricardo's theory cannot be applied in a world in which a country's comparative advantage changes over time. This is made plain by the evidence of economic history, as much as by the experience of the contemporary world. Japan for instance, *developed* its comparative advantage in car production over the course of some decades in the last century, allowing it to race ahead of the American auto industry. The same happened in different industries in South Korea and later in China. Comparative advantage is always a dynamic phenomenon, certainly in today's world, and utterly sensitive to state policies. The *zaibatsu*s of Japan and the *chaebol*s of South Korea (both state-backed conglomerates of big businesses violating all free-market axioms) are ample testimony to the fact that comparative advantage can be shifted in favour of the developing country with the help of state policy.[9]

In passing, it may be noted that the specialization that results from free trade is hardly an unmixed blessing. It locks countries into trade patterns, which later become dependency traps, especially in an ecologically endangered world, and thus faces risks of disruptions in long, global supply chains.

There are lessons from the past, too, suggesting that comparative advantage under free trade was demonstrably a fiction in many instances. Britain never grew any cotton when it was industrializing in the eighteenth century. Yet, it was the leading textile power. Records show that the British textile industry benefited immensely from trade barriers and the forced decline of Indian handicrafts, the colonial state playing the catalytic role in the process of market creation. Many a cruelty was visited upon Bengal weavers to kill the international competition from muslin production that Manchester textiles were facing.[10]

The inescapable fact of economic history, which few contemporary economists take into account, is that no country of substantial size has ever industrialized successfully under conditions of free trade. This is the basis for the famous infant-industry argument—that countries in an early phase of industrialization need the protection of trade barriers—now in (unjust) disrepute with policymakers across the world, as import substitution has given way to import liberalization. Incidentally, contrary to widespread belief, the developing world grew much faster during 1960–80 (when it practised protectionism) than during the next two decades (when it was made to follow free trade policies by the IFIs).[11]

If we take the orthodox view that industrialization along the resource-intensive lines begun by the West is the way to 'develop' a country even in an ecologically imperilled age, what it means is that the free trade prescriptions handed down by the IFIs really have no basis in theory or fact. Their rationale actually lies in two undiscussed non-negotiables: the rich nations cannot survive any more without international trade, given the dependency traps in which economic growth under specialization has left them, and, secondly, the globally mobile banks and TNCs are hungry for markets and profits in countries other than their own.

In practice, free markets are not so much 'free' as *deregulated*— out of public democratic control. A better way to describe the way our globalized world works today is that it is founded not so much on free trade, as on *deregulated international corporate commerce*. (A large fraction of international trade nowadays happens *within* the TNCs.) This architecture of political–economic dominance has been a long time in the making.

Origins of today's globalization

To understand present-day globalization we need to know that the impetus for it came from the Euro-American world and that it has been going on in different forms at least since the era of European colonialism. The Industrial Revolution from the eighteenth century greatly expanded the technological horizons of globalization by developments in transport, navigation and communication, not to forget armaments, which drove the creation of modern empires. Vast colonial empires were set up by the European powers, in the name of the Christian mission, 'progress' and 'civilization' and, of course, free trade. All the empires were, in strong measure, trading empires. This fact continues to reign over us today, with the rhetoric of 'free markets' not letting up even after a historic collapse of markets in the financial crisis that began in 2008.[12]

During what is known to economists as 'the first wave of globalization' (1870–1914), led by the British Empire (Pax Britannica), virtually the whole world was inducted into extensive international trading relationships. The First World War put an abrupt end to that. Importantly, finance was not a developed segment of the economy. So globalization was restricted largely (though not exclusively) to trade and direct investment by Britain and other European powers. Countries like China and (British) India, which were forcefully inducted into a 'free trade' system, experienced deindustrialization and underdevelopment.[13]

We may note in passing that international labour markets were much freer in those days than is the case today, with immigration to the US loosened by the requirements of the domestic labour market. At that time many countries did not even require passport checks and visas at their entry points. The world at that time was closer to Adam Smith's vision of a 'free market' than today's world, with its myriad restrictions on human mobility. Throughout his famous book *The Wealth of Nations*, Smith advocated free movement of labour. Foreseeing our times accurately, he clearly states that society's laws give 'less obstruction to free circulation of stock [capital] from one place to another than to labour'.[14]

The second wave of globalization came about after the Second World War, under American dominance (Pax Americana). During what is referred to by economic historians as 'the golden age of capitalism' (1945–71), much of the world (with the important exceptions of China and the Soviet bloc countries) was brought under the same umbrella of economic relationships yet again. Europe and Japan rebuilt their economies after the war with financial assistance from the US.

Despite efforts to the contrary, many newly decolonized countries in Asia, Africa and Latin America remained under the domineering influence of the Western economies, and they supplied cheap raw materials and resources to them. In later years, they would be invited to take on huge amounts of debt from Western banks, ostensibly in order to fuel their own growth and development, but in effect serving to transfer control over resources from the Third to the First World—a phenomenon which has only grown with time and which some writers describe as 'neo-colonialism'.[15]

Ironically, the word globalization did not acquire currency until quite recently. Even in the West, a generation ago (1980), no one had heard of globalization. When the writers of this book were growing up in north India in the 1970s and 1980s, the word was certainly unheard of. You could go through five years of economics at university without encountering the word. No professional economist—certainly not in India—was advocating globalization as a means of growth or poverty reduction.

So when did things change? The term came into common usage in economic contexts in the West very slowly during the 1980s and truly gained importance, becoming a buzzword, only in the 1990s after the fall of the Berlin Wall. As Washington smelt a historic opportunity for its transnationals, it began to advocate globalization as the only way to organize economies. Capitalism and communism were seen to have been at war for three-quarters of a century, and capitalism was finally declared winner of the Cold War. Now it was propagated by the great powers to the world as the superior economic system, by sheer virtue of having outlived its rival.[16]

It was the United States, under George Bush Sr, that *imposed* globalization in its present form upon the world—as part of 'the new world order' after the First Gulf War in 1991.[17]

Globalization has far less to do with free trade than with the extension and consolidation of markets within the broad canvas of the American empire—whatever the cost to the world and to ordinary Americans. By the 1980s, after two centuries of growth in the Western world, capitalism encountered saturated markets in Europe, the US and Japan. The 1970s had been a troubled decade for the capitalist system, as it struggled with oil crises, recession and inflation. There were two great oil price hikes— in 1973 and 1979—by the Organization of the Petroleum Exporting Countries (OPEC), the oil producers' cartel.

The period 1979–82 saw the deepest recession in the West since the 1930s. This was also the time the Bretton Woods currency exchange rate system broke down when in 1971 the US refused to convert dollars held by foreigners into gold. Till then the gold exchange standard, with the value of the dollar designated by a fixed quantity of gold, was the basis for converting one international currency into another. From 1971 onward, the dollar became the default reserve currency of the world. In effect, we have come to live under the Dollar Standard, a fundamental cause of today's global crisis.[18]

When Soviet communism ended in 1989, the TNCs began looking towards Russia, Eastern Europe and South-East Asia. But the 1997 financial crisis in South-East Asia and the 1998 crisis in Russia dashed many hopes and destroyed much wealth. Then they turned their gaze towards China and India for further expansion. China, on the 'reform' path since the late 1970s, had already begun to attract investment from the TNCs by the mid-1980s. In the 1990s, the enormous populations, first of China, and later of India, were seen in Western corporate boardrooms as the 'markets of the future'. Large middle- and low-income countries—Brazil, Russia, India, China, South Africa (BRICS)—were classified as 'emerging markets'. (East and South-East Asia had already 'emerged'—and crashed.)

One feature of these markets deemed unique was the enormous significance of politics in shaping the climate for foreign investment. They had large, poor populations who would find it difficult to access the opportunities opened up by globalization. Any large-scale unrest due to the impact of unfavourable state policies was bound to disrupt the markets. Thus the IFIs placed these political regimes under observer institutions to ensure that they maintained a peaceful environment for smooth international business.

Globalization also means the establishment of international production and supply chains, led by the TNCs, across the globe. A product today involves inputs and processes that span oceans and continents. Rubber could be collected in Malaysia, processed in Thailand, treated in China, vulcanized in South Korea, made into car tyres in Mexico and sold to car manufacturers in Japan or the EU. Part of the reason for this has to do with the rapidly growing volume of intra-firm international trade (between subsidiaries of a TNC located in different countries), a phenomenon explained at least in part by the corporate desire to evade taxes. Such global supply chains, as we will see, have huge ecological implications.

However, the economic integration of the globe has proceeded most rapidly in financial markets. Production, trade and direct investment have been slower to get globalized, for obvious reasons: money can be transferred today at the click of a mouse whereas goods and machinery take the long sea route. The fact that finance is so mobile today actually underscores the instability of the global capitalist system, making it immensely more vulnerable to breakdowns.

Since times before the present crisis, seasoned observers and financial regulators have been deeply anxious about the astronomically large, growing and increasingly autonomous, deregulated global financial markets—typified by the hedge fund phenomenon since the beginning of the twenty-first century. More and more publicly quoted companies have sold out to private equity, making supervision difficult. Firms quoted publicly on the stock exchange are under supervision by the authority that regulates the stock market. In India this institution is the Securities and Exchange Board of India (SEBI). Private equity firms escape supervision by avoiding public listing.

Gambling on everything—from currencies, companies and real estate to natural disasters and pension funds—has become the norm in global financial markets, turning capitalism into what traditional economic wisdom used to fear: a casino. It also means that funds for investment in physical capital are less readily available, since the returns are low and slow by comparison.

Globalization and power

Contemporary globalization is, above all, founded on unequal power relations that span the globe and the countries that constitute it. It is historically inseparable from the era of colonialism, being premised on the inequalities of power and wealth that date from those days. Now, as then, it is underwritten by military dominance. As the *New York Times* columnist Thomas Friedman wrote years ago,

> the hidden hand of the market will never work without a hidden fist. McDonald's cannot flourish without McDonnell Douglas, the designer of the F-15. And the hidden fist that keeps the world safe for Silicon Valley's technologies to flourish is called the US Army, Air Force, Navy and Marine Corps.[19]

This dominance ensures that today the dollar serves as the world's reserve currency. Globalization, with its unjust economic outcomes, is regarded by many to be imperialism by another name. The erosion of freedom and human dignity and the assault on human cultures is inevitable in such an 'obligatory', coercive form of globalization.[20]

Such globalization is no more inevitable than the power of the interest groups, corporations, institutions and governments who have lobbied so successfully for it over the past generation. In fact, were it not for the breakdown of the Bretton Woods fixed exchange rate system in 1971 and the consequent emergence of a regime of floating exchange rates (which enabled speculation in financial markets, because of new uncertainties in the values of exchange rates), it is doubtful if the present form of globalization—involving such massive, destabilizing international capital flows—would have emerged.

Corporations wield ultimate power in our world today. They elect and often bring down governments, even if it seems that the *people* are voting them in and out—for they control the range of eligible candidates (the power of money shaping campaign financing) and fund lobbies that actively push for favourable economic policies in ostensibly democratic countries like India and the US. Corporations also have great influence over the policies and actions of a country's central bank, the overarching monetary authority that certifies the currency, as well as over the regulatory authority for the stock market. This happens because such authorities necessarily have to consider the consequences of their decisions on big businesses and how the latter would influence the markets.

However, it is in the contradictions of the marketplace that global capitalism encounters its nemesis in the form of recurring and deepening crises. This is what has happened since 2007–08.

Of emerging and submerging economies: A coupled India

While there have been periodic crises in the history of capitalism, the present juncture is unique. There are not many moments in history characterized by the overwhelming uncertainty and flux that surrounds us today. The deep global recession persists, taking a heavy toll of jobs, homes and businesses across the world. In times like this, afflicted by a succession of crises, our sense of reality shifts from day to day. An idea can seem absurd one day, unavoidable the next. Such extraordinary conditions create a general mentality of seeking comfort in the dogmatic prophecies of continuous growth uttered by the international community of like-minded institutions and experts.

Global 'free market' capitalism seemed to be coasting towards ever greater prosperity till August 2007, when the long-sustained bubble of the American housing market burst, suddenly drawing much of the world economy into a common vortex of serious troubles. The worst crisis that the capitalist system has faced since the 1930s has already claimed gigantic banks and corporations like Lehman Brothers, Merrill Lynch, General Motors and Chrysler.

It was believed in many quarters that 'emerging' economies could be insulated from the dire state of the financial system in the wealthy nations, or even help mitigate the recession there. This view cannot be sustained any longer. Even if the Indian and Chinese economies have recovered somewhat since 2009, capital flows have receded from Asian markets and the demand for Asian exports in Western markets has declined sharply after the crash.

How could India remain unaffected by the crises abroad? The truth is that so far Indian policies have all been externally oriented. Foreign-investor-friendly policies can only 'couple' the economy more closely with the world economy. Policies for the opening up of Indian markets, resources and investment opportunities to globally mobile TNCs have neglected the home market.

A stronger home market, built on the foundations of a strong agricultural and rural economy would have indeed insulated us from the decline in fortunes elsewhere. But that has not happened because of the systematic neglect of agriculture and other rural sectors, like village industries. Agriculture, while employing more than half the country's population, is able to contribute only 17 per cent to the GDP, at least partly on account of how poorly farmers are rewarded for their efforts. So, even doubling its growth rate from 2.5 per cent to 5 per cent adds only 0.4 per cent to the overall growth rate. Thanks to the present state of long-standing policy neglect of agriculture, the demand from the rural population cannot be expected to bail out the rest of the economy.[21]

Given the interdependence in the world economy, the options before policymakers in a country like India are quite limited as long as they adhere to the fundamental tenets of globalized economies. If there were ever any doubts that national sovereignty over economic policy has been ceded to global financial markets over the past two decades, the present crisis has cleared them up. Many policy norms have been flouted to tackle the ongoing crisis, not only in India but in much more economically powerful nations. Everywhere the lure of the market has overshadowed any other consideration in the daily conduct of statecraft. Soon after the Lehman collapse, the Indian prime minister had to acknowledge that 'we are not in complete control. There are bigger players and we are victims of that. The crisis is not of our making.'[22]

The ideology of free markets has failed the test in a dramatic fashion. In the immediate aftermath of the crisis the ex-chairman of the US Federal Reserve, Alan Greenspan, said: 'I have found a flaw . . . Those of us who have looked to the self-interest of lending institutions to protect shareholders' equity, myself included, are in a state of shocked disbelief.'[23]

Thousands of statements like the above can be quoted from political and business leaders around the world, pleading helplessness in the face of the crisis. Judging from such statements, would it be fair to imagine that our leaders are blissfully ignorant? That, to use Donald Rumsfeld's infamous language, they don't know that they don't know? That they often don't even know what they should find out or what questions they should ask? And if so, should they be in a position to make effective policies to avoid serious harm to the exposed public? There is far too much that is opaque and unknown (even to the so-called 'experts') about the way contemporary economies are working, rendering policymaking a hazardous exercise at the best of times and altogether perilous in today's globally interconnected environment.

If the fall of the Berlin Wall in 1989 demonstrated the economic failure of state socialism, the collapse of Lehman Brothers in September 2008 proved the failure of deregulated libertarian capitalism. It is now more obvious than ever that neither the market nor the state can actually handle the problems that each of them creates. Governments everywhere have first tried to save the system, not those bearing the brunt of its failures.

Time for another world

Missing from all the policy debates of the last few decades is, ironically, the role of citizens, communities and their institutions. We have merely been at the receiving end of decisions taken by governments and corporations—for the most part unaccountable to the public. Now that governments and markets are both failing miserably, can human society be galvanized into collective democratic action to ensure that socially and ecologically sane decisions are made? The present crisis of the system may be an indicator that we are at a major political crossroads. The question is how decisions are going to be taken in the future, and by whom.

For India and the world to prove equal to the challenges being thrown up, we need to assess the overall impact of the current phase of globalization. This we attempt in Part I of the book. As we discover the problems that have emerged due to or have been aggravated by globalization, we will naturally be led to consider the alternatives to the economic model that has led us to the brink. This we will do in Part II of the book.

According to the pundits, 'the India story' has been one of unmitigated success. 'Development', many contend, could not have yielded better results. However, as we shall see, there is a growing dark side to the boom which, quite apart from the global economic forces just mentioned, threatens not just the apparent gains of recent years but also the framework of the Indian political system itself. It is necessary, for instance, to grasp the enormity of the ecological and social havoc to which the forces unleashed by 'development' are giving rise. If we fail to acknowledge these facts, they will overwhelm us sooner than later.

Development under globalization has been such a multidimensional phenomenon, with consequences for spheres as far-flung as politics and environment, economy and culture, that one cannot possibly do justice in one book to the full range of issues. It is also beyond our expertise to examine each major area in detail. Our goal is much more to establish the key links and assemble 'the big picture' from the many disparate and scattered facts being reported, than to repeat scholarly work being carried out by others.

To explore the complex issues of globalization, we have adopted specific approaches. First, we address the *interrelatedness* of the different phenomena involved. The standard 'economic' way of looking at globalization abstracts the economy from the real social world in which it operates. It is as if there exists an automaton—the economic agent—acting as a more or less efficient wealth-producing machine, with no goal other than the maximization of private benefits, which, therefore, maximizes social wealth. The reality is quite different. The economy is embedded in an environmental, political and cultural context, which cannot justifiably be ignored. Thus, breaking from the standard approach adopted by most scholars, we will venture across disciplinary boundaries, attempting to take a more integrated view. We will see that a fragmentary approach to understanding the key problems is in fact what has rendered our political classes and the policymaking elite incapable of grasping, or unwilling to act on, the multiple, interrelated crises we face.

Secondly, we live in a vastly more interconnected world, so it is only appropriate that we take a *global—earthly—*approach rather than a narrow nationalistic one. This involves many things. For instance, it implies that certain options that were open to the rich countries on *their* road to affluence may not be open to us in our quest to get rich or to eradicate poverty. A blindly imitative 'do-as-they-did' attitude or a tamely subservient 'do-as-they-tell-us-to' approach will fail everyone in the end.

Such an approach tells us that we ought to industrialize in much the same way and have the right to the same carbon emissions per capita that they have enjoyed. We cannot do so, precisely because they have already exhausted what might have been a sustainable quota of per capita emissions for each person alive and to come. Humanity's profligacy has already exceeded the earth's capacity, as has India's as a nation; we will elaborate on this in later chapters. The challenge is to find answers to problems that originated in and were exported by the West, and compel it to accept and facilitate these solutions, rather than allow ourselves to continue on this profligate, irresponsible path. The West's path of 'development' has been violent to the earth and to other peoples—ours cannot be.

Thirdly, India's present challenges cannot be understood or addressed unless they are viewed from a *historical* perspective. What does this mean? It implies that while acknowledging the significant departures one also takes note of the continuities between the pattern of economic growth and development that prevailed in India before 1991 and what has been happening since. The same approach must inform our understanding of trends before 1947 and after, since there are significant continuities. For example, a largely unamended Land Acquisition Act of 1894, written for colonial purposes, is still in place to take over land from communities for industrial purposes, and the same centralized bureaucracies the British had set up are in place even today. The ecological challenge especially compels such an approach, since the same energy-, water- and resource-intensive model of industrialization has persisted through these decades and is widely advocated by our elite with ever greater fervour.

Taking a historical view of things also means reckoning with the future imaginatively. We will be living in the future, while continuing to dwell in the past. Many of the unfolding challenges—ecological, economic, political and cultural— necessarily draw us into speculative thinking, given the paucity of information and the multiple uncertainties that fog our vision today. This should not deter us from making reasonable speculations. We will take the liberty and the risk of doing so, inviting the reader to consider what might seem extreme possibilities only till they see the very real dangers of the future.

Fourthly, throughout the text there will be occasion to illuminate our arguments with appropriate theory and on-ground examples. At the heart of the book is the contention that the inherent logic of an unrestrained market economy organized to maximize economic growth is today fundamentally at odds with the goal of ecological sustainability and social equity. There are already very serious ecological problems impacting rural and urban communities across the country, portending a dismal future for them.

As the supply-lines of urban India are readily traced to rural hinterlands, which also serve as its waste-dump, it is only a matter of time before the frontier of devastation reaches urban areas and the metros. Moreover, urban India is all too vulnerable to sabotage by disaffected rural communities who are routinely witnessing the raw end of development under globalization.[24]

Fifth, the book raises key philosophical and cultural concerns about the fundamental *values* at stake in the path of industrialization and development under globalization that the Indian elites, mimicking the dominant trends in the world outside, have embraced. Human society cannot remain immune to the dominant values—of competitiveness and aggression, greed and covetousness—required by a 'successful' industrial economy. While these human feelings and drives obviously predate modern industrialism, the latter reinforces them.

Consumer society is founded on perverse premises that play havoc with human relationships. The book reflects on other values—cooperation, compassion, integrity, frugality, simplicity, responsibility, equity and loyalty—that have been traded away or pushed to the background.

The obsession with endless economic growth is actually a fetish, wherein humanity is being asked to resolve psychological, metaphysical or spiritual challenges through material consumption, which drives up the GDP of a nation. We suggest that this is more an escape from our real problems than an honest attempt to tackle them.

Finally, and most importantly, the book adopts the perspective of the most imperilled and marginalized (human and non-human) communities of India—without pretending to speak for them. This is not to deny the significance of other angles of vision. But we focus on the existential situation of such communities for several reasons. One, because elementary ethics commands attention to their problems in a world where a part of humanity has enriched itself like in no previous age of human history. Secondly, we suspect that the fate we inflict on the poor today may well come back to haunt us in the not-so-distant future. If we continue to impose the ecological costs of our city-centred way of life on the poor, the day will soon come—has already come (if we think of the Mumbai floods of 2005 or of pesticides in our food)—when the seriousness of the ecological crisis knocks at our own doors. Worse things are possible tomorrow; it will be too late by then to address the disasters. Thirdly, if our leaders and the elite claim that we are 'one nation', it is about time we began to heal the rapidly widening chasm between Bharat and India and resuscitate the vitality of what is actually a civilization—endangered today by the ambitions of a corporatized nationhood.

In sum, the book argues for a radical transformation in our policies, priorities and attitudes if we are to negotiate and survive the troubled terrain into which we have foolishly strayed. The goal of ensuring sustainable livelihoods for the mass of our people, and of saving life in all its myriad forms, can only be met by collectively evolving a radical ecological democracy as an *economic* and *ethical* alternative. A business-as-usual approach to development under globalization is doomed to fail everyone. Time is short and we cannot afford to wait for all the facts to flood in and make it difficult to stay afloat. What we already know is quite enough, if we can summon the courage to draw the right conclusions and collectively compel our governments and institutions to act with foresight and wisdom.

This book does not argue against globalization. On the contrary, by taking account of facts like growing militarization, the loss of freedom and the increasing restrictions on the free movement of people, it argues that true globalization—in the sense of a mature cultural understanding among the peoples of the earth—is yet to happen. What it argues against is the unsustainable globalization that lies behind the rhetoric of 'free markets' and is at the bottom of so many of the problems that the world faces today.

Another world is not merely possible. It is long overdue, if the world is to survive at all.

2

THE DRUNKEN STUNTED DOG

IMBALANCED GROWTH IN INDIA

'A time will come when countries will beg to be exploited.'

—Sukhamoy Chakravarty, economic adviser to
Mrs Indira Gandhi, in the mid-1980s[1]

'Reform is sometimes the first step to the abyss,' freedom fighter
Aurobindo Ghosh once said. The famed India story is morphing
into a rather strange and restless beast. Queried about his
impressions of the Indian economy in recent years, a visiting
overseas economist (who shall remain anonymous) replied:
'Imagine a puppy which is fed a special kind of diet which distorts
his growth so that one of his legs grows astonishingly fast, while
the other three get stunted to various degrees. Now imagine
that the puppy grows into a dog of sorts, gets drunk and begins
to spin around the house in ecstasy—the hangover and the diseases
lying in wait . . .' The special diet is the policy package pushed
by the World Bank and the IMF (International Monetary Fund).
The dog's drunkenness refers to the delirious stock market, and
the hangover and diseases will 'follow the next big crash'.[2]

The most shocking aspect of the dazzling Indian growth story is its primary structural feature, unique in the history of the modern world, given the size of India: while the wealthy make hay and the top quarter of the population is doing visibly better (at least in purely material terms), three-quarters of the population of the country has been largely excluded (or rejected) from the processes of prosperity that have unfolded over the past two decades. Market-friendly—and, even more, investor-friendly—policies since 1991 have meant that the growth process had a built-in exclusion to it from the very beginning.

Using varying definitions of the middle class, McKinsey Global Institute puts the proportion of the middle class within the total population at 5 per cent in 2007, while the National Council for Applied Economic Research (NCAER) estimates it at 11.4 per cent. No one seriously estimates the size of the middle class today at more than 25 per cent of the population, even using the most liberal definition. Differences in estimates arise from differences in growth projections. Some extraordinary estimates of the Indian middle class claim the exact opposite—that only a quarter of the population is being left out of the present growth.[3]

If there were truth in these estimates, the TNCs (transnational corporations) would have shown more interest in making foreign direct investment (FDI) in India with an eye on the market for real goods and services (as against financial products). However, during 2000–10, the total (cumulative) FDI that has come into India is a mere $164 billion, 43 per cent of which came from Mauritius (perhaps from NRI sources). Less than 10 per cent of FDI has come from the EU countries, 7 per cent from the US, 5 per cent from the UK and 4 per cent from Japan. By comparison, UNCTAD (United Nations Conference on Trade and Development) data records that China and Hong Kong together got $794 billion in FDI during 1999–2009. Another index of how the transnationals rate the nature of India's future growth is that while 8 per cent ($13 billion) of the FDI during 2000–10 has been in telecom, only 4 per cent ($6.5 billion) is in automobiles.[4]

There is other data to corroborate the fact that three-quarters of the population is being left out of the mainstream development process. If development were truly a widespread phenomenon, cutting across social classes, we would see, among other things, a rise in the growth of taxpayers in the country. Instead, the growth in the number of taxpayers in the country is slowing down (from 3.2 per cent per annum between 2001–02 and 2005–06 to 2.4 per cent per annum between 2002–03 and 2006–07). In 2006–07, it stood at a mere 31.3 million as against an Indian workforce of 450–550 million today. Thus, only 5–7 per cent of the working population is paying income tax. Even assuming that the number of working people evading the income tax net is 10 or 20 per cent more than 31.3 million, we still have only 7–9 per cent of the working population within the income tax bracket.[5]

Even more reliable numbers all point in the same direction. According to the government's annual *Economic Survey*, as much as 93 per cent of Indians still make their living in agriculture and the informal economy—at some distance from the so-called modern world. However, Bharat is crucial not just to India's success but to its very survival. The work performed by this majority is crucial to the existence and operation of the modern economy. And yet, the cognitive priority that this proportion of the people receives in the *Economic Survey* is such that while details are presented about the employment of the middle classes and the elite in the organized sector of the economy, the employment (and unemployment) in the overwhelming unorganized sector is relegated to the chapter on 'Social Sectors', where health and education also make a token appearance. In that chapter we discover that well over half of the country's population continues to be dependent on agriculture for a livelihood. Such narrative improprieties are an essential part of the Indian growth story.[6]

If we are to understand the roots of these processes of exclusion and rejection, it is necessary to go back to 1991 and trace the history of the reforms.

Reforms by stealth: The brave new world order

Nineteen ninety-one is a watershed in the recent history of the world. It was in that year, two years after the fall of the Berlin Wall, that the Soviet Union gave way and the Cold War between the two superpowers, which had dominated human affairs for half a century, formally came to an end. The end of official communism was widely interpreted as a victory for capitalism. Soon thereafter, the surviving superpower raised the pitch for globalization (under Bush Sr's 'new world order'), though it was already a growing reality at an informal level in much of the world. Not surprisingly, it was also in 1991 that the Congress government introduced major economic reforms in India.

The forces that went into the introduction of reforms in India are many and multifaceted. They can be understood as a complex mix of domestic and international pressures. One of the clearest statements of the goals of the reforms was given in 1993 in a paper brought out by the ministry of finance:

The fundamental objective of economic reform is to bring about rapid and sustained improvement in the quality of life of the people of India. Central to this goal is the rapid growth of incomes and productive employment . . . the only durable solution to the curse of poverty is sustained growth of incomes and employment . . . Such growth requires investment: in farms, in roads, in irrigation, in industry, in power and, above all, in people. And this investment must be productive. Successful and sustained development depends on continuing increases in the productivity of our capital, our land, and our labour.

Within a generation the countries of East Asia have transformed themselves. China, Indonesia, Korea, Thailand, and Malaysia today have living standards much above ours . . . *what they have achieved we must strive for.* (Emphasis added)[7]

With the benefit of hindsight, many commentators and economists have argued that government controls were stifling entrepreneurship (and with it, the economy itself) and that this was the rationale for the reforms that followed. While this was certainly happening to small entrepreneurs, it was hardly the case with Indian big business which rarely had to face serious hurdles from the state. This was not the reasoning offered at the time. The proximate cause of the reforms lay elsewhere.[8]

India suffered a severe payments crisis on its external account in the summer of 1991, in the wake of the oil price hike after the First Gulf War. The country had survived two bigger oil price hikes in the 1970s without having to go to international lending institutions. Why did it need to go this time around? The Rajiv Gandhi government had indulged in some reckless borrowing in the 1980s and spent heavily on weapons purchased abroad. Also, the import bill had been climbing through the 1980s, thanks mainly to trade liberalization. In the event, there was only enough hard currency at one stage to pay for two weeks of imports. Given that India was (and is) still heavily dependent on imports of oil and capital goods from abroad, it needed to borrow from abroad to pay for these.[9]

Was it purely coincidental, or was it perhaps due to economic mismanagement that India found itself in an economic crisis in 1991 and had to contract huge loans from the IMF and the World Bank? The secrets of big changes in state policies are hard to fathom. However, based on our awareness of what has happened in one developing country after another since the 1970s, we can hypothesize that there is more method, than chance, in the madness of reforms led by the Washington Consensus. Some economists have smelt out the truth here. Charan Wadhwa, for instance, has written: 'As in many developing countries, India also launched its massive economic reforms in 1991 under the pressure of economic crises.'[10]

India's decision-makers resorted to negotiating a loan equivalent to $2.2 billion from the IMF. The 'structural adjustment' loan of $500 million from the World Bank was an inevitable adjunct to this, given that the two international financial institutions (IFIs) work in tandem with each other when it is a matter of coming to the 'assistance' of governments in poor countries (and thereby positioning themselves to influence policy there). The IMF loan was meant to address the short-term needs of what economists call 'stabilization policy' (controlling inflation by balancing the government budget and bringing the country's external accounts into balance). The Bank loan was meant to address the 'structural' macroeconomic problems that were diagnosed as the underlying cause of the payments crisis of 1991.

It must be appreciated that India's international solvency (its ability to meet its sovereign debt obligations) was in question at the time. The government had to send gold to Britain as collateral for the loans it was contracting. The IFIs, by granting the money, were underwriting India as a creditworthy nation. All underwriters extract their pound of flesh, and the Bank and the Fund—accountable ultimately to their bond- and share-holders and the US Treasury—certainly do. Country after country that relied on the Bank–Fund assistance experienced the loss of autonomy and sovereignty over economic policymaking. As expected, the same transpired in India.

Internationally, there were other pressures at work. The reforms—trade liberalization, privatization of public enterprises and social services, and globalization of finance chief among them—had much to do with the changed international geopolitical environment and the ideological mood it gave birth to. As the Eastern Bloc communist nations went into crisis, capitalism was proposed, as part of the Washington Consensus, as the unavoidable alternative for all countries in the world. Slogans for 'free markets' became dominant. Even socialist economies, including China, were making the transition from a planned to a market economy.

On the ground, there was no consensus of any sort. There was not even an open debate. The opportunity thrown up by the exchange crisis in India was seized upon by eager reformers both within and outside the country. The ensuing reforms were prompted by the crisis. They were not the outcome of a clearly planned strategy.

What is most remarkable is the speed at which the reforms proceeded in the 1990s, aided no doubt by the arrival of the IT/telecom revolution, which has defined the technological core and shaped the character of the latest phase of globalization. Had reforms been publicly deliberated over, as befits a proper democracy, their course may have been different. However, policy changes of epic scope were introduced, largely behind closed doors. Given the conspicuous absence of open debate, it is fair to describe the radical policy shifts as 'stealth reforms', though, interestingly, many a commentator describes them thus with an approving nod![11]

There was hardly even a murmur from the political parties (except sometimes when they were in the Opposition) or the institutions of civil society or the media. 'After the unlamented demise of bureaucratic socialism, the Indian elite . . . entered the brave new world of globalization,' writes Ashis Nandy.[12]

In retrospect, these changes have proved to be the most significant policy departures from the past, often going against the spirit of the Indian Constitution, if not its letter too. Two of the principles laid down in (the non-justiciable) Directive Principles of State Policy (under Part IV of the Constitution), which are meant to guide our elected rulers, are:

- To ensure that 'the operation of the economic system does not result in the concentration of wealth' (number 39c)
- To ensure that 'the State shall endeavour to promote cottage industries on an individual or co-operative basis in rural areas' (number 43)[13]

No one with any knowledge of the consequences of globalization during the past twenty years can seriously contest the view that, far from letting such principles guide the policies and their implementation, they have actually been rudely overturned by the reforms.

Buckling under structural adjustment

What do 'structural adjustment'[14] policies typically entail? In brief, they demand a complete reorientation of the indebted nation's macroeconomic policies with the overarching goal of meeting the country's external debt obligations. This results in moneylenders, albeit big and powerful, seizing effective control of a country's economic policies—when all they should be rightfully concerned about is whether the debt is being serviced.

After June 1991, the Narasimha Rao government was asked to implement a series of measures ('loan conditionalities') involving macroeconomic stabilization, coupled with fiscal 'adjustment' and structural policy reforms.

The standard 'belt-tightening' tools—involving devaluation of the currency (it becomes cheaper to buy with foreign currency) and the use of deflationary fiscal and monetary policies (which reduce the economic obligations of the state vis-à-vis society)— were deployed in order to achieve the goals of 'stabilization'. This meant a sharp reduction in the government's fiscal deficit (excess of spending over tax collections) due to cutbacks in social spending. A tight monetary policy was adopted. Many parts of the economy shrank as a result.[15]

Further reforms in areas like the liberalization of banking and insurance are in the pipeline. A change still in the offing is a commitment to lift international capital controls by making the rupee convertible on the capital account in order to facilitate large international movements of capital. This last step could prove extremely hazardous for India if the external payments situation deteriorates seriously, especially if recession persists in the global economy.

The most devastating consequence of debt-leveraged imperialism is that the so-called multilateral institutions increasingly influence policy. Policies are being written with a view to please the 'sentiments' of global financial markets. Hence, the overwhelming obsession with 'growth': it enables faster multiplication of monetary wealth for the world's powerful investor elite. This loss of sovereignty over economic policy—which India had escaped, by exception in the developing world, till the 1980s—has dramatic consequences for ordinary working people in the country. They are yet to see the benefits of the reforms, even as the elite get further enriched and the ranks of the dollar millionaires grow.

State against citizen: Traffic cop turns into a competing motorist

The reforms have dramatically transformed the character of the Indian state. The legitimate role of the state in any society that values justice is to protect the interests of vulnerable groups against the operation of powerful interests and lobbies, and to secure areas of common interest such as a healthy environment and space for wildlife/biodiversity to thrive. The state ought to be the great balancing agent. In a capitalist society the most powerful and organized private interests tend to be large corporations. It is the duty of the state to ensure that they do not ride roughshod over the livelihoods of exposed communities and the needs of the citizenry.

It is the state's responsibility to protect the access of the poor to resources and social services, as much as their jobs and wages. This was the historical origin of the modern welfare state in the West. In a poor democracy like India the social responsibilities of the state become enormously more important. And exposing the poor to the ravages of the world market is inconsistent with the spirit of our Constitution.[16]

Since the days of Nehru the state had played a critical role in seeking to ensure a modicum of socio-economic justice, even if it often did not succeed in this task. While certainly making life annoying for businesses, it controlled to a degree the abuse of private corporate power.

Consider a few instances that show the changing economic character of the state. Water, especially drinking water, was still a public resource; in principle, accessible to everyone. There was a functioning, well-developed (even if frequently corrupt) public distribution system (PDS) which made affordable food available to the poor. It is easy to forget that by the early 1980s, India was largely self-sufficient in the production of foodgrains, a status it has decisively lost since then—in the name of free trade. Medical facilities were meagre, but had not yet been privatized. The price of drugs had not shot through the roof as it has during the last couple of decades, thanks to the new patenting laws. Doctors and private hospitals had not hiked up their fees to levels unaffordable for most people. The vocabulary of 'inclusion' has emerged in recent years, almost as a half-hearted afterthought to compensate for lapses that were entirely foreseeable.

In other areas, a diverse industrial base had been built with substantial indigenization of technology. State investments in the public sector, just like in every other country, were crucial to this. High-quality institutions of technical education (Indian Institutes of Technology [IITs], Indian Institutes of Management [IIMs], medical colleges) had groomed a substantial cadre of trained manpower—engineers and doctors who have since chosen to join the private sector or leave the country. Ironically, corporate India owes so much of its famed successes to the physical and social infrastructure built by the state since 1947.

It is a fact that the state's industrial licensing and other policies throttled entrepreneurship (especially by small investors) till the 1980s. However, there is a persistent tendency for the votaries of reforms to demonize *all* state policies before 1991. It is far too easy and convenient to take for granted and forget the foundations on which the corporate profits of recent years rest. In this, as in many other respects, the corporate sector in India has followed the long-standing American example, where corporations have deployed their lobbyists to systematically use the government to privatize benefits and socialize costs, especially for the development of high-investment technologies from the days of the nineteenth-century telegraph to today's Internet.[17]

As subsequent chapters of this book will show, in many cases the Indian state has rapidly mutated from being a regulator of corporations (a function necessary in any modern society, as the great financial crisis proves) to becoming their active agent, evident for example in its aggressive promotion of SEZs (Special Economic Zones). In yet other cases—like where it has gone in for public–private partnerships (PPPs) or where public sector investments in areas like hydel power have brought about large-scale displacement and loss of livelihood for rural communities—the state has in fact turned into a competitor for scarce resources. This is most evident in the state's continuing use of the dated 1894 Land Acquisition Act to accumulate land banks across the country, in the name of a vaguely defined 'national interest' (see chapter 7).

The ethos of mainstream Indian politics changed after the reforms began. Governments now just want to obtain the people's rubber stamp in every election and proceed with agendas hatched in alliance with the organized private sector. Recent trends in governance reveal a close tie-up between the state and the corporate world, as is clear from the attention the government accords to various business lobbies like the US–India CEO Forum, CII (Confederation of Indian Industry), FICCI (Federation of Indian Chambers of Commerce and Industry),

ASSOCHAM (Associated Chambers of Commerce and Industry in India) and NASSCOM (National Association of Software and Services Companies).[18]

The change in the character of the state and the shift in the balance of power within Indian society—away from public accountability (howsoever limited) towards unaccountable private power—are the most distinct political consequences of the reform process that began in 1991. This trend is mirrored by experiences in many other parts of the world during the era of neo-liberal globalization.

The notable positive changes—such as the promulgation of the Right to Information Act, the panchayati raj constitutional amendments and the use of the Web to make official information public—that have come about are a result of public demand and protest rather than being voluntarily included in overall state policy. Even these positive steps have had to struggle against the increasingly repressive nature of the state after globalization, when serious violations of human rights have become altogether banal and routine.[19]

A 'Confucian' rate of growth

It is claimed that prior to the reforms India was growing at the 'Hindu rate of growth', a modest 3 per cent every year. Subsequently it has moved to what might be called a 'Confucian' growth path, where impressive rates of 8 or 9 per cent per annum have become common. Is this contrast valid? When the data is examined closely, we find that India was growing at 5–6 per cent between 1974 and 1990. The only substantial period after the reforms when the growth rate (6–9 per cent) consistently exceeded this was between 2003 and 2008, before the onset of the ongoing global recession.[20]

Let us outline the more salient aspects of the peculiar form of economic growth that India's mainstream economy has experienced since the early 1990s.

The grass is greener outside: External orientation of policymaking

Most economists and policymakers around the world, even after the 2008 crash, have consistently advocated open economies to ensure growth and development. A striking aspect of the Indian growth process over the past two decades is the enormous international orientation of its character. Policies have been as closely tailored to the needs of international business (both Indian and foreign) as is possible.

However, an international orientation of policies does not have to lead to the withdrawal of the state from large areas of economic and social responsibility. As the Cambridge economist Ha-Joon Chang has made abundantly clear with evidence marshalled from around the world, no large country has ever grown rapidly in the early phase of economic growth without engaging with the world economy in a strategic manner, using a high degree of state intervention: 'The distortion of facts in the official history of globalization is . . . evident at country level. Contrary to what the orthodoxy would have us believe, virtually all the successful developing countries since the Second World War initially succeeded through nationalistic policies, using protection, subsidies and other forms of government intervention.'[21]

The 'successful developing countries' Chang has in mind are the East Asian nations, none of whom actually conformed to the neo-liberal prescription of reduced state intervention in the economy. South Korea, Taiwan and Singapore have all had highly interventionist developmental states. Chang assembles plenty of evidence of state-backed capitalist development in Japan and Western countries too.

The policy elite seem to have forgotten the economic significance of the period from 1947 to the mid-1980s, when the state was laying down, howsoever poorly, the foundations of modern economic growth in India. India is now trying to catch up with the rich world by following the rules laid down by them. It is not allowed to protect the domestic economy— in agriculture, no less than in industry and services—against foreign competition.

The externally oriented growth strategy crafted for India took a dim view of purchasing power in the domestic market. It was argued that India was too poor to grow by itself. Given its allegedly limited capacity to save, it needed not only capital from abroad but also the markets of the Western world to sell its exports. It is factually incorrect to contend that the Indian savings rate and the limited size of the domestic market were impediments to growth. As we have seen earlier, India was growing at 5–6 per cent between 1974 and 1990.

As far as savings and capital for investment are concerned, it is noteworthy that domestic savings and investment are even today not too far apart, suggesting, at least in principle, the redundancy of foreign capital for growth. It is true that in a free society the state, through its economic policies, has only limited influence over how private savings would be invested. And yet, appropriate policies can be imagined which would direct savings towards productive investments. In many years, savings have exceeded investment. India had already achieved a savings rate of about 23 per cent of the GDP when the reforms started in 1991. This was high for a poor country, and certainly much higher than the rates of saving in the West, especially the US (which has typically had a negative savings rate till the crash of 2008). In fact the savings rate, even after the reforms, hovered around 23 per cent all the way till 2002–03, before crossing 30 per cent for the first time in 2004–05. In 2006–07, while the national savings rate was 35.7 per cent of the GDP, the rate of investment was only marginally higher, at 36.9 per cent, suggesting that, somewhere, foreign capital inflows were performing some altogether different role in the economy.[22]

In January 2008, the PM's Economic Advisory Council (EAC) admitted to the redundancy of foreign capital inflows for domestic investment:

> Rising levels of investment have been financed from domestic sources— through a combination of higher retained corporate earnings and improved fiscal balances of government. There has been little absorption of net foreign savings . . . Thus, the capital inflows which were in excess of the current account deficit have in an accounting sense become part of the foreign exchange reserves of the central bank and [been] 're-exported' overseas.[23]

A key lesson from the ongoing global crisis is that an externally oriented growth strategy for countries as large as India or China is flawed at the root. While China now faces serious dilemmas in relation to its dependence on the American market, there are reasons to question India's policies as well, especially in view of the future. First of all, the markets of the affluent nations are saturated, while the unemployed labour force in a country like India is huge. Secondly, exports to the rich nations are usually capital-intensive (unless one thinks of super-exploitative sweatshops) and so cannot support too much employment. Thirdly, there is stiff competition from other poor countries also trying to sell in the markets of the wealthy nations. Fourthly, when India attracts big inflows of foreign capital, it raises the value of the rupee, thereby making Indian exports less competitive in global markets. To compensate for this, suppliers often suppress wages or even retrench workers. Finally, too much portfolio investment (FII, or foreign institutional investment) generates exchange rate instability in a developing country, causing problems for exporters and importers, again adversely affecting wages and/or employment.

As a result of indiscriminate integration with the global world economy, India suffered like many other Asian economies from the financial crash of 2008. Reliable aggregate data is not available, but estimates suggest that anywhere from half a million to possibly ten million workers may have lost their jobs since September 2008, most of them in export sectors and export-related areas of the informal economy. The layoffs have been in areas like gems and jewellery, textiles, leather goods, handicrafts, and also in areas like aviation. Yet, many mainstream economists and policymakers are keen to emphasize that India has been less hurt than China during the present global crisis because it relies less on the international market. While exports constitute only around 20 per cent of the Indian GDP, they make up twice that proportion in the case of China. As noted economist Amit Bhaduri puts it: 'When the market boomed they took credit for liberalising the market, then as the market crashed they took credit for not liberalising the market.'[24]

Growing dependence on trade: A digression

Consider open-economy trade policies. More international trade leads each country to specialize in its areas of comparative advantage. Such specialization (because it involves large sunk costs in both capital and training of skilled labour), once achieved after a period of time, usually *compels* trade thereafter. We lose the freedom of opting out of trade. This loss of freedom is a liability in an ecologically critical and politically fragile situation of the kind we find ourselves in. The reason is that trade involves transport costs and possible disruptions. Transport is energy-intensive. Freight rises when the price of fossil fuels goes up—as it must, if externalities like climate change are to be duly reflected in it.

The world has been living off a highly subsidized global energy infrastructure. (The International Energy Agency estimates that global energy subsidies add up to 0.6–0.7 per cent of the world GDP, the bulk of them for fossil fuels, especially oil.) There is perhaps no country which has not kept the price of energy under check in order to make it cheaper for producers to generate it and/or affordable for the population to buy it. Indian governments certainly have. Through subsidies from public sector oil companies, tax credits, incentives for energy investment, government support for research and development (R&D), and a host of other mechanisms (in the US, through military expenses), the price of energy everywhere has been kept artificially low. This makes it apparently 'optimal' to import things which would normally be produced at home, taking away not just domestic investment opportunities but also jobs, and hurting the environment in the process.[25]

If we wish to have energy prices reflect the external costs of production, this status quo is long overdue for a change. Do we wish to expand our dependence on foreign trade in the manner of the West just at a time when ecological, political (arising from the Middle East) and financial uncertainties (such as wobbling exchange rates for key currencies) are more than likely to endanger our supply-lines in the future?

In India there are at least four major additional problems with the deregulated path of economic development. The first is that another country—it could be any populous developing country like China, Brazil or Bangladesh—could offer even more lax terms to entice big capital, and succeed. This would lead to loss of jobs when the TNCs fly their capital away.

Secondly, laws pertaining to competition are usually still only national in jurisdiction (with the exception of the EU), well behind the globalized character of the times. So TNCs from rich countries are able to walk into Third World markets with ease, especially since governments have turned much more pliant during the last two decades. This means that even the purported advantages of lower prices on account of greater efficiency don't accrue to Third World consumers. Too few firms control too large a share of the market, exercising a degree of market power that makes standard economics look ridiculous. Thus, it is no surprise that five corporations control 90 per cent of the international grain trade, three countries produce 70 per cent of the exported corn and the thirty largest food retailers control one-third of the world's grocery sales.[26]

Thirdly, integration with an international trading system historically and structurally dominated by the TNCs of affluent countries almost inevitably implies high trade deficits for poor countries. (China—not so poor today and cluttered with Western TNCs who export from there— is the notable exception, because of its singularly exceptional trade and financial relationship with the US.) This happens not only because of the poor prices earned by developing countries when they export to the affluent nations but also because they must open up their economies to imports from abroad, while their own access to rich country markets is curbed. Export promotion efforts in industrializing nations help but little. India's share of world exports fell from 2 per cent at the time of Independence to 0.5 per cent by 1990. Even after liberalization it has risen to a still modest 1.1 per cent in 2007, in no small measure because industrialized nations use increasingly subtle forms of protectionism against goods from abroad.[27]

The last one is a more serious problem, with which all countries need to wrestle. International competition can reduce costs in two distinct ways: by improving efficiency of resource-use or by lowering standards (for instance, environmental ones). Without strict regulations and controls, competing profit-maximizing firms have an intrinsic tendency to cut and shift costs in any way possible.

After globalization, there is a 'China Price' for every product. Labour and environmental standards are notoriously lower in China than in the rest of the world (though there are some signs recently of rising wages)—the reason why so many thousands of TNCs have located there. This is precipitating the well-known race-to-the-bottom, which is globally harmful in a world saddled with ecological problems.

The fallout of the TNCs' preferring China has affected India adversely. India too has been bringing standards down to entice capital, SEZs being just one instance of this. Ultimately, the whole world pays for deregulated globalization because the ecological consequences of the growth of large economies under such conditions will be shared by everyone to different degrees.

The mainstream economist may hope that deregulating world markets would lift standards everywhere and bring them to levels that prevail in the West. But the direction of capital mobility away from the developed world during the last twenty years gives the lie to this hope. There is a far greater possibility—as we witness the unravelling of the welfare state in the West, not to forget a greater incidence of environmental disasters—that more and more parts of the world will resemble the ravaged ecological and social landscapes already created by the most spectacular growth story in history.

Standards around the world—whether they have to do with the environment or labour—cannot be improved unless states become strong enough to resist corporations, including the TNCs. Internalization of social and environmental externalities is where corporations pay for reducing or minimizing the social and environmental damage their operations cause. While internalization is the great expectation economists have from markets, it proves costly to the firms involved. These firms have to pay higher taxes, fines and compensations for the damage they cause if standards are raised. It may be Union Carbide in Bhopal, India, or BP in the Gulf of Mexico. The issue is the same: can the government under whose jurisdiction the disaster happens act tough and force the TNCs to pay? Usually not.

Deregulated globalization has taken away from nation states their power to enact and enforce policies that could—at least in principle—internalize external costs. Deadlocks are now routine in climate negotiations. Liberating the world from fossil fuels is very difficult because those who benefit from the underpricing of carbon wield too much power. In the deregulated environment to which they have got accustomed, TNCs are able to find any number of ways to pre-empt a breakthrough. States often do not have the laws to help them contest the TNCs. When they do, they find it hard to muster the staying power, the political will or the financial/legal resources to enforce them in a world so inordinately dominated by corporate muscle.

As of 1995, trade in services too came within the ambit of multilateral trade negotiations for the first time. Surviving the opposition of developing countries, the WTO (World Trade Organization) succeeded in creating the framework for an agreement called the General Agreement on Trade in Services (GATS). Its implications for India—which, from being a loud opponent, has become a votary of GATS—are very large. Sectors of the economy sensitive to it are banking, finance, accountancy, insurance, legal services, real estate, retail, media, higher education, health, energy and water delivery, to name the most prominent ones. The consequences of this trend unfolding in India become apparent when we recognize the neon-lit names of the world's leading banks and real estate firms on our metropolitan horizon, not to forget the aggressive efforts being made by institutions like the ADB (Asian Development Bank) and the World Bank to push for the privatization of water services, health and education.[28]

Private finance and public policy

The most disturbing truth about the Indian growth story is that policies continue to be written to keep foreign investors interested in India, overriding all other priorities.

Global market dynamics and Indian policy management challenges are subtle. The strange, debt-heavy growth model that India has adopted has created a dependency on the fortunes of the affluent world and drawn it under the tyranny of global finance. Policymaking gets tightly constrained by global forces. India has been led to live beyond its means, much like American consumers were led to live beyond theirs—perhaps the key explanation for the 2008 crash. Debt-led growth comes with its own basket of problems and the men and women who rule the world understand this only too well.

Indebted economies like India must accelerate export production and sell in the buyers' markets in the West not only in order to bridge the trade deficit but also to meet their debt obligations. Over a period of time, workers in the export sector come to be badly exploited, as does the environment (discussed in chapters 4 and 5)—from excessive mineral extraction or over-fishing. A good part of India's GDP (between 15 and 20 per cent) is owed to foreigners, and 6–8 per cent of our export revenues go towards meeting foreign debt obligations every year. Over a quarter of the government budget is directed towards repayment of public debt.[29]

We are told not to worry about foreign debt since there are plenty of foreign exchange reserves. However, unlike China, whose enormous reserves are based on an export surplus, giving their policymakers remarkable room for manoeuvring, Indian foreign exchange reserves are based entirely on inflows of speculative capital owned by foreigners and NRIs, who see India as a desirable destination for their investment—at least for the time being. They can 'park' their funds in Indian financial markets for returns that exceed those of almost any other market in the world. Strictly speaking, the money is not owned by Indians resident in the country. In one three-month period in 2007, Indian markets gave a flattering return of over 33 per cent to investors (adding $400 billion to their kitty), at a time when the 'mature' markets of the West were often yielding negative returns.[30]

Notwithstanding the hyped-up IT success story, the truth is that Indian export performance has been modest at best, and certainly quite inadequate for making policy formulation relatively autonomous of global financial interests. The slow growth of export revenues and the persistence of external trade deficit are open secrets, but have hardly been written about. It means that the net contribution of foreign trade to the Indian economy has been negative all along and is, in fact, deteriorating. During the decades since 1947, Indian exports exceeded imports only twice—not after liberalization, but during the 1970s.

The last time that India enjoyed a trade surplus was in 1976–77. After the reforms began, India's merchandise trade deficit has expanded (at constant prices) rapidly from $6 billion in 1990–91 to $57 billion in 2007–08 (over 5 per cent of the GDP). The surplus from trade in services, including IT ($37.6 billion, 3.5 per cent of the GDP), was not adequate to make up for this in 2007–08. Import liberalization has allowed much demand to 'leak away' from the Indian economy. The trade deficit worsened from 2.3 per cent to 7.8 per cent of the GDP in the five years preceding the crash. If India spent Rs 8 out of every Rs 100 of its GDP on imports in 1991, by 2000 the proportion had increased to Rs 14 and in 2008 it was Rs 30. More than ever before, India is now a heavily import-dependent economy.[31]

The fact that India has been financing its growing trade deficit with funds from abroad has a huge bearing on the Indian state's autonomy over policymaking. It means India has to keep interest rates high for elite foreign investors and exchange rates stable in order to reduce the risk for those who invest in rupee-denominated assets. This has made the Indian government extremely sensitive to the 'sentiments' and mood swings of the stock market since these are dependent on capital inflows to finance the excess imports (many of them critical items like oil and capital goods). The Mumbai stock market index, the SENSEX (Sensitive Index), has seen a meteoric rise in recent years, curbed only by the crisis that began in 2008. From a value of 1000 in 1990 it rose to 20,000 in 2007, before the crisis knocked it rudely back. Since then, however, it has recovered much of its value, albeit subject to many and growing uncertainties.[32]

For the government, there is always a lurking fear that speculative portfolio investments would be withdrawn if the investor elite find the policies restrictive. Countries competing for global finance—Russia, China, Brazil, South Africa, Indonesia—could drain such capital away from India. If such a thing were to happen, India will once again confront the situation it faced in 1991, when the hard currency reserves it had left were adequate only for two weeks of imports. This is one of the deepest concerns for any Indian policymaker and a primary reason our media has suddenly become obsessed with reporting high growth rates in recent years.

'Confidence' in a government's policy is after all a shaky thing, as the 1997–98 Asian financial crisis demonstrated resoundingly and the present global crisis reminds us. One way to keep the confidence of global investors is to stay on the right side of the IFIs, the ultimate underwriters of so much international financial investment. They strongly influence the views of globally powerful banks, institutional investors and credit rating agencies regarding 'emerging' economies. In practice, this involves fulfilling their 'guidelines' and 'conditionalities'.

The other side of the story also needs to be told. Why are investors from rich nations so keen to invest in emerging markets? Aren't there plenty of areas for lucrative investment in what the punters call 'mature markets'? In brief, the answer is no.

Capitalism is a restless economic system. International capital is on a ceaseless quest for new investment opportunities. The objective of the financial system is the allocation of capital and risk across investments. Before the breakdown of the Bretton Woods monetary system in 1971, the financial sector of the advanced capitalist economies did not form such a big chunk of the overall level of economic activity and was tightly regulated everywhere. From the early 1970s a new hyper-financialized reality has been unleashed. In the era of floating (and thus, uncertain) exchange rates, speculation in international currency markets became lucrative and grew rapidly. New financial 'products' were devised to raise the level of returns.

With rapid developments in information technology and telecommunications, things took a further leap in the 1990s. With globalization, financial liberalization was enforced in the growing economies of Asia and Latin America (China being a significant, if partial, exception) under the supervision of the IFIs. This meant lifting of capital controls and the entry of speculative capital from rich countries into emerging markets.

In a financially globalized world the hunt for higher and quicker returns takes the form of aggressive investing in growing economies. *Growth* of output, not its overall *level*, is fundamental to the investor. If the real economy is growing at only 1–2 per cent every year, the financial (bond and stock) markets can't yield very high returns. This has been the story of developed economies in recent decades. Having 'mature markets', they are not only saturated in the real sense of producing more than enough goods and services for their people—their populations too having stabilized—they also have little scope for growth in the financial sector.

Investors from rich countries take an obsessive interest in the economies of the poor and developing countries because, starting from a small base, they are rapidly growing entities—in real terms. This means financial wealth can multiply much faster in countries like ours. The 'emerging markets' of the BRICS (Brazil, Russia, India, China, South Africa) nations shot to prominence after the end of the Cold War for this reason.

Consequently, the 'climate for investment' became important and Third World governments were constantly goaded into making areas under their jurisdiction safe for such business. Global China and India today are creations of a business media sponsored by powerful investors who rule Wall Street and the City of London. In these emerging markets, annual returns upwards of 50 per cent are quite common, and some funds yielding returns above 100 per cent are not unheard of. In such a world, why would anyone wish to invest in real economic activity, where returns are low and slow by comparison, except to have a secure reserve of wealth outside the world of financial paper? As a result, real economic activity has suffered even in the rich countries.[33]

The top ten performers among the world's stock markets are all from 'developing' countries, which includes the BRICS nations. In the first five months of 2009 these ten nations yielded, on average, returns of between 37 and 72 per cent. India was ranked third at 48 per cent, even if it is only the seventy-fifth best country to do business in, according to *Forbes* magazine (revealing that an economy like India can generate high financial returns while still being a difficult place for the real economy of actual physical production to function smoothly). By contrast, the G-7 nations (excluding Canada) yielded, on average, returns of just between 1 and 5 per cent during the same period, despite being places designed for business.[34]

Let us be clear what this means. Annual returns of 30, 50 or 100 per cent are orders of magnitude more than the returns the real economy can ever yield. Thus, if someone is able to extract those returns from a country, it actually implies a hidden exploitation of those who contribute to the production of its wealth, since the financial claims of market winners are *real*, denoting actual command of goods, services and resources. This is the updated, twenty-first-century version of global capitalist exploitation through increasingly opaque finance.

There is a powerful seduction at work here. Under finance-led globalization, capital flows across international boundaries have exploded and the everyday sale and purchase of currencies in foreign exchange markets around the world have increased dramatically. As we saw in chapter 1, the enormous bubble of finance floats atop a relatively modest stream of real wealth. There isn't nearly as much real wealth in the world as is imagined by so many. The reason for the great financial crisis of 2008 was the realization of this overarching fact by the average herd investor, who merely follows the market trend. The superficial stock market data—with its capricious, periodic highs and lows—is all too misleading.[35]

Finance, even more than IT, is at the core of the Indian growth story. FIIs have exploded in the Indian stock markets. They first arrived in 1993. By 2006, they were transacting Rs 28,55,000 crore ($634 billion), which was over two-thirds of the country's GDP and more than six times the value of 'primary market transactions' (which create equivalent physical assets). By now the ratio would be far greater. The share of what is called the 'derivatives' trade has also been rising fast. Derivatives are financial assets whose value is derived from that of underlying assets (like mortgages, commodities or something else). These were two and half times the value of spot transactions in 2006.[36]

FII inflows tend to be very volatile. A lot of the capital that comes into the country also leaves very soon. Hence, the Indian government's nagging concern about keeping them here. As the global financial environment becomes more uncertain, such volatility and insecurity are likely to grow. If India's foreign exchange reserves were to come from an export surplus, there would be no such worries.

There are a variety of investors who 'play' in international capital markets. They are usually not individuals, so much as the managers of banks, corporations and various 'funds' (like mutual funds and pension funds), and others who manage the money of wealthy investors. In recent years, 'hedge funds'—which invest the money of very big investors—have appeared on the market. These investors are interested in extremely high returns—well above what stock investments normally yield. Hedge fund managers thus have the licence to borrow (often as much as thirty times their capital) and play with huge sums of money, investing across a wide range of asset portfolios in world markets. Even after the battering of 2008, they reportedly manage more than $1 trillion of funds globally, an amount comparable to India's total stock market capitalization (the financial worth of all listed companies taken together) as well as its GDP.

Given the enormous risk of destabilization that hedge funds pose to emerging markets, the Indian government had kept them away from stock markets here. However, they managed to invest in FIIs in India indirectly through intermediate mechanisms. Finally, SEBI (Securities and Exchange Board of India) legalized them in 2007. Before the crash their valuation on Dalal Street had grown to five times their invested value. A lot of NRI investments are routed via Mauritius which has a 'double tax avoidance treaty' with India. In fact, Mauritius tops the list of countries invested in the Indian stock market. The US comes second.[37]

Another important high-powered international investor category is private equity. They do not participate in stock markets (hence, 'private' equity), choosing instead to invest directly in certain existing firms. This is why they are classified as FDI. They seek to make big profits through capital gains (resulting from appreciation of asset values). The American private equity firm Warburg Pincus invested $292 million in

Bharti Tele-Ventures between 1999 and 2001. It sold its share in 2004–05 for $1 billion, retaining a stake of $700 million. The implicit return calculated over a five-year period is almost 500 per cent. Clearly, while Indian big business gained from the entry of foreign capital, the latter gained far more, and more easily. Private equity firms have already invested billions in India, awaiting resumption of high growth.[38]

It is crucial to note the parasitic character of most of the capital inflows into India. The bulk of it is not used for real investment in the Indian economy. According to the *Economic Survey* of the Government of India, the gap between domestic saving and domestic investment was close to zero between 2002 and 2008, suggesting that India's investment was financed almost entirely from domestic sources. This means that the net capital inflows from abroad during these five years, amounting to over $120 billion, actually drew massive returns from India without contributing in any way to the creation of new productive capacity. What were these surplus foreign funds used for? They added to the dollar reserves of the RBI (Reserve Bank of India), helping finance surplus imports. India was, in effect, seduced into living beyond its means. Money also entered the Indian banking system through the RBI and was used to debt-finance elite purchase of housing and consumer durables, inevitably contributing to inflation in the process.[39]

As a result of its continuing high external deficit, a high government budget deficit and high consumer price inflation, India is regarded by many observers—such as *The Economist* magazine—as one of the 'riskiest emerging markets', making it all too possible that portfolio investment might suddenly leave India in a moment of crisis, replicating the events of 1991.[40]

To recall, the two main justifications given for the opening up of the economy after 1991 were that (i) more foreign trade would give a boost to the Indian market and (ii) the entry of foreign capital would increase domestic investment. Both these claims, the evidence suggests, were unfounded. More foreign trade has amounted to import liberalization much more than to growth in exports (which have increased slowly), leading to a serious worsening of the external deficit and a net drain on the economy. Capital inflows have not contributed to investment. Instead, they have contributed to the extraction of high, exploitative returns from India—something which would have been the envy of colonial Britain—while allowing high levels of elite consumption. In either case, the rich countries have been able to derive great advantage from India's increasingly open and vulnerable economy.

Another consequence of the entry of FIIs into India is that they now own significant chunks of Indian firms. Between 1993 and 2007, while net FII inflows into India added up to $70.8 billion, their market value was $251.5 billion by December 2007. In December 2007, FIIs held 37 per cent of the free-float shares in the top 1000 firms listed on the Mumbai Stock Exchange. Growing control of Third World corporations by financial interests from the rich countries has of course been taking place in other Asian economies as well, such as South Korea. In 2004 foreign investors owned half the shares in the top ten Korean firms, including Hyundai, Samsung and POSCO.[41]

The net result is that global finance profoundly influences the real domestic economy (producing actual goods and services), whose activities are relegated to a lower priority. This mirrors a worldwide trend in which the centre of gravity of the economy as a whole has moved away from real production towards finance.

It is worth noting here that the acquisition in recent years of foreign industrial firms by several Indian big business houses—

for example, Tatas' acquisition of Corus—does not quite mean what it seems to. As leading firms in industrialized economies shift their focus to the high-turnover financial sector, it is understandable that they wish to offload much of their stake in areas of industrial production. Such sources of profit are low and slow, involve problems with labour unions and sometimes have publicly visible environmental consequences.

What is crucial to understand from the point of view of those with a genuine concern for the economic betterment of people in India is that purely financial transactions result in a mere change of ownership. They contribute little or nothing to the productive or job-generating capacity of an economy. When shares change hands in the secondary market, the transaction does not reflect the creation of any real assets.

Thus, a finance-led boom of the sort that India has witnessed since the beginning of this century brings windfall gains to the global and Indian investor elite, but deprives many important sectors of badly needed funds by diverting them instead to the financial sector. Moreover, under the liberalized tax regimes that have been created as 'incentives' for financial investment, both capital gains (when assets are sold) and returns on financial assets are very lightly taxed. This adds fuel to fire as secondary market transactions grow in volume compared to primary transactions.

With the high margins on financial investments, fund managers can pay themselves exorbitant bonuses and offer high salaries to other finance professionals. Some of the most capable and educated young people from India's top institutions, like the IITs and the IIMs, are lured into jobs in finance that pay in six or seven figures every month. Compensation is often negotiated in stock options (part ownership of the firm's shares), which move up in value in a stock market boom. Understandably, employees start working very soon to merely raise the market valuation of their firm, rather than for the purpose of directing the company's activities towards real productive ends. Greed in this case, as in so many others, actually undercuts *industrial* capitalism.

Summing up the impact of the rise of finance in India, expert in international economics Sunanda Sen writes:

> Financial reforms in India have neither been for growth in terms of the creation of physical assets nor for a fair distribution of the financial flows which are not only equitable but also productive. Instead the country has provided opportunities for speculation in financial assets in a manner as had never been witnessed before. This has been considerably facilitated by communication technology, with investors having the facilities to manage their portfolios at the press of a button![42]

Is it then any surprise that the reform era has altered in dramatic ways the role of the state? Sunanda Sen once again:

> The logic of capitalism today redefines the priorities of the state machinery, pushing the agenda on its role as the facilitator of the market. The process entangles, as a necessary adjunct, the interests of advanced countries where international capital originates. The advanced countries today have a much greater stake, as compared to what it used to be some decades back, in the functioning of the developing country markets. IFIs or the WTO, which are usually run in the interests of the same set of rich industrialised nations, often operate as intermediaries between the latter and the developing ones. This makes it even easier for the advanced countries to have close surveillance over the policies in the developing countries and to steer those in a direction which is of interest to their own countries.[43]

The political influence of global finance capital on India was demonstrated by an episode in January 2005 when the RBI governor hinted at the possibility of mild taxation of FII flows, in order to 'enhance' their quality. Overseas investors applied pressure on the finance minister to get the statement officially 'rejected'. The RBI's diminishing control over monetary policy is obvious from its inability to stem the appreciation of the rupee (with higher FII flows) in 2007 and the consequent loss of jobs in the export sector. Clearly, the maintenance and growth of employment is not high on the agenda of our policy elite. The IFIs to whom they are obliged have tacitly dictated other priorities. The RBI's impotence in the new climate has been evident once more during the recent depreciation of the rupee.[44]

While foreign capital inflows may not have brought much benefit for the bulk of the Indian population, their sudden outflow can certainly bring much harm. The experience of Latin America in the 1980s and 1990s, that of East and South-East Asia in 1997–98, of Russia in 1998 and of Argentina in 2001 suggests that the sudden departure of foreign capital easily leads to a quick devaluation of the currency, inflation and unemployment. Given India's precariously poised external accounts, this must remain a serious worry for Indian policymakers.[45]

Policy space is taken up not just by measures that open the economy to foreign goods, services and capital. The conditionalities imposed by the IFIs ensure that fiscal and monetary policies suit the interests of financial markets. This is why, for instance, Indian governments have had to accept the Fiscal Responsibility and Budget Management (FRBM) Act (2003) which restricts deficit spending, thereby capping public expenditure on health, education, public housing, environmental protection and social services (though the 2008 collapse forced the government to make an exception—to boost *business activity*, not specifically to generate employment). Under pressure from international creditors, working through the IMF and the World Bank, India's policymakers have consistently had to focus on minimizing the primary deficit on the government budget. This hovered around zero, till the global crisis hit in 2008. But if we add to the primary deficit the large interest payments on foreign debt made by the government since the 1990s, the fiscal deficit balloons to 3–6 per cent of the GDP per year. Arguably, this (together with the growing trade deficit, 1–4 per cent of the GDP) constitutes the flip side of the institutional capital inflows into India (1–3 per cent of the GDP).[46]

Likewise, no policy that slows down financial transactions, such as a turnover tax, an increase-in-the-capital-gains tax or tax on transactions in securities is allowed on the agenda. (In India, incidentally, taxes constitute only 10–11 per cent of the GDP, in sharp contrast to industrialized countries, where the figure is between 30 and 50 per cent.) These steps, it is argued, will upset 'investor sentiment' and drive away foreign capital inflows. But measures like easing the convertibility of the rupee, it is pointed out, will vastly improve such sentiment.[47]

Since India has integrated with the global economy in a time of high finance, it has had to adjust at telescopic speed to the terms set by the world's wealthiest investors, working through a long network of funds, credit rating agencies and, of course, the IFIs. As the 2008 crash revealed, much more powerful governments than India's are helpless before the tyranny of global finance. The hands of our 'democratically' accountable leaders are actually well tied behind their backs, the reason why no government since 1991 has really tinkered with the policy framework of what has been called neo-liberalism (read 'climate for investment').

After the General Elections of 2004 we got a taste of what it means for the policy levers of an ostensibly sovereign country to be remote-controlled. After the UPA (United Progressive Alliance) victory, the stock market nosedived out of fear that the country's economic policies would be radically altered— even though nothing fundamental had changed in the underlying economic realities. Funds started leaving the country. However, once political assurance arrived in the form of an announcement from the top economic team, the prime minister, the finance minister and the deputy chairman of the Planning Commission, all known for their pro-corporate and market-friendly views, the stock market settled down quickly. The ultimate guarantor of the climate for investment is the state. And in playing this part it has also ceded autonomy over the nation's economic policies.

As noted earlier, an important argument cited in favour of globalization in the 1990s was that it would enlarge the pool of capital available for domestic investment. What has actually happened is the exact opposite. Either speculative foreign capital makes extractive investments in India or Indian capital is found investing overseas in a whole range of acquisitive and new ventures. This is what 'going global' sometimes means for an Indian TNC.

According to the RBI, India's FDI abroad in 2007–08 was $17.4 billion, up sharply from $4.5 billion in 2005–06. (This may be compared with the FDI coming into India in 2007–08: $34.4 billion.) The bulk of the investments abroad has been via acquisitions like Tatas' purchase of Corus and JLR (Jaguar Land Rover), or Hindalco's purchase of the bauxite major, Novelis.[48]

It is one thing for some Indian companies and big businesses to be successful global players, another thing for the Indian economy and people to benefit from that. Lakshmi Mittal tops the list of billionaires of Indian origin. He is the owner of the largest steel company in the world. But his contribution to the Indian economy is negligible, since most of his operations have so far been in other countries, like Kazakhstan or the EU.

Indian big business is creating jobs in Britain (where Indian companies are now the second biggest employer after the US) and in the US, even in China. Indian big business has created no less than 300,000 jobs in the US during 2004–07, according to our commerce minister. Creating jobs and wealth in India for ordinary Indians is lower down their rung of priorities.[49]

Indian big business can acquire copper mines in Zambia and bauxite mines in Australia. It can buy oilfields in Equatorial Guinea and sell bottled water in the West. It can set up software production units in Eastern Europe, close to markets in the EU. It can create R&D establishments in Britain, inviting British scientists to work for them. It can produce hundreds of millions of dollars worth of shoes in China and sell them in the EU, paying taxes in both places. But does any of this help create opportunities and employment for Indians back home? Not unless the profits are remitted and invested at home. Of this there is little guarantee, especially if the conditions (like difficulties associated with land acquisition in India) which led the companies to do business abroad continue to prevail.

The latest buzz in the business world is the rapid acquisition of farmland by Indian, Chinese and Middle-Eastern firms in East Africa. The purchase of agricultural land in countries like Ethiopia, Kenya and Madagascar, which suffer frequently from famines, has been strongly criticized by food policy experts. They argue that the investing countries' food security ought not to come at the expense of that of the host nation. Nor does the latter deserve to have its ecological balance disturbed by industrial agriculture. More than eighty Indian companies spent over $4 billion in 2008 buying land in Ethiopia alone. Export of food and flowers from there is the stated goal, though speculation in farmland in a time of rising commodity prices globally appears to be the real aim. Ignoring local political risks, the Indian government appears to be supporting the acquisition of farmland in foreign countries as an alternative to the purchase of food in international markets. Aren't there simpler food alternatives in India itself, if government policy is properly designed and implemented? (We return to these issues in chapters 6 and 10.)[50]

These are aspects of globalization few had anticipated. It may have made a few Indians rich and famous around the world. But it has only meant lost managerial skills (a new kind of brain drain) and loss of financial and other scarce resources for the Indian economy.

'No vacancy': Jobless growth

For a country the size of India, the well-being of the people hinges more fundamentally on the possibilities of productive and rewarding work opportunities than on overall economic growth. When Indian economic policies were redirected towards a more open economy in the early 1990s, the resulting growth in output was expected to be pro-poor as well. In other words, growth in employment was expected. Has that actually happened?

Between 1983 and 1994, when economic growth was 4–5 per cent every year, employment in the organized sector grew at 1.2 per cent. Between 1994 and 2005, when growth increased to 5–6 per cent (sometimes crossing 7 per cent), employment growth turned negative (–0.3 per cent). It turned imperceptibly positive by 2006 (0.12 per cent). But once the data is in for all the hundreds of thousands of workers laid off during the current recession, the employment growth could again turn negative. Importantly, in the pre-reform period, the rate of growth of employment was well above the rate of growth of population. During the post-reform period the opposite has been the case.[51]

In 1991, when the reforms began, the organized sector employed 26.7 million people, of whom 7.7 million worked in the private corporate sector. In 2006 the numbers had remained virtually unchanged (total employment was 27 million with 8.8 million in the private corporate sector, including the big spurt in the IT sector). Moreover, as the National Commission for Enterprises in the Unorganized Sector (NCEUS, also referred to as the Arjun Sengupta Committee) has shown in its reports, almost all the *net* increase in employment in the organized sector has been of the casual variety, without job or social security. Following the neo-liberal prescription of flexible labour markets, there is a clear trend towards the informalization of the workforce. Meanwhile, between 1991 and 2006, India's labour force grew from about 325 to 440 million.[52]

The committee came to the important conclusion that making labour markets more flexible is unlikely to generate more employment: 'Empirical findings suggest that the so-called labour market inflexibility had hardly been a factor in determining either the growth of employment or labour intensity in organized manufacturing.' For the future, NCEUS projects that of the 13–14 per cent of workers with access to formal sector employment in 2017, almost half will be employed in an informal capacity (without benefits), much like today.[53]

The primary explanation for the stagnation in organized sector employment lies in the very nature of the capital-intensive technology used in modern industry and services. Mechanization and automation account for this. India today produces more than three times the industrial output it made in 1990 with the same number of workers in the organized sector that it employed then. The above numbers are confirmed by evidence from the shop floor. Here are some of the many examples that can be cited.

Edward Luce of London's *Financial Times* reports that in 1991 the Tata Steel plant in Jamshedpur—India's largest private sector steel company—employed 85,000 workers to produce a million tons of steel worth $800 million. In 2005 it churned out 5 million tons worth $4 billion, employing the services of only 44,000 people. While the output multiplied five times, employment was halved.[54]

Stephen Roach, the chief economist of Morgan Stanley, offers similar stories. In 2004 the Bajaj motorcycle factory in Pune—using Japanese robotics enabled with Indian IT—turned out 2.4 million two-wheelers annually with approximately 10,500 workers. In the mid-1990s the same factory had needed a workforce of some 24,000 to produce only a million units. More than double the output has been produced by less than half the workers.[55]

A detailed study of some traditionally labour-intensive sectors of Indian industry (apparel, leather, gems and jewellery, sports goods and bicycles) shows that labour-intensity of production (units of labour used per unit of output) has steadily declined from a ratio of 0.72 in 1990–91 to 0.30 in 2003–04.[56]

When the government or the corporate sector makes an aggressive pitch for a certain project (for instance, involving land acquisition for SEZs), the number of jobs to be created is made to sound impressive. But the foremost goal of modern businesses is profit, not jobs. Competition pushes them to retrench workers and mechanize where necessary in order to maximize profits. 'When I expand, it is always in a capital-intensive and not a labour-intensive direction,' businessman Dinesh Hinduja once told a journalist.[57]

Jobless growth is not just an Indian phenomenon. Western nations have frequently had to retrench workers because of growing automation, and developing countries like China and those in East Asia have also been facing a serious problem of jobless growth. In China, where nearly half the GDP comes from the industrial sector, the number of workers engaged in manufacturing fell from a peak of 98 million in 1995 to 83 million in 2002, constituting only about 12 per cent of the workforce. The number of workers engaged in manufacturing in all the G-7 countries taken together is just a little more than 50 million.[58]

Redundancy, even more than exploitation, is increasingly the condition of labour around the globe. It seems that the economist Joan Robinson's characterization of the modern worker's situation, articulated decades ago, is all too real today: 'The only thing worse than being exploited by a capitalist is to be exploited by no one at all.'[59]

The argument is often made that looking merely at the organized sector to judge job-creation is misleading, since so many opportunities come up in the unorganized manufacturing sector for each job created in the formal sector. This claim is not supported by facts. The links between the organized and the unorganized sectors are not of a kind where the growing wealth of one simply spills over into the other.

Usually, the wealth of one grows at the *cost* of the other. In a time of cut-throat competition, manufacturers often improve their competitiveness by suppressing wages or retrenching labour. The organized sector is engaged in a one-way exploitative relationship with the unorganized sector via processes such as outsourcing and subcontracting. Moreover, small industries—the primary employers in the unorganized sector—have not only suffered from competition from larger firms, they have also suffered from policy neglect and lack of credit from banks, which focus more on big business and consumer loans.

An OECD (Organization for Economic Co-operation and Development) study of the Indian economy documents that while the capital available to each worker in an enterprise with more than 100 workers grew from 1998 to 2004, and is today thrice of what it was in 1993, it actually declined by 14 per cent in smaller firms—evidence that investment is stagnant in small industry. Further, because of big capital inflows from abroad the rupee appreciated against foreign currencies, making Indian exports expensive, due to which small industries lost export markets. The net result is that jobs in unorganized manufacturing, which employs five out of six workers in manufacturing, have not grown much. Between 2000–01 and 2005–06, *before* the recession, the number of workers employed in this sector *fell* from 37.1 to 36.4 million.[60]

So, if India's labour force has expanded by well over 100 million since the early 1990s, where have people found work? The answer lies in the dramatic growth of 'self-employment' and employment in unorganized services. They appear to have absorbed over 60 million new workers since 1993, most of them severely underemployed and underpaid. The remainder are—even officially—unemployed.[61]

Given current trends, there are well-founded fears even in corporate circles, of India heading for an 'unemployment explosion' in the future. TeamLease Services, one of India's leading staffing companies, estimates unemployment rising to a terrifying 200 million people or 30 per cent of the labour force by 2020, 90 per cent of the unemployed being in the fifteen to twenty-nine age group, with all its attendant sociopolitical implications. Without policies sensitive to labour, India's famed demographic dividend is fated to become a destructive curse. This is why policies like the MGNREGA (Mahatma Gandhi National Rural Employment Guarantee Act) take on such significance today.[62]

There is a critical observation to be made about the destruction and loss of traditional livelihoods—not merely jobs—in so many rural areas of the country through the forcible displacement and dispossession of working communities. There is no official reckoning of livelihoods lost in such cases. Only the jobs promised to the latter are totalled up and attractively presented to the public, as though there were nothing lost on the other side of the ledger. We shall return to this issue in the next chapter and in chapter 7.

Imbalanced growth

Stories of successful economic growth and development are rooted in relatively balanced growth between the different sectors of the economy. The linkages between the different sectors get stronger as growth happens. The economy gets increasingly unified over time, as against getting fragmented into sectors growing at extremely unequal rates, often at odds with each other.

In particular, students of development economics know the importance of structurally balanced growth in the relative expansion of agriculture vis-à-vis industry and services. For instance, if the latter two sectors do not grow fast enough, they become incapable of absorbing the surplus labour from agriculture. Conversely, if agriculture does not keep pace with industry and services, there are food shortages and, possibly, shortfalls in agricultural raw materials for industry.

In industrialized economies, over the past century and a half, as productivity per unit of labour in farming has grown with mechanization, labour has shifted or been pushed out from agriculture into industry and services. Most developed countries today have only a minuscule share of the workforce, often less than 2–3 per cent, in agriculture. At one time, more than half the workforce used to be engaged in farming and traditional activities. Even manufacturing, thanks to rapid automation, absorbs less than 10–20 per cent of the workforce now, the bulk of the people finding employment in the modern service economy.

Orthodox development economics, generalizing from the experience of the West and Japan, holds that in the course of economic growth a greater share of the GDP begins to accrue from industry and services. Agriculture and the large unorganized sector are expected to fall in importance as labour is absorbed into the more 'high-value-added' activities in the formal, contractual economy.

In India, as in many other poor countries, we notice something else altogether. Consider the numbers in Figure 2.1. We would expect that the fall in the share of workforce in agriculture was on account of a transfer of labour to the manufacturing sector. Instead, we notice that while manufacturing's share of the workforce rose from 10.7 per cent to just 12.2 per cent (though less than a sixth—2 per cent of total employment—of the manufacturing employment in the country now comes from the organized factory sector), the share of services in employment increased from 17.6 per cent to 24.8 per cent. Output data reveals a similar story: the share of services

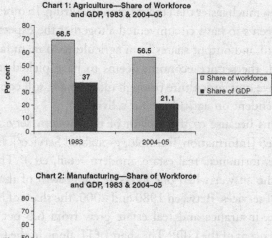

Chart 1: Agriculture—Share of Workforce
and GDP, 1983 & 2004–05

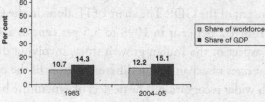

Chart 2: Manufacturing—Share of Workforce
and GDP, 1983 & 2004–05

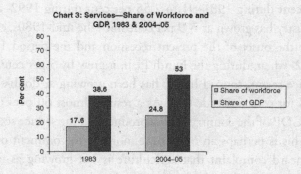

Chart 3: Services—Share of Workforce and
GDP, 1983 & 2004–05

FIGURE 2.1: Three figures showing distribution of workforce and GDP across the three main sectors of the Indian economy.

Source: EAC, *Review of the Economy 2007–08*, based on NSS (National Sample Survey) data.[64]

has risen much faster than that of manufacturing. In other words, India seems to have circumvented altogether the expected shift of labour and output shares from agriculture to manufacturing. Instead, the service economy seems to have picked up those who have quit agriculture (though most people still continue to be dependent on agriculture for a living).[63]

Is this because of the growth of the modern service sector (IT, ITeS [Information Technology–enabled Services], banking, finance, insurance, real estate, modern retail, etc.)? This *seems* to be the answer when one looks at the growth of the output share of services. Between 1980 and 2000, the share of banking, finance, insurance and real estate grew from 6.6 per cent to 12.6 per cent of the GDP. The share of IT alone in the GDP has grown from 1.2 per cent in 1998 to 5.5 per cent in 2008.[65]

This aspect of the Indian growth story, involving drastically divergent rates of expansion in different sectors of the economy, demands wider recognition. The neglect of agriculture has meant that the annual growth rate in agricultural output fell from 3.3 per cent during 1981–91 to 2.55 per cent during 1992–2004. Industry has grown at 7–9 per cent since the mid-1980s, except after the onset of the present recession and the period 1997–2002, when, during the Ninth Plan, it grew by 5 per cent. The service sector, topped by IT, has been growing at double digit rates for over a decade now. As a result, almost 60 per cent of the GDP of the country is now produced in the service sector.[66]

This is perhaps an opportune moment to comment on the oft-heard complaint that agriculture is not growing as fast as industry or services. (One may note that the complaint is not so much that the growth in agriculture has slowed down compared to what it itself used to be or could potentially be.) Any comparison of growth rates between agriculture and the other two sectors must reckon with the fact that the former is bound by natural cycles, like those of water and the seasons, in a way that industry and services are not. You can increase the number of daily shifts of labour in the case of industry and services, and raise their growth 'artificially', especially if you are accessing a 'large' stock of non-renewable energy sources. On the other hand, in agriculture, while productivity can be increased, there are definite natural limits to what can be achieved in a given state of technology. Increasing the number of daily shifts of work, for instance, will not increase production (might even reduce it). Thus, it is a little inappropriate to crudely compare growth rates across sectors. Yet, much of the policy discussion and commentary tend to do so.

Returning to the question of the sectoral distribution of employment: what explains the rise in the share of services in total employment? Employment in the organized sector as a whole has stagnated since 1991. Even IT, the flagship of the growing economy, has registered a growth in employment of just a few million workers over the past decade. The answer is to be found in the unorganized sector, that is to say, in Bharat, rather than 'Shining India'. The informal or unorganized sector is that part of the economy which consists of unincorporated private enterprises, mostly owned by individuals or partnerships, which employ fewer than ten people. It is also sometimes called the 'non-factory sector', because more often than not, the work is done in homes and sweatshops, usually in uncongenial settings. The 'enterprises' are usually unregistered.

The service sector is unevenly divided between a high-income, low-employment segment (like IT, ITeS, finance, hospitality, media and real estate) and a low-income, high-employment part (such as rickshaw pullers, tea shops and small retail). There is virtually no link between these two parts of the service economy which government documents lump under the same heading. In the former case, the forward linkages of the organized service economy are more with the rest of the world than with the domestic economy. For instance, growth in banking and finance is usually driven more by global than by domestic market forces. Such an economic pattern only reinforces the inherent dualism in the economy.

It is the residual unorganized sector which has served as a default option for many hundreds of millions of people for whom the organized mainstream economy has no work. But employment 'growth' in the unorganized sector is actually an illusion. It is largely a form of compelling underemployment for so many who do not have the education or the job opportunities that the elite and the middle classes enjoy. Yet, the unorganized sector produces half the country's output, while employing more than nine out of ten Indians. The growth of the informal economy in both urban and rural areas testifies to the failure of the development model to generate jobs.

The old black hole: The growing informal economy

One of the more overwhelming images of India is that of a colourful, teeming mass of people engaged in many different kinds of work. Farmers, small shopkeepers, tea-shop-owners, road-builders, construction workers, cart-pullers, head-loaders, basket-weavers, herders, rickshaw-wallahs and fisherfolk are only some of the kinds of working people on the streets of our towns and cities. This vast majority makes up the informal economy, outside the protection of job and social security. They live on what they earn each day.

How many working people are we thinking of when we speak of the unorganized sector? The overwhelming majority. In 2004–05 the government-appointed NCEUS identified that 420 million people belonged to this group. Of these, almost 29 million were informal workers in the organized sector, their wages on an average 40 per cent more than their counterparts in the unorganized sector. Over a third, 140 million, were women. In contrast, the NCEUS could identify only 35 million working people in the formal, organized sector of the economy. In other words, over 92 per cent of the working people in India are informal workers.[67]

Agriculture still constitutes the mainstay of the informal economy, employing between 230 and 260 million working people, a growing proportion being women. What is striking about the informal economy is the huge number of enterprises that constitute it. For every enterprise in the formal sector, there are as many as fifteen in the informal economy. Since levels of investment are low, the physical capital available to each worker is very little when compared with the formal economy. Consequently, labour productivity is limited. Education levels are much lower because of historical, structural deprivations. As a result of these factors, even if people work very hard— usually much harder than in the formal sector—they are poorly paid and most of them live in conditions of extreme poverty.

It is important to recognize that only a small fraction of India's informal workforce can be meaningfully seen as a 'reserve army of labour'—the fraction that stands the odd chance of finding work in the formal economy. This Marxist notion usually assumes that people in this category are in and out of formal employment, depending on the demand for labour. However, what is true about India's informal workers is that the vast majority of them are typically 'out' of formal employment permanently. Both because of mechanization and a deficit of skills (given the structural and tragic mismatch between their education and the skill requirements of the modern sector), they stand very little chance of finding regular (or even casual) work in the formal economy. In this sense, unemployment in India is mostly structural, unlike in Western countries where it tends to be cyclical. (As Western economies recover from recession, they tend to absorb the unemployed.)

Working conditions in this part of the economy are a world apart from those in the modern, organized sector. If one is an air-conditioned, chrome-plated building adorning downtown India, the other is a dingy sweatshop or a dilapidated hovel in a lane in a battered slum. Apart from the fact that there is no job security or social benefits like health insurance and pension funds, workers typically work much longer hours than in the formal sector, usually without overtime pay. When they have regular employment, they rarely get leave from work. They are typically paid by piece-rates, rather than fixed wages. In either case, remuneration is exploitative.

Social divisions and hierarchies, based on caste or gender, make exploitation even more convenient. One study of Lucknow *chikan* embroidery workers found that in some cases village women were getting as little as Re 1 per kurta, because women's embroidery at home is not seen as 'real work' by the mahajans who make the payment. Informal workers are often employed in hazardous conditions in chemical factories or ship-breaking yards, without a semblance of occupational safety. There are rarely any formally drawn labour contracts, most of the workers being illiterate.[68]

Women workers are often preferred because they are found to be more docile and diligent. In recent times, many are new to any sort of a job and so, easy to treat as casual labour. They already constitute a 'flexible labour market' that free-market economists long for. One reason why the NCEUS has found rising participation rates in the labour force is because more and more women now have to work outside the home. Times are tough. Opportunities for a certain class of women may have grown in the ITeS/BPO (business process outsourcing) sectors, but in manufacturing their working conditions are super-exploitative.

A study of women in Mumbai's slums shows that they are increasingly working in industrial, subcontracting units in which occupational hazards abound. The units compete with each other to get contracts from large companies in the formal sector, resulting in highly exploitative wages. There are no separate toilets for women. There are no maternity benefits or welfare. There is no social or employment security. The cumulative pressure of work under oppressive conditions combined with the load of housework and child-rearing has led to great deterioration in the mental and physical health of women. Since this is a 'lawless sector', where women (and men) have no legal rights, there have been urgent calls for protective legislation.[69]

In the rural unorganized sector, conditions for working women are even worse. Near the border of Uttar Pradesh (UP) and Madhya Pradesh (MP), landless *kol* women can be found carrying large head-loads of firewood to railway stations. A whole day's work that involves travelling on foot for 10–20 km may fetch them Rs 30. Those who work in the stone quarries of the thakurs and the brahmins earn similar wages and face sexual indignities to boot. They are often forced into sexual compromises in order to protect their men from upper-caste violence. Kols are meant to have protection under the law, but local government officials are often in league with the landed upper castes.[70]

In UP there are anywhere from 40,000 to 60,000 people (85 per cent of whom are women) from Dalit and Muslim communities whose livelihood comes from scavenging and cleaning human excreta. They are usually daily-wage workers who earn Rs 60 to Rs 100 a day. They labour in the most inhospitable surroundings and are socially isolated. They have no protection of any kind in their 'employment'. This too is part of the nation's 'informal' sector.[71]

In some parts of the informal economy, children contribute much of the labour. When they are not looking after their younger siblings at construction sites, they are found rag-picking, serving tea to truck drivers on highways, weaving carpets in Mirzapur or doing fine zari-work in Gujarat—their nimble fingers preferred to those of adults. Roughly one in five children under age fourteen, according to UNICEF (United Nations Children's Fund) surveys, works as a domestic servant. The working environment for children is even more degraded than it is for adult workers. A UNICEF study of the Varanasi carpet-weaving industry found utterly dehumanizing conditions where children were made to toil:

> Most of them are kept in captivity, tortured and made to work for 20 hours a day without a break. Little children are made to crouch on their toes, from dawn to dusk every day, severely stunting their growth during formative years. Social activists in the area find it hard to work because of the strong Mafia-like control that the carpet-loom-owners have on the area.[72]

It would be a terrible blunder to see the informal manufacturing sector as unrelated to the modern, organized part of the economy, as though they sat on two different islands. The Indian informal economy today is the hybrid outcome of the encounter between a resiliently feudal society and the advanced globalized capitalist economy. It is how the rest of India has had to adapt to mainstream economic development and rapid global integration. The informal sector has been integrated into the globalizing capitalist economy on terms that suit the middlemen and the formal economy. The latter actually draws huge ('informal') subsidies from the former, thanks to the cheap production of finished and semi-finished goods. It always has. There would hardly be a reader of this book who does not benefit from the exploitative conditions that prevail in the Indian informal economy.

To add insult to injury, the growing informalization (and feminization) of the workforce is everywhere a phenomenon accompanying globalization and the creation of production and value chains that stretch right across the world. It is not incidental to the dynamism of the global capitalist economy. In fact, the possibilities of exploiting cheap, unprotected labour and raw materials is precisely what tempted the TNCs to move their production operations to places like Mexico, China and India in the first place.

The export of jobs from the rich nations—of which we have heard so much in recent years—was inevitable given the gap in wages and benefits enjoyed by the labour aristocracy in the West and the poorly compensated workers in Asian or Latino sweatshops. ILO (International Labour Organization) reports have repeatedly testified to the growth in informalization of labour since the early days of globalization. It has greatly cheapened the cost of production for global brands like Walmart or Nike. Both consumers and MNCs (multinational corporations) from the affluent countries benefit from this lucrative arrangement. In India there is data to show that the share of contract labour (in total employment) in the factory sector grew from 13.5 per cent in 1990 to 23.2 per cent in 2002, testimony to the fact that flexible labour markets already exist.[73]

This phenomenon of outsourcing or subcontracting has increased dramatically with the fierce competition unleashed by globalization and the ruthlessly exploitative 'China price'. Under this new international division of labour, corporations from rich countries hire Third World subcontractors who in turn employ workers on cheap wages. In this complex, layered system, subcontractors avoid the costs entailed in assuring job and social security by parcelling out contracts to production units in the informal economy, which compete fiercely with each other. Indian products have gained competitiveness in international markets, even in the formal IT sector, largely by controlling labour costs in this way. Large global retailers and brands have set up elaborate global production and supply chains that reduce their purchase costs. Thus, a long chain of dependency, which starts in the scattered sweatshops and working homes of some of the poorest urban classes in the Third World, ends in the corporate boardrooms of branded MNCs in Atlanta or New York.

An investigation carried out in 2010 by the London *Observer* found super-exploitative conditions in which working people are employed in factories in New Delhi. These units serve some of the top brands in the Western world: Gap, Next and Marks & Spencer. Hired through middlemen, workers toil up to sixteen hours a day.

Workers also say that those who refuse to work the extra hours have been told to find new jobs. Those in the factory supplying Gap and Next also claim staff who refused to work extra hours were threatened and fired, a practice defined under international law as forced labour and outlawed around the world. Workers said they had been required to put in up to eight hours a day in overtime, for which they claim to have been paid at half the legal minimum rate required by the Ethical Trading Initiative and Indian law. Some workers at the same factory said they had to work seven days a week, a practice condemned by their union as 'slave labour'.[74]

Gap may feign innocence, but it is not new to the game of taking advantage of dirt-cheap labour in India. In 2007 one of its suppliers in New Delhi was found to be using child labour in the most abysmal and abusive conditions, involving everything from unpaid work to threats and violence. Big textile exporters rely on cheap fabrics in Third World sweatshops to carve global market niches. The same is true of leather goods, gems and jewellery. Incidentally, 30 per cent of Indian merchandise exports come directly from the much neglected small-scale sector, which is normally not on the radar of either the media or the government.[75]

One study of leather goods producers in Kanpur found that nearly 80 per cent of the final price of exported shoes goes to a long line of middlemen who enter the value chain in the post-production phase. Only 2 per cent of the export price of a shoe actually ends up with the workers who make them. No one seems to want to do anything about the exorbitant margins of profit for the long line of intermediaries.[76]

In the five years from 1999–2000 to 2004–05, the number of informal workers in the Indian economy, including those employed in the organized sector, grew by 58 million

(15 per cent of the labour force of 1999–2000). The growth in formal workers over the same period was only 1.4 million. The NCEUS rightly underscores the fact that almost all the growth in employment during this period has been of the informal variety.

Moreover, unemployment has grown significantly between 1993–94 and 2004–05. NSS data shows that the annual rate of growth of employment fell from a high 2.34 per cent between 1983 and 1993–94 to a dismal 0.86 per cent between 1993–94 and 1999–2000, while the labour force was growing at more than 2 per cent per annum during the 1990s. NSS data for 2004–05 also reveals that only 60 per cent of the population in the working age group (fifteen to sixty-four) was 'usually employed'.[77]

More than 50 per cent of the workers in India's half-billion labour force are self-employed. Almost 90 per cent of India's non-farm enterprises are in the unorganized sector and 30 per cent of the non-agricultural output is produced in this sector. Half the country's GDP, inclusive of agriculture, is produced by it. 'It would indeed be instructive,' the NCEUS writes, 'for policy-makers to reflect as to how much of public expenditure, public systems and public policy are devoted to this vast segment of the Indian economy on which the majority of Indians depend for their livelihood.'

A recent ILO–WTO study argues that 'social protection is crucial' for informal workers to gain any benefit in a globalizing world open to trade. It shows that 'the higher the incidence of informality, the greater the vulnerability of developing countries to shocks like the ongoing global crisis. Countries with larger informal economies suffer more frequently from shocks and experience lower sustainable growth rates.' Workers in the unorganized sector can be laid off with the slightest change in the mood of the market.[78]

Whereas the formal economy—since it uses extraordinarily well-developed and capital-intensive technology for mass production—requires moneyed mass markets of at least (globally) middle-class consumers, access to cheap resources, and precise and limited amounts of highly skilled and trained manpower, the needs of the default informal economies are altogether different. They have been pushed from subsistence to survival everywhere over the past few decades. They have very limited assets, if any. If they do, they approximate the free-market model of mainstream economic theory far more closely than big business which requires, inevitably and everywhere today, state backing.

Contemporary capitalism is unthinkable without the modern state. Informal market economies, constituting mom-and-pop stores, micro-enterprises and family farms survive without state support. This sector has an ambiguous relationship with large corporate capital. Enterprises that constitute the starting point of the supply chain for global brands are indispensable for the formal sector. However, those that compete with the formal sector, even if they operate in markets with very different income and demographic characteristics, are considered obstructions to the formal sector. How would large-format corporate retail make a niche for itself as long as small family businesses and *kirana* stores take care of most everyday human needs? How would global agribusiness expand its frontiers as long as small and marginal farmers are producing and selling most of the grain in the market? The examples can be multiplied.

The redundancy of labour in the modern world is emphasized by a scholar of peasant societies, Teodor Shanin:

> The modern formal economy needs only about a quarter of the global workforce. The other three-quarters are engaged in survival through the informal economy. The core of the informal economy

is not peasant farming, but family and neighborhood relationships of mutual support. So while the informal economy is seen—if it is seen at all—as the political economy of the margins, when you put it all together, you can see it is not marginal at all.[79]

The 2005 Economic Census in India, which, before the mammoth NCEUS effort, was the country's only regular data-gathering exercise that covered the informal economy, shows that there were as many as 42 million enterprises (61 per cent of them rural) engaged in non-agricultural production around the country. They employed 99 million people in 2005. This means that the average number of people employed per enterprise was only 2.35. (Contrast this with the formal sector where hundreds, often thousands or tens of thousands, of workers work in the same factory shed.) In this case, only 1.5 per cent of the enterprises surveyed by the census employed more than ten people. Seventy-three per cent of the workforce in the surveyed units was in rural areas. The annual growth rate of these enterprises between 1998 and 2005 was as high as 5.5 per cent in rural India and 4.8 per cent overall.[80]

How are we to interpret these numbers? They could mean that the economic reforms have given a strong impetus to entrepreneurship around the country. However, a different interpretation is more credible. Most such enterprises employ just two or three people. They have dreadfully low levels of investment and access to credit. Given that more than half the workers in the country end up self-employed, what appears to be happening is that masses of working people, either permanently retrenched from jobs in the formal economy or left out of mainstream growth processes or actually losing land and other resources (from land acquisition, indebtedness, stronger competition, environmental destruction, etc.), have had to resort to self-employment at whatever wages they can obtain in order to survive. It is difficult to call someone who is barely able to feed the family two meals a day by hawking vegetables or slaving twelve hours a day at a construction site an 'employee'. It is more accurate to see them as India's large and growing residual underclass.[81]

What sort of wages are being earned by informal workers? The tables below (computed from NSS data) tell their own story:

TABLE 2.1: Average Real Daily Wages of Regular Workers, All India, 15–59 years, in Rs/day at 1993–94 prices

Workers	1993–94	1999–2000	2004–05
Rural Male	58.5	80.2	83.8
Rural Female	34.9	71.8	49.4
Urban Male	78.1	102.3	101.0
Urban Female	62.3	84.6	76.1

TABLE 2.2: Average Real Daily Wages of Casual Workers, All India, 15–59 years, in Rs/day at 1993–94 prices

Workers	1993–94	1999–2000	2004–05
Rural Male	23.2	28.6	31.1
Rural Female	15.3	18.5	20.2
Urban Male	32.4	38.1	37.3
Urban Female	18.5	23.0	21.8

Source: J. Unni and G. Raveendran, 'Growth of Employment (1993–94 to 2004–05): Illusion of Inclusiveness?', Economic and Political Weekly (EPW), 20 January 2007. Data includes agricultural workers.

Real wages declined or stagnated for most categories of workers over the period from 1999–2000 to 2004–05. What do these numbers really mean? If we take five members and two wage-earners per family (one male, one female), we can see that for casual workers—the majority of the workforce in urban areas—the daily per capita income in 2004–05 (at 1993–94 prices) was under Rs 12 a day. In rural areas, it was just over Rs 10 a day. Both are below the *official* poverty line. And this is only for the days of the year that both working members in a family found work. It is to be noted that these are *averages*. In other words, there are many not earning even this much. Small wonder then that the high economic growth of recent years has made no impact on the living standards of the poor.

According to the anthropologist Jan Breman, a veteran scholar who has, for half a century, researched the lives of the poor in south Gujarat:

> It is hard to believe that the neo-liberal lobby, which advocates the unfettered working of the market and the transition to an informal labour regime, has so easily created an ideological climate in which it is possible to systematically ignore the brutal way in which the men, women, and children at the foot of the economy are dealt with. Protection and security, and the right to a minimum wage and decent work have become taboo words, and are seen as indications of politically incorrect thinking.[82]

Two significant pieces of legislation were drawn up in 2005 concerning the welfare of workers in the unorganized sector: the Unorganized Sector Workers' Social Security Bill (on payment of a modest premium, it offers workers health insurance, maternity benefits, life insurance and old-age pension) and the Unorganized Sector Workers (Conditions of Workers

and Livelihood Promotion) Bill, their aim being to improve the
conditions of employment, such as applying limits on the
number of working hours and actually enforcing the legal bans
on child and bonded labour. Other than the fact that the
legislation took several years to be passed (finally passed only in
December 2008), only one consolidated act was passed, watering
down most of the provisions of the second legislation (which
had been recommended by the NCEUS). In the context of the
continued insistence on 'flexible labour markets' under the neo-
liberal scheme of things, this makes sense.[83]

All this only shows, once more, where the policy priorities of
the state lie. (The SEZ Act, by contrast, was passed within a few
days of being tabled, in May 2005.) Underscoring the urgent
need for legislative intervention in the unorganized sector,
Breman points to 'the enormous gap between the logic of the
proposals and the economic policy currently being pursued in
India'. In his view it 'would require the restoration of a public
domain which, in the relentless drive for privatization, has all
but disappeared'. It remains to be seen how well even the diluted
law for unorganized sector workers is implemented.[84]

3

TRICKLE-DOWN?

PERSISTENT POVERTY AND
GROWING INEQUALITY

What's good for the rich, it seems, is also good for the poor. The overwhelming justification for economic growth at any cost during the past two decades is not that it suits the interests of the wealthy elite and the middle classes but that it addresses in the best possible way the long-standing challenge of mass poverty. It enlarges the national pie which can *then* be distributed more lavishly between rich and poor alike. If we enable the rich to get richer, it is argued in effect, they will help make the poor less poor.

It is supposed to work roughly like this. Unless the state corners resources and sets the market aside, it is only the wealthy who are in a position to invest. As investment grows, the output expands. The economy grows and develops. It industrializes and builds the service economy. It draws more and more people away from 'unproductive' agriculture and traditional livelihoods into the high-value-added modern, mainstream economy. Farmers and artisans are educated out of their traditional ways and absorbed by the modern sector, in the end achieving far higher standards of living than before.

Agriculture, hitherto in the hands of peasants, is taken over by the allegedly more efficient corporate sector, much like in the affluent countries. The process is facilitated at critical stages by public interventions in the form of welfare spending on health and education, among other things, based on the growing tax revenues that economic growth affords. In the end, everyone is better off, thanks to the rising tide that lifts all boats. This is the famous 'trickle-down effect' which is meant to terminate poverty.

We should expect two decades of blistering growth to have had a positive impact on the lives of people in India. What does the actual experience suggest? Let us examine the evidence, beginning with the wealthy classes.

The economic condition of the people

Wealth (inclusive of all assets), the basis of income especially for the rich, is far more unequally distributed across the population than income. Moreover, the wealthy in India are not merely rich within the country. They have become globally wealthy. The UN published for the first time in 2006 the most comprehensive global study of personal wealth. It reports that the richest 1 per cent of adults around the world own 40 per cent of global assets, and that the richest 10 per cent of adults account for 85 per cent of the world total. In contrast, the bottom *half* of the world adult population owns barely 1 per cent of global wealth. The top 10 per cent of India's population owns 53 per cent of the country's wealth. The bottom 10 per cent controls a mere 0.2 per cent. Also, for the sake of contrast, we may wish to note that per capita wealth in 2000 was $144,000 in the US, while in India it was only $1,100.[1]

According to an executive director of the global financial giant Morgan Stanley, between 2003 and 2007 India witnessed an increase in wealth of over $1 trillion (more than a year's GDP). Of this amount, $570 billion (more than half) was held by domestic shareholders, who constitute a mere 4–7 per cent of the total population, according to SEBI (Securities and Exchange Board of India).[2]

Before the financial crash, there were more dollar billionaires in India than in any other country except the US. Even after the crash, there are four Indian billionaires among the top ten richest people in the world. Without taking account of the large black economy of the country, which would magnify the inequalities considerably, the reported per capita income of the wealthiest Indians—the top 0.01 per cent, amounting to 112,500 people—in 2007 was about $150,000 (Rs 72 lakh) per annum. The per capita income of the top 1 per cent of India's population (the 11.25 million people who own cars and laptops) was $8000 (Rs 3.8 lakh) per annum.[3]

Clearly, the wealthy have been doing extremely well. But are they also doing *better*—relative to the rest of the population—than they were before 1991? The answer is yes. The share of wages in GDP has in fact halved since the 1980s and is now among the lowest in the world. During the same period, while the share of corporate sector shareholders in GDP grew by 13.5 per cent, the share of agriculture (on which more than half the population still relies for a livelihood) in GDP *fell* by 4 per cent. Indian corporate sector firms have profit margins of, on an average, 10 per cent—twice the global average.[4]

The stagnation in workers' wages is responsible for the decline in the share of labour. The ILO (International Labour Organization) reports that in India labour productivity (output generated by a unit of labour per hour) increased by 84 per cent between 1990 and 2002. However, real wages in manufacturing fell by 22 per cent in the same period. Journalist P. Sainath points out that 'this was also a period when CEO salaries had begun clocking all-time records. Even now, top-end compensations in India are growing much faster than in the U.S.' The annual salaries (excluding capital income) of each of the top ten corporate executives in India were between $2 and 6 million in 2006.[5]

Free-market enthusiasts would like everyone to believe that economic growth is a 'positive sum game' which benefits everyone in a lesser or greater degree. The evidence we have assembled so far suggests that the rich have certainly made their sums far more positive than before. How have the poor been faring?

There is debate on the dominant trends in poverty in India after the reforms. At one extreme of the debate are the market-friendly economists, many of them present or erstwhile employees of the IMF (International Monetary Fund) or the World Bank, who have spotted a definitive reduction in poverty over the last two decades. At the other extreme are serious sceptics who point to obvious indicators which have shown no significant improvement, many of them actually getting worse with the years. It includes experienced observers of local situations, with an eye for changes in the qualitative dimensions of poverty, like changes in the availability of work, security of employment, working conditions, public services, and so on.

The first group—the leaders of the poverty measurement industry—published sometime back a volume called *The Great Indian Poverty Debate*. The contributors were economists, concerned with measurable changes in poverty. Despite the sceptical note on which the volume ended, the editors stuck to their view that poverty had declined significantly through the 1990s. They based this on an alleged rise in real wages and the growing purchase of consumer durables.[6]

This approach to poverty has been criticized by, among many others, economist Ashwini Saith and anthropologist Jan Breman. The core of their criticism is that the dominant approach, by focusing only on numerical data on income or expenditure, obscures the underlying cause of poverty: social inequality and power relations. The informal economy, where the bulk of Indians live and work, 'is interpreted on the basis of a formal sector methodology'.[7]

A recent study carried out by the UNDP (United Nations Development Programme) and Oxford University considered the multidimensional character of deprivation around the world. To calculate the multidimensional poverty index (MPI), it took account of ten indicators in addition to family incomes: years of schooling, child enrolment, child mortality and nutrition, electricity, flooring, drinking water, sanitation, cooking fuel and assets. On these broader criteria for the estimation of poverty, as much as 55 per cent of India is still poor.

Even in the more prosperous states like Haryana, Gujarat and Karnataka, the number of poor people exceeds 40 per cent of their population. Within specific deprived groups, the situation is much worse: 66 per cent of the Scheduled Castes and 81 per cent of the Scheduled Tribes are poor. A comparison between the state of Madhya Pradesh (MP) and the Republic of Congo in Africa (both with about 70 million population in 2007) is revealing. Both had a similar proportion of the poor (69.4 per cent for MP and 73.2 per cent for Congo). There are more MPI poor people in eight Indian states alone (421 million in Bihar, Chhattisgarh, Jharkhand, MP, Orissa, Rajasthan, Uttar Pradesh and West Bengal) than in the twenty-six poorest African countries combined (410 million).[8]

There are enough reasons for believing that the official numbers on poverty are serious underestimates, derived by keeping the poverty line unreasonably low, in order to reflect a lower number of poor people. What is usually taken for the poverty line is more reasonably regarded as a 'starvation line', given that it excludes essential items like water, housing, transport, health and education and, in the countryside, such things as fuel and fodder, basic to rural survival and, till recently (or often), falling within the ambit of the non-monetized economy in several parts of the country. Many such items have now been privatized and commodified, dramatically hiking costs for the common people.

There are also severe problems with the World Bank approach to the estimation of the extent of poverty. Everyone knows that no one could live anywhere on the equivalent of what would have been dry-as-a-crust-of-bread $1.08 a day in 1993 in the US. So the World Bank recently raised the number to $1.25, a princely increment of $0.17. Using this new figure, in August 2008 the World Bank released a set of revised estimates of poverty entitled *The Developing World is Poorer than We Thought*.

Even after the raise, it found that in 2005 there were 468 million *more* poor people in the world than they had earlier believed to be the case. In India, the number of people below this new poverty line turned out to be 456 million, as against a previous estimate of 320 million. Moreover, raising the poverty line just slightly, to $1.45, the World Bank found that the number of Indian poor increased to 590 million, well over half of the total population.[9]

Nonetheless, even if the *numbers* of the poor are far greater than originally estimated, the World Bank insists that the *incidence* of poverty has been steadily going down in India and the rest of the developing world since the early 1980s.

Consider some more obvious statistics, such as the Human Development Index (HDI) that incorporates per capita income (which, being an average, hides enormous variations in income), literacy rates and life expectancy. (It may be noted that this says nothing directly about poverty.) When the reforms began in 1991 India was ranked 123rd among countries around the world in terms of the HDI. In 2007 it had slipped to the 134th place, even if in absolute terms its HDI grew from a measure of 0.49 to 0.61 between 1990 and 2007. Other countries, including Honduras and Equatorial Guinea, fared better.[10]

The early years of SAP (structural adjustment programme) reforms were extremely rough on the poor. India added 56 million to the ranks of the poor in the early 1990s which, in the words of an experienced observer, may have been 'the worst time for the poor since Independence', given that deregulated foodgrain prices shot up by 58 per cent between 1991 and 1994. The virtual dismantling of the public distribution system for food in the late 1990s, as per IMF–World Bank requirements, played havoc with the large number of poor families, seriously impacting nutrition levels.[11]

For daily-wage earners—by far the biggest category of workers in the country—real wages, which seemed to be on a gentle upward trend between 1993–94 and 1999–2000, have since then either stagnated at low levels or have even fallen sharply in some cases. The percentage of regular workers earning a salary below the national minimum wage of Rs 80 per day is well over half in rural India and almost half in the unorganized sector of urban India. A third of unorganized workers in the organized sector also earn below the national minimum wage. Among casual workers, the story is far worse.* Five out of six such workers

---

*Regular workers are people who have full-time work on a daily basis. Casual workers are daily-wage earners, without the certainty of employment from one day to the next. By unorganized workers in the organized sector we mean people who work without job or social security in the formal economy.

in the countryside, and well over half in urban areas, earn below the national minimum wage.[12]

All this evidence has been corroborated recently by a most shocking statistic. According to an important government committee on employment in the unorganized sector (NCEUS, referred to in chapter 2), 77 per cent of India (836 million people) in 2007 lived on less than Rs 20 a day. The overwhelming majority of such people should certainly count as poor by any reasonable definition, the only exceptions being those few who have remained outside the monetized economy and still have their natural resource base intact. The official poverty line normally used by the government is lower than Rs 20 a day, which explains why poverty estimates are often said to be in the region of 20–30 per cent of the population. With the extraordinary growth of the last decade, poverty should have been declining fast. But it hasn't.[13]

Other measures of poverty, based on hunger, focus on nutrition. Such measures typically count the daily intake of calories. The per capita intake of calories fell between 1993 and 2005 in both rural and urban areas. In rural areas it fell by 5 per cent, and in urban areas, by 2.5 per cent, as Table 3.1 shows.

TABLE 3.1: Per Capita Intake of Calories, 1993–2005

Area	1993–94	1999–2000	2004–05
Rural	2153	2149	2047
Urban	2071	2156	2020

Source: NSS (National Sample Survey) Report No. 513, quoted in 'India's Runaway Growth: Distortion, Disarticulation, and Exclusion', *Aspects of Political Economy*, No. 44–46 (April 2008), Research Unit in Political Economy.

The original basis for the computation of poverty, first proposed by the UN and later adopted by India, was a basket of goods that yielded at least 2400 calories per capita every day in villages and 2100 calories in urban areas. Agricultural economist Utsa Patnaik of Jawaharlal Nehru University (JNU) has applied this norm rigorously to compute the extent of food deprivation. It turns out that as much as 87 per cent of India's rural population was unable to get its minimum requirement in 2004–05, rising from 75 per cent in 1993–94. The corresponding figures for urban India are 64.5 per cent and 57 per cent, again showing a worsening of calorie intake and poverty over the decade.[14]

Official economists try to explain away the fall in calorie intake by suggesting that with 'greater prosperity' diets have changed, since there is now less need for manual labour, more mechanization on farms, and so on. Calorie intake does not fall in other countries with rising prosperity, certainly not from such low levels of income. Data of the Food and Agricultural Organization (FAO) indicates that overall calorie availability per capita has increased in developing countries from 2134 calories in 1970 to 2722 in 2005. For the world as a whole, FAO data shows that average calorie intake has increased from 2549 calories in 1979–81 to 2798 in 2000–03, again showing a straightforward positive correlation between rising incomes and calorie intake. For rich countries it is typically well over 3000 calories a day.[15]

Has India bucked the trend? Interestingly, the World Bank does not give calorie intake numbers in its official Country Data. Nor would 200,000 farmers have committed suicide if rural 'prosperity' had reached them (see chapter 7). NSS data itself shows that calorie consumption rises with income levels: the class that spends the most consumes double the calories of the classes with the lowest expenditure in both rural and urban India.[16]

Further, the proportion of the Indian population that is more than 10 per cent below the NSS nutritional norm has increased between 1993–94 and 2004–05 in both rural (from 42 per cent to 49 per cent) and urban areas (49 per cent to 53 per cent).[17]

Without getting into too many technicalities, the reason why government figures continue to understate the extent of poverty is because they are based on an outdated consumption basket from the early 1970s (for instance, excluding domestic fuel/ energy), corrected only for subsequent inflation. Effectively, this means that the poverty line used in 2004–05 was Rs 12 a day in rural India and Rs 18 a day in the cities. At this official poverty line, calorie intake in rural India would be 1820 per capita daily, almost 25 per cent less than the nutritional minimum 2400 a day. The official figure of 27.5 per cent poverty in 2004–05 is based on such flimsy foundations.

Meanwhile, many items in the rural basket, such as fodder and firewood, which were gathered gratis from the commons, now have to be bought. Likewise, in urban India, people spend more money on transport in order to get to work, because of slum evictions. In both rural and urban India large amounts are being spent on health and education, because of the failure of public provision.[18]

Further corroboration of these pessimistic trends comes from data on the per capita availability of foodgrains. Availability is production plus imports minus exports. Numbers from the government's *Economic Survey* tell a story of their own. Since 1991, there has been a decline of over 10 per cent in the per capita availability of food, indicating that growth in food production is falling behind population growth. Availability of protein (in the form of pulses) has declined to about half of what it was in the early 1960s, even as per capita cereal availability increased slightly. Consumption (typically lower than availability because some cannot afford the available food) of pulses per capita declined annually at 3.2 per cent per annum between 1991 and 2003. It may seem from the figures below as though things have picked up after 2001 (perhaps on account of changes in policy). However, the underlying reason for this is that India had a succession of poor monsoons around 2001, which particularly depressed the figure for the latter year, making it seem as though by 2007 things had really improved. Nothing fundamental changed about policies towards agriculture between 2001 and 2007 to warrant such an inference. (The 2007 figure can be compared with any other year since 1961 to see what has happened.)[19]

TABLE 3.2: Per Capita Availability of Foodgrains
(in grams per day)

Year	Cereals	Pulses	Total
1951	334	61	395
1961	400	69	469
1971	418	51	469
1981	417	38	455
1991	469	42	511
2001	386	30	416
2007	407	36	443

Source: Economic Survey 2008–09, GoI, New Delhi, 2009, http://indiabudget.nic.in/es2008-09/chapt2009/tab117.pdf

Perhaps the most damning evidence of the failure of reforms to improve the condition of the poor comes from statistics on health and nutrition. Gujarat is one of India's most prosperous states, with the fastest rates of growth (often above 12 per cent) in the country during 2005–10. According to government data, the proportion of stunted children (under age three) in the state continues to remains very high. It was 44 per cent in 1992–93, and 42 per cent in 2005–06. The proportion of underweight children has also remained about the same during the reform period (47–48 per cent). For India as a whole, while growth has been relatively slower, there has been marginal improvement in some areas of children's nutrition. The proportion of stunted children has fallen from 46 per cent to 38 per cent. The number of underweight children has decreased from 52 per cent to 46 per cent since 1992–93. However, the incidence of anaemia among children below age three has risen from 74 per cent to 79 per cent between 1998–99 and 2005–06. Among women of child-bearing age (fifteen to forty-nine) it has increased from 49.7 per cent to 57.9 per cent during the same period.[20]

It is thus no surprise that on the Global Hunger Index (GHI), calculated by the International Food Policy Research Institute in Washington DC, India was placed sixty-fifth in a ranking of eighty-four countries in 2009, well behind Nigeria, Cameroon and Burkina Faso, regarded as among the poorest in the world. Industrialized, 'vibrant' Gujarat has a hunger index far worse than Nepal, Kenya, Pakistan and Zimbabwe.[21]

No matter which way the poverty measurement industry spins the numbers, the elephant in the room is too large to shrink. It appears that widespread hunger persists in India not despite growth, but perhaps *because* of it, or rather because of its specific character. As we contended earlier, the big change brought about in the pattern of India's economic policies after 1991 was towards a perceptibly more external orientation of the economy. Among many other things, this has meant far less attention to agriculture;

the virtual dismantling of the country's food security system (PDS); land acquisition from farmers for the stated purpose of industrialization (like SEZs [Special Economic Zones]); taking away much fertile land from the cultivation of food (towards non-food cash crops or out of cultivation altogether); and a far greater emphasis on the generation of exports to service the country's foreign exchange needs. From the perspective of agriculture and food security, this has meant a diminution of the sown area under foodgrains.

Despite the slight increase in the productivity of the land, the production of foodgrains has not kept up with population growth. Between 1990–91 and 2005–06 the cultivated area under foodgrains (cereals and pulses) fell by 5 per cent from 127.8 to 121.6 million ha, with jowar (an indigenous millet) falling 40 per cent from 14.4 to 8.7 million ha (while India's population grew by 30 per cent!). In good measure, this decline can be attributed to displacement by non-food export crops.[22]

The patterns of exclusion and rejection

None of the trends of growing inequality and persistent poverty outlined above can be understood unless we also see the many processes of socio-economic exclusion at work in the country. In addition to what has already been said, especially with regard to jobless growth and exclusion from decent, well-paid employment, we consider a brief sample of some of the other key processes at work.

Financial exclusion: The law of gravitation of credit

Money lies at the heart of a market-driven world. To be excluded from it is to be left out of most things one needs. Extension of credit by the banking system is the very basis for investment and growth in any sector of the economy. The pattern of allocation of credit between different sectors tells us a lot about the nature of the growth process an economy is going through. Credit becomes doubly important for those who have lost their lands and access to common-property resources and are bereft of other assets. It is the only real opportunity for the asset-poor to change their long-term fortunes. When we look at bank credit numbers in India since the early 1990s we find that money has followed money.

Let us first look at the effective credit 'subsidies' that big business has got in India. RBI (Reserve Bank of India) data shows that in 2001–02, 11,000 large borrowers accounted for as much as Rs 40,000 crore of the bad debts of commercial banks, an amount equal to almost 2 per cent of the GDP in that year. Large borrowers numbering 1741 still owed Rs 22,866 crore to public sector banks. While small borrowers, like peasants, are sometimes arrested, physically threatened or beaten up to recover bank loans, big borrowers simply have their debts rescheduled or even forgotten in order to prevent default and retain creditworthiness.[23]

Banks were nationalized by Mrs Gandhi's government in 1969 with the express purpose of ensuring that priority areas of the economy (on which the largest majority of people relied) received the credit necessary for their survival and growth. Agriculture and the small industry sector come under the category of 'priority sector lending'. Their share of total bank credit fell from 27.4 per cent to 17.9 per cent between 1990 and 2006. More than half the country is still dependent on agriculture. The share of agriculture in outstanding bank credit fell from 15.9 per cent in 1990 to 11.4 per cent in 2006. Meanwhile, the share of personal consumption loans (for housing, automobiles, consumer durables, credit card expenses, etc.) shot up from 6.4 per cent to 23.3 per cent during the same period, housing alone rising from 2.4 per cent to 12 per cent.[24]

Credit starvation is the norm among small and marginal farmers in agriculture. According to the NSS surveys, about half the farmers are heavily indebted today. In some states, like Andhra Pradesh (AP) and Tamil Nadu, the proportion goes up to 75–80 per cent. In 1991 the proportion of such farmers across the country was 27 per cent, according to the same surveys. A key explanation for this growth in indebtedness (and the resulting suicides) lies in the fact that farmers have been forced to resort to non-institutional sources of credit, such as local moneylenders, who extort exorbitant rates of interest. (Banks have supplied only about a quarter of the credit to farmers in recent years.) The much-publicized loan waiver for farmers that the UPA (United Progressive Alliance) government announced in 2008 did not touch this source of indebtedness.

The drying up of credit to priority sector areas like agriculture and small industry is a consequence of the new banking norms that have been ushered in after the reforms began. They mandate very strict creditworthiness among borrowers who are to be considered for bank loans. Interest rates charged from small industries and artisans have also been generally higher than for other loans, even if there are fewer non-performing assets among them. As banks grow in size, thanks to mergers and acquisitions in the wake of 'liberalized' measures, credit for priority areas is expected to decline further. Already, the trend is towards the closing down of public sector bank branches in the countryside. According to the RBI, the number of bank branches in rural India was 1443 in 1969, before nationalization. It peaked at

35,360 in 1993. Since then, 4750 bank branches have shut down in the countryside (roughly one every working day) between 1993 and 2007, while the number of branches in the cities has more than doubled during the same period. The number of rural bank accounts fell from 32.5 million in March 1991 to 25.4 million in March 2004. After bank nationalization in 1969, the proportion of rural credit from moneylenders (and other informal sources) had come down from 75 per cent (between 1951 and 1961) to less than 25 per cent (in 1991). The share of formal sector lending had more than doubled. These trends have been reversed after 'liberalization'.[25]

Financial exclusion has a regional dimension which deserves comment. If we examine the credit extended by banks as a proportion of their deposits, the ratio varies greatly from one part of the country to another. It is 92 per cent in the western region and as low as 49 per cent in the eastern states. Lack of access to credit influences migration patterns, as people head for areas seen to be 'rich' (and thus also having privileged access to credit). 'The migrants from UP [Uttar Pradesh] and Bihar are merely following the capital that has flowed out of their states.' One state's rising share often comes at the cost of another's falling share, inhibiting the latter's capacity to create new capital.[26]

If we take a closer look at loans to small industries we find that micro-enterprises, which provide the bulk of employment in the industrial sector, have been suffering from a veritable drought of credit. The number of small industry bank accounts fell by over 52 per cent, from 2.18 million in March 1992 to 1.43 million in March 2003. The share of small industry in total bank credit declined during the same period from 12 per cent to 5 per cent, less than half of what it was in the early 1970s. The NCEUS pointed out that 92 per cent of all micro-enterprises and 95 per cent of all self-employed units received no assistance from the banking sector whatsoever. When they do get loans, they are charged rates of interest significantly higher than those charged from large enterprises. According to RBI Deputy Governor Rakesh Mohan, in 2005 the cost to banks of loanable funds was 7.5–8.5 per cent, but interest rates varied 'from 3–4 per cent on the lower side to 24–25 per cent on the higher side'. Clearly, some privileged borrowers were getting credit at a steep discount. The then RBI governor Y.V. Reddy stated very clearly that banks were overcharging farmers and small businessmen while underpricing the risk of loans to large borrowers. Even allowing for a degree of risk-adjustment, this isn't what would be considered a rational allocation of scarce credit according to the operation of the free market. It appears that it is an almost deliberate policy to run down agriculture and the small industry sector, while promoting big enterprises and rich consumer credit.[27]

The bias against small borrowers is very clear from other data as well. The number of small borrower accounts (credit limit less than Rs 25,000) declined 42 per cent, from 62 million in March 1992 to 36 million in March 2003. As a proportion of bank credit, the share of small borrowers fell from 25 per cent in the late 1980s to 5.4 per cent in 2003. If 'micro-enterprises'— typically run by one or a few poor people or a family in the far corners of the informal economy—were booming, we would hardly see this precipitous fall. The data lends support to the view expressed by Jan Breman who objects to labelling the majority of the people in the informal economy as 'self-employed' or 'micro-entrepreneurs'. People classified as such in government reports and surveys are more often eking out a meagre existence as a hawker or a *thelawallah*—forms of livelihood they have been driven to, not chosen. Alternatively, 'what is portrayed as own-account work is often barely disguised forms of wage-labour'.[28]

As a result of the credit drought that has been precipitated in the countryside, farmers have had to go back to the informal market dominated by moneylenders. The astronomical rates of interest have typically left them in a debt trap, whereby they have to take new loans to pay off the old ones. It was this disaster the government tried to alleviate through the farm loan waiver in the 2008 budget—a singularly misinformed, high-publicity strategy to 'help' farmers in distress.

During the last decade, microfinance institutions (MFIs) have sought to fill this credit vacuum. Started by Nobel Prize–winner Mohammed Yunus in Bangladesh in the 1970s, MFIs have been advertised as the miracle cure for rural poverty across South Asia, if not also around the world. Their primary innovation consists in the fact that they free poor borrowers from the need to furnish collateral when contracting a loan, inducing the community to monitor and vouch for an individual's credit standing. MFIs have exploded in India since the beginning of the century. High growth is anticipated in the future as well.[29]

An MFI is typically sponsored by a capitalist who notices the business opportunity present in a rural credit market. Needless to say, his/her goal is to maximize profits. (However, it may be noted that not all MFIs look to maximize profits. There are some community-managed MFIs whose overriding goal is to create assets for the poor.) The rates of interest that an MFI charges are of course lower than those charged by local moneylenders (otherwise they would not be able to break into the market), but they are still considerably higher than what public sector and cooperative banks used to charge before the new credit policies of the 1990s. Annual rates of 30 or 40 per cent are quite common. Elsewhere in the world, as in Mexico, MFIs have been known to charge rates as high as 60–80 per cent. Little wonder then that globally powerful private equity firms have expressed much interest in MFIs—also the reason why they get such positive business press. If MFIs can turn out new kinds of financial products, which can be hawked by banks and international financial firms in the global capital markets, it may well turn out to be a fertile 'marriage of international speculative capital and domestic usury'.[30]

Along the same lines, journalist Laxmi Murthy writes: 'In the rapturous hype over micro-credit, one crucial question begs to be asked: since a majority of people have neither the skills nor the inclination to be entrepreneurs, why is there a seeming boom in micro-enterprises? . . . Micro-credit offers brisk business to financial institutions.' Microfinance conferences are routinely supported by the World Bank, the International Fund for Agriculture and Development and transnational banks such as Citicorp, Chase Manhattan and American Express.[31]

MFIs are under huge pressure from their sponsors to make— and recover—loans at all costs. There are features of MFI practice in India that cast doubt on their usefulness to the rural poor. They sometimes charge interest for the entire period for which the loan is contracted, even if it is returned early. In many cases, borrowers have been led right back into the arms of moneylenders in order to pay back an MFI loan. In a case we came across in Kakinada district in AP, a set of women farmers had to go back to selling liquor (something they had themselves fought hard to get banned earlier) to return the loan. Peer-driven loan recovery in women's groups frequently undermines long-standing community ties and women's solidarity. The pressure to return the money often involves extreme measures such as stoppage of any further credit, seizure of security deposits, use of offensive language and threats of violence. This has sometimes led the borrowers to abscond or escape. There have also been cases of suicide, as in parts of AP.[32]

While bank-linked self-help groups (SHGs) have a better record of helping the poor—since they are not fundamentally conceived as profit-maximizing institutions—they too are known to charge rates of interest as high as 18–36 per cent. There is hardly an honest income-generating activity the poor can undertake in the Indian countryside, which would return a profit so high as to make debt at such exorbitant rates worthwhile. In other words, a debt trap for the poor—whereby they would be borrowing more to return old loans—is all but inevitable and can easily be foreseen. The leaders of these institutions are well aware what pains the poor have to undergo for the MFIs to achieve the high return success rate (90 to 98 per cent) of such loans.[33]

The fact remains that—just as it is for the private corporate sector—there is no substitute for state support (in the short run) when it comes to the provision or facilitation of credit to farmers and other vulnerable groups.

In retrospect, it is quite clear that the exit of priority sector lending and public sector banking from the rural areas, mandated by the international financial institutions (IFIs), has in effect made way for a new form of international financial exploitation of the Indian poor by the world's wealthy. MFIs and SHGs would not have been able to compete against the credit supplied by public sector banks (at rates of, say, 16–18 per cent). If credit was being withdrawn from agriculture and small industry, where was it being directed? It is possible to see much of the boom of recent years as having been fuelled by consumer credit extended to the city-based elite and the middle classes. Outstanding credit for cars and two-wheelers more than doubled between 2002–03 and 2006–07, from Rs 46,000 crore to over Rs 100,000 crore. Eighty-nine per cent of cars sold in 2006–07 were bought with loans, which covered 79 per cent of the value of the purchase. It is also worth pointing out that much of the consumer credit expansion of recent years has been made possible by the flow of capital from abroad. The impressive growth rate of the economy is thus based on foundations that are more narrow and shaky than they appear at first sight.[34]

While our policymakers and business elite spout the rhetoric of inclusion, the fact remains that sharp cleavages have appeared in the nation's credit markets as a result of the withdrawal of the state. Even as the poor remain creditworthy because of their working capacities, they are not treated as such by banks and lenders interested in high and fast returns in an age of short-termism. These returns can only come from the wealthy. That formal banking services will not be made accessible to the vast majority, even as urban consuming classes are pampered with soft loans, is now quite clear.

There is no such thing as a 'business democracy', the great economist Michal Kalecki once wrote. Merely having entrepreneurial talent is hardly enough to get a successful business going. Money, as Adam Smith knew well, is easy to make, when you already have some of it. No one extends credit to you otherwise, especially in an age that finds it hard to wait. Financial exclusion is therefore par for the course in an economy driven overwhelmingly by market principles.

Enormous transfers of the control over real ecological and economic wealth are now taking place through financial mechanisms. Given their scale, these can only be stopped through state intervention—perhaps forced by people's uprisings. Even a routine thing like the printing of money to balance the government's budget is a way of redistributing control over resources from those with fixed incomes to those with upwardly variable incomes, since it relies on inflation. When banks create money which ends up financing mining projects, to take a different example, they too are abetting the redistribution of resources away from the poor who lose their ecosystems and do not have access to credit that the rich do. If we understand money and credit as claims on resources, and also notice the structural financial exclusion faced by the poor in a climate when the rich have been borrowing and buying at will, we can better understand the transfers of wealth that have been taking place over the past few decades in a deregulated world.[35]

Food and health care: Inflation undermines survival

Inflation is a sustained rise in prices. It is also, at bottom, a process of *redistribution* of real income—away from creditors (to whom money is owed) and those with salaries and fixed incomes, towards debtors (who owe the money) and those whose compensation has a significant variable component: of profits or capital income, which typically rise with inflation. Modern economies suffer constantly from inflation. When it affects the prices of food and essential items, it redistributes real incomes and wealth in the economy even faster.

Seen in this light, inflation in the prices of essential commodities and services is a market-ruled process of growing economic exclusion, though it is never recognized as such. At a time when biofuel is displacing the cultivation of food in so many countries, driving up the world price of grain in the process, money becomes a universal weapon of mass discrimination. (Prices in India cannot remain unaffected by world prices in a world of open economy agriculture.) In a country like India in which hunger and malnutrition are so widespread and deep-rooted, rising prices of essential items like food, medicines or housing effectively exclude large numbers of people from the most elementary wherewithal of subsistence.[36]

India had become self-sufficient in foodgrains by the early 1980s. The rate of growth of foodgrain production (2.5 per cent per annum on average) well exceeded the rate of population growth till the time that the reforms began in the early 1990s. Since then, the rate of growth of production of foodgrains has fallen sharply to 1.2 per cent per annum, while population has continued to grow at 1.6–1.9 per cent per annum. This, as we saw earlier, has caused a significant reduction in the per capita availability of food since the beginning of the reform era.[37]

For people to have food security (access to adequate food from self-cultivation or from the market at affordable prices), it is not enough that overall production in the country is sufficient. The distribution network of food also has to be in place. It is for this reason that a sophisticated system of food management, involving state-subsidized foodgrains, had been evolved in the country in the decades after Independence. Foodgrain was purchased by the Food Corporation of India (FCI) by offering minimum support prices—MSP—to farmers and distributed via the PDS (public distribution system) at a lower issue price through half a million ration shops across the country.

Till 1997, there was a PDS (howsoever corrupt, unnecessarily centralized and supplied with poor quality grain) universally accessible to all rural and urban households with an address on which to get a ration card. In 1997, in line with the requirement of reducing food subsidies in order to trim public expenditure (as stipulated by the IMF/World Bank conditionalities), a new, Targeted PDS was introduced. Under this, a distinction was made between households above and below the poverty line (APL and BPL), with lower prices for the latter set of families.

In a bid to cut the food subsidy bill of the government, the issue price (at which grain is sold) was raised several times over the years after 1997, for both categories of households accessing the PDS. This led to a sharp divergence between the procurement of foodgrains from farmers by the government and the off-take from the ration shops—as fewer and fewer people could afford the grain—the difference adding to the 'excess' food buffer stocks in the FCI's godowns. In the years from 1997 to 2004 this difference exceeded 100 million tonnes, half the annual production of the country for a year. It generated the shameful anomaly of India exporting large quantities of food (often contributing to cattle-feed in the EU), even as hundreds of millions of people went hungry within the country. Studies also show that a significant proportion of deserving poor households were wrongly excluded from access to food. The inevitable result was a significant rise in malnutrition in many parts of the country, while the reduction of malnutrition slowed down in other regions—a high price to pay to reduce an item on the government budget which usually takes up well under 1 per cent of the GDP.[38]

The phenomenon of the government turning into a de facto hoarder repeated itself in 2010, for the same reasons as before but also because the storage and distribution facilities of the FCI seemed to have deteriorated even further. In August 2010, in the midst of double-digit inflation in food items, the FCI was sitting on a stock of 17 million tonnes of wheat, much of it rotting away or being consumed by rats. This could have fed 210 million hungry people in the country for a year.[39]

Meanwhile, inflation has been clawing into the standards of living of the working poor around the country. According to the RBI, since March 2007, year-on-year consumer price inflation in food prices has ranged between 9 and 14 per cent for all categories of workers (including urban industrial workers and agricultural labourers), rising particularly sharply in the first half of 2008 when food prices were rising globally. Between April 2007 and April 2008, for instance, the retail price of rice increased by over 20 per cent, *tur dal* (split pigeon pea) by over 15 per cent, mustard oil by 28 per cent.[40]

Apart from such things as the rise in the price of oil and the increasing use of land for biofuels, speculation in commodities, which has become a key area for financial investment in recent years, has contributed to inflation. This has been prodded by governments around the world deregulating markets in grain and commodity futures—agreements between two parties to transact at a predetermined price at a future date. In India, in April 2003, the NDA (National Democratic Alliance) government lifted the ban on forward trading in fifty-four commodities, including several agricultural ones. Further market liberalization has happened in the form of new instruments such as 'commodity derivatives' and 'options', all of which favour the speculative buyer, rather than the producer, of agricultural commodities.

Speculation is bad enough when carried out by small-time hoarders and traders who control many of the *mandi*s around the country. It is still more harmful when big business partakes of it. It received a huge impetus as a result of the entry of transnational agribusiness in the commodities bazaar. Importantly, the legal limit for the amount of grain that can be stored for private trading was quietly raised a few years back from 10,000 to 50,000 tonnes. The government has often upbraided small speculators. But big global players, like Cargill or Archer Daniels Midland (ADM), have obviously never been shown up in public. The amount of grain such hoarders may be holding at any point of time ought to be public information— but that would be to give the game away from the private traders' perspective, and they are protected by laws. The game is rooted in uncertainty and asymmetries of information. The annual profits of the food MNCs (multinational corporations) engaging in commodities trade have risen in recent years at annual rates of 30 to 90 per cent![41]

What is striking is that even after overall inflation rates have come down because of the fall in global oil prices and the recession—often approaching deflation—the rise in food prices in India continues.

What accounts for this? Uncertain harvests, as in 2009, thanks to the failure of the monsoon, are part of the answer. The production of pulses, for instance, did fall a little short of demand. But imports of over 2 million tonnes should have made up for this. Why did prices continue to rise? The price of tur dal rose by as much as 33 per cent in just a month, rising to Rs 60–80 per kg in July 2009 in the four largest metros of the country. The price increase from 2008 was of the order of 50–90 per cent. It is possible that the expectation of rising prices led, once again, to hoarding and speculation. In states where the government raided hoarders and released supplies in the market, prices fell.[42]

Sowing was inhibited by the poor monsoon. The area under paddy—a *kharif* crop—shrank by over 6 million ha across the country in 2009. This, along with lower yields than normal, was expected to lead to a fall in annual rice production by 17 per cent. This announcement by the minister of agriculture was enough to drive up the price of rice to more than Rs 40 a kg. The story with respect to sugar was similar.[43]

Even many lower-middle-class families in the big cities have had to compromise on their diets as a consequence of the rise in food prices. A Delhi car driver we spoke to, an employee on corporate payroll, used to earn Rs 11,000 a month (plus benefits) in 2009. The second earning member in his family is his elder son, who works in a designer showroom in Gurgaon, earning Rs 6500 a month. They together managed to save on average about Rs 1500 every month, part of which was sent to their extended family that lives in a village in Bihar. They lived in a two-room house of their own with four other family members, in a resettlement colony between Delhi and Gurgaon. Here is what their monthly family budget looked like:

Food	Rs 6000–7000
School fees	Rs 3000–3500
Transport	Rs 1000–1200
Mobile telephone	Rs 1000–1200
Electricity	Rs 500–600
Cooking gas	Rs 600–900
Clothes/Footwear	Rs 1200–1300
Health expenses	Rs 500–1000
Miscellaneous	Rs 1000–1200 (including debt-servicing)

Some of these expenses were obviously spread across the year. It is notable that the family spent 37–44 per cent of its monthly income on food. Such a family, with a per capita daily expense of almost Rs 90 (which places them in the top 15–20 per cent of the country's population by expenditure), now has to choose between dal and vegetables at every meal. The impact on protein intake for small children is obvious.

In 2010, during one of the runaway food inflation episodes, the *Times of India* reported:

> In Ahmedabad's Gokuldham settlement, Mona Rajput has had to make the painful decision to stop giving milk to her four-year-old son so that her five-month-old infant can get some. In a country in which half of all children are already malnourished, the seemingly unstoppable rise in food prices is threatening to sow the seeds of a dangerously malnourished future generation.[44]

Food is not the only item of importance in a poor household's budget. Housing is almost as significant, especially in the cities. The rise in rentals in the metropolitan areas has been quite dramatic. Between 2001 and 2007, the government's Housing Price Index roughly trebled in Delhi, Mumbai and Bengaluru.[45]

In addition, the poor spend significant—and growing—proportions of their income on health, education and transport (especially in the cities). With the rapid increase in the incidence of slum evictions, the urban poor now have to commute longer distances and spend more to get to their place of work every day. It is quite revealing that in Delhi, shifting people from jhuggis to 'better' locations has often reduced their real income by as much as 50 per cent.[46]

In its Approach Paper to the Eleventh Plan, the Planning Commission notes that 'a very large shift, of at least 5% of total private consumption, has occurred over the last decade from food to health, education, conveyance'. This is, in all likelihood, an underestimate. All these items have been rising in price since the beginning of the reform era, significantly due to privatization, as the case of health spending demonstrates.[47]

The rising prices of drugs, tests and hospitalization have increased the burden on the poor. RBI data shows that between 1993–94 and 2003–04, while the prices of all other items in the consumer's basket almost doubled, the cost of drugs grew 2.5 times. This was before the new product patent law under the WTO (World Trade Organization) was brought in, in 2005. After signing the WTO's TRIPS (Trade-Related Aspects of Intellectual Property Rights) Agreement, India amended its patent law. Earlier it was the process through which a drug was made that was patented, now it is the product itself that is patented, prohibiting cheap generic drugs. The new law further raised the price of drugs, as handsome royalties are paid to patent-holding MNCs. NSS surveys show that even in 1995–96, 24 per cent of rural patients and 21 per cent of urban ones had to forgo medical care because they couldn't afford it. At the time of the previous survey, less than a decade earlier, these numbers were 15 per cent and 10 per cent respectively, clear evidence of the growing lack of access to health care, as the drug industry was being reoriented to suit the needs of international business.[48]

According to a 2006 WHO (World Health Organization) study, 43 per cent of low-income families in India had to either go into heavy debt or sell off their assets to meet their rising medical bills. Lack of clean drinking water, basic sanitation and proper nutrition—84 per cent of the surveyed families could not afford fruits or vegetables—made people more vulnerable to diseases and higher health expenses. In some cases, poor families had to spend as much as half their monthly family income on health. Even in absolute terms the amount was higher, on average, than for middle-class families.[49]

Reporting on the rural health-care crisis in AP, journalist P. Sainath writes:

A common thread running through the farmers' suicides plaguing the state has been very high medical spending. Just five households affected by such deaths had health costs totalling around Rs 4,00,000. Health spending is amongst the fastest growing components of rural family debt ... For years, the state boosted the private sector in health, promoted corporate hospitals and pioneered the 'user fees' system in government ones.

Out-of-pocket expenses for health care in India (80 per cent of the total) are perhaps among the highest in the world. The state, claiming to provide 'universal health care' provides only 20 per cent of the expenses. This amounts to barely 1 per cent of the GDP. Even in the US, which has the most private-sector-dominated health-care system in the industrialized world, the state takes care of 44 per cent of health expenses. In the UK the figure is as high as 86 per cent.[50]

The irony is that even countries like China, Malaysia and Sri Lanka, which spend a smaller proportion of their GDP on health (2.4–3 per cent) than India, emerge with better health indicators. The reason probably is that despite spending so much, the majority of people in India do not get the quality of health care that better (state-managed) systems are able to provide in the countries mentioned. If government policies can eschew market mania, and improve public delivery systems, there is quite obviously scope for a far superior social allocation of health resources.[51]

However, the thrust of health care has moved in the market-friendly direction after the reforms. In 2007 India attracted the second largest number of medical tourists in the world—450,000. Many of the hospitals where such visitors are treated were granted subsidized land by the state, in exchange for a promise to create a certain number of beds for the poor. Thus, the Indian taxpayer is actually subsidizing health care for the middle classes of the West—who have sometimes been denied affordable care in their own countries.[52]

As brands like Fortis, Novartis and Apollo begin to throng the landscape of metropolitan India, providing 'world-class' health care to global citizens of privilege, it is easy to forget the languishing primary health centres, the unaffordable tests and consultations, and the exorbitant drug prices that the indigent majority is left to fight over. Along with the dismantling, disprivileging or loss of traditional systems of health care, it means that the poor have been left in a no-man's-land, cut off from sources of traditional healing and without the means to access the modern system.

The manufacture of demand: India's Watergate?

Given growing urbanization, the supply of water—to both urban and rural areas—has become a hotly contested issue. Cities are making increasing demands on their rural hinterlands.

Consider the case of Delhi. It has the highest amount of water available per citizen in the country. According to the NCR (National Capital Region) Planning Board, it is estimated at 340 litres every day. But the distribution of water is astonishingly unjust. The three-quarters of the capital that lives in slums, unauthorized and resettlement colonies, and urban villages, has to collect or buy water at a premium. It has to manage on 30–90 litres per person every day, often waiting in endless queues under the sun. At the other end of the social scale, the prime minister's house on Race Course Road squanders 73,000 litres a day (admittedly hosting many people daily, but still using much more water per person). Ministers' homes consume 30,000–45,000 litres. An average room in a five-star hotel guzzles 1600 litres a day.[53]

Delhi's problem is not inadequate supply. Every neighbouring state has had to yield to Delhi's needs. Contrast Delhi's consumption of 340 litres per capita every day with Singapore (162 litres), Hong Kong (172), Munich (130) and Copenhagen (125). In these cities water consumption has been controlled. Official sources say that about 40 per cent of the water supplied to Delhi is wasted. Yet there is no move by the government to enforce conservation by big consumers or bring in a graduated tariff, calibrated to correspond with their ability to pay.[54]

For the last several years, there has been a lot of pressure on the government to privatize the supply of water in Delhi. In 2007 RTI (Right to Information) activist Arvind Kejriwal of the group Parivartan, in a deposition to the People's Tribunal on the World Bank, claimed that one institution applying this pressure was in fact the World Bank, though the latter claimed that it was the Delhi Jal Board which wanted to contract a loan from the former. In his deposition Kejriwal pointed out a whole series of secret manoeuvres and blatant irregularities that the World Bank was promoting in its dealings with the Delhi government, including tampering with bidding procedures, to have the water supply contract for the whole city of Delhi given to the firm Pricewaterhouse Coopers. This was of course in violation of the World Bank's own guidelines. Thirty-five IIM (Indian Institute of Management) professors wrote in protest to the government. The story broke in the media in late 2004, and a lot of citizen pressure succeeded in aborting a water privatization plan, which would have hiked the price of water for the average citizen by possibly a factor of nine, thereby pricing out of the market the majority of citizens of Delhi. The World Bank wanted the twenty-one water zones of Delhi to be parcelled out to certain companies who would have operated the system for a huge profit, other than fees of as much as $25,000 a month per consultant handed out for each of the water zones. The hand-holding and 'looking over the shoulder' that the World Bank was doing with the Delhi Jal Board was so obvious that Kejriwal was led to ask the question: 'Are we citizens of an independent country?'[55]

The National Water Policy of 2002 is biased towards privatization of water. In his speech to the National Water Resources Council, the PM stated that

> the policy should . . . recognise that the community is the rightful custodian of water. Exclusive control by the government machinery . . . cannot help us to make the paradigm shift to participative, essentially local management of water resources . . . Wherever feasible PPPs should be encouraged in such a manner that we can attract private investment in the development and management of water resources.[56]

The problem with such an official perspective is that it puts very disparate and unequal non-state actors—whether they are MNCs or slum-dwellers—on par. They are all seen as part of the same 'community', interested in participatory management.[57]

Wherever water has been privatized in a Third World city in recent times, the high user charges have effectively priced the poor out of the fulfilment of the most elementary of human needs. The primary justification for privatization is of course that it allows for cost recovery of water provision in a complex urban setting. But it seems to do a lot more than that, such as padding the returns to shareholders of water companies, while letting the governments and the taxpayers shoulder the risks of big private investments. Besides, privatization is not the only way to recover costs. There are other models in existence which involve government responsibility, using taxpayer money.

Ironically, in the US, less than 10 per cent of the water is supplied privately even now. The argument that participating corporations bring in large amounts of funds for infrastructure is a fictitious claim. Typically, companies raise the debt in capital markets and then recover the interest and the principal through high user charges. As most multinationals do not wish to risk their investments in Third World countries, it is the IFIs who channel their infrastructural aid to poor countries through these companies. Further, client governments offer any number of concessions to these companies—dollar-indexed assured rates of return, loan guarantees, assurance of minimum demand, etc. After privatization, water rates have more than doubled, often trebled, in such places as Ghana, Argentina and the Philippines.[58]

Even where outright privatization of water has not happened, the government's attention has been taken off the importance of providing drinking water to the people. Serious shortages in public supply have to be made up somehow and this makes room for private water suppliers. UN data shows that in Mumbai in 1997, informal vendors were charging forty times as much as public supply. In Delhi, the figure was sometimes nearly 500 times. The inequity in water distribution is obvious if one remembers that the rich and the middle classes have supply connections. Slum-dwellers rarely do. In Mumbai, which has managed to stall privatization till now, daily-wage earners often pay up to 20 per cent of their wages for water. Slum demolitions have made it even harder and more expensive for people to obtain water.[59]

The privatization of water in the countryside has taken an altogether more vicious form in India. In the state of Chhattisgarh, for instance, a 23-km stretch of a river (Sheonath) was sold to a company called Radius Water Limited in 1998, putting in jeopardy the agricultural and other water needs of fifteen villages. After much protest the deal was withdrawn in 2003. Meanwhile, Jindal Steel & Power Limited has been granted permission to build a private dam on Kukrut River, again affecting adversely the water needs of ten villages upstream and downstream. The Jindal Group has also been extracting water from the Kelu River as though it were their private property, impacting availability of water for agriculture for hundreds of families.[60]

The proposed sale of a 200-km stretch of the Nira River (for Rs 1000 crore) in Maharashtra has been put on hold since 2009 after a lot of protest from CSOs (civil society organizations) and the affected farming population.[61]

Perhaps the most interesting water story remains to be told. The silver lining for corporate business in the drinking water crisis in India is the opportunity it has created for the bottled water industry. It did not exist in India when the reforms began in 1991. Bisleri relaunched its product (after a failure in 1967) in 1994, under the seductive slogan 'Bisleri, veri, veri extraordinari!' After enough massaging of the potential market, the idea came of age that water was scarce, and it was acceptable to sell and buy water.

The global bottled water market is itself quite new. This is the fastest growing segment—worth over $100 billion—of the global beverage market, with a share of 38 per cent. But while the global market for bottled water is expanding today at 4.5 per cent annually, the Indian market is growing at a stunning

20–40 per cent every year, doubling every four years. From 2 million cases sold in 1990, the sales have multiplied seventy-five times, to almost 150 million in 2010. There are more than 200 brands and 1800 bottling plants across the country. India is the world's fastest growing bottled water market in the world, according to the Earth Policy Institute. Between 1999 and 2004, the number of bottles sold in China doubled. In India they trebled. The market is expected to be $1500 million by 2013. The growth of the bottled water market is explained of course by factors like the rise in water-borne diseases and erratic water supply, but even more by aggressive marketing and cuts in excise duty by the government.

India's drinking water crisis is severe today. At least part of the blame for this has to be shouldered by the bottled water industry. It has contributed both to falling water tables and groundwater depletion as well as to its pollution across many regions of the country.

Bottling plants for fizzy drinks have had a profound effect on the availability of clean groundwater in many rural areas of the country. Public protests against the Coca-Cola bottling plants in Plachimada (Kerala), Mehdiganj (UP) and Kala Dera (Rajasthan) are well known by now (see chapter 10). In Kala Dera Coca-Cola paid the government the princely sum of Rs 5000 a year during 2000–02 to access the groundwater. The increased contamination and pollution has also meant a rise in water-borne ailments.[62]

From the point of view of the poor majority of the country, the rise of bottled water has actually come at the expense of public drinking water supply, effectively pricing them out of the market. Per capita consumption of bottled water in India is still just six litres per year (compared to a global average of twenty-four litres). This constitutes less than 1 per cent of the drinking water consumed in the country every year—the reason why so many companies see such high potential in the Indian water market.[63]

The reason for the high profits (between 20 and 205 per cent, according to informal sources) is that the invaluable raw material—water—is acquired for next to nothing (at Re 0.25, including treatment costs, in a Rs 10 bottle). The chief costs are packaging, marketing and transportation. Packaging (bottle, cap and carton) can take as much as 35 per cent of the final price. Labour, establishment and marketing costs are contingent on the location. But a 1-litre bottle can be produced at a cost of Rs 5–7, including taxes. The amazing thing is that people are still willing to pay Rs 10 or Rs 12 for a bottle, leaving a tidy profit margin of 40–140 per cent for the manufacturers. A tribute to aggressive marketing in tropical conditions—bottled water is 'purer', 'safer', 'sweeter', 'more convenient', 'healthier', 'Himalayan', 'mineral-rich', 'sparkling' or 'has more oxygen'. Economic theory predicts that 'supernormal' profits are competed away by competition and new entrants in the long run. Either a decade is not long enough to be 'the long run' or the theory is false.[64]

The lure of huge profits has attracted big players into the water-bottling business. Other than the market leader, Parle's Bisleri, there is Pepsi with its Aquafina brand. Tata Tea has recently acquired a big stake in Mount Everest. Coca-Cola, which sells water under the Kinley label, has bought a part of Glaceau. Even WIPRO has entered the bottled water business with its purchase of the FMCG (fast-moving consumer goods) firm Unza.

If the major costs—groundwater depletion, pollution and disposal in the case of bottled water production—are not taken into account, bottled water would be *systematically overproduced* in a market economy. Importantly, once consumption habits are formed, neither the producer nor the consumer has any interest in paying the 'external' costs of the production of bottled water. They would not even care to know what the true costs are. We will typically not have information on these costs by looking at government or company data. To find the real costs of bottled water production, we would have to check with the rural communities who suffer the externalities.

Nor do the bottling companies and the governments that grant them licences want the public to see the enormous energy footprint that bottled water leaves everywhere. It takes *2000 times* as much energy to mine, process, bottle, ship, cool and sell water than it would take to get it from a tap! (This calculation excludes the energy cost of bottle disposal.) It also takes three to seven bottles of water itself to produce one bottle. Some calculations indicate that bottled water costs up to 10,000 times more than tap water in terms of real resources consumed. At $10 a gallon, it costs more than petrol in the US! And in a world where the bottled water trade across the oceans is growing (often because imported bottled water has less pesticide content), the energy implications should be a cause for alarm not only for anyone aware of 'peak oil' shortages but also for everyone concerned about climate change. There are infinitely simpler ways of addressing people's drinking water requirements than shipping fancy mineral water from across the oceans in oil-guzzling vessels or mining out and polluting the groundwater of poor rural communities.[65]

'Garib hatao': Driving the poor off the land

One aspect of socio-economic exclusion and rejection is so fundamental that it almost escapes notice. It has to do with being deprived of land. Both the mainstream and the default economies ultimately subsist on land, though (what with all the illusions about the 'knowledge economy') it is easy to imagine that wealth in modern economies is independent of it. But when all is said and done, access to land is *the* primary bone of contention in globalizing India—whether it is in the forested regions of central and eastern India, where adivasis are trying to defend their ancestral rights against mining companies, or in slum neighbourhoods like Dharavi in Mumbai where more than a million working people are trying to hold out against the ambitions of powerful developers interested in making a quick buck on prime real estate.

Everyone has to have a patch of earth to have a home. The same is true about an office, a coal-mine, a factory or a supermarket. The only question is how much the land is worth in a certain context. And how other things are valued in relation to it. For instance, as everyone familiar with the real estate market in India knows, the moment there is a change in land use (typically from agriculture or some other traditional use to industry, infrastructure or modern services), there is a dramatic rise in the price of land. Nothing intrinsically has changed about the patch of earth in question. But it rises in monetary value.

What explains the magic? In a market-driven world, the people with the money have determinate impact on prices, especially when they need a limited resource. They determine 'value'. Those with traditional access to land do not have the financial resources to defend their (mostly unrecognized) land rights, which are often held in common, as distinct from modern conceptions of private property. On the other hand, some of those who want land in specific desired locations have plenty of money. When they also have the government on their side, it is easy to foresee what is likely to happen. In this sense, it is indeed very true that 'there is no money in agriculture', a line all too often heard nowadays. The story is not too different in other countries around the world. Everywhere, the conflict between agriculture and industry, between traditional livelihoods and the modern growth-oriented economy, has played out to the lasting disadvantage of the former. There is a ring of inevitability to it which seems to paralyse all analysis and moral sense.

What has happened in India during the reform era is that the poor are losing control of the only asset they own—land—in both rural and urban settings, perhaps at an even faster pace than before the reforms. In the countryside, the term used to denote the phenomenon is borrowed from physics: 'displacement' (which includes dispossession even when actual physical uprooting may not be involved). Its urban counterpart is also a mechanical euphemism: 'eviction'.

The developmental logic driving both these processes in sequence is the same: the breakneck expansion of the formal, mainstream economy, gargantuan in its demands on energy, water, land and other resources. It is important to note just how much both these processes have accelerated after 1991. Both displacement and eviction have been going on since long before 1947. But the growing population pressures of recent decades and the ambitions of the metropolitan elite have speeded up both processes, uprooting the poor in virtually every case.

Consider first, development-induced displacement. It is important to note that there is no official database on it. When we measure something it implies that we care about it. The fact that successive governments in independent India have not found it necessary to keep track of the number of people uprooted by industrial, mining or infrastructure projects is in itself a comment on where priorities lie—and whether they really believe their own rhetoric about the concern to reduce poverty. It reflects the facile assumptions on which policies are based.

Nonetheless, in the absence of official figures, community organizations and intellectuals have made independent estimates of the number of displaced people (DPs) and project-affected people (PAPs), the latter being those whose livelihood is adversely affected or lost because of a development project even if they are not physically removed from their habitat. The estimated number of DPs and PAPs between 1947 and 2000 ranges between 21 and 60 million for the whole country (7 million in West Bengal alone), though some authors put it even higher. (Forty per cent of the people displaced or affected are adivasis, 20 per cent are Dalits and 20 per cent are Other Backward Classes [OBCs], constituting 8 per cent, 16 per cent and 30–40 per cent of the total population of the country, respectively.)

In other words, a population the size of somewhere between Scandinavia and France has been asked to move to make way for development projects in the first five decades of Independence. This is part of the price that the mainstream economy has exacted from the default economies. Only 9 to 36 per cent of the DPs and PAPs have been resettled when one looks at the record of the different states. The low rate of resettlement is perhaps explained by the fact that 80 per cent of these groups (including the proportions of adivasis, Dalits and OBCs) have been historically voiceless, even if they have gained a modicum of influence during the past two decades.[66]

The pace of displacement may have greatly accelerated since the reforms began in 1991 (though the figures are not available). This can be judged from the fact that the rate at which development projects are being cleared has grown dramatically. It is also indicated by the pace of land acquisition. During the first decade of the twenty-first century, AP had acquired half as much land for industry as it did in the first forty-five years after Independence. In the period 1951–95, Orissa had acquired 40,000 ha for industries. Over the last decade its land acquisition demands ballooned to 100,000 ha. Between 1986 and 2006 the ministry of environment and forests (MoEF) gave environmental clearance to over 4000 projects, a rate of roughly one project every two days over two decades. In just the first two years after the issuance of the new Environment Impact Assessment (EIA) notification in 2006, it cleared over 2000, at the rate of two to three a day. The protests over land acquisition and displacement are naturally growing pari passu, in many cases taking the form of left-wing extremism.[67]

A parallel process is unfolding in the cities of India. As so many of those who have lost land and/or livelihood in the countryside move to the cities in search of work, they find space to live only in the mushrooming slums. However, most of these settlements are not legal; poor people simply cannot find legal housing. Typically, they are patronized by political parties seeking to expand vote banks.

Since the reforms began, 'selling' Indian metros to global capital and finance has become an overriding priority. It means clearing up the 'eyesores' in every Indian city. Slum demolitions are now routine, clinical affairs, often carried out on the sly, without prior notice, under the umbrella of the police. There is little debate, even in the media, despite strident political protests. Court appeals usually fail to win justice for those affected. Judgements that tended to be pro-poor till the 1990s have since then reversed direction. It is an outright denial of housing rights for large segments of the urban population, in obvious violation of the Supreme Court's interpretation of Article 21 of the Indian Constitution, which protects life and personal liberty.[68]

How many people have been evicted during the past two decades? Again, as with displacement, the state does not keep records. Between November 2004 and January 2005 alone, according to the UN Rapporteur on Housing Rights, in one of the biggest ever demolitions, 80,000 hutments were razed to the ground, often at night, in Mumbai alone. Nearly 300,000 people—all of them below the poverty line—lost their homes in a drive to eliminate 'post-1995 encroachments' as the city progressed on its journey to become 'India's Shanghai', as the Maharashtra chief minister once announced quite proudly.[69]

The national capital too has witnessed a spate of slum evictions during the last two decades. What is offered here is only a small sample of the slum-clearance drive which has taken possession of city authorities in their urgency to make Delhi 'world class'. In the year 2000, for instance, 75,000 people lost their jhuggis to government bulldozers. Most of these people were not relocated. In 2004 Delhi's biggest slum cluster Yamuna Pushta, on the banks of the river, was demolished, rendering 150,000 people homeless. The driving force behind this eviction was the 2010 Commonwealth Games. Only a quarter of the evicted families have been resettled on the northern outskirts of the city, disrupting their lives and livelihoods. In 2006, 7500 people lost their homes in Mandawali and 3000 near the Bhatti mines. The list goes on and on.[70]

At the time of the 2001 census there were 1100 slums in Delhi, most of them located on land formally owned by the Delhi Development Authority (DDA), the Municipal Corporation of Delhi, the New Delhi Municipal Corporation or the Indian Railways. The fact that even these meagre dwellings were callously ground into the earth points to a further entrenchment of exclusion since the reforms began, when one takes account of the livelihoods and the ways of living (including medical clinics, schools, power lines) that were disturbed or destroyed in the process.

The Khanna Committee set up in 2006 to investigate unauthorized construction and misuse of land in Delhi found that 75 per cent of the people of the city were living in unauthorized areas, half of them in resettlement colonies and slums. It attributed this to the failure of the DDA 'to build adequate housing units for low-income communities'.[71]

Very similar stories are reported from other cities around the country. In Hyderabad, a city with 800 notified slums, each with 10,000–15,000 people on an average, the Telugu Desam government under Chandrababu Naidu carried out a series of evictions in 2003 and 2004. The Congress government which succeeded it followed through with the same aggressive policy. Thousands of families were evicted within the space of a few years, mostly without being resettled. If they have been relocated at all, it has been on the far outskirts of the city, disturbing livelihoods in the process. And yet, unauthorized colonies that have come up for the rich, such as Sainik Farms in Delhi, are not touched.[72]

The so-called 'left' governments are not any better. In Kolkata, on Human Rights Day (10 December) in 2002, 4000 families were brutally evicted from Beliaghata by the ruling CPM (Communist Party of India [Marxist]) coalition, despite their having ration cards as proof of residence. The same government had settled them there in the early 1980s. No family has been resettled yet. The event came to be remembered as the 'December Ten carnage'. In later years, evictions have been carried out in a large number of other neighbourhoods in Kolkata.[73]

Action Aid has reported a long series of forced evictions from cities like Ahmedabad, Bengaluru, Hyderabad, Chennai and, of course, Delhi and Mumbai. Now, under the Jawaharlal Nehru National Urban Renewal Mission (JNNURM), slum evictions are expected to become more frequent and ruthless. Housing rights writer Kalyani Menon-Sen says, 'Evictions have increased as a consequence of the JNNURM, the externally-aided flagship programme that makes aid to State governments for urban development conditional on implementation of measures for opening up and privatising land and housing markets.'[74]

Unlike countries where the state takes responsibility for public housing, in India the poor are deprived even of what they are able to muster on their own. While public housing is almost nil in most Indian cities, private players do not see any profit in investing in housing for the poor.[75]

As migration and urbanization continue to increase, the size of the slum population in the country is growing to overwhelming proportions. NSS surveys show that there were 49,000 urban slums in India in 2008–09. According to UN data, 55 per cent of our urban population lived in slums in 2003. This made it 158 million people in that year, the world's second largest urban slum population after China. Wherever in the world SAPs have been implemented, they have led to a rapid urbanization of poverty. Such large numbers of people are not about to magically disappear tomorrow. They signify a quiet, undeclared apartheid society shot through and through with a myriad ugly forms of discrimination.[76]

The red thread: Inequality-led exclusive growth

The reigning wisdom in mainstream economics is that in the early stages of economic growth a country experiences a rise in inequality. This, it is argued, is necessary for the future of the economy since the rich are in a position to save and invest more of their income compared to the poor. With greater investment, growth picks up, employment grows, tax collections go up and welfare programmes for the poor and marginalized classes in society can be implemented. This reverses the earlier rise in inequality. It is said, with some justification, that historically this has been the experience of economic growth and development in the affluent countries, modelled by economists as the famous Kuznets Curve.

Let us be clear about what is involved here. Nations like Britain, Germany, Japan and the US were able to reduce inequality over time because the norm of the welfare state came to prevail. Firstly, economic growth was broad-based, involving most segments of the population. Exclusion was not the norm. Secondly, to the extent that this growth did not directly benefit significant segments of the population, the fiscal norms of welfare states prevailed and ensured a semblance of redistribution, so that the benefits of growth were shared to a significant degree.

It is crucial to note the change in policy climate around the world over the last generation, since the Thatcher–Reagan years. Firstly, as per neo-liberal prescriptions, the welfare state has been rapidly unravelling in the Western world, giving rise to inequalities yet again. Secondly, the neo-liberal diet has been imposed on most developing nations too (China and, to a lesser degree, South Korea, being partial exceptions). The prescription is to let the rich have lots of cake today so that the poor may possibly get some bread tomorrow.

In accordance with this, in India the policy elite and almost everyone in the educated classes believe that poverty has been declining steadily since the inception of the reforms and has reached manageable proportions of around a quarter of the overall population. The 2007–08 *Economic Survey* claims that the proportion of the poor in the total population has declined from 36 per cent in 1993–94 to 27.5 per cent in 2004–05—a view supported till very recently by the World Bank, using an international poverty line of $1 a day. True, India has spawned more billionaires during this period than any other country, except the US. But have they, as mainstream economic theory expects, contributed enough to the alleviation of poverty through their investments? And have these investments brought employment opportunities for the poor? As we have seen, the answer to these questions is 'No'.[77]

What if the truth is the opposite of what is widely accepted? What if three-quarters of the population is actually being left out—or worse, preyed upon—by the growth process of the mainstream economy during the past two decades? For our purposes it is enough to know that poverty—even if *perhaps* on the decline—has not been falling quite as swiftly as it was supposed to, compared to the rate of decline in some other developing countries (like China, which has exercised autonomy and has not been under the policy rule of IFIs). If economic growth is meant to be the decisive salve for poverty, the latter is still too high for a country that has been growing impressively at 8 or 9 per cent in recent times. More recent official estimates by the Planning Commission put the proportion of the poor population across the country at 38 per cent. The Sengupta Committee figure of 77 per cent of Indians spending Rs 20 a day or less is corroborated by a number of other figures. Malnutrition in the country has been consistently high and in fact rising in some parts of the country (such as Jharkhand, MP and even Kerala). The incidence of anaemia among children and women of child-bearing age has grown perceptibly during this period.[78]

The urban–rural divide has also been growing. The ratio of urban to rural per capita income increased from 2.34 to 2.85 between 1993–94 and 1999–2000. If one looks at the provision of 'community, social and other services' (health, education, etc.), government data reveal that while in 1993–94, 42 per cent of the public expenses under this category went to rural areas, in 1999–2000, rural areas received just 29 per cent, even though more than 70 per cent of the country lives there.[79]

The rise in wealth at the top and the concomitant heightening of inequality have been so rapid that a recent IMF paper warns that 'the ability of the government to pass and sustain reforms momentum depends on popular support. If large parts of the population are left behind, even if only in relative terms, the viability of future reforms may be threatened'.

It states that 'overall consumption inequality increased in the 1990s, particularly in urban areas and . . . while inequality was stable in urban India and declining in rural India in the 1980s, this trend was reversed in the 1990s . . . the urban–rural gap widened . . . in almost all states growth became less equalizing in the 1990s . . . the bottom 50% of India's population experienced faster growth in the previous decade'.

The IMF document concludes that 'there is no evidence of correlation between the speed of growth and its inclusiveness'.[80]

Such candid admissions from an institution like the IMF— which would not be inclined to interpret the evidence along these lines unless the facts were truly telling—calls for a deeper understanding of what has been transpiring. How does one conceptualize the nature of the growth process in the Indian economy over the past few decades? What is the primary mechanism at work?

High growth, it appears, is feeding on inequalities. The growth has been *demand-deepening* (within the wealthy and the rich classes), rather than *demand-widening* (cutting across classes). As inequalities have grown, purchasing power has come to be concentrated among the elite and the middle classes, mostly in urban areas and the metros.

Our taste is for a class of goods and services which transit readily from the category of 'wants' into 'needs' at the hands of invasive advertising and socially competitive, invidious consumption. They either have to be imported or can only be produced by large, often (but not only) multinational, corporations within the country. Given the availability of cheap consumer credit, the demand for these goods rises even faster than incomes.

The growing demand for luxury goods and services thus feeds a particular pattern of consumption demand and corporate industrialization that renders increasingly redundant the skills and talents of village artisans and small producers, no less than the modest output of small industries. What's more, land is taken away from agriculture and farmers in order to facilitate industrialization (via things like SEZs), infrastructure and mining, thereby exacerbating inequalities in society, both between rich and poor and between cities and villages. It also generates pressures for further migration to urban areas.

In the words of well-known economist Amit Bhaduri,

Over time an increasingly irreversible production structure in favour of the rich begins to consolidate itself. Because the investments embodied in the specific capital goods created to produce luxuries cannot easily be converted to producing basic necessities (the luxury hotel or spa cannot be converted easily to a primary health centre in a village etc). And yet, it is the logic of the market to direct investments towards the most productive and profitable sectors for 'the efficient allocation of resources'. The price mechanism sends signals to guide this allocation, but the prices that rule are largely a consequence of the growing unequal distribution of income in the society. The market becomes a bad master when the distribution of income is bad.[81]

As we shall see in the next few chapters, such a process of industrialization, driven by the growing demand for luxury items from a small fraction of the people relies on unsustainable levels of exploitation of the environment, given its appetite for water, energy and non-renewable resources. We will also see how rural India gets a raw deal in this transfer of resources from the hinterland to urban India. In effect, the metros thrive on the ecological subsidies routinely extracted from the countryside.

Any other model of industrialization or development is rendered unthinkable by this powerful process at work. This globally driven model—backed by powerful governments, the IFIs and the WTO, not to forget the sensation-peddling, corporate-dominated media—has generated a virtual consensus in favour of something understood as 'development'. There is a veritable consumer carnival for the upper crust of the population often new to the wealth at its disposal. They can now take safaris in Africa, attend conferences every other month in Canberra or Copenhagen, have birthday parties in the Maldives (while it's still there) and go shopping for deodorants in Singapore. However, the hard reality is that the motor driving the process of this predatory growth rides on the destroyed or threatened lives and livelihoods of peasants and adivasis, or on the bloodied shoulders of maltreated, over-exploited female workers in the subcontracted economy.

The myth-making excesses of the media have resulted in a sensory, intellectual and moral numbing of the public imagination. Cricket, Bollywood and the infotainment offered by the 24/7 media exercise a hypnosis powerful enough to keep the bewitched classes from making use of their peripheral vision.

People are kept busy with 'activities' centring on consumption, distancing them from issues that concern their underprivileged fellow citizens. Significant numbers of our metropolitan elite have managed to effectively secede from the majority of the country. Thus, large swathes of our media practise conscious and inadvertent censure of the overwhelming and distasteful realities, besides creating a zone of false euphoria over India's 'success'. This is not to tar everyone with the same brush. Yet, even those media channels and newspapers that sometimes carry accurate reports on matters like farmer suicides or the uprooting of large communities due to large-scale industrialization find themselves swamped by issues—both genuine and false—that primarily affect or interest the elite. And, as a rule, advertising—which builds a sense that everything can be solved by buying more—gets a lot of play, especially on television. So, the care and attention demanded by a serious report on the condition of our people becomes very difficult to sustain. As a result, fundamental processes of moral cognition are short-circuited, and denial becomes the last refuge for most prominent members of our educated classes—whether they are political leaders, policy heads, bureaucrats, businesspersons or journalists.

'You can wake up a man who is sleeping,' Gandhi wrote, 'but you can't wake up someone pretending to sleep.'

This growth can never trickle down

Even if a lot of well-meaning businesspersons and policymakers in powerful decision-making positions wish it, the benefits of this unprecedented economic growth can never trickle down in any significant manner to the mass of the people. Based as it fundamentally is on a 'club membership' system, it will keep further enriching the already rich and fail to make any dent in poverty. Unless its pattern and direction are radically changed by conscious, collective, ecologically sensitive, democratic political processes, growth will continue to be exclusive and create further unemployment. It will continue to worsen social tensions and increase corruption, crime and insurgency that we have already been witnessing. It will resemble the growth of dying cancer cells rather than that of a healthy body, leading possibly to a violent dismembering of the Indian nation as we have known it.

For growth to be inclusive in an increasingly privatized, capitalist society, it must, at the very least, ensure that the poor find growing purchasing power in their hands. One or more of the following conditions must be met: (1) New employment is generated in the organized sector at a pace somewhat comparable with the rate of growth of the working population. (2) The indirect employment effects (in the informal economy) of growth in the organized sector must be substantial and make up for the failure of the organized sector to create adequate employment. Moreover, such informal jobs have to be rewarding—over-exploitation only deepens structural poverty. (3) If the gains of growth accrue largely to the rich, the government must be able and willing to redistribute a significant fraction of them to the poor, through appropriate fiscal policy. This possibility is the last surviving hope of the growth economist, who has traditionally defended inequality-generating growth on the grounds that its overall benefits can always be split in an egalitarian fashion after they have accrued (to the rich)—through taxation.

The evidence presented earlier in this chapter leaves us in serious doubt as to the viability of either (1) or (2). We have seen that growth has been largely jobless as far as the organized sector of the mainstream economy is concerned. We have also seen that the linkages between the organized sector and the rest of the economy (where they exist) are usually too exploitative to bring any lasting benefit to the poor majorities who work in agriculture and the informal economy. (The mainstream economy is increasingly more integrated with the global economy than with the domestic informal economy.) On the contrary, the patterns of exclusion and rejection that result from the demands placed by the mainstream economy on the rest of the population are so extreme as to worsen the material condition of the vast majority even further. Poverty is not so much a natural as a cumulative product of exploitative historical and contemporary socio-economic processes that have been with us particularly since the days of colonialism. Given the sheer number of people who have been paralysed by debt, dispossessed, displaced or otherwise impoverished, it would scarcely be an overstatement to say that development, far from reducing poverty, has actually been creating new, modern forms of it.

What about secondary employment generated in the informal sector as a consequence of the enormous growth in the organized sector? Reliable data are hard to come by. But even if we assume that between 1991 and 2006 ten new jobs were generated in the informal sector for every new job created in the organized private sector (ignoring the effect of the public sector where the number of jobs actually declined), about 11 million (net) new jobs were created *over a decade and a half* in the informal sector. Apart from the backlog of scores of millions of unemployed and underemployed people, the *annual* accretion to India's workforce alone has been roughly the same number during this period!

We are also ignoring here the huge amount of unemployment, forced employment or exploitative self-employment for the poor that has resulted from their losing traditional forms of livelihood (in agriculture, fisheries, forest-work or elsewhere), because their resource base has been taken over for mining, industrial or infrastructure projects. Such people—who number in the tens of millions—have been integrated at the bottom end of the monetized economy in some of the most exploitative tasks imaginable. Farmers have often been rendered penniless by such processes and turned into poorly treated, ill-paid drain-cleaners in the cities.

If it is any consolation, a recent ILO study on employment and economic growth in Asia concludes that even China has experienced 'employment-hostile growth' since the mid-1990s. And for further consolation we may look to the West, where the complaint of jobless and job-destroying growth has been loud and persistent for at least two decades.[82]

Are state policies to blame for the failure to create jobs? Yes, if one keeps in view their role in signing on to a deregulated model of globalized growth and development which is *structurally* exclusive. It is vain to hope that the rich can enable the welfare of the poor, even if they invest productively the money saved in taxes. The global imperatives of the cost-cutting, quality-enhancing and capital-intensive technology that they must necessarily adopt renders them powerless to create new jobs, despite their most noble intentions. The trajectory of technology, as it has evolved historically in labour-scarce Western economies, dictating thereby the basic patterns of economic growth, militates against such possibilities. A 'kind' capitalist—who, from the largeness of his heart, gives work to many workers at high wages—will soon find himself out of the market in a world of lean and mean competitors.

This phenomenon has had a striking outcome in India. While employment has stagnated over most of the last two decades, the real output of the non-agricultural part of the economy (which is expected to provide new jobs) grew by a factor of at least three: only a slight increase in the number of organized sector workers produced three times as much output, thanks to automation of production processes. This is an astonishing fact. In other words, even taking account of the accretion of low-paid employment in the unorganized sector, if someone had the good fortune to be employed in the organized sector, their remuneration went up, on an average, by a factor of at least three. If not, they await the materialization of trickle-down hopes. This difference is surely part of the explanation for the dramatic rise in inequalities in the country during the past two decades.

We are left with the last possibility of trickle-down growth. Is it possible that the increase in tax collections by the government—enabled by the higher pace of economic growth— will be channelled in a sustained way over a long period of time towards the neglected areas of public expenditure, like water, health, education, housing and employment generation? This may happen up to a point and in a few cases. Given its positive effect on election results in 2009, the allocation for the important MGNREGA (the Mahatma Gandhi National Rural Employment Guarantee Act, the government's flagship scheme for the people) has grown significantly in recent years. From 2.1 per cent of annual public expenditure, a modest Rs 11,000 crore in 2005–06 (the year the scheme was launched), it has grown to Rs 39,100 crore in 2009–10 (3.8 per cent). At Rs 100 a day for 100 days a year, almost 40 million rural workers can potentially avail of the scheme, as against 11 million workers when the scheme was launched (we abstract the leakages due to corruption). But the higher allocation for MGNREGA also means there is less left over for other social programmes, given very tight budget constraints and the Fiscal Responsibility and Budget Management (FRBM) Act. In general, the record of Indian governments devoting large fractions of tax collections on social spends is, euphemistically put, dismal.[83]

The persistence of mass hunger, malnutrition, poverty and unemployment in a context so inundated with wealth for a few reminds one of the economist-diplomat John Kenneth Galbraith's sharp observation—faith in trickle-down is a bit like feeding race horses superior oats so that starving sparrows can forage in their dung. Political psychologist Ashis Nandy points out that 'the dominant model of development, whatever else it can do, cannot abolish poverty' since, among other things, 'it seeks to push a polity towards a stage when poverty, even if it persists as a nagging social problem, no longer remains salient in public consciousness'. A 'developmental regime' helps in cultivating a 'social deafness and moral blindness towards parts of the living world around us'. There are few hurdles to the elimination of poverty more obstinate than its consistent denial by the educated classes.[84]

What does global evidence on poverty reduction over the last few decades of growth reveal? London-based New Economics Foundation (NEF), using World Bank data, estimates that between 1990 and 2001, for every $100 worth of growth in the world's income per person, just $0.60 found its target and contributed to reducing poverty below the a-dollar-a-day line. To achieve every $1 of poverty reduction therefore required $166 of additional global production and consumption, with all its associated environmental impacts. *This means that to reduce poverty by $1 involved paying the non-poor an additional $165!* If one takes the evidence between 1981 and 2001, the additional amount was much less at $44. 'Poverty reduction' is costing more with the passage of time. The NEF concludes:

> This approach is both economically and ecologically inefficient. It will be highly improbable to reconcile the objectives of poverty reduction and environmental sustainability if global growth remains the principal economic strategy. The scale of growth this model demands would generate unsupportable environmental costs; and the costs would fall disproportionately, and counter-productively, on the poorest—the very people the growth is meant to benefit.

According to the NEF, the rate of global poverty reduction achieved between 1981 and 2001 could have been achieved through the annual redistribution of a mere 0.1 per cent of the income of the richest 10 per cent of the world's population.

This also implies that population growth is not the real cause of the global ecological crisis. If there had been no economic growth during 1981–2001, but the aforesaid redistribution had been carried out, the rich would be imperceptibly less rich than before and the poor would be a shade less poor. However, nature and our progeny would be far better off. It shows that redistribution is, at least ecologically speaking, a far more effective way to reduce poverty than is economic growth.[85]

Most economists separate the goal of economic growth from the distribution of the benefits that growth will bring. They believe that we must first expand the pie, then we can consider ways of distributing it equitably. Now we can see the serious flaw in such a view. The truth is that the *way* the pie gets created determines in good measure what and how much is produced and how it gets divided. If high growth is based on an exorbitant financial sector and increasingly capital-intensive industrial technologies, which structurally exclude large numbers of working people, it is a formidably uphill task for the government to correct the inequalities that result merely through taxes and spending programmes. There are demands after all from the mainstream economy on the tax collections—for things like infrastructure, defence, security, higher education, etc.—which usually take priority over social spending. If growth was to be employment-led and ecologically and culturally sensitive, resulting as a *by-product* of an expansion of people's creative participation in a sustainable economy, it would take care of both demand as well as inequalities. The removal of poverty can truly become feasible only when the priorities are redrawn—high growth cannot be an end in itself, or even the first objective.

Rabindranath Tagore was no economist. But he did understand this simple truth. We would do well to recall his words in his long-neglected essay, 'The Robbery of the Soil':

> Most of us who try to deal with the problem of poverty think only of a more intensive effort of production. We forget that it brings about a greater exhaustion of materials as well as of humanity. It gives to the few excessive opportunities for profit at the cost of the many. It is food which nourishes, not money; it is fullness of life which makes one happy, not fullness of purse. Multiplying material wealth alone intensifies the inequality between those who have and those who have not, and it inflicts so deep a wound on the social system that the whole body eventually bleeds to death.[86]

4

A HOUSE ON FIRE

INDIA'S ECOLOGICAL SECURITY UNDERMINED

'The multiple environmental crises that confront our country have created in many ways an alarming situation. Climate change is threatening our fragile ecosystems. We are staring at the prospect of an impending drought. Water scarcity is becoming a way of life. Pollution is a growing threat to our health and to our habitats . . . There are fundamental choices that we have to make about our lifestyles; about how we wish to produce and consume, the things we ought to do and the things we ought not to do. I sincerely believe that the greatest challenge facing humankind today is the challenge of arriving at a new equilibrium between man and nature.'

—Prime Minister Manmohan Singh,
Address at the National Conference of Ministers of
Environment and Forests, 18 August 2009[1]

In 1992, soon after heralding the new economic policies constituting globalization, India's prime minister Manmohan Singh (then finance minister) delivered a lecture on the environmental aspects of the reforms, under the aegis of the

Society for Promotion of Wastelands Development.[2] His main argument was that environmental protection requires resources, which a poor country like India could not afford; hence the new policies were sound in that they would create the financial resources to invest in the environment.

However, things have not played out as Singh envisaged (or wanted the audience to believe). Singh's argument rested on the assumption that additional financial resources would be generated without causing further irreversible damage to the environment—a far from valid premise. If environmental problems are created faster than the rate at which additional resources to tackle them are generated, if they just cannot be solved by pouring money in or if they are irreversible (e.g. the destruction of natural rainforests), the problem in the end is worse than when one started.

As we explore below, the current phase of globalization has had a severe impact on the country's natural environment and, consequently, on those communities who depend directly on nature for their subsistence and livelihood.

Had Manmohan Singh's assertion worked, by now we should have seen a spate of measures and programmes to protect India's environment. But while the budgets of official environment departments have risen somewhat (those, too, nowhere near needed), and there have been some encouraging recent steps, and though 'sustainable development' has been the official motto for a number of years, the ecological crisis has only intensified. This chapter attempts to show that this is an inherent and inevitable outcome of globalization. Just as the 'trickle-down' theory does not work for the poor, so too the assertion 'having the resources to invest' does not work for the environment.

Two caveats

Before presenting the evidence regarding the ecological impact of globalization, two clarifications are necessary. First, nothing below is meant to indicate that we are per se against the basic activity being critically analysed. It is not our intention to say that there should be no mining, no floriculture, no fishing, no exports and imports, and so on. What is crucial is to ask not only whether we need these, but to what extent, for what purpose and under what conditions. These questions are simply shoved under the carpet in the current model of 'development' under globalization.

Second, it should be clear that many of the trends we describe below are not necessarily a product of the globalization phase in which we currently find ourselves. Indeed, many of them have roots in the model of 'development' we have adopted in the last six decades. However, this phase of globalization has not only greatly intensified these trends, it has also brought in new elements that considerably enhance the dangers of this model to India's environment and people. Where possible, we will point to such new elements.

A bit of history

A highly encapsulated historical account here would help lay the context for the current environmental situation. While there is evidence of environmental degradation (e.g. the conversion of forests for agriculture) through all the centuries during which the subcontinent was being settled, many historians note that a significant intensification took place during the colonial period. The British state commercialized huge tracts of forest and made cash-cropping a widespread phenomenon, both of which had massive impacts on biodiversity. Perhaps even more significant, it took over effective control of the vast 'commons' that were till then under community management (even if many of them may have been nominally under various rulers). This twin legacy of commercialization and state takeover of natural resources continues to be a dominant part of the context in which we see India's environment today.[3]

Unfortunately, after Independence the Indian government continued the policies introduced by the colonial state. Forests, for instance, were seen primarily for their timber and other commercial values, and the centralized bureaucracy managing them was only made more powerful. In the first two decades after Independence, there was very little change in this approach.

It is in the 1970s and 1980s that we see the beginnings of a major shift. A number of people's movements became prominent, challenging the commercialization and degradation of resources. The Chipko Movement empowered villagers in a part of the western Himalayas to protest the felling of timber by outsiders, resulting in a series of successes, including a prohibition on tree-felling for fifteen years starting 1980. This was also the period when a number of mass movements against big dams arose, most prominently against the Bhopalpatnam, Ichampalli, Bodhghat and Narmada projects in central India, and the Silent Valley in the south. Traditional fisherfolk across India's coasts mobilized against mega-scale commercial fisheries. Simultaneously, there was considerable rethinking within the political and bureaucratic classes. The government brought in path-breaking policies and laws, including acts to protect forests and wildlife and to control air and water pollution. There was a paradigm shift in policy towards forests, putting their ecological and social values above commerce, and an umbrella law to protect the environment was promulgated. Post-Independence, the

1970s and '80s were clearly a period of unprecedented rise in official acknowledgement of the ecological crisis.

In the last couple of decades, however, we see a reversal of the trends of the 1970s and '80s. All the 'commons'—forests, wetlands, grasslands, coasts and marine areas—have once again come under severe attack. It is not a coincidence that this period is also the period of economic globalization.

As a prominent example of this historical roller-coaster ride, let us see what has happened to India's forests. The colonial and post-Independence period, up to about 1980, witnessed rapid deforestation. According to official (Forest Survey of India) estimates, the country lost some 4.24 million ha of forest from 1951 to 1980, or approximately 140,000 ha every year.[4] With movements like Chipko and the promulgation of the Forest Conservation Act 1980, however, deforestation was considerably controlled. This is shown by data obtained from the MoEF (ministry of environment and forests) using Right to Information (RTI) applications. In the period 1981 to 1990, the annual rate came down to about 17,000 ha (if one excludes regularization of encroachments, for which there was one big year, 1990). This relatively lower rate remained for the first few years after the new economic policies were brought in in 1991, but once the effects of these policies (especially with industry and infrastructure demanding more land) started kicking in, the rate again increased substantially. From 1999 to 2007, the annual diversion became about 53,000 ha; this came down a bit in 2008–09, when about 43,000 ha of diversion was approved or accepted 'in principle'. Well over half the total forest land diversion for non-forest purposes, which has taken place since 1981, has happened in the new millennium.[5]

The ecological impact of growth in the reform era

Infrastructure, mining and materials: Demand is the god

With a single-minded pursuit of a double-digit economic growth rate, demand achieves the status of a god that cannot be questioned. The question is no longer *how much* we should produce or extract and for what purpose (keeping in mind the limits of natural resources and social systems), but how we can most cheaply produce or extract whatever is demanded, or how to sell with the help of aggressive marketing and advertising.

The last couple of decades have therefore seen a massive increase in new infrastructure creation, such as several thousand kilometres of roads, dozens of ports and airports, urban infrastructure and tens of mega and large power stations. This has meant the increasing diversion of land, mostly of natural ecosystems like forests and coasts, or agricultural fields. It has also meant a spurt in extraction of necessary raw materials, like minerals. Between 1993–94 and 2008–09 mineral production in India has risen by 75 per cent. Total figures of mineral production are not possible to give in terms of quantity, since different minerals have different measures.

TABLE 4.1: Growth in Extraction of Some Key Minerals from 1997–98 to 2008–09

(in '000 tonnes)

Bauxite	6108	15,250
Coal	297,000	493,000
Iron ore	75,723	225,544
Chromite	1515	3976

Source: Ministry of Coal and Mines Annual Report 2001–2002; Ministry of Mines Annual Report 2008–09.

India now ranks high in the global production of a number of minerals: the second largest for barites, chromite and talc/steatite/pyrophillite; third for coal/lignite and bauxite; fourth for iron ore and kyanite/sillimanite; and sixth for manganese ore and crude steel. It is also fully or largely self-sufficient in the case of most minerals and exports an increasing amount (see section on exports below).

Most of the minerals being demanded are under forested or poor rural areas, rich in biodiversity, and where communities are heavily dependent on the area's resources. Of the approximately 113,000 ha of forest land that has been diverted for mining since 1980, over 70 per cent has been in the period 1997–2007, a clear indication that globalization has dramatically raised the demand for minerals.[6]

The ecological and social impacts have been horrifying. The blasted limestone and marble hills of the Aravallis and Shivaliks; the cratered iron ore or bauxite plateaux of Goa, Madhya Pradesh and Orissa; the charred coal landscapes of eastern India; and the radioactive uranium belt of Jharkhand are all witness to the worst that economic 'development' can do. Tens of thousands of hectares of land have been rendered completely barren and unproductive, with only a small percentage restored (usually a euphemism for reclamation by a handful of mostly exotic species of trees, nowhere near the original vegetation). Mining wastes poison streams and rivers. Ore fines and toxic substances, carried by rainwater into nearby watercourses, make the water unfit for human use. The mining of major minerals generated around 1.84 billion tonnes of waste in just one year (2006), most of which has not been disposed of properly. Companies annually pump out millions of litres of water to drain mine galleries and release it into nearby watercourses. This causes flooding, silting, waterlogging and pollution. They also lower the surrounding water table, reducing the available groundwater. Iron ore mining alone is estimated to have used up 77 million tonnes of water in 2005–06, enough to meet the daily water needs of more than 3 million people.[7]

The local communities are the worst sufferers. Mining forces them into an extremely brutal environment, highly accident- and disease-prone. The worst affected are the adivasis of central and eastern India, whose lands and forests have been extensively destroyed by mining and associated industries. Displaced communities have undergone an overnight transformation from relatively self-reliant communities to callously abused people. Women and children, as always, suffer the most.

Increasingly, mineral-based production units like coal-fed power plants, steel plants and cement factories are located near the mines. Every mining enterprise leads to the conversion of agricultural or forest land to other purposes such as roads, railways and ropeways for mineral transport, infrastructure for administrative purposes, and so on. In effect, the total land affected by mining is many times larger than what is actually mined or leased out, all to the detriment of local communities and the environment.

Even areas specially designated for wildlife conservation are not spared. A 2003 report by the environmental group Kalpavriksh documented at least ninety wildlife sanctuaries and national parks, and hundreds of other ecologically sensitive areas with unique biodiversity and wildlife, being threatened by existing or proposed mining.[8]

Added to the negative impacts is the fact that mining does not appear to be contributing to the welfare of the local people, even by conventional economic or human development standards. Three states with substantial dependence on minerals (between 8 and 10 per cent of the GDP or about 6–13 per cent of the total revenue receipt)—Jharkhand, Orissa and Chhattisgarh—are characterized by low per capita income, lower growth rates and higher levels of poverty and food insecurity compared to the rest of the country. These three also have the most 'backward'* districts in the country: Jharkhand with nineteen of twenty-two, Orissa twenty-seven of thirty and Chhattisgarh fifteen of sixteen. In Orissa, while the mining sector has prospered, agriculture has markedly declined in several ways: a reduction in cropped area and area under foodgrains; underutilization or neglect of agricultural land and labour; degradation and diversion of cultivable land; and stagnant productivity. As for employment, the Indian mining industry employs just about 560,000 people, and this too is coming down as mechanization increasingly displaces labour. Between 1991 and 2004, the value of mineral production in India increased fourfold; employment, however, dropped by 30 per cent. The argument that economic growth necessarily leads to more jobs for people needs to be revisited (as also demonstrated in the previous chapter).[9]

Since 1991, some of the world's largest mining companies have invested in India. This includes Rio Tinto Zinc (UK); BHP (Australia); Vedanta (UK/India); Alcan (Canada); Norsk Hydro (Norway); Meridian (Canada); De Beers (South Africa); Raytheon (USA); and Phelps Dodge (USA). Many of these have as bad, or worse, environmental and social records as India's own mining companies.[10]

Though Indian laws and policies relating to mining contain a number of environmental safeguards, these have been violated repeatedly. For instance, the National Conservation Strategy and

*Denoting areas with high levels of poverty and lack of basic facilities.

Policy Statement on Environment and Development, 1992, recommends restriction on mining and quarrying activities in sensitive areas such as hill slopes, areas of natural springs and areas rich in biodiversity. But a considerable portion of the mining approved since then has been in precisely such areas.

On top of this, the direction of policy change has been towards making life much easier for mining companies. For example, after the government approved guidelines allowing private companies to get prospecting licences in areas up to 5000 sq km—as against the existing limit of 25 sq km—permits for mineral reconnaissance went up from 53,000 sq km to 466,556 sq km (about 14 per cent of India's total landmass!). In 2008 a new National Mineral Policy encouraged the move towards greater mechanization, privatization and foreign investment; suggested that environmental regulations become voluntary; and assured companies of automatic mineral licence after prospecting. In 2006 a new EIA (Environment Impact Assessment) notification specified that mining projects up to 50 ha, and coal mining projects up to 150 ha, are to be dealt with by state EIA authorities, which have the discretion to decide that they do not need any EIA and public hearing at all![11]

A serious lack of regulation in the mining sector is clearly indicated in the spate of exposés regarding illegal mining that came into public view in 2009 alone. Activists and the media have reported instances, some very large-scale, from seventeen different states in the country. The dimensions are appalling: in Karnataka alone, 11,896 cases of illegal mining were detected between 2006 and 2009; in Andhra, 35,411 cases. Some states, like Andhra Pradesh and Orissa, shamed into action, have halted operations in many illegal mines and arrested the concerned officials. The Central Bureau of Investigation too has launched inquiries into the issue. Such action is welcome, but unlikely to make any major dent, simply because the lack of regulation is an inevitable consequence of an economy *driven* by the demand of both India and the rest of the world, and of a state willing to bend over backwards to accommodate corporate interests.[12]

In this kind of scenario, the estimates given by mining agencies of the total mineral reserves known, or estimated to remain, are scary. Bauxite production in 2008–09 (estimated) was 15,250 thousand tonnes. But estimated or inferred total reserves in India are, at 3,289,817 thousand tonnes (in the states of Orissa, Andhra Pradesh, Madhya Pradesh, Chhattisgarh, Maharashtra, Gujarat and Jharkhand), more than 200 times this amount! Limestone production in 2008–09 was (only) 2300 million tonnes; total reserves are estimated at 175,345 million tonnes. And so on for most minerals.[13] If India is to feed its own and the world's enormous appetite for minerals, millions of hectares of its land would have to be laid waste.[14]

Exports: Selling our future (and past)

Changes in macroeconomic policies—such as in interest rates, tax rates and social spending—have profound consequences for the environment and people's livelihoods, howsoever indirect. These go unnoticed since we do not have even a conceptual framework—let alone systems of national accounts—which incorporates such connections. For instance, currency devaluations lead to greater pressure on the environment, as an exporting 'developing' country necessarily gives up more of its resources in order to obtain a given amount of hard currency through international trade. Cheaper credit or tax incentives for investment usually accelerate the pace of environmental damage, especially in a context in which the state is loosening environmental regulation. When financial markets are opened up to trading in commodities and commodity futures (bargains based on expected future prices), metals and other non-perishable raw materials become very attractive as items to hoard, speculate and make money on. Every time the government signs an MoU (memorandum of understanding) with a mining company, the share values of holders of equity in it rise, prompting further exploration and mining.

In 2004 a Foreign Trade Policy for 2004–09 was set forth, with the aim of doubling merchandise exports by 2009. As the ministry of commerce stated, 'The government has set a long-term vision of making India a major player in the world trade.' In line with this, exports grew at an annual rate of over 25 per cent from 2003–04 to 2007–08, jumping to US$163 billion, representing 1.4 per cent of global trade.[15]

Whether an economic development model that depends heavily on exports is itself desirable is a question we address elsewhere in this volume (see chapters 9 and 11). At any rate, a responsible policy would have at least the following key principles:

- Access of the country's citizens to the products being considered for export is not jeopardized by reduced physical availability or increased costs;
- The exploitation of natural resources to extract/produce these products is ecologically sustainable;
- The rights of local communities from whose areas the resources are being extracted are respected; and
- These communities are the primary beneficiaries of the exports.

Unfortunately, exports under globalization have violated each of these principles, not surprising when targets are set in terms of monetary figures of growth rather than the quality of the impact of such growth on human welfare. The clearest examples of this are the cases of fisheries and aquaculture, floriculture, commercial agriculture and mining, which are all among the fastest growing export sectors.

Marine fisheries

Exports of marine products have risen from 139,419 tonnes in 1990–91, to 602,835 tonnes in 2008–09 (in value terms, from Rs 893 to 8608 crore).* While the rise was extremely steep in the pre-1991 period also (from a small volume of 15,732 tonnes in 1961–62), the globalization phase is significant in many ways. As more and more tonnage is removed from the seas, it gets harder to continuously increase extraction. A growing demand from countries to which India previously did not export and the introduction of new technologies have fuelled a steady growth in extraction and export. From a handful of products being sent to about a dozen countries, we now export about 475 items to ninety countries.[16]

The Marine Products Export Development Authority (MPEDA) estimates that India can still significantly increase its exports because, of the fishery potential of 3.9 million tonnes, only about 2.9 is being tapped (as of 2007–08). But at what cost? Of the total marine product exports, about 21 per cent is of shrimps, constituting 44 per cent of the total value.[17] India is now the second largest aquaculture producer (in quantity and

---

*The base year for the financial figures is not given. Total marine fish catch rose from 2.3 million tonnes in 1990–91 to 2.9 million tonnes in 2007–08; adding to this inland fish catch, the total production in India rose from 3.8 to 7.3 million tonnes in the same period.

value) in the world. There are a number of studies of serious ecological damage and disruption of the livelihoods of traditional fisherfolk and farmers along the coasts. Unlike traditional aquaculture (which is a very old activity, mostly for subsistence), commercial-scale intensive shrimp farming, driven by the fact that most (95 per cent) aquaculture is now export-oriented, is known to be extremely polluting and disruptive of the delicate salinity balance of coastal areas. The National Environmental Engineering Institute (NEERI) carried out quick studies on directions given by the Supreme Court in the mid-1990s. It showed that in the states of Andhra Pradesh and Tamil Nadu, the social and environmental costs of shrimp aquaculture were 3.5 *times* the earnings (annual losses: Rs 6728 crore; annual earnings: Rs 1778 crore). The costs include damage to farmland and salt pans, wage losses to farmers, fall in rice production and losses in fishing income.[18] As more and more areas get converted to shrimp farming, local fish that are the staple food of local communities, like mullets (Mugilidae) and pearlspot (*Etroplus suratensis*), are eliminated.[19] This example shows the scale of hidden external and social costs that may lie behind the apparent economic success in so many areas. (See chapters 7 and 8 for a discussion on externalities.)

It is therefore worrying that while the current spread of brackish-water aquaculture is about 167,000 ha, the *potential* that organizations like MPEDA estimate, is about 1.2 million ha.[20]

A serious 'side effect' of the rapid emergence of aquaculture is that trawlers earlier engaged in catching shrimp from the wild have switched over to 'high open-bottom trawls, which catch all species of fish in the entire water column which, in turn, denies non-trawl gear groups access to their traditional fisheries resources'. Also, aquaculture requires collection of shrimp from the wild, which has a 'significant impact on marine biodiversity' by reducing recruitment to fish stocks.[21]

In 1996, acting on a number of complaints and expert studies, the Supreme Court prohibited all aquaculture on the coasts, other than 'traditional and improved traditional types of technologies'. It ordered all other aquaculture farms to be demolished by March 2007. It also directed the government to set up an authority to regulate further aquaculture development.[22]

But only in 2005, a Coastal Aquaculture Authority (CAA) was set up, and shrimp farming has actually continued to grow, often in violation of the relevant laws. Guidelines for sustainable aquaculture have been issued by MPEDA, standards on particular aspects have been put out by CAA, and there is an increasing policy emphasis on environmentally safe methods, but it is unclear how much impact these are having on the ground.[23]

Aquaculture is not the only aspect of fisheries that has caused environmental damage. As marine capture fisheries have also grown to about 3 million tonnes in 2008, there is evidence of over-fishing in the territorial waters (though not in the deeper seas) and over-harvesting of several species.[24] Such over-fishing, according to the Report of the Working Group on Fisheries for the Tenth Five-Year Plan, is mainly due to the use of the seas as 'open-access' with no tenurial rights given to traditional fishing communities.[25] Technologies, too, have changed, with bottom trawling becoming very common and traditional gear being replaced, as also the erosion of traditional knowledge that maintained sustainability.

Again, globalization has had a significant hand in all this. According to available data, fishery stocks in most of the world's seas have been exploited, one of the exceptions being the Indian

Ocean. It is obvious that the major fishing companies and the rich fish-eating nations are eyeing these waters. The government claims that big operators under the new policies will be allowed to fish only in deep waters, where traditional fisherfolk do not go. But past experience has shown that trawler owners find it convenient and cheaper to fish closer to shore.[26] Also, trawlers continue to be illegally used in the fish-breeding season. Physical clashes between trawler owners and local fisherfolk are common.

Minerals

Mining for exports (adding to the burgeoning domestic demand) is another major thrust area for investments. Exports of most minerals have risen significantly. In the case of lead ores and concentrates, they went up from a mere 543 tonnes in 2003–04 to an astounding 1,102,514 tonnes by 2007–08. Limestone exports shot up from about 200,000 tonnes in 1995–96 to 879,000 tonnes in 2007–08; sand (non-metal bearing) from 32,523 tonnes to 413,598 tonnes. And so on. In just a few cases, such as iron ore, has export growth been unsteady or has declined.

Moreover, a growing percentage of many of the minerals we produce is being exported. In 1995–96, only 1.4 per cent of the bauxite produced was exported; by 2007–08 it had gone up to 47 per cent, with a huge jump in exports after 2003–04.[27]

Lifting restrictions on exports

In tune with the increasing emphasis on export-led growth, successive policies since 1991 have reduced the export restrictions on materials and products. By 2002 all quantitative restrictions were removed (with the exception of very few sensitive items). Additionally, various forms of support such as transport assistance have been made available to a number of export items.

The items thus freed up or supported have environmental and social implications. This includes several crops and agricultural products, flowers and marine products. While not all of these are by themselves problematic, the policy does not seem to have considered the ecological sustainability of the spurt in production, the impact of homogenization and the impact on domestic availability to the poor.

Import liberalization and consumerism

Along with the liberalization of exports, the Indian economy has opened up to an increasing amount and variety of imports. The demand for key imports is often used to justify the export-push since foreign exchange earnings come from the latter.

Hazardous wastes and materials

The last decade or so has seen India emerging as a major importer of hazardous and toxic wastes from the industrial countries. There are over 100 broad kinds of wastes we now import, ostensibly for recycling and reuse in a range of chemical and metal-based industries, of which a few dozen are hazardous. It is difficult to get consolidated figures of such wastes, as the database of the Department of Commerce is disaggregated into categories that overlap between toxic and non-toxic wastes. But the available figures are indicative enough. For instance, import of waste parings and PVC (polyvinyl chloride) scrap shot up from about 33 tonnes in 1996–97 to 12,224 tonnes in 2008–09. Plastic wastes as a whole rose from 101,312 tonnes in 2003–04 to 465,921 tonnes in 2008–09. Import of metal wastes on the whole rose substantially.[28]

A growing proportion of the imported waste is from the computer and electronic industry. According to an investigation by Toxics Link, an NGO (non-governmental organization) working on waste issues, about 70 per cent of e-wastes found in the recycling units of Delhi were those dumped by industrial countries into India.[29] In the latest of revelations, Toxics Link found that the company Attero had received permission to import 8000 tonnes of e-waste in 2009.[30]

Many of the imported wastes are extremely hazardous for human and environmental health. Metal scrap and ashes, for instance, can release arsenic, lead, cadmium and other well-known causes of cancer and life-threatening ailments. They also contain ammunition and other material from various war-ravaged regions of the world, including Unexploded Ordnance (UXO) from West Asia, Somalia and Rwanda. India even imports depleted uranium and thorium wastes, whose radioactivity can be deadly. In 2001, mercury, known to be highly lethal, was found to have been dumped in a scrapyard behind a settlement in Tamil Nadu. When investigated, it was found that the culprit was Hindustan Lever Ltd, which had imported thermometer-making machinery and elemental mercury from Bethlehem Apparatus (US), and had simply discarded whatever was not usable. Protests by the community led the Tamil Nadu Pollution Control Board to take action, including ordering the scrap (416 tonnes!) to be sent back to Bethlehem Apparatus.[31]

The lack of standards and care in the processes of recycling or disposal is also serious. Underpaid labourers, usually in the unorganized sector, work in extremely hazardous situations. Vulnerable women and children can be commonly found in waste recycling units. A variety of diseases relating to these working conditions—like heavy metal poisoning, skin ailments, lung diseases, limb injuries, etc.—afflict such workers. Moreover, most of the dumps where wastes are discarded are near settlements of the poor, creating serious health problems through water and air pollution. Often the technologies for waste treatment and recycling that are exported along with the wastes from the industrial countries are well below the standards of technologies they themselves employ (like for incinerators and gasifiers). Workers even get killed, as in the case of ten labourers who died when 'scrap metal' (containing spent ammunition and other war remains) blew up at the Bhushan Steel and Strips Ltd factory, Ghaziabad, in 2004.[32]

In 1995 India was even considering opposing the ratification of the Basel Convention, which bans trans-boundary movement of toxic waste, but public pressure fortunately persuaded it to withdraw its opposition. Yet, it continues to allow serious violations of the convention, letting the quest for profits prevail at all costs. In 2009, responding to repeated demands from civil society, the MoEF notified the Hazardous Waste Rules, but these have serious loopholes such as not being applicable to Export Processing Zones (EPZs) where most of the waste import and reprocessing takes place.

Interestingly, in a bid to bypass waste legislation, as also to avert rising public criticism of the waste trade, new free trade agreements (FTAs) are terming it as trade in 'non-new goods'! For instance, the draft India–EU FTA says that neither party shall apply to non-new goods those measures—including enforcement measures—which are more restrictive than to new goods.

India is also a major destination for ship-breaking, potentially a highly contaminating and hazardous activity. Alang in Gujarat is the world's biggest such facility. The ecological and human costs of pollution and poor working conditions in Alang have repeatedly been pointed out.[33]

It is not only materials and wastes that are being imported, but entire production processes. India too has joined the increasing number of 'developing' countries that welcome polluting or extractive industries which produce goods needed by consumers in the West. For instance, foreign pharmaceutical companies have set up production facilities in many states, and often have much more lax standards (or enforcement of standards) than in their parent countries. At Patancheru, Andhra Pradesh, severe water pollution has been linked to production of drugs headed for Sweden.[34] This is yet another manifestation of the ecological imperialism that comes with the terrain of deregulated corporate globalization.

An unintended problem associated with increasing trade is the entry of invasive alien species. The UN International Maritime Organization estimates that at least 7000 species are being carried in ballast (ship) tanks around the world, including bacteria and other microbes. The economic damages and control costs of invasive alien species in five countries (USA, South Africa, UK, Brazil and India) are estimated at $336 billion per year. There is poor study of this in India, itself a matter of serious concern given the widespread knowledge that invasives (both indigenous and exotic) have caused havoc to many of our ecosystems and wildlife populations, and to agriculture and pastoralism.[35]

Consumerism and waste

Since the 1980s, but more so in the current globalization phase, lifestyles have become increasingly consumerist. The 'good life' is characterized as the ever-increasing accumulation of material products, and 'activities' like shopping encouraged as fashionable.

To judge the overall ecological impact of a product one has to observe the entire product cycle from the stage of mining (or agricultural production) to waste disposal. In this respect, the phenomenal rise in the use of plastics, detergents and other non-biodegradable or hazardous materials in the last few years is striking (see below).

The links between consumerism and the environment are not well-studied, but there are some indications. Based on surveys by the Central Statistical Organization (CSO) and the National Council of Applied Economic Research (NCAER) over the 1980s and 1990s, Tata Energy Research Institute (TERI) has documented the rapid rise in the use of non-renewable materials (like minerals), manufactured consumer goods (including those with direct environmental impact like refrigerators and air conditioners using CFCs [chlorofluorocarbons]), transport vehicles, and so on. This is not just a result of rising populations, but probably has more to do with changing lifestyles. For instance, consumer preferences are changing from non-packaged goods to packaged ones—TERI estimates that consumption of packaged paper will rise from 2.7 kg per person per year in 1997 to 13.5 kg per person per year by 2047. This would mean a total paper use of 23.1 million tonnes for packaging alone, and the consequent rise in solid wastes. The composition of wastes being generated is also changing, with compostable ('wet') waste reducing in proportion to total waste, whereas non-compostable waste is increasing. Hazardous waste generation is now mind-boggling, at about 4.4 million tonnes in 2006. Electronic waste, a phenomenon purely of the last couple of decades, was estimated at 146,180 tonnes in 2005 and likely to go up to 800,000 tonnes by 2012.[36]

Another indication of the impact of consumerism comes from the energy sector, linked to climate change. In 2007 Greenpeace India produced a report on climate change issues in India, showing that a tiny percentage of India's population was responsible for an inordinate amount of carbon emissions, but this was hidden by the low-emission rates of a huge number of Indians, which brought down the per capita figures.[37] Greenpeace surveyed 819 households across several income classes and calculated their carbon emissions based on energy consumption from household appliances and transportation. India's average per capita carbon emission is 1.67 tonnes every year (compared to the global average of 5.03). But Greenpeace found that the emission of the richest class (those with per capita income above Rs 30,000 a month) is 4.97, just a fraction below the world average. In contrast, the emission of the poorest class (income below Rs 3000 a month, almost half of India's population) is only 1.11 tonnes. The richest in India produce 4.5 times more carbon emissions than the poorest (according to an estimate by Praful Bidwai, it could be about 16.5 times!). More to the point, these emissions should be compared to the 2.5 tonnes per capita limit that scientists consider to be necessary if we want to restrict the temperature rise to below 2°C. All 150 million Indians who earn above Rs 8000 per month are already above this limit.[38]

Greenpeace found that the biggest difference was in the extent of use of electrical appliances. While general lighting, fans and TVs are common to all classes (though used much more by the middle and upper classes), several appliances are found predominantly in well-off households (those with per capita incomes above Rs 8000 a month, comprising a mere 6 per cent of the total population). This includes air conditioners, electric geysers, washing machines, electric or electronic kitchen appliances, DVD players, computers and the like. Secondly, these classes depend much more on transportation that uses fossil fuels, including gas-guzzling cars and airplanes.

The report's conclusions regarding energy consumption can easily be extended to any form of consumption: minerals, food, water, industrial products, as also to polluting outputs, such as solid and liquid wastes. We tried some rough back-of-the-envelope calculations on the overall ecological footprint—with the assumption that the footprint is directly proportional to wealth—and came to some startling estimates. The per capita footprint of the wealthiest Indians (top 0.01 per cent) could be as much as *330 times* that of the poorest 40 per cent. It is over twelve times that of the footprint of the average citizen in a 'developed', high-income country. The footprint of the richest 1 per cent (inclusive of the wealthiest) of Indians is two-thirds that of the average citizen of a rich country and over seventeen times that of the poorest 40 per cent of people in India. Thus, a person who owns a car and a laptop in India (to use a convenient yardstick applicable as an average rather than universally) consumes roughly the same resources as seventeen poor Indians, or roughly the same as 2.3 average 'world citizens'* (the world per capita income being about $10,000 or about Rs 4.5 lakh per annum in 2007).[39]

*The assumption made here is that a rupee of GDP that accrues to the wealthy leaves the same resource and carbon footprint as a rupee of GDP earned by the poor. Thus, if the GDP that accrues to the top 10 per cent of the country's population is 30 per cent and that going to the poorest 10 per cent is 3 per cent, the ecological footprint of the rich is roughly ten times that of the poor (even though the rich tend to use ecologically more damaging goods and services). The other assumption is that every rupee earned by the rich is spent, if not on direct consumption (including imports), then on investment (assuming savings are fully invested) or spending by the government (from taxes levied). In making international comparisons—which must correct for different costs of living across countries—we have taken recourse to the standard

The plastics explosion

Since 1991, the production capacity of various forms of plastics in the country has shot up from less than 1 million tonnes, to well over 5 million. In the 1990s the growth of plastics consumption was twice (12 per cent p.a.) that of the GDP growth rate based on purchasing power parities (6 per cent p.a.). The average consumption of virgin plastics per capita grew fourfold within a decade.[40]

It is indisputable that plastics have been extremely useful in a number of applications. However, what is disturbing is that a substantial proportion of plastics use is wasteful, unnecessary and dangerous. Plastic packaging and wrapping is now used for everyday products that simply do not need it; plastic carry-bags have become ubiquitous in towns and villages alike; and the explosion of pouches for everything from shampoo to mouth fresheners is uncontrolled.

By 2000–01 India was producing 5400 tonnes of plastics waste per day (more recent figures are not available). Perhaps up to half of the plastic used is recycled and the rest is simply dumped. Impacts are severe, from the choking of waterways—held to be partly responsible for the devastating floods in Mumbai in 2005, which left over 1000 people dead—to the death of animals (terrestrial and aquatic).[41]

Belatedly, some steps have been taken to curb the menace. Carry-bags (all or under a certain thickness) have been banned

---

international dollar PPP (purchasing power parity) method used in World Bank calculations. Thus, $1 in India in 2007 commanded as much goods and resources as $2.88 in the US in the same year. So, for instance, an individual with the Indian *rich's* per capita income of $8000 annually commands as much as an *individual* earning $23,000 ($8000 × 2.88) per annum in the US.

in many cities or regions, though implementation remains patchy in most cases. At the time of writing, the government is considering the much-needed regulations on plastic packaging.

Headlong into unsustainability?

Given the way India has treated its environment in the last few decades, environmentalists and social activists have been warning that we are on an unsustainable path of 'development'. This conclusion, born out of observation and experience, was recently confirmed in a report by the Global Footprint Network and the Confederation of Indian Industry (CII).[42] Released in 2008, this document assesses how much pressure India's citizens are putting on the earth's resources, and whether we could sustain our levels of natural resource use if we had access to only what is available within our borders. The facts are not pretty:

- India has the world's third largest ecological footprint, after the USA and China;
- Indians are using almost twice of what the country's natural resources can sustain (or twice its 'bio-capacity');
- The capacity of nature to sustain Indians has declined sharply by almost half, in the last four decades or so.

In the foreword to the report, the chairman of the CII Green Business Centre, Jamshyd Godrej, said: 'This report . . . shows that India is depleting its ecological assets in support of its current economic boom and the growth of its population.' Words that would have sounded like old hat from an ecological activist come as a surprise from an industrialist.

There are not too many other assessments of the sustainability of India's 'development' path. TERI carried out a study on losses due to environmental damage in the late 1990s. It concluded that environmental costs in India exceed 10 per cent of the GDP as a result of loss in agricultural productivity; loss in timber value due to degradation of forests; health costs due to polluted water and air; and costs due to depleted water resources. Further, the economic loss due to soil degradation resulted in an annual loss of 11–26 per cent of the agricultural output. Another report on future scenarios for India, also by TERI, pointed to worrying trends in resource depletion, waste generation, and so on.[43]

Cambridge economist Partha Dasgupta goes beyond the GDP and the HDI (Human Development Index) indicators of development, includes the changing state of the productive base (which includes natural resources) and concludes that development in the period 1970–2000 has been 'unsustainable or barely sustainable'.[44]

Climate change: Impact and response

Climate change is linked to globalization in a number of ways, though the root cause lies in the more general phenomenon of modern 'development' (see chapter 9). The period since the 1980s, when globalization started being imposed on developing countries (also known as the global South), has seen the greatest rise in climate change emissions from a host of sources. Carbon dioxide emissions have nearly doubled since 1985, as a result of substantial jumps in global trade (requiring transportation of goods and people); the rise of some key Southern economies (South-East Asia, China, India) riding on the backbone of fossil-fuel energy; and growth- and trade-related natural resource destruction (especially deforestation, including devastatingly high rates in the world's rainforests). Rising environmental consciousness has only recently begun to make a dent in these trends—too late to avoid emissions that are already, according to most scientific assessments, on their way to increasing global average temperatures to staggering levels.[45]

Several recent assessments provide a range of scenarios of the impacts India will face. A rise of close to one metre in sea levels, which could occur by the early twenty-second century, could inundate about 5764 sq km, displacing over 7 million people. Some of this may already be happening in areas like the Gulf of Kachchh and the Sundarbans. Changes in rainfall patterns, with the overall amount increasing, but a decrease in both the amount and the number of rainy days in many areas, will cause worse droughts and floods than so far experienced. (As so often with water, the issue is one of imbalances, rather than overall quantity.) This and increased temperatures could, according to most assessments, reduce foodgrain production (by up to 20 per cent for some crops), though some say it could increase. The receding and faster melting of the Himalayan glaciers (the rate of which is a topic of serious scientific disputes, but very few challenge the fact that this is happening) will threaten river-based livelihoods across northern India. Water shortages (or excess during floods) will increase suffering and regional conflicts. Changes in marine water temperatures will affect the productivity of the seas, cause rich coral systems to start dying and change fish movement patterns in ways that fisherfolk will find difficult to cope with. The productivity of other ecosystems, including forests, could also be adversely affected, and desertification may intensify. Intense heat-spells, cyclones and storms and other 'freak' weather events are likely to increase. Already, across India, local communities are reporting strange occurrences in the weather; in crop outputs and responses; in pastures; in marine systems; and other phenomena that have not been felt in living memory. While these may not count as 'scientific' observations in a formal sense, they are powerful and widespread enough to warrant belief, or at least a close examination.

Impacts on human beings will be increasingly highlighted over the next few years, but what could remain neglected are impacts on other species. It is impossible to predict precise impacts, but as all natural ecosystems will be stressed by climate change, negative consequences are inevitable. For instance, 70 per cent of the country's vegetation may find the changing ecological conditions hard to cope with, and habitat changes will force animals to move into areas where they are more vulnerable. In the Sundarbans, for instance, changes in salinity due to rising sea levels and possible decrease in the flow of freshwater from inland could threaten several species.

Both because it will have to bear the brunt of climate change impacts and because it is itself becoming a major contributor to emissions, India needs to take action. While its global position has justifiably been one of demanding accountability and action from the Northern countries (with variations in the specifics of the argument), its domestic policy remains weak and vacillating. The more authentic and robust principle for Indian climate policymaking has to be its own *bio-capacity*, rather than what is fair according to India's 'right to development' vis-à-vis the industrialized world. When it comes to the crunch, its own bio-capacity will limit it, no matter that the right to development may continue to be unjustly distributed (both across and within countries).

Only very recently has the government acknowledged the need for domestic action, with the release by the prime minister of a National Action Plan on Climate Change (NAPCC). There are some good elements, such as a significant focus on solar power and energy efficiency through dedicated missions. But even these have conceptual and implementational problems, like lack of focus on other renewables, little emphasis on decentralized solar generation and several missing sectors in energy efficiency. Many of the other elements, like missions on sustainable agriculture and water, remain stuck in tired, outmoded strategies with little bold, out-of-the-box thinking. The water mission includes a continuing dependence on big dams, completely ignoring their immense ecological and social costs and the fact that many proven alternatives exist. In agriculture, a major chance to shift away from chemical fertilizers (responsible for about 6 per cent of climate emissions in India) to organic inputs has so far been missed (the mission is still under development). Some basic issues are avoided or cursorily dealt with, like the inequities in how much 'climate space' is occupied by different sections of India's population and the obscene consumerism of the ultra-rich (whose rates of emission are already well above the globally acceptable limit). A fundamental fault of the NAPCC is that it has been drafted and continues to be worked on through its individual missions, with minimal public input and transparency. Overall, it does very little to challenge the fundamental structural flaws of the 'development' and growth model that brought about the climate change crisis in the first place. Simultaneously, environmental regulations continue to be diluted or ignored, mirroring a global trend in which countries entering the globalization phase are forced or cajoled into reducing the state's role in regulation.

Multiple crises: Food, water and livelihoods

Damage to the natural environment translates into daily crises for several hundred million people in India. This is not only because they are directly dependent on nature and natural resources; there are other social, economic and political forces at work, and their interplay is complex. Nevertheless, it is an important, and often neglected, cause of insecurity and disruption in people's lives.

A very large section of India's population is going through severe and multiple crises: food insecurity, water shortages, inadequate fuel availability and dislocation of livelihoods with limited alternative options. In some form or the other, all these have existed prior to the current phase of globalization, and even prior to modern forms of 'development'. But such deprivations are precisely what 'development' and globalization were meant to alleviate; on the contrary, they have been exacerbated, or have stayed as severe, for many people and regions.

A number of recent official and civil society studies have revealed the shocking state of food insecurity (we deal with this in chapter 3). Crucial sources of nutrition such as traditional cereals (e.g. millets) and pulses, have declined both in availability and affordability (e.g. a 26 per cent decline in per capita availability of pulses since the early 1990s).[46]

But a substantial number of these would also be people whose natural resource base has been degraded or destroyed, taking away their source of wild or cultivated foods. Several studies show that in the case of forest-dwelling and pastoral communities, wild plant foods (fruits, leaves, grasses, seeds, tubers, flowers) are crucial for food security, especially as nutritional inputs, in times of crop failure or for special occasions including illnesses. If one adds wild meat, the dependence is even higher (though reduced after a prohibition on most hunting has been imposed with varying degrees of effectiveness). This dependence would be even higher for fishing communities, both coastal and inland. Such wild foods are sourced from natural or semi-natural ecosystems, whose degradation has therefore had a direct impact on food security.

Soil degradation affects almost half of India's lands, severely bringing down agricultural productivity and in particular affecting the marginal and small farmer. The globalization phase has also seen agriculture entering into an extended period of crisis, with abysmally low and declining growth rates and, more importantly, declining ability to sustain livelihoods. Policy distortions and a lack of clear focus have also resulted in substantial conversion of food-producing lands to non-food cash crops, with pulses and traditional grains being the worst sufferers (see chapters 3 and 7). To top it all, farmers are enticed or forced to sell off the topsoil for brick-making, forever destroying the productive capacity of their farms. This has reached outrageous proportions around many cities, such as Bengaluru, from the surrounds of which over 4000 truckloads of soil from farms and tank-beds are removed *every day* for the city's construction purposes. Then there is the ugly reality of widespread displacement that 'development' has entailed, taking people away from their traditional production landscapes and seascapes (one estimate has put this at 60 million since Independence; see chapter 3). And finally, as millions of people get pushed out of the ecosystem and small-agriculture-based subsistence livelihoods into the market economy, food can only be obtained with cash or credit, which, as we have seen, are scarce resources for them.[47]

Water insecurity is as serious. The total use of water in India (at about 750 billion cubic metres or bcm) is still well within the water available (about 1869 bcm), but it is projected to catch up soon after the year 2025 and then overshoot by 2050. This, of course, is if we only consider human use; if we account for all other functions of water for natural ecosystems and for other species, we realize we are already in a grave situation. All the more so if we consider the significant inequities in water distribution and availability among various regions and peoples.[48]

For several million people in both rural and urban areas, access to adequate potable water even for drinking is a struggle, and access to water for agriculture a losing battle. Proximate causes include mismanagement and excessive use of surface wetlands and subsurface aquifers; degradation of catchment areas that trap rainwater; repeated droughts; excessive concentration of population (in cities); pollution of surface and groundwater sources. At the root of these lie policy failures (relating to wetland and groundwater conservation and management; pollution; and pricing of water), appropriation by powerful corporations and the elite (see for instance the case of Coca-Cola in the box on 'Corporate social irresponsibility', chapter 5), and other fundamental causes, some of them discussed in chapter 3.[49]

Of particular concern is groundwater. Its exploitation for agricultural, industrial and urban purposes has, in many parts of India, reached levels where water tables are dropping alarmingly. A free-for-all has prevailed with regard to the digging of tube wells. Over half the groundwater blocks in rural India are not recharging as fast as withdrawal. In a reply to a question in Parliament, the government has stated that in one-third of the country's districts, groundwater is not fit for drinking due to high levels of iron, fluoride, arsenic and salinity. Punjab, Haryana, Karnataka, Gujarat, Tamil Nadu and Rajasthan are among the states worst hit by over-exploitation or pollution.[50]

Water-related conflicts are already cropping up in various parts of India: between villages, between villages and cities, between citizens and corporations, and between states. The Cauvery River dispute between Tamil Nadu and Karnataka is by now iconic (in a perverse way), but there are many other examples, such as a dispute between Karnataka and Goa on the proposed damming of the Madei River.[51]

And finally, there is the crisis of livelihoods. As ecosystem disruption and land/water degradation intensifies, or as access to natural resources and traditional consumers declines, communities who have been traditionally self-employed (as farmers, hunter-gatherers, fishers, pastoralists, craftspersons, etc.) are increasingly impacted. There is no comprehensive estimate of the loss of livelihoods and employment that has taken place so far, itself an indication of how neglected this issue is. But the decline in the farm sector (as documented in chapters 3 and 7) is enough cause for worry, as indebted marginal farmers turn into agricultural labourers and a good many farmers—40 per cent by one estimate—express their desire to quit agriculture, as it has been rendered unremunerative.

A whole host of traditional occupations (e.g. shoemaking or public entertainment like circuses and street shows) are becoming obsolete as there is no demand for their produce or services— with mass-produced 'modern' goods and more mechanized services replacing them—other than a few that have been able to create a niche in the modern market. Traditional fishers along India's coasts have been increasingly displaced (economically, if not physically) by the spread of industrial or large-scale commercial fisheries; degradation of the marine environment; decreasing access in areas where ports, resorts, sports facilities or urban centres are coming up; the mechanization of fishing (including by those from their own communities); loss of markets, and so on.

Traditional forest-based livelihoods are badly impacted not only by forest degradation but also by access restrictions under

forest and wildlife legislation. Ironically, this sometimes leads
to illegal practices that do more harm to the forests than their
original occupations are believed to have caused. Inland fisher
communities, perhaps even more marginalized than their coastal
counterparts, lose out when their wetlands get badly polluted,
dammed, converted into protected areas or appropriated by
private contractors.[52]

The worst hit are the nomadic groups: their migratory routes
disrupted, their lifestyles and cultures marginalized,
misunderstood or denigrated, and their own younger generations
turning away under myriad influences. The Anthropological
Survey of India estimated that there are at least 276 non-pastoral
nomadic occupations (hunter-gatherers and trappers; fishers;
craftspeople; entertainers and storytellers; healers; spiritual and
religious performers or practitioners; traders, and so on). Most
of these are threatened, some already extinct or dying, and the
people displaced from these livelihoods are either getting
absorbed into the insecure, undignified, low-paid and
exploitative sector of unorganized labour or are simply left
unemployed. The same holds good for many of the 40 million
pastoral nomads of the country, badly affected by the degradation
of pastures, the cutting off of migratory routes by infrastructure
or 'development' projects and changes in a once-harmonious
relationship with settled communities (though some politically
more powerful pastoral communities have managed to hold
their own).[53]

Finally, there is the massive impact on non-human nature.
Hundreds, possibly thousands, of species of plants and animals
are being pushed to the edge of extinction as their habitats are
gobbled up by the same land-grab process that is displacing
communities. This loss of wildlife is part of the erosion of

agricultural biodiversity, as agricultural and other policies force massive homogenization in cropping and animal husbandry patterns.[54]

'Development' in general and globalization in particular have contributed to these crises in many ways. The state has sponsored or backed the appropriation of fields, pastures, forests, wetlands, groundwater and other natural resources by the corporate sector or for use by the elite, as documented earlier in this chapter or elsewhere in this book.[55]

ADDING FUEL TO FIRE

UNDERMINING INDIA'S ENVIRONMENTAL
GOVERNANCE

Understanding the environmental destruction detailed in the previous chapter involves not just an appreciation of the commercial and industrial forces behind it. It also entails a realization of the changing framework of environmental governance, which is supposed to regulate such forces.

Internal liberalization: Towards a free-for-all?

All industrial countries of the world have gone through a process of tightening environmental standards and controls over industrial and development projects, for the simple reason that project proponents and corporate houses on their own have not shown environmental and social responsibility. In every industrialized country of the world, development projects, even privately owned ones, are subject to stringent regulations regarding use of natural resources and the adverse social and environmental impacts of their activities, including environmental clearance procedures, siting considerations, monitoring exercises and penalties for violations. (There are, of course, routine and often systemic faults in enforcing these regulations, and there is almost no control on how corporations originating in these countries behave outside.) Such regulations have been put into place after learning the hard way that an uncontrolled growth process is a recipe for ecological and social suicide.

In India, a reverse process is going on: that of loosening, in policy and/or in practice, the environmental safeguards so painstakingly built up over the 1980s. This loosening is due to severe opposition from industrialists and politicians, whose objections are simple, if not simplistic: when all other regulations are being removed, and the economy is moving into fast gear, why impose environmental regulations? There appears to be an inability or unwillingness to distinguish between circuitous red tape and necessary green tape.

Environment clearances and impact assessment

Not long after the 1991 reforms process began, environmental regulations came to be seen primarily as a hurdle. For example, there was a considerable delay in issuing a notification that made environmental clearances legally mandatory for certain types of development projects. This notification, drafted and twice opened for public objection in the early 1990s by the MoEF (ministry of environment and forests), was finally gazetted as the EIA (Environment Impact Assessment) notification in 1994, but in a considerably diluted form. A provision that development projects near ecologically sensitive areas would need separate clearance was dropped, among other such changes.

The world over, EIAs are crucial tools to assess the ecological feasibility and desirability of projects and processes, and can be significant in taking a country towards the goal of sustainability. The 1994 notification was weak and subject to various kinds of implementation failures, but it nevertheless injected a degree of environmental sensitivity into the planning of development projects. However, it continued to be seen as a nuisance by industrialists, politicians and many development economists— as a last vestige of the hated 'licence raj'. Pressure from these circles continued to mount on the Central government, bolstered by the findings of the Committee on Reforming Investment Approval and Implementation Procedures set up by the Union cabinet, which concluded that environmental clearance procedures were a major cause of delays.[1]

A World Bank–funded process to assess environmental governance also pointed to the need to 'reform'—a euphemism for 'weaken'—regulatory measures. Thus, in 2006 the government brought in a completely 're-engineered' notification on environmental clearances, making it much easier for industries and development projects to obtain permission and weakening democratic participation in development decision-making. It proposed that several kinds of projects could now get clearance at the state level, but did not build in any mechanism to ensure that local community institutions of governance were involved. Without this, handing over power to the state governments only made the situation worse, given that a vast number of projects are sponsored or proposed by these governments themselves. The notification also weakened the provisions for compulsory public hearings, disallowing interested third parties, who would not be directly affected, to take part; the public would now have access only to 'draft' EIAs, and local authorities could even dispense with hearings if they felt the situation was not conducive. The notification also took tourism off the list of projects needing environmental clearance (see below).[2]

The scale and pace at which industrial and developmental projects are being given environmental clearance now makes any meaningful regulation impossible. For instance:[3]

- The MoEF clears 80–100 projects every month, with environmental and social conditionalities that project proponents are supposed to adhere to.
- As of early 2009, MoEF has over 6000 projects to monitor through six regional offices and a staff of two to four officers per office for the task.
- Projects granted environmental clearance are monitored only once in three to four years.
- No centralized record of non-compliance is maintained by the MoEF.
- Less than 50 per cent of the projects cleared in 2003 had monitoring reports generated by the MoEF.
- Only 150 of the 223 projects cleared in the year 2003 had at least one compliance report submitted by project authorities.

Forest clearance

The impact of globalization on environmental regulations is nowhere clearer than in the realm of forestry. The Forest Conservation Act (FCA) has become a Forest *Clearance* Act. While after 1980 the process of diverting forest lands for non-forest purposes had sharply declined, it has again risen substantially in the globalization phase. Thus, out of the total forest land diversion that has taken place since 1980–81, about 55 per cent has been after 2001; about 70 per cent of the forest land diverted for mining since 1980–81 was between 1997 and 2007.[4]

Many chief ministers have demanded, from time to time, that the FCA be scrapped altogether or amended to devolve some diversion powers to the states. While the Central government has resisted these demands, it does not appear to be able or willing to resist the increasing pressure for diverting forest land for non-forest purposes.[5]

Coastal and marine areas

Coastal and marine areas have been regions of contestation for decades, with the introduction of commercial trawlers and industrial-scale aquaculture being strongly opposed by local traditional fisher communities since the late 1970s. But the rapid rise in large-scale commercial exploitation is only one source of conflict. The coasts are increasingly being viewed as suitable sites for industries, tourism complexes and trade hubs (as ports). Once again, this period of globalization has dealt a heavy blow to fledgling attempts at conserving the ecological and livelihood integrity of this part of India, which sustains a third of its population.

In 1991 the Coastal Regulation Zone (CRZ) notification was promulgated as a means to regulate activities that could be detrimental to ecological and livelihood interests. The CRZ notification was a bold step to try safeguarding the ecologically sensitive coastal areas of the country. Though by no means perfect, and despite perfunctory implementation by most states, the notification was instrumental in stopping or delaying many destructive projects. It also provided some level of protection to traditional fisher communities, maintaining their right to access the coast and seas and giving them a shield against activities like the takeover of stretches of beach by tourism facilities or industries, or damage to fisheries by mangrove and coral reef destruction.

For these reasons, the original CRZ notification became a nuisance for industrial and commercial interests. Their pressure on the government resulted in as many as nineteen changes to the original notification. Almost all of these were with the intention of relaxing regulations for setting up ports and allowing mining, oil and natural gas exploration, and SEZs (Special Economic Zones; see chapter 8) in what were previously 'no-development' zones. But it seems that even this was not enough for, in 2005–06, the government initiated a move to change the notification altogether, based on the report of a committee headed by M.S. Swaminathan. The proposal for a new Coastal Management Zone (CMZ) notification allows states to determine what should and should not be allowed in various zones along the coast and legitimizes all structures that have come up in violation of the CRZ notification. Civil society organizations (CSOs) and fisher communities (through networks like the National Fishworkers' Forum) have severely criticized the proposal for being a sell-out to commercial and industrial interests. Responding to this, the MoEF has allowed the CMZ draft notification to lapse and, as of the time of writing, promised widespread consultations before coming up with a new notification.[6]

Meanwhile, in widespread violation of the CRZ notification, or by using its many loopholes, a number of ports, industries, sports and tourism complexes and other projects have come up on India's coasts. The Orissa coast is currently being carved up for a series of ports (over a dozen are planned). The one at Dhamra being set up by Tatas is, according to several conservation groups, likely to be immensely harmful for one of the world's biggest nesting sites of the threatened olive ridley sea turtle (*Lepidochelys olivacea*). Sand mining for possible thorium deposits is also being considered for large stretches of Orissa's coast. What could finally happen to this area is indicated by what has already happened to the coasts of the Gulf of Kachchh in Gujarat. The state government has permitted cement industries, oil refineries and a host of other projects to come up along this coast, leading to widespread destruction of coral reefs, mangroves and beaches, significant marine pollution (including periodic oil spills) and the displacement of traditional livelihoods dependent on these resources. This includes significant incursions into the Marine National Park and Sanctuary, established supposedly for the strict protection of the area's rich marine biodiversity.[7]

Tourism: Nothing 'eco' about it

Tourism has received a major boost in the reform era.[8] From about 140 million domestic tourists in 1996, the figure almost quadrupled to 527 million in 2007; in the same period, foreign visitors increased from 2.29 million to 5.08 million.

Several parts of India previously restricted to visitation (some off-bounds only for foreigners) have been opened up for tourism in the last few years. This includes ecologically, culturally and strategically sensitive areas like Ladakh, Andaman and Nicobar Islands, Lakshadweep and many parts of north-eastern India. Other areas, already open before globalization, are groaning under mass, unregulated tourism activity. Hundreds of cases of violations of the law, e.g. of the CRZ notification by tourist resorts on the coast, have been reported in the last few years (over 1500 cases from Kovalam beach area in Kerala alone); precious few have seen prosecution or other deterrent action by the government.

Even areas supposedly under strict protection for wildlife are not spared. Tiger reserves and other protected areas like Kanha, Bandhavgarh, Corbett, Periyar, Ranthambhore, Bandipur and Nagarahole are ringed by resorts. They put enormous pressure on the staff and facilities of the reserves, repeatedly violate both the letter and spirit of regulations meant to minimize tourism impact and contribute virtually nothing to the upkeep of the reserves. Ironically, these are often the same areas from where villagers have been evicted or their access stopped under the guise of 'protecting' wildlife.

The environmental and social impacts of unregulated tourism are immense: wrecking of natural ecosystems and disruption of wildlife corridors; dumping of enormous amounts of garbage (converting most hill stations, for instance, into plastic dumps); disturbance by vehicular traffic; displacement and dispossession of local communities (e.g. stopping the access of fishers to the coast); the takeover of the already scarce water and land resources; and the sudden introduction of new cultures that disrupt local ways of life.[9] In Kerala the rapid increase in tourist houseboats (to over 2000) has caused significant pollution of the state's famed backwaters.

The government has bent over backwards to make things easier for the tourism industry. The first call for relaxing the CRZ regulations came from this industry. In 2006 the new EIA notification removed tourism from the list of projects requiring mandatory EIAs and Central government clearance. Not surprisingly, this was followed by a rush of proposals and investments. Several states have taken the cue from the Centre (some even preceding it). Himachal Pradesh relaxed its Land Reforms Act to allow non-Himachalis to buy land for tourist resorts (the earlier restriction had helped to restrain indiscriminate construction). Maharashtra promulgated a regulation to provide incentives for new townships in the name of tourism (resulting in the controversial Lavasa and Amby Valley townships for the rich, partly on adivasi lands).

The Eleventh Five-Year Plan does not even mention the negative impacts of this regulation on the tourism industry. On the contrary, the government has been actively considering extending the concept of SEZ to tourism, by creating Special Tourism Zones (STZs). These zones would have several facilities like single-window clearance and 100 per cent tax exemption for ten years, and would have to be large enough to be able to provide 2000 to 3000 hotel rooms.

Opening up protected areas

The last couple of decades have seen a spate of proposed and actual diversions of land within national parks and sanctuaries, including outright de-notifications (or deletions). Though the control of such wildlife-protected areas is in the hands of state governments, a Supreme Court judgement in 2000 has made it mandatory for proposals of diversion to be referred to the National Board for Wildlife (NBWL). Before this, however, in the case of wildlife sanctuaries, state governments could slice off areas to allow non-conservation-related activities. For instance, in 1992, the Himachal Pradesh government de-notified the Darlaghat Sanctuary to make way for a cement factory. CSO protests reduced the damage, as the government re-notified a portion of the sanctuary, but over 300 sq km were still sacrificed. The same government also carved out 1000 ha of prime wildlife habitat from the Great Himalayan National Park in 1999 to make way for the Parbati hydel project.[10]

From 1998 to 2009 the NBWL considered 290 proposals for diverting a massive 294,014 ha of land within about 100 protected areas. Of these, fifty-four were cleared, entailing a diversion of 9,884 ha (and some road length), while twenty-three projects of over 2,643 ha were rejected. The majority were kept pending, many of which will continue to come up till accepted or rejected. Interestingly, the NBWL did not reject a single mining proposal from 1998 to 2008 and turned down only one in 2009. Mining alone took over 2,102 ha of land within protected areas.[11]

Some of the diversions are shocking and perhaps symptomatic of the mood even among some of the well-known conservationists who have been members of the NBWL. Uranium prospecting, for instance, has been allowed inside the Rajiv Gandhi (Srisailam) Tiger Reserve in Andhra Pradesh, the same reserve from where there is now a proposal to relocate the Chenchu tribal people, who have inhabited these forests for centuries. A number of irrigation and hydel projects have been allowed in the protected areas of Andhra Pradesh, Himachal Pradesh, Jharkhand, Uttar Pradesh, Arunachal Pradesh and Uttarakhand (its Askot Sanctuary alone—home to the endangered musk deer—has half a dozen hydel dam proposals!).[12]

Corporate social irresponsibility

A classic case of how 'corporate social responsibility' has become convenient greenwash is that of Coca-Cola. While it portrays itself as sensitive to ecological and social concerns, and claims to help solve rural water problems in many parts of the world, the company has meant something very different for several dozen villages in India. Around several of Coca-Cola's bottling plants in Kerala, Rajasthan and Uttar Pradesh, villagers have complained of water salinity or hardness, a drop in groundwater levels and new diseases in livestock and people. Studies by official agencies have found shocking negligence, including discharge of untreated sewage into neighbouring fields and a canal, and dumping of hazardous sludge in the open. The situation has turned so serious that in most of these areas villagers have mobilized to demand closure of the plants, succeeding at some of the sites (see chapter 10).[13]

Privatizing the intellectual commons

India under globalization has also seen the increasing privatization of knowledge. While there have always been knowledge monopolies (like some medicinal remedies closely guarded by healers or scriptures accessible only to priests), most knowledge has traditionally been part of the commons, available to all those who choose to seek and use it. The modern era has, however, seen a greater propensity to think of information and knowledge (and products arising therefrom) as private, belonging to individuals or individual entities who have 'discovered' or 'invented' it. And thus the growing domination of 'intellectual property rights' (IPRs) in various fields over the last few decades: writing and publishing; music and other cultural products; science and technology; agriculture; health care; and environment.

Since the early 1990s, the Indian government has abandoned its earlier stance of keeping knowledge related to natural resources and sectors like agriculture and health in the commons. It has succumbed to pressure from industrial countries and corporations to introduce a range of IPRs. This has happened especially after India joined the WTO (World Trade Organization) in 1995, after considerable hesitation, and despite nationwide protests.

The WTO's immediate impact was on the Patents Act, which has since then been amended thrice (1999, 2002, 2005) in the globalization phase, to make it fully compliant with the Trade-Related Aspects of Intellectual Property Rights (TRIPS) Agreement of the WTO. Although it has some saving graces—such as the non-patentability of traditional knowledge and inventions derived from it, and the need for patent-seekers to disclose the source and geographical origin of the biological material they are using—the amended act has opened up virtually all sectors of the economy to monopolistic intellectual and commercial practices. It also allows for the first-time patenting of micro-organisms (except those discovered in nature); this has made it possible to patent all life forms in the future, for which there is considerable global corporate pressure. Genetically modified (GM) seeds are also not exempt; because of this, farmers whose crops get contaminated by a neighbouring GM crop can face charges of violating the GM company's patents (as has already happened in the infamous *Monsanto v. Canadian farmer Percy Schmeiser* case). A number of other provisions of the amended Patents Act enable corporations to consolidate their monopolistic power.[14]

In fact, IPRs on biological resources (and the knowledge related to them) became possible with the Protection of Plant Varieties and Farmers' Rights Act (PPVFRA) in 2001. Pressure for such a regime was already mounting on the government since the opening up of the Indian seed sector to domestic and foreign companies. India's obligations under TRIPS/WTO gave the final push in favour of the PPVFRA despite intense civil society (including farmers') opposition. Though it contained exemptions for farmers, this act brought in the possibility of corporations and others claiming monopoly rights over new varieties of plants (which would relate mostly to crops).[15]

Once we are on the road to accepting IPRs on life forms, it becomes that much harder to resist the global trend to make such IPRs more and more monopolistic, affecting both farmers and the crop genetic diversity, which they have developed and continue to depend on. India could well have pioneered a system of protection that gave common/public/community rights to plants, which obliged breeders to publicly share their inventions while assuring them financially adequate and socially acceptable returns. But it did not. The system could have emphasized diversity rather than uniformity in the use of crops, and used public good rather than private profit as the major incentive for creativity (as has so far been done in the public sector seed development programme). But it did not.

During this period, two other laws with a somewhat different orientation were passed: the Geographical Indications Act 1999 and the Biological Diversity Act 2002. The former provided for the protection of brands related to collective or community knowledge, practices or products, where these were identifiable with a particular region, e.g. Kolhapuri sandals or Darjeeling tea. The latter (amongst its various aims) provided for protection of traditional knowledge against piracy. However, it did not challenge IPRs on life forms and related knowledge and allowed for access to biological resources for various purposes including privatization. Rules framed under it gave communities the prime task of documenting their knowledge, without a corresponding framework empowering them to ensure that such documents were not misused or pirated, and without allowing them to be part of the overall governance of biodiversity and related knowledge. The act's implementation has taken it even further into the globalization framework: the more progressive provisions on conservation of biodiversity, sustainable use of biological resources and the protection of traditional knowledge have hardly been implemented, and most of the focus has been on clearing applications from industries and formal sector researchers for access to biodiversity.[16]

Weakening environmental and social governance

The most worrying and long-lasting impact of globalization has been the weakening of environmental governance. This is manifested in a number of ways, especially as in the legislations listed above. Over a hundred CSOs across India have repeatedly pointed this out to the prime minister and the minister for environment and forests in a series of open letters from 2004 to 2006.[17]

At the policy level, too, the government has disprivileged the environment to make way for rapid growth. In 2006 it brought in a National Environment Policy (NEP), which is fundamentally flawed as it focuses on development (not the natural environment) as a right and lays a lot of emphasis on market instruments to safeguard the environment. The process of framing the NEP itself was highly non-participatory, and two years of protests and alternative suggestions by civil society groups were simply ignored.[18]

There has been a marked decline in openness to civil society participation in environmental governance. In one of the open letters issued in April 2005, CSOs revealed that membership to the various expert committees in the MoEF—set up under the Environment Protection Act for including critical independent voices in decision-making—was restricted mostly to people who would not raise uncomfortable questions.[19] Only one CSO with an independent record was among the sixty-six members of six committees. Interestingly, as if anticipating such criticism, the MoEF had even issued a circular in April 2004 with guidelines defining 'experts' in such a way as to exclude civil society groups and individuals who may not have high academic qualifications, even if they had the experience that counts.[20]

Shockingly, a number of members and chairpersons of the expert committees (e.g. of those on river valley projects and on mining) have been exposed as being on the boards of companies that were proposing projects for clearance to these committees! For instance, in mid-2009 CSOs revealed that P. Abraham, chairman of the MoEF's expert appraisal committee on river valley and hydropower projects, was on the boards of the power companies engaged in the construction of several of the hydel power projects being cleared by the committee. This revelation led to his resignation, and a promise by MoEF to 'increase transparency in environmental clearance' procedures. Such conflict of interest has also come up in the case of committees set up under the National Biodiversity Authority, to give permission for accessing Indian biological resources, and continues in a number of other expert bodies of the MoEF.[21]

There has been some reversal of this trend of excluding independent voices or opaqueness to CSOs, with the new minister of state for environment and forests who came in with the UPA (United Progressive Alliance) government in 2009. Some of his initiatives such as withdrawal of the MoEF's 2004 circular on environmental experts and the resignation of the chair of the EIA committee on river valleys are welcome signs. But going against the grain as they are, it is not clear how long the initiatives will last or how deep they will go in strengthening environmental governance. A new institution in the form of a National Environment Tribunal is aimed at providing faster legal recourse to litigants, but has been criticized by many CSOs as being a superficial move. The same criticism has been levelled at a proposed move to separate the environmental clearance function from the MoEF by creating a National Environment Protection Authority. In both cases—given that the overall context of fundamentally flawed legislation and the approach to environmental sustainability of development projects and processes are not being changed—the reforms are not expected to provide any lasting solution.[22]

Besides the attack on environmental governance, there is an increasing propensity to dilute or sidestep the social guarantees given to some of the most vulnerable sections of Indian society. The opening up of forest-dwelling adivasis' and farmers' lands for mining, industries and other development projects is an example of this, as are relaxations against transfer of farmland to non-farmers and of land ceiling regulations (see chapter 8).[23]

The government has even been tempted to take away the rights that citizens have to judicial recourse. In a bid to thwart increasing CSO use of the Supreme Court, the government, in 1997, drafted a bill to regulate the use of Public Interest

Litigation (PIL). The bill proposed to charge a deposit of Rs 1 lakh for each PIL, which a successful petitioner could get back if the judge so decided, but which an unsuccessful petitioner would lose. It also proposed that only affected parties could file a PIL (unlike at present, where any person/group can approach the court on behalf of affected parties). These and other provisions, if the bill had come into force, would have killed the possibility of most affected communities and persons being able to file PILs. Indeed, the intention seemed to be to curb litigations against foreign and Indian industries. In a meeting with chief ministers and power ministers in October 1996, the then prime minister said that people were using the PIL to block projects cleared by his government and asked whether these were Public Interest Litigations or Political Interest Litigations.[24] Fortunately, the bill was never advanced as public pressure mounted on the government, and Supreme Court judges reacted sharply against the bill. However, in 2010, even as this manuscript is being finalized, the government has proposed a National Litigation Policy, which has the following clause: 'PILs challenging public contracts must be seriously defended. If interim orders are passed stopping such projects then appropriate conditions must be insisted upon for the Petitioners to pay compensation if the PIL is ultimately rejected.'[25] This is a move to discourage PILs against development projects, with the risk of having to pay potentially massive amounts as 'compensation' serving as a major deterrent.

The corporate party

Industry's own views have been clear for many years: relax various environmental, labour and other regulations. A particularly interesting version of this is in relation to the situation of 'Naxalism'. In a November 2009 report of its Task Force on

National Security and Terrorism, FICCI (Federation of Indian Chambers of Commerce and Industry) argues that 'the growing Maoist insurgency over large swathes of mineral-rich countryside could soon hurt some industrial investment plans . . . just when India needs to ramp up its industrial machine to lock in growth and just when foreign companies are joining the party, the Naxalites are clashing with the mining and steel companies essential for India's long-term success'.[26]

FICCI's schizophrenia is palpable; on the one hand, it talks of 'the grievances of the rural peasantry, especially against their displacement due to development projects and the cornering of the benefits of natural resources by a few'; on the other, it says: 'India's affluent urban consumers have started buying autos, appliances, and homes, and they're demanding improvements in the country's roads, bridges and railroads. To stoke Indian manufacturing and satisfy consumers, the country needs cement, steel, and electric power in record amounts. . . . There is a need for a suitable social and economic environment to meet this national challenge. Yet there's a collision with the Naxalites . . . Chhattisgarh, a hotbed of Naxalite activity, has 23 per cent of India's iron ore deposits and abundant coal. It has signed memoranda of understanding and other agreements worth billions with Tata Steel and ArcelorMittal (MT); De Beers Consolidated Mines; BHP Billiton (BHP); and Rio Tinto (RTP). Other states too have similar deals. And US companies such as Caterpillar (CAT) want to sell equipment to the mining companies now digging in eastern India.'[27]

Has spending on environment increased?

At the start of the globalization reforms in 1991, the then finance minister, Manmohan Singh, had stated that India needed to increase its rate of economic growth to raise the resources needed to protect the environment. Quite apart from the fundamental issue of whether one can bring back what has already been destroyed (e.g. the several hundred thousand hectares of natural forest that have been submerged under dams, mined out or chopped for industry), one needs to ask: has funding for environmental protection substantially increased in proportion to the problems that globalized development has caused?

It is not possible to get a comprehensive answer to this question, for funding related to the environment can come in various forms, including that which is embedded within non-environment sectors like rural development. We will return to this question briefly. Meanwhile, however, one simple indicator that can help answer this question is the trend of funding for the MoEF. This agency is the central body responsible for safeguarding the country's environment and ostensibly for pointing India towards a path of sustainability. How has the MoEF fared in its budgets since 1991?

The picture is not encouraging. The MoEF's allocation from the Union budget has never, ever, gone even near the mark of 1 per cent of the total Union budget. It has fluctuated between a little less than 0.5 per cent (in the early 1990s) to a high of 0.72 per cent in 2000–01, to an all-time low of 0.36 per cent in 2009–10 (just as environmental challenges were escalating). Indeed, it has steadily declined as a share of the total budget, since 2004–05, at the same time that the government has repeatedly professed its commitment to sustainability.

While the total budget has risen over five times in the period 1995–96 to 2009–10, the MoEF budget has risen only four times. In other words, assuming the resource-intensity of the GDP has remained virtually the same over this period, our ecological problems have been growing significantly faster than the financial resources earmarked to address them. This gives the lie to the original reasoning that growth was necessary to generate resources for environmental protection. To set things on the right course, the state should be allocating a *rising* proportion of its annual funds to environmental protection, especially as ecological damage mounts steadily and, in some cases, exponentially. Only this would be consistent with the promise that economic growth will lead to environmental benefits (not, for the moment, taking into consideration that money cannot possibly reverse or compensate for irreversible ecological damage).

It is difficult to glean environmental aspects from other sectors. One clear indication could be the funding for non-conventional energy sources. From a total of Rs 157 crore in 1992–93, funding for these sources as a whole has gone up to Rs 1205 crore in 2008–09 (again, uncorrected for inflation). When compared to the total budgets in the energy sector, the amounts allocated for non-conventional sources pale into insignificance. In this same period, energy was allocated Rs 20,290 crore and Rs 93,815 crore respectively; in other words, non-conventional sources were given about 0.8 per cent of the total energy budget in 1992–93 and have crept up to a still-meagre 1.28 per cent in 2008–09. Most of the rest of the budget went into thermal power—acknowledged to be highly polluting and the biggest source of greenhouse gases; a substantial portion also went into hydropower, much of it into big dams, known to be ecologically (and socially) extremely damaging.[28]

Integrating environment into socio-economic planning: A mirage

The Government of India produces an annual *Economic Survey*, reviewing major trends in the economy and providing an outlook for the coming year. Since the early 1990s, the survey has included a section on environment, previously absent. However, the section has remained an insignificant aside, getting one or two pages out of around 200, and tucked away in a couple of chapters (usually, Infrastructure or Industry). The first two chapters, which set the stage for the survey as a whole by reviewing the state of the economy and the major challenges faced, have never incorporated environmental issues, other than the odd passing mention related to a specific sector like agriculture. Not once has the survey provided an assessment, or even an indication, of the need to measure the economic losses caused by environmental damage. Clearly, rather than becoming a central tenet of planning for economic development—as has been repeatedly promised by the government—ecological concerns continue to be paid only lip service.

Many issues of the survey in the mid-1990s painted a generally dismal situation regarding forests, land, water and pollution, and pointed to the need to step up action for conservation and pollution control. In more recent years, the focus has been mainly on pollution, land degradation in relation to agriculture and, in the latest, climate change. However, none have linked the year's major economic developments with the status of the environment; they do not, for instance, analyse whether the impact of these developments was ecologically detrimental or corrective. Nor do they do the reverse: analyse the implications of the environmental situation for future economic development in India.

The Government of India has repeatedly stated that sustainable development is a goal of our planning process. But a statement of intent is one thing; putting in place actions—and related indicators and criteria that could assess progress—is another. The MoEF produces an annual report that details the actions taken to protect the environment, from forest and wildlife conservation to pollution control. But there are yet no criteria or indicators, used either by the economic planning wings of the government or by the MoEF, to assess whether we are indeed on a path of sustainability or moving away from it. Extensive tables of data appearing at the end of the surveys, including indicators for development, contain almost no environmental factors other than access to safe drinking water. As shown above, independent assessments and the widespread observations of environmental and social action groups point to pronounced trends of unsustainability, and there is little available in official reports to suggest that these are off the mark. The only possible exception is the contention that India's energy-intensity (energy used per unit of GDP) is improving.[29]

The contradictions of a government that publicly commits itself to sustainability yet shows little evidence of moving towards it become even more glaring in the case of individual sectors that the *Economic Surveys* deal with. For instance, both the 2007–08 and 2008–09 surveys mention, in the chapters on Agriculture, the serious degradation of land due to overuse and misuse of chemical fertilizers. But in the same breath they talk positively about moves to encourage fertilizer use. There is no focus on the need to shift to organic cultivation, other than a passing mention of 'organic and bio-fertilisers'. Somewhat more positive is the clear acknowledgement of the need for micro-irrigation, planning to meet local conditions and revival of millets. But these are piecemeal solutions to the agricultural crisis gripping the nation, a crisis the surveys acknowledge, but a crisis whose recommended solution comprises the same strategies that created it in the first place.

Some reflection on environmental concerns appears in the surveys' treatment of sectors like energy and transport. For instance, the 2008–09 survey stresses the need for energy efficiency, with an aim to reduce demand by 5 per cent, and notes the setting up of a national mission on the subject (under the National Climate Action Plan). But it makes no mention of non-conventional renewable sources and in fact targets thermal, nuclear and large hydro sources for nearly 100 per cent of the production. It also repeats a favourite bugbear of politicians and development economists that 'environment and forest issues' are a major cause of delays in the development of sources like hydropower.

For perhaps the first time, the 2008–09 survey mentions that 'consumption issues' have to be looked into, in relation to climate change and the need for 'ecological sustainability of India's development path'. This could be one wedge for the much fuller entry of environment into economic assessments in future, but, for the moment, those who are in charge of India's economy do not appear to be particularly interested.

There is not even a promise of accurate environmental accounting (of the impact of growth of the GDP). It is obvious that the GDP (or even HDI [Human Development Index]) is a poor index of sustainable development. Such calculations pay no attention to environmental costs and risks. GDP stands for gross domestic product. The letter 'G' represents the fact that the depreciation of the economy's productive base is not taken into account by today's pre-eminent measure of economic activity in a country. It can hardly be concluded that an economy's productive base grows alongside its GDP. The loss of climatic balance, biodiversity, top soil, arable land, forests, water bodies, minerals and energy sources is never reckoned in the

GDP. No one notices the shrinking of the resource base if all eyes are on the growth of the GDP and stock values. If the productive resource base continues to shrink (unless there are large compensating increases in the *productivity* of the resource base), at some point economic growth will turn negative, causing unexpected falls in the standard of living. All may appear to be well when in fact it is not. If we have already crossed critical tipping points there is no way of knowing! But there is plenty of evidence from other sources to show that we are well into the path of unsustainability.

Moreover, as students of national income accounting know all too well, there are serious problems with using growth of the GDP or per capita income as measures of material well-being. This is especially problematic in an economy which is supposed to be expanding on the back of growth in services. When pollution (and thus, clean-up expenditure) rises and medical expenses go up, boosting the GDP figures, we are supposed to believe that the nation is doing better. If old people are looked after in homes for senior citizens rather than by their families, this adds to 'economic growth' because a social service is being commercialized. The same applies to the situation when mental affliction grows in society and psychiatrists acquire more clients. Likewise for a thousand other instances in which a hitherto unmonetized part of social life (which is valued for the enormous contribution it makes to human happiness *precisely because it is priceless*) gets converted into a paid service. It is absolutely vital to recognize that in a society like India, where communities have been traditionally strong (albeit hierarchical, unjust and problematic in various ways), a breakdown of community life will all too often express itself in the form of a spurt in growth led by the (mostly unorganized) service sector. The perversity of such a measure of human welfare as the GDP or per capita income (or even HDI) then becomes all too obvious. This should surprise no one. The original purpose of aggregate GDP was to measure the economic strength of a state, not the well-being of the people who lived under it.

Has globalization not benefited the environment at all?

There are undoubtedly a number of environmental benefits that globalization brings. Several technologies relating to renewable energy, pollution control, energy efficiency, and so on, have been part of the overall inflow through globalization. The electronics and communications boom too has facilitated a much faster and greater exchange of information and ideas, including the possibility of campaign alerts to which people around the globe can respond almost instantly. A good example of this is the increasing international pressure generated against proposed mining by the UK company Vedanta Alumina on a hill considered sacred by the Dongria Kondh adivasis of Orissa (officially classified as 'Primitive' and hence entitled to special protection of culture and homelands). Though the locus of the protest is the tribe itself, supporters have used the electronic media to repeatedly send out information across the world, which is one reason for a number of investors pulling out of Vedanta.

One also has to contend with the argument that globalization makes way for globally benchmarked TNCs (transnational corporations), which bring in environmentally superior technologies (like the latest pollution control equipment, clean coal methods, etc.) as compared to dinosaur-era industrial plants that would otherwise dominate Third World development. The case of China and its bad environmental experience with

Township and Village Enterprises (compared to the relatively 'cleaner' TNCs) is often cited. It is also argued that through globalization better environmental standards can be imposed worldwide—a proposition one can rightfully challenge with the overall evidence of a race to the bottom. It is the First World countries whose standards are today threatened by Chinese competition—as witnessed by the weakening of the American EPA (Environment Protection Agency) under Bush—rather than Third World countries' standards being lifted because of globalization. Corporations are not naïve. There is a strong business logic for outsourcing and subcontracting. It preys on, among other things, labour and environmental standards.

There is no indication that the benefits of globalization are anywhere commensurate with the losses it entails, as outlined in this chapter. Whatever indications are available, quantitative or qualitative, all point to growing ecological unsustainability of the country as a whole and increasing environmental insecurity for hundreds of millions of its citizens. At least partly this is because the forces that globalization has exacerbated or unleashed—encouragement to private profit, growth at all costs, a boost to wasteful consumerism, the ascendant power of the corporate class, and so on—are not going to be tackled or quelled simply by deploying environmentally appropriate technologies or spreading rapid-fire information. At best, these will delay the ecological collapse and social disruption that globalization is leading us into, helping us gain time to work towards creating a radically different society. We will explore the contours of such alternative visions, including the role of globalization in its proper sense, in the second part of this book.

TOWN AND COUNTRY

AN OLD STORY GETS MUCH WORSE

'It is an unchangeable fact that the India of tomorrow will find expression in its cities.'

—From an advertisement for 'Lavasa Future Cities', *The Times of India*, 1 November 2009

India disowns Bharat

Villages have virtually disappeared from the radar screens of powerful administrators. At a 2009 conference of chief ministers and high court chief justices on the operationalization of *gram nyayalaya*s (village courts), the chief minister of Gujarat, Narendra Modi, was one of the two chief ministers (Sheila Dixit of Delhi being the second) who claimed that there were no villages in their state. No villages at all. The fact that the 18,000 villages in Gujarat are not in Modi's sight explains succinctly why the state has one of the world's worst records on rural poverty and malnutrition. It also relates to Gujarat's status as India's most polluted state, which is easy to ignore because the consequences are borne by the invisible villages. Its famed 400-km-long 'Golden Corridor' from Vapi to Mehsana hosts some of the worst offenders, bringing terrible health consequences for the villagers living close to industrial estates in the area.[1]

The mainstream of Indian educated opinion today has strong views on the demise (actual or desired) of the village. Most among the globalized, educated urban classes in India have turned their back on the village, even though 800 million people still live in the countryside.

City-dwellers are mostly ashamed of rural India. It is seen as inescapably backward in both economic and cultural terms; a place that has become redundant in modern times. This view is held very widely among many political leaders, bureaucrats, journalists, scholars and the educated public alike. For them there is really no option for India but to urbanize rapidly and move people out of 'low-paying' occupations in the countryside—as though urbanization per se constitutes progress and development and will automatically raise living standards, and as though such a massive historic change were even possible with such a large rural population.

This misperception is greatly compounded when one considers that cities constitute what may be called 'the spatial nervous system' of globalization, with metros and megacities (more than 10 million people) constituting the key nodes. Throughout the world, globalization has suddenly heightened the role of cities and pushed villages further into oblivion.

One of the more striking socio-psychological consequences of globalization has been that it has rapidly changed the *meaning* and function of places and their relation to each other. As countries have been led to relate to the world market, they have redefined themselves exclusively according to what they can sell to and buy from the rest of the world. The market has become the frame through which every place sees and evaluates itself. Within each country, almost every village, every region has found itself in rapidly changing economic circumstances in which it must constantly think of markets in cities and regions far from itself, just in order to survive. The links a place has traditionally had with local and regional markets are weakening. In India, globalization has brought the rest of the world—especially the Western world and East Asia—to the centre of urban public cognition, while rural India has fallen off the radar screens.

Since the early days of the Industrial Revolution villages have got a raw deal at the hands of cities. While supplying almost all the food, industrial raw materials and much of the labour to the cities, villages have been at the receiving end of urban industrialization in every country—capitalist, socialist or communist. When peasants have been allowed to farm at all, they have ultimately been led to or coerced into producing for the domestic or the overseas market, never having much influence over the price at which they have had to trade their product. In India the price of food and agricultural output has always been influenced by more powerful actors—local traders, moneylenders, city merchants, the government or international institutions like the Chicago Board of Trade (one of the world's oldest grain exchanges). Forest-dwelling pastoralists and adivasi populations too have been under attack everywhere. The same is true of fisherfolk whose livelihoods are being rapidly displaced by corporate trawlers, commercial aquaculture and coastal construction.

As the processes of globalization have unfolded over the Indian landscape, the economic and cultural distance between cities and the countryside has grown dramatically, even as new technologies have superficially 'penetrated' the countryside (by the presence of things like mobile phones and telecom towers). Every schoolchild till the 1980s used to learn that India (certainly Bharat) lived in its villages, a view dear to Gandhi. Now, it is clear to young people in the metros that India has moved to the shopping malls, its rhythms marked by measures like teledensities and stock values. Even young people in villages have come to internalize such a view, thanks to the impact of urban-dominated television and a metro-centric education system. For most young people, 'life is elsewhere': if they are from a village in Maharashtra, life is in Mumbai, and if they are born in Mumbai, then it is often in Paris, New York or Hong Kong.

Of course, these far-reaching psychological changes build on an old trend. The shift in attitudes of the Indian educated classes since the 1980s is a result of the reinforcement of the logic of colonialism. It had led Tagore, almost a century ago, to remark: 'The city, in its intense egotism and pride, remains blissfully unconscious of the devastation it is continuously spreading within the village, the source of its own life, health and joy.'[2]

The primary global developmental logic

The logic of development, first put in place by our colonial masters, works like this. In the last few centuries, the well-off policy elite—with the ultimate decision-making authority—have always resided in the cities. They are persuaded by a certain vision of the nation's development. While this vision does not explicitly reject the countryside, it pays but lip service to it, assuming that its proper role is to serve the larger interests of 'the nation'—ultimately assumed to be urban. It is a modern notion, drawn from the legacy of colonial exploitation and the experience of Western societies. As we have seen, it focuses on aggregate magnitudes like stock market indices, growth of the GDP and exports, the severe shortcomings of the vision hidden behind averages like per capita income. It is not bothered by the iniquitous concentration of income and wealth. Importantly, it is unmindful of the chasm that separates standards of living in the city and the countryside. It is oblivious of the utter dependence of cities on the rural hinterland for resources and uncaring about misusing the villages as sites for raw material extraction or industrial and urban waste disposal.

The understanding is also that, unlike in industrialized economies, which have been able to drastically reduce labour in agriculture, there is still far too much pressure on the land in Indian villages. Since it is believed that land is no longer where the money is (real estate bubbles and bonanzas notwithstanding), over time the surplus labour from villages ought to move to the cities or industrial complexes—where industry and the growing service economy are (supposedly) waiting to absorb working people displaced from farming or allied activities. The overwhelming concern with growth stems, at least in part, from a vision in which industry and services must expand very fast if they are to absorb a growing population of the unemployed.

However, expectation is one thing and its realization quite another. For decades now, the story of surplus labour absorption in India has been a rather dismal one. While people continue to get displaced from their land in the villages, or to leave it 'voluntarily' as agriculture, forestry, fisheries and handicrafts are rendered difficult survival propositions, they try their hand at other occupations in the village itself (without any assistance from the state) or migrate to the cities or other rural areas that need cheap labour. Such cheap, exploited labour is the secret behind the successful sweatshops which contribute significantly to Indian exports. At the same time, the vast majority of people who arrive in urban India fail to get a regular job. They end up working as poorly paid, daily-wage labour, or find some exploitative means of self-employment to support their families. At best, they get work as casual labour in the organized sector.

The part of the story rarely told is that in economic policies agriculture has been, now consciously, now inadvertently, *rendered* unviable for small and marginal peasants who constitute over 80 per cent of India's farming population. This happens through a variety of mechanisms—low prices offered to farmers for their produce; denying them affordable credit and irrigation; creating dependency on highly priced inputs (that leaves them in a debt trap); and allowing processes that reduce land productivity, including environmental degradation. The rural poor are also at the receiving end of land- and resource-grab in multiple forms by both the government and private mafia. The net result is that over a period of time, the distribution of income and purchasing power comes to rest increasingly in the hands of well-off city-dwellers, corporations and a small rural elite. This feeds into the familiar story of inequalities, resource poverty and urbanization. As the pattern of demand changes in line with prevailing inequalities, what the economy produces also changes. This has adverse social and environmental effects. Amit Bhaduri summarizes this process:

> There are insidious consequences of such a composition of output biased in favour of the rich that our liberalised market system produces. It is highly energy, water and other non-reproducible-resources-intensive, and often does unacceptable violence to the environment . . . Many are forced to migrate to cities as fertile land is diverted to non-agricultural use, water and electricity are taken away from farms in critical agricultural

seasons to supply cities, and developmental projects displace thousands. Hydroelectric power from the big dams is transmitted mostly to corporate industries, and a few posh urban localities, while the nearby villages are left in darkness.[3]

Even very well-informed people, perhaps from habitual prejudice, do simple-minded calculations to underscore the primacy of the cities. For instance, it is argued—superficially—that cities are where the bulk of the country's GDP is generated (ignoring all the underpaid inputs, like labour, from the countryside into urban areas). So that is where decision-making should logically be located. Arguments are made to the effect that there isn't adequate electoral representation for cities and metros in the country. In an interview to London's *Financial Times*, business executive Nandan Nilekani tries to explain why infrastructure in India is so poor in comparison with China. He points out that there is 'a disconnect . . . between the economic power and the political power'. Bengaluru with only 10 per cent of the population of Karnataka contributes 60 per cent of the state's GDP. However, it has only 7 per cent of the State Assembly seats. Nilekani betrays an envy of dictatorial China which is common to elite thinking today: 'In China you don't have that problem. India is the only example of urbanisation (on this scale) happening with universal adult franchise.'[4]

He omits to mention that Bengaluru generates this wealth by blatantly exploiting the countryside (for minerals, water, forest produce, food and dozens of other requirements) and throwing its waste back into it; and that, regardless of its share of Assembly seats, it arrogates to itself enormous decision-making power and influence.

Urbanization or megalopolisization?

Urbanization has traditionally accompanied industrialization everywhere in the world. Yet, the character of urbanization in the Third World has been very different from what happened in the West. On the one hand, as urban studies scholar Mike Davis points out, 'the scale and velocity of Third World urbanization utterly dwarfs that of Victorian Europe.' On the other hand, in a qualitative sense, Third World cities are virtually the default outcome of the structural developmental logic pushed by state policies.[5]

While the above is broadly true, the story of Indian urbanization is again a bit different from how it has unfolded in other Third World settings. Census data shows that even now, at the beginning of the second decade of the twenty-first century, only 30 per cent of India's population is urban. Moreover, the rate of urbanization is proceeding at a much slower pace in India compared to other Asian economies, such as China, South Korea or even Indonesia. Even though the urban population in India is expected to double in the first three decades of this century (it was 285 million at the time of the 2001 census, it is expected to be 575 million by 2030), a look at the 2001 census data is instructive. The pace of urbanization, contrary to what everyone has been led to believe, is actually slowing down since the 1970s. (This is not inconsistent with the growing displacement, as a lot of the migration is now taking place between rural areas or involves temporary moves to urban areas for such activities as construction, thereby contributing to the growth of 'footloose labour'.)[6]

Before we explore the riddle of its slowing rate, consider some other numbers which reveal a somewhat unusual pattern of urbanization. Megacities are those that contain more than

TABLE 6.1: Pace of Urbanization in India

Census decade	Urban population (Percentage of total at the end of census period)	Annual percentage rate of urban population growth
1941–51	17.3	3.5
1951–61	18.0	2.3
1961–71	19.9	3.2
1971–81	23.3	3.8
1981–91	25.7	3.1
1991–2001	27.8	2.7

Source: Census of India, 2001, http://censusindia.gov.in/Census_Data_2001/Census_Newsletters/Newsletter_Links/eci_3.htm

10 million people. According to the think-tank City Mayors, of the twenty-one megacities in the world in 2006, there were only two in the affluent countries (Tokyo and New York) and five in the subcontinent, including three in India: Mumbai, Delhi and Kolkata. More than five out of 100 Indians live in one of these three cities. Chennai, Hyderabad, Bengaluru, Ahmedabad and Pune will become megacities during the next decade. Moreover, of the 110 million people who lived in thirty-five Indian cities (of more than 1 million) at the time of the 2001 census, well over half were concentrated in six cities. The 2001 census lists 5161 'towns' as well. Putting these numbers together, we arrive at an interesting statistic: of the 5161 'towns', 5126 had an average population of less than 40,000, while the remaining thirty-five averaged almost 3 million! It is what statisticians call a 'bi-modal distribution'. The average Indian city with above 1 million population (such as Lucknow) is thus seventy-five times larger than the average small town in its hinterland!

The reasons for this odd phenomenon are twofold. Firstly, the definition of a 'town' for census purposes is a settlement of at least 5000 people with a density of more than 400 per sq km in which 75 per cent of the male working population is involved in non-agricultural occupations. (This category includes everything from bicycle-repair shops to small retail and hawking. It is a mystery as to why women are excluded from the definition.) Perhaps the description 'semi-urban' would be more accurate to describe the 17 per cent of India that lives outside both villages and big cities. That will leave only about 13 per cent of India in the big cities. Since it excludes the *kasba*s and the *mofussil* towns outside the metropolitan loop, this number is actually a more accurate index of India's urbanization.

Secondly, it is a pointer to the imbalanced form of urbanization (without commensurate labour-absorbing modern industrialization) that has been happening in India. It means that the disparities between the few dozen-odd metropolitan growth poles and the small towns are almost as large as those between the metros and rural India. It is what one might call a passive adjustment to globalization in a 'cyberized' age. Globalization today is anchored in large metropolitan spaces that are internationally linked through air travel, Internet, television and telecom networks. State policy has given birth in Third World countries to megalopolises which concentrate all the wealth and power necessary to order the space around them, attract masses of people looking for work from far-off regions and leave enormous proportions of the population to fend for themselves beyond (and often within) the urban agglomerations in the global limelight. In India urban growth has been concentrated around a handful of privileged regions. Too little policy attention has been paid to smaller urban areas.[7]

For contrast one may look at China, which has had 'dual-track' urbanization, the state backing the growth of mid-sized towns. China has seen extraordinary urbanization since 1978. It has moved a population the size of Europe from villages to urban areas. The number of official 'cities' has grown from 193 to 640 during these three decades. But the population share of the metros has actually *declined*. With a comparable overall population, while India has only thirty-five cities above 1 million people, China has as many as 166. Through conscious planning, the state has encouraged migration to smaller towns and cities, rather than to the metros. It has enabled this through directing investment towards smaller urban centres. This is the reason that the only two Chinese megacities—Shanghai and Beijing—have much smaller populations than any of our megalopolises. Among other things, it means less congestion and pressure on urban infrastructure. In this sense at least, urban growth in China certainly offers an instructive contrast to India, though it is very similar in being inequitable and ecologically unsustainable.[8]

What is also important to note about the Chinese story is that the small towns have been able to develop into fair-sized cities because China has far greater fiscal resources than India. The resources are greater not just in absolute terms but even relative to the respective GDPs. China's GDP is two-and-a-half times that of India's. But it can spend more on infrastructure and public services than India because it collects twice the percentage of GDP in taxes (19 per cent, as against only 9–10 per cent; in the affluent countries it ranges from 30 to 50 per cent). India's low tax collections are on account of corruption, evasion and 'a system riddled with exemptions, discretion, and arcane rules'. It is also worth noting that while the marginal personal income tax rate in India is 30 per cent, in China it is 45 per cent.[9]

Striking also is the rate of growth of Indian megacities during the past half-century, compared to the previous half-century. The following table tells its own story:

TABLE 6.2: Population Growth in Indian Megacities

(All numbers in millions)

Metro	1891	1941	1991	2001	2021 (Projected)
Mumbai	0.82	1.68	12.4	18.7	28.5
Delhi	0.17	0.7	9.4	13.1	23.0
Kolkata	0.68	2.1	10.3	12.1	20.0

Source: Collated by the authors from Census of India data, http://censusindia.gov.in/; KMDA data, http://www.kmdaonline.org/html/about-us.html; Urban Development, Govt of West Bengal, http://wburbandev.gov.in/pdf/Chronology_Development_KMPC.pdf; DMRC data, http://www.delhimetrorail.com/corporates/ecofriendly/Chapter%201.pdf; and 'Bombay faces population boom', BBC, 20 December 2000, http://news.bbc.co.uk/2/hi/south_asia/1093424.stm

The growth of these cities during the second half of the twentieth century has been explosive. Mumbai, for instance, took fifty years to double its population from 0.82 to 1.68 million between 1891 and 1941. Over the next six decades (1941–2001) it multiplied eleven-fold. During the same period Delhi expanded to eighteen times its size in 1941 and Kolkata six times. Thus, even if India's pace of urbanization is mathematically slower than that of other Asian economies, the *character* of urbanization—which is, in effect, megalopolisization—makes the absolute scale and speed of it a formidable challenge.[10]

Development economist John Mellor says:

One of the major problems of contemporary developing countries is the unhealthy structure of urbanisation—a tendency for the urban population to concentrate in one or a few of the major population centres. That was not a characteristic of the developed countries when they were at similar stages in development. Their urban centres were more numerous and the urban population more diffused over those centres.[11]

The great urban divide

Well over half of urban India lives in slums. Was it always like this? In *Planet of Slums*, Mike Davis points out that the story was quite different before Independence. Urban slums grew slowly in the first half of the twentieth century, but not because rural India did much better in those days. Like China today, British India tightly regulated the entry into urban centres. This was done with the help of encroachment and zoning laws, which held squatting and street-vending in check. Nandini Gooptu points out the role of Town Improvement Trusts when it came to slum clearance and the removal of 'plague spots'. (Plague, cholera and influenza took a huge toll in those days: the British were as negligent towards public sanitation as the rulers of independent India.) Colonial and native middle-class areas of the city were kept tidy with the help of such laws and practices. In this sense, the evictions in India since the mid-1980s are a throwback to the colonial era when such things were carried out even more stringently.[12]

Some Indians do not hesitate to say that the growth of slums is the price of democracy in independent India. Certainly, their role as vote banks is perverse. And yet, the solution to the problem is not demolition and relocation to remote sites. That only manages to render the 'problem' artificially invisible.

One clear answer to this is state support of economic activity in villages and small towns, but the wind is blowing in the opposite direction. The government's flagship urban development programme, the JNNURM (Jawaharlal Nehru National Urban Renewal Mission), for instance, targets only the sixty-three largest cities, spending Rs 1,20,000 crore over a seven-year period beginning 2005–06.[13]

India is likely to overtake China, which currently has the world's largest slum population, during the next decade. The first-ever human development report for Mumbai (2009) finds that the two Mumbais within the city occupy completely different economic, physical and social spaces even though they share a geographical territory. 'The contrasts in living standards are of a magnitude not seen anywhere else in the country.'[14]

Eighty per cent of the half a million people who migrate to Delhi every year end up living in slums. Delhi's slum population is expected to cross 10 million by 2015. The situation is no different in any other Indian metropolitan region which is a growth pole in the current economy. In every such area (numbering fewer than a dozen) the influx of rural migrants exceeds many times the capacity of the region to generate jobs— even if double-digit growth rates are maintained for two decades. In other words, unless there is a radical change of course, we will continue to witness the growth of slums, unemployment and the urbanization of poverty. We will also continue to see violent evictions and, possibly, reprisals, as the experience of slum growth in Latin America shows. In a country like India, chauvinistic movements of the kind that have begun in Mumbai are likely to flourish, as there are misperceptions about the root causes of urban unemployment, and interested parties are quick to make political capital of the problem.[15]

Slums are an inevitable outcome of the developmental logic outlined earlier. If people experience both despair and hope in them, it is because of the *direction* of the movement of people from the countryside, where economic life has become most arduous, to cities where, even if there are no steady jobs, there is at least the *hope* of one. Casual employment is certainly much easier to find in cities. Migration—whether it is internal or international—is almost always undertaken in hope. Even if real urban incomes for the majority remain stagnant, or urban unemployment continues to rise, migration shows few signs of abating, given how difficult life has become for the rural poor. For a host of reasons, for an individual or a family, the reversal of migration from cities is usually unthinkable even if jobs are not forthcoming or wages are low. They are on a one-way street.

The migration to megacities puts enormous pressure on urban infrastructure, especially for the poor. Provision of essential services, such as drinking water, sanitation, basic housing and electricity is light years behind the burgeoning needs. As human settlements grow in size, number and distance from places of work, transport needs also grow beyond the control of urban planners.

Who sows? Who reaps?: Indian agriculture disabled

Ever since the early days of modern economics, agriculture and 'allied activities' (livestock, forestry, fisheries, etc.) have been classified as 'primary sector' activities. Industry has always been seen as part of the 'secondary sector', while services constitute the 'tertiary sector'. What makes the activities of the primary sector primary? The answer is already known to everyone. While human society can live, even thrive, without the products of the secondary and tertiary sectors—such as home theatres or spas—

it cannot survive long without food. 'Everything else can wait, but not agriculture,' Jawaharlal Nehru had said.[16]

The tragic shame of globalizing India today is that farmers, who pass their days working so hard to keep others alive, are themselves unable to survive the onslaught precipitated by the globalization-driven policies followed since the mid-1980s. Since at least 1997 this is evidenced most palpably in the disturbing phenomenon of farmer suicides around the country. However, in order to appreciate the causes underlying this trend, it is important to wind back a bit and examine the powerful long-term forces that have been impacting Indian agriculture.

The performance of agriculture has always been critical to the wider economy for a number of reasons. It supplies cheap food for growing urban populations, a pool of cheap unskilled labour to other sectors and cheap raw materials to industry (such as cotton for textile mills). Assuming it shares a little in the growing prosperity, it provides a market for industrial consumer goods. And ultimately, it becomes a source of demand for industrial capital goods (tractors, turbines, etc.) needed to boost productivity within the industrialized model of agriculture.

In a country like India, in which well over half the population is still dependent on agriculture for a significant proportion of its livelihood, the performance of agriculture becomes a matter of even wider interest. Between 1983 and 2005, government data shows that while the share of the workforce occupied in agriculture fell somewhat, from 68 per cent to 56 per cent, the share of the GDP emerging from agriculture fell much more sharply from 37 per cent to 21 per cent, signalling the relative decline of the sector and the stagnation of labour productivity.[17]

Plenty of other data can be cited to show that Indian agriculture as a whole has been in persistent decline and deepening crisis for at least a decade and a half. In the early 1980s, agriculture was growing faster than the economy. The growth rate of agricultural GDP has fallen sharply from 3.3 per cent during 1980–95 to just 2 per cent in the period 1995–96 to 2004–05, even though the monsoon gods have mostly smiled on rain-dependent farmers. The growth in crop yields has declined sharply for every major crop when one compares these two periods. In the case of critical food crops like rice, wheat, coarse grains and oilseeds, the growth rate in yields has become less than half of what it was in the earlier period. In the case of pulses, the growth rate in yield has actually turned negative. The numbers make for a very dismal comparison with competing nations like China.[18]

The primary reason for the stagnation in yields of major crops in India is the cruel neglect of small farmers and agriculture by successive Indian governments since the mid-1980s, along with severe ecological degradation. The falls in public outlays on investment in agriculture have been precipitous. Without such investment, both dry-land and irrigated agriculture suffer.

Consider some numbers. Public investment in agriculture, which grew at 19 per cent per annum in the 1970s began to *decline* at 5 per cent every year in the 1980s and by as much as 7 per cent annually between 1986 and 1993. As a result of callous policies, investment in this sector as a proportion of total investment in the economy shrank from 17 per cent in the 1970s to 12 per cent in the 1980s to just 9 per cent in the 1990s. Less than 5 per cent of plan expenditure in all the recent Five-Year Plans has been earmarked for agriculture, even if almost 60 per cent of India's working population lives off it. To this day, six decades after Independence, most of Indian agriculture (60 per cent) is still rain-fed. The dramatic fall of public investment in critical areas like decentralized irrigation or in dry-land farming has meant that farmers have increasingly had to resort to private 'solutions' to what is by nature a public problem—with terrible attendant consequences. Agricultural economist Mihir Shah points out that as much as 75 per cent of the increase in irrigation during the last two decades has come in the form of tube wells, as farmers resort to competitive pumping of groundwater. This is lowering water tables all around and creating a severe water crisis.[19]

The Green Revolution—which since the late 1960s ushered in HYV (high-yielding variety) seeds for rice and wheat—is also to blame for the long-term decline in crop yields, even if it increased production in the short run. Areas like Punjab, Haryana and western UP (Uttar Pradesh), which rode the crest of the Green Revolution wave in the 1970s, multiplied their short-term yields manyfold with the help of HYV seeds. They are now in the grip of 'acute ecological and economic distress', in the words of famous agricultural scientist M.S. Swaminathan, ironically one of the key figures behind the Green Revolution. The soil has become heavily chemicalized. According to the department of land resources, two-thirds of India's agricultural lands are 'degraded' or 'sick'. Fertilizers have caused serious nutrient imbalances. Groundwater, where it is still accessible, has become salinized or heavily contaminated with nitrates that can cause various diseases. Also, people from villages in Punjab universally report that 'food tasted better before the Green Revolution'.[20]

The routine neglect of agriculture is also reflected in the changes in area under different crops. When farmers do not find supportive government policies they either change the cropping pattern, give up agriculture altogether or, as seen more recently, they tragically end their own lives. According to the government's *Economic Survey* (2010), the area under foodgrains in 2008–09 was 3.5 per cent less than the area in 1990–91. The decline in land under coarse grains—which constitute the staple of poor diets in so many parts of the country—has been striking: 24 per cent! Meanwhile, the increase in area under non-foodgrain cash crops and horticulture, many of them for export, was 20 per cent.[21]

When you couple the declining sown area under food crops with stagnant yields, it becomes clear why there is cause for serious concern. Perhaps the most telling statistic is the one about the per capita availability of foodgrains across the population. The data presented in chapter 3 indicates the sharp decline in the availability of both cereals and pulses in the country. Imports have clearly not been able to bridge the gap between the high rate of population growth and the falling rate of food production.

When those responsible for keeping us alive take their own lives

It is in the light of such sobering data that the phenomenon of farmer suicides needs to be seen. The National Crime Records Bureau data shows that on average about 17,000 farmers have killed themselves in India every year since 1997. Every hour, on average, two farmers commit suicide. In total, at least 200,000 farmers have killed themselves around the country over thirteen years (up to 2010). This is a phenomenon without precedent in this part of the world, including the colonial era, and all of recorded history. It is the largest wave of suicides historically, according to veteran journalist P. Sainath. Moreover, it is important to mention that India perhaps represents a heightened form of a global trend. Farmers are killing themselves at higher rates than the rest of the population in most parts of the world, including in affluent nations like the US, the UK and Australia. In those countries too they have been stripped of their livelihood by the ruthless expansion of international agribusiness. In India, the difference between farmer suicide rates and suicide rates in the rest of the population is very large. Also large is the difference between farmer suicide rates before the mid-1990s and those today.[22]

Farmer suicides are merely the flashpoint of what is by now widely perceived as a chronic crisis in Indian agriculture. Even government experts and stalwarts acknowledge it. According to Swaminathan, 'We are on the verge of a disaster. We will be in serious difficulty if food productivity is not increased and farming is neglected . . . The future belongs to nations with grains and not guns. The current food inflation is frightening.'[23]

So why are farmers killing themselves in thousands every year? What underlies the enormous agrarian crisis? While a full diagnosis lies beyond the scope of this book, if we are to assess the impact of globalization in India, we need to have a good sense of the causes behind the devastation agriculture has suffered in the reform era. After all, there was no such crisis during the 1970s and 1980s and no farmer suicides. What has changed?

The most fundamental change is that Indian agriculture is rapidly being tailored to the demands being placed on it by the global economy led by domestic and foreign TNCs (transnational corporations). This is referred to as the 'corporatization of agriculture'. What does this mean? It implies that transnational agribusiness has been eyeing (and grabbing ever greater chunks of) the Indian food market since the economy was prised open for the giant corporations. This leads to many things in turn. Agriculture is being rapidly 'industrialized' and made dependent on the expensive inputs sold by such corporations. The economics of small subsistence farming is being manipulated (obviously with the help of government policies) to make it unviable, so that once the peasants are dispossessed (or sometimes displaced) the big corporations can take over arable land and have large, profit-making plantations as in the Western world or in parts of Latin America (this is only in its nascent stages in India). Corporate majors are keen to have fully integrated—'farm-to-fork'—production and retail chains, whereby everything from the supply of seeds and other inputs to the retail marketing of processed items via branded metropolitan outlets will be in their control.

Everyone appears to concur that small-holder agriculture has no money in it. In 2000 itself the National Agricultural Policy had formally recognized that agriculture had become 'a relatively unrewarding profession'. Farmers themselves, in a government sample survey done in 2005, revealed that 40 per cent of them wished to quit farming. Few observers have considered asking how this situation has come about and what the role of government policies has been in generating it. The fact is that government policies have been indifferent, often hostile, to the interests of small farmers. Instead of protecting the latter, the policies have rapidly been transformed into enabling steps for the profitable entry of domestic and foreign transnational agribusinesses into agriculture.[24]

Income for agricultural workers and farmers depends on four things: land per worker, productivity of the land, price of inputs and the price the output earns. With population growth and land-grab for industry and infrastructure, the land available per worker is falling. Productivity, as we have seen, has stagnated or risen too slowly. Moreover, the government has not been rewarding farmers adequately for their efforts in terms of remunerative prices or support with marketing, as per the conditionalities laid down by the IMF (International Monetary Fund) and the World Bank. All this has been happening while input costs keep going up, especially for farmers caught in the Green Revolution model of agriculture which makes them increasingly dependent on industrial inputs. The net outcome of the interplay of these four factors is summed up by Prime Minister Manmohan Singh: 'The rates of growth of agriculture in the last decade have been poor and are a major cause of rural distress. Farming is increasingly becoming an unviable activity.' Farmer suicides were termed 'IMF suicides' in South Korea some years back. The term is as appropriate for India and other parts of the Third World, given the role the IMF has played in shaping economic policies in these countries.[25]

The Situation Assessment Survey of Farmers (SASF) carried out by the government in 2005 revealed some startling data. Agricultural earnings for rural households were, in general, inadequate to meet their consumption expenditure, covering only about 35 per cent of it for the average household. Apart from tending to its own field, the average farmer household, according to the SASF, engages in various other economic activities—labouring in others' fields, dairy and non-farm businesses like petty retail. The monthly sum total of the average farmer's earnings from all these activities (Rs 2115) still came to an amount significantly less than his/her consumption expenditure (Rs 2770). The latter amounted to a meagre Rs 503 per capita per month, or less than Rs 17 a day. This is why farming households have had to go into debt even to meet their consumption needs.[26]

Such data gives the lie to government claims that rural poverty has been falling in the country. If it has, it has not been falling anywhere near fast enough. Recently, both the World Bank and the IMF have had to retract their earlier line and admit that the chances of poverty reduction in a country like India are minimal without paying due, and focused, attention to agriculture.[27]

One of the myths of globalization is that large farms are more productive since they enjoy economies of scale. (Thus, agribusinesses should be allowed to take over farming.) This is untrue. There is plenty of data to show that land productivity on small farms is actually significantly higher (for reasons that need not detain us here) than on large plantations (two to ten times higher in different parts of the global South, according to some agricultural experts).[28]

The 'farm-to-fork' logic for consolidation of production and retail chains by a few large firms is rebutted by Sainath in the following words:

> Remember the excuse trotted out for letting Big Retail sell agricultural produce? It would do away with the 'middleman,' giving farmers and consumers a better deal. Yet prices of fresh produce are costlier at big retail's outlets. You still get a better deal from the petty vendor on the street. Often, that pathetic 'middleman' they're crushing is a poor woman street vendor, the last and weakest link in the chain of intermediaries between farmer and public. The new middlemen wear suits.[29]

The rise in the price of food in recent years has been projected by the media as having benefited the farmer. The truth is quite different. All the cream has been skimmed off by powerful big retailers, at most by wholesalers, while farm-gate prices and the farmers at their receiving end have languished.[30]

When it comes to farmer suicides, it is notable that the bulk of them have occurred not in the poorest states in the country

(Bihar, UP, etc.) but in some of the more well-off regions (Maharashtra, Andhra Pradesh, Karnataka, Punjab, Kerala, etc.). Commercialization is assumed by many observers to inevitably be of benefit to farmers. The truth is that greater market orientation has exposed farmers to far greater risks and sunk them deeper into the quicksand of debt. How exactly has the economics of farming been manipulated against the small-scale cultivator?

India became a signatory to the WTO (World Trade Organization) when it came into existence in 1995. Soon thereafter, India signed the Agreement on Agriculture (AoA). This obliged it to expose its hitherto protected farmers to the winds of global competition, including, especially, competition from highly subsidized grain (and cotton) from the rich countries. The rich nations subsidize their agriculture to the tune of over $1 billion a day, even as they hypocritically advise developing countries to keep their faith in 'free' trade.[31]

The AoA was resisted widely in the country before it was accepted by our government. Protests by farmers' organizations like the Karnataka Rajya Raitha Sangha had begun in the early 1990s itself. They challenged the Dunkel GATT (General Agreement on Tariffs and Trade, precursor to the WTO) proposals for the opening up of agricultural markets in poor countries because of the threat to millions of rural livelihoods. On Gandhi Jayanti in 1993 half a million farmers in Bengaluru also pledged to protect their seed sovereignty. They challenged the patenting of agricultural seeds and plant resources by private TNCs, opposing their entry into Indian agriculture and vowing to protect agricultural biodiversity. Over the past decade and a half, farmer protests have continued, but government policy, conforming to WTO 'obligations', has refused to change so far.

The Indian government had traditionally supported farmers by offering them good prices for their produce, much like the way farmers are supported in every part of the industrialized world. Under pressure from the international financial institutions (who have repeatedly ticked off the Indian government for food and other subsidies), these prices have not been allowed to keep pace with inflation after the reforms began; instead, subsidized grain has been dumped into Indian markets to the quiet delight of globally powerful agribusinesses, contrary to all principles of comparative advantage or free trade. The miseries of our farmers today bear out Adam Smith's apprehensions from two centuries ago:

> Were those high duties and prohibitions taken away all at once, cheaper foreign goods of the same kind might be poured so fast into the home market as to deprive all at once many thousands of our people of their ordinary employment and means of subsistence. The disorder which this would occasion might no doubt be very considerable.[32]

India's hard-earned self-sufficiency in foodgrains—achieved by the early 1980s (albeit through a model that has proven to be unsustainable, though more sustainable ones were available)—is today lost once again. Far from gaining greater shares in agricultural export markets, Indian farmers have actually lost significant shares in the domestic market as imports of agricultural products have grown faster than exports. 'Access to markets? Yes, we want access to our own markets,' says the Latin American farmers' organization Via Campesina.[33]

A detailed study of the impact of globalization policies on adivasi communities in Kerala shows a clear trend towards pauperization and unemployment caused by the cheap imports of agricultural produce. Whether cultivating their own crops or labouring on plantations owned by others, adivasis were badly hit when import of tea, coffee, pepper and other crops was liberalized. This was made worse by a steady decline in foodgrain distribution through ration shops. Foodgrain prices in the ration shops increased steadily. The study also shows that women are worse affected by these factors than men.[34]

Meanwhile, farmers have also come to depend heavily on industrial inputs, including seeds, fertilizers, pesticides, diesel oil, power and farm machinery. The costs of these inputs have risen substantially, catching the farmers in a sharp pincer movement and leaving them in deep debt traps that local moneylenders exploit to their advantage. According to Sainath, it took Rs 2500 to cultivate an acre of cotton in Vidarbha in 1991. It costs Rs 20,000 today. 'The gains from these higher costs are cornered by the corporate world in sectors like seed, fertiliser and pesticide. Soaring input costs have been crucial to farm bankruptcies, debt and suicides.' The proportion of rural households in debt almost doubled from 26 per cent to 48.6 per cent during just the first decade of the reform era.[35]

The tipping point in the suicide story could be a single crop failure, expenses for a family wedding or an unforeseen health bill. To add fuel to the farmers' fire, the government, again under 'advice' from the IFIs, has been withdrawing credit to small farmers (see chapter 3). According to Sainath, while the number of urban commercial bank branches doubled in the period from 1993 to 2008, almost 5000 commercial bank branches were shut down in Indian villages, leaving farmers once again at the mercy of moneylenders. Data from the All-India Bank Employee Association (AIBEA) indicates that in the case of every socially marginal category—Dalits, women, small farmers, adivasis—the proportion of the population with bank accounts fell significantly between 1991 and 2004. Between 1992 and 2006, when the share of personal loans (for things like cars and consumer durables) in bank loans and advances grew from 8 per cent to 23 per cent, the share of agriculture fell from 15 per cent to 11 per cent of the total.[36]

In recent budgets of the Central government a new twist has been given to making credit available to farmers. Sainath reports that 'more and more of "agricultural" credit will go not to farmers but corporations'. Indeed, 'even External Commercial Borrowings (ECBs) will henceforth be available for cold storage or cold room facility'. Several of the loans disbursed as 'agricultural credit' are in excess of Rs 10 crore and even Rs 25 crore. And even as large loans steadily grew in number between 2000 and 2006, agricultural loans of less than Rs 25,000 fell by more than half. The evidence on the handover of agriculture to globally powerful corporations becomes more blatant with each passing year. Of the 2010 Central budget Sainath has written: 'This is a budget crafted for, and perhaps by, the corporate farmer and agribusiness.'[37]

The Rs 70,000-crore loan waiver given by the government in its 2009 Central budget to indebted farmers came in for a lot of criticism in the mainstream media. The waiver, restricted to bank loans, ignores the fact that almost two-thirds of the debt incurred by farmers across the country is to local moneylenders and other informal sources of credit. Moreover, loan waivers are one-off events whose effect lasts only till the moment when the interest cycle starts again. Besides, Sainath points out that the corporate sector has enjoyed waivers of as many as fifteen times as much since 1991—over Rs 5,00,000 crore being written off in 2010 alone (if one includes all direct and indirect forms of relief to the organized private sector, often hidden under such heads as 'Statement of Revenue Forgone').[38]

Nor does the full-scale corporatization of Indian agriculture stop at budgetary concessions. It means diverting more food-producing land for the generation of biofuel, even though it is claimed that only 'wasteland' is being used for the purpose. This fuel is then used for private vehicles, whose increasing demand has begun to determine land-use patterns. It means giving a free hand to powerful mega corporations when it comes to the introduction of GM (genetically modified) foods into India. (However, mercifully, massive public resistance and a responsive environment minister have succeeded in staying the entry of Bt brinjal/eggplant for the time being.) It means writing or changing land-related policies that will facilitate the transfer of land from small farmers to big corporations—often for non-agricultural uses. It means helping domestic companies and transnationals carve a market for their seeds, fertilizers, pesticides and farm equipment. And so on.

Some of the most egregious steps towards the corporatization of agriculture have been undertaken by the Indian PM and the US President during 2005–06 through the signing of the India–US Knowledge Initiative in Agriculture (KIA). This 'Initiative' is being touted as the beginning of the Second Green Revolution in India, led by biotechnology. This, it is being claimed, is the answer to agrarian decline in India. It has been working over the past several years, in several phases, to usher in changes in the country's regulatory regime, which would suit the business interests of the world's leading TNCs. Some of the prominent members on the KIA board are representatives of major agribusinesses and TNCs like Monsanto, Archer Daniels Midland (ADM) and Walmart. It is clear which interests will prevail when it comes to the food and large retail sector. There is more than a touch of irony in large private players—usually the target of regulation—being present in a body that is helping make new regulations.[39]

Regulation in four areas is being targeted: 1) genetically modified organisms; 2) contract farming; 3) seeds regulation; and 4) intellectual property rights (IPRs). Manufacturers of GM crops are finding it difficult to market their products in the Western world because of tight regulations. India (and China) are interesting to them because of the sheer size of their potential markets for such crops. In 2007, after the KIA had come into effect, the Genetic Engineering Approval Committee issued a statement to the effect that no approval was needed any longer from it for the import of GM food products into India. This was in keeping with mounting US demands from the WTO for the removal of restrictions against trade in GM crops.[40]

At the time this book is being written, the Biotechnology Regulatory Authority of India Bill is set to be presented to Parliament for approval. This bill has been described by agricultural scientists as 'draconian' due to provisions that make it illegal to question the safety of GM crops. Information on GM crops is kept outside the purview of the RTI (Right to Information) and even state governments (more than ten of whom had protested Bt brinjal) will not be permitted to intervene in their production and marketing. The irony is that as per the Indian Constitution, land and agriculture are state subjects, outside the direct purview of the Central government.[41]

On another front, there is pressure from the KIA to push farmers to switch to crops and plant varieties that are more suitable for processing via contract farming. In the US—whose regulatory regime is sought to be replicated under Indian conditions—companies enter into marketing agreements with farmers that allow farmers little choice over inputs (like seeds) or over the price at which they sell their output to large companies. Similar reports are coming from those parts of India which have already been inducted into contract farming.[42]

Legislative changes—via the Seeds Bill for instance—are being brought about to favour private industry and make it extremely problematic for farmers to maintain their age-old right to seed sovereignty. There has been pressure for many years to criminalize the recycling of seeds which farmers have traditionally practised in order to sustain themselves. Fortunately, this has not happened yet. Also, state governments are now finding it hard to control the pricing of seeds, their interventions being seen as 'unwarranted' from the KIA perspective. Agriculture expert Kavitha Kuruganti writes that 'what is "unwarranted" from the US perspective is a constitutional right that state governments have over agriculture'. She points out rightly that 'farmers' rights and viability of farming as a profession will be closely linked to IPRs in farming'. The KIA also undermines the operation of such environmental policies and legislation as the Biological Diversity Act (2002).[43]

In sum, the state's approach to agriculture and small farmers is a harbinger of times to come. By giving obvious preference to a few corporations over millions of indigenous small farmers, it is failing to perform its duty under the nation's Constitution. If domestic companies and TNCs ultimately win this battle, the small farmer of old will be decimated over the next few decades. Tens, if not hundreds, of millions of dispossessed and displaced peasants will join the ranks of footloose labour, which is lucky to find work for even half the year. Perhaps the numerical growth rate in agriculture will become impressive after this massive destruction of traditional livelihoods. The chosen few among the globally agile TNCs will come to control and dominate the

Indian food chain—from the seed and input supplies and the grain fields all the way up to the wholesale and retail of processed foods in metropolitan supermarkets.

However, given the size of the population under consideration—over 700 million—this scenario is somewhat unlikely to *actually* transpire. The pressure of population on the land is growing, not diminishing, especially since jobs in others sectors of the economy are not forthcoming. People are not going to quietly accept the rapid worsening of their lot. The more plausible eventuality—which is already playing out in some parts of the country—is that Indian agriculture will become a zone of long-term conflict and violence as powerful global players challenge the age-old foundations of Indian agrarian life with the sometimes open, sometimes tacit, backing of state policy.

The neglect of agriculture since the dawn of the reform era is working against the broader economic interests not just of the rural population but of the country as a whole. Agriculture is germane to the well-being of a poor country. And it is the very foundation of a strong developing economy. This much is obvious—now even to the World Bank and the IMF. What is less obvious is that the well-being of agriculture has a profound impact on industry and other sectors of the economy, especially in the countryside. The linkages have long been understood by development economists. It is surprising that in the excitement around globalization and the reforms these elementary lessons have been forgotten.

The government needs to invest in agriculture, at least in proportion to its significance in the national income, if not to its significance in employment—especially in land and water regeneration, decentralized irrigation and dry-land agriculture. Alongside, once the RBI ensures affordable credit for farmers, land productivity and food production will grow (unless land continues to be seized from agriculture at a high rate). If reasonable prices are offered to farmers for the sale of their crop, which to some extent is already happening with organic produce, farmers' incomes would grow as well. As farmers become better off they too will be able to spend a larger fraction of their income on non-agricultural goods, generating demand for the products of industry and services. Many of these things can be produced in rural areas themselves. Consumer goods and small retail would be the direct beneficiaries of such an approach. As non-agricultural demand in the countryside increases, one can reasonably expect rural non-farm employment (RNFE) to grow too. This would happen particularly because consumer goods, small retail and other sectors are more labour-intensive than other (more modern) sectors of industry and services.

The growth of RNFE will give a further impetus to local food production as the effective demand for food increases. This will in turn boost other sectors of the local rural economy. And so on. A 'virtuous cycle' can thus be set in motion. In conjunction with potentially successful government programmes like a better-designed and more effectively implemented scheme under MGNREGA (Mahatma Gandhi National Rural Employment Guarantee Act), it can change the socio-economic face of the countryside.

There is only one problem with such an approach to agriculture. It leaves virtually no opportunity for the giant food companies (both domestic and foreign) and seed companies to make growing profits by controlling India's food chain. Nor will corrupt politicians and bureaucrats get the opportunities they are used to. On the contrary, as local rural economies create a dynamism of their own, they will render the Indian peasantry relatively autonomous. Leaders of farmers' movements in India are not interested in continuing their dependence on external help of any sort. As a Karnataka farmer says, 'We, the farmers, need to stand on our own two legs. We don't want financial assistance . . . we don't want to be dependent on the WTO, the IMF and the World Bank.' What these institutions and their client corporations are most afraid of is precisely such independence.[44]

We will return to the possibilities of such a radical agricultural revolution in Part II.

'Rurbanization'

The crisis in agriculture is rapidly altering the shape of the countryside. The drive from New Delhi to Meerut in western UP is about seventy kilometres. It used to take under two hours a generation ago. Today it can take up to three or four. The entire route—predominantly rural and agricultural earlier—has become urbanized. It is cluttered with flour and sugar mills; brick kilns; property dealers; tea shops; *kirana* stores; truck, car and two-wheeler mechanics; bicycle repair shops, and so on. This has led to an explosion of heterogeneous traffic—from trucks and buses to bullock carts and cycle rickshaws, not to mention pedestrians—which makes the road resemble a city artery rather than a highway.

Does it mean that the entire stretch has become *truly* urbanized? No. Just a few hundred metres from the highway, the landscape is still entirely rural. Fields are planted with wheat or sugar cane and cattle forage on the fallow lands. More importantly, modern urban infrastructure—covered drains and hygienic sanitation, public toilets, a steady supply of drinking water, a reliable supply of power, good roads and other civic amenities—is conspicuous by its absence in most of the places cars speed by. There is the occasional emblem—with two children riding a pencil—of the Sarvashiksha Abhiyan (Education for All) visible every now and then in one's peripheral vision, signalling the marginal presence of the state schooling system. But it's not like schools and colleges are exploding all around. Nor are hospitals. As one observer puts it, 'The town is not coming out to the country, as much as the country is reaching out to the town, leaving behind a host of untidy rural debris.'[45]

India is not atypical here. The failure of development around most of the Third World is generating what Mike Davis calls a 'hermaphroditic landscape, a partially urbanized countryside'. It is a form of human settlement not readily classified as either urban or rural. It intermeshes the two in a dense, complex web of transactions which tie urban cores to their environs. Geographer David Drakakis-Smith, writing about Delhi, points out that 'extended metropolitan regions . . . represent a fusion of urban and regional development in which the distinction between what is urban and rural has become blurred as cities expand along corridors of communication, by-passing or surrounding small towns and villages which subsequently experience *in situ* changes in function and occupation'.[46]

Cities around the world are defined not just by large agglomerations of human population. They are also marked by a way of life which is organized for a somewhat healthy coexistence under such demographic conditions. Thus, it would be much fairer to describe the stretch from New Delhi to Meerut as 'rurban', as some people have suggested. A human settlement pattern of such character is hardly uncommon around the country. On the contrary, between the collapsing villages and the overcrowding cities, it is possible to see them becoming the very norm.

The crisis in agriculture and employment is leading to a dramatic change in the nature and meaning of settlement patterns across the country. Agricultural stagnation has meant that people who would ordinarily describe themselves as 'farmers' are routinely engaged in non-farming occupations in order to survive; this makes official figures about the proportion of the population dependent on agriculture somewhat difficult to interpret. It is no longer possible to speak in clear-cut terms of 'rural' and 'urban' populations when tens of millions of households have evolved everyday survival strategies that straddle both the countryside and the city.

While the money-order economy is not new, it has developed far greater complexity in 'the new India'. Construction labour, to give just one example, often moves back and forth between urban and rural areas, depending on the availability of work and time of the year. The same family is often engaged in agricultural labour during harvest season, before returning to their temporary hovels at urban construction sites. A family may have an elder son working in West Asia, another one (temporarily) at a city supermarket and yet another dividing his time doing petty trading between the city and the village; all this, even as the youngest son tries to produce enough off the land to feed the ageing parents, and a daughter tries to earn something as a nurse or housemaid. Such stories are found everywhere and create a nightmare for census taxonomists.

Traditionally, migration has been seen as a positive sign, resulting from the rising productivity of agriculture and the parallel creation of industrial and service sector jobs in the cities. It is clear by now that in India these are not the primary forces behind such migration. Distress migration has grown as productivity in agriculture has stagnated and little respectable job creation has happened in the cities despite years of high growth. As the numbers presented in Table 6.1 indicate, the speed of such migration, reflected in the rates of urbanization, is perhaps slowing down. According to the Census of India, as of 2001, seven out of ten Indians still lived outside urban areas.

The destination of migrants appears to have changed quite radically in recent times. More significant than rural–urban migration is the intra-rural movement of labour. There is far more migration from one part of rural India (say Bihar or Orissa) to another (perhaps Punjab or Gujarat) than it is even possible to measure. As the scholar Jan Breman has pointed out, circulatory (and seasonal) migration is a massive, growing phenomenon across the entire subcontinent, facilitated by the fact that transport costs are borne by the migrants themselves. From the point of view of employers, workers from outside the region are typically more desperate and docile—and thus cheaper—than local labour.[47]

This crisis has generated a situation whereby there is a huge, growing number of working people who constitute what one author, writing in the parallel context of the global economy, describes as 'the reserve army of migrant labour'. Displaced and dispossessed, they are fully mobile, footloose labour, as willing to work as contract labour for agribusinesses as they are to serve on a construction site or an over-exploitative sweatshop. In any of these circumstances they find it hard to earn survival wages.[48]

CRONY CAPITALISM, LAND WARS AND INTERNAL COLONIALISM

'If you look at the areas where we have so many billionaires, many of them are not software entrepreneurs; it's things like land, real estate, natural resources and areas that require licences . . . there are other areas which are less competitive and where proximity to government helps. That's a worrisome factor . . . there is a danger . . . if we let the nexus between the politician and the businessman get too strong.'

—Raghuram Rajan, chief economist, IMF[1]

The frequency and intensity of protests by Indian farmers has grown in recent years. As we have seen in the previous chapters, they have a dozen things to be angry about. But few things raise the temperature more than land acquisition, perhaps the most explosive issue in India today. As metropolitan India continues to live off the countryside, the latter increasingly rebels against it.

To take just one of a thousand examples: in August 2010 some 25,000 farmers from western UP (Uttar Pradesh) marched to Delhi and stalled traffic to protest the seizure of their cropped lands for Chief Minister Mayawati's Yamuna Expressway, linking Delhi and Agra. It is not the only mega project which is in such trouble. At the time of writing, Mayawati has had to put on hold forced acquisition and the allocation of land to developers to build townships along the expressway. A range of compensation schemes are being proposed to the farmers to resolve the conflict.[2]

Land from the tiller: The Indian enclosure movement?

One of the fundamental commitments made at the dawn of independent India—and dating to the concerns of the freedom struggle during the early decades of the twentieth century—was that the state would ensure the availability of land to the rural poor and the marginal peasantry by carrying out extensive land reform. This was seen as basic to the goal of distributive justice. To this end, for instance, zamindari (absentee landlordism) was legally abolished after Independence. In fact, the promise of 'land to the tiller' informed many electoral campaigns in the decades after Independence. Availability of fertile land to the peasantry was seen as a necessary prerequisite to food security and the removal of rural poverty. Land reforms were not particularly successful in most parts of India. Nonetheless, the intention was important and progress *was* made in some states.

This intention has been completely forsaken in policy circles after the reform era began. The hypocrisy is blatant when you compare the rhetoric of political parties with their actual performance. The UPA (United Progressive Alliance), for instance, in its Common Minimum Programme announced before the 2004 elections that 'landless families will be endowed with land through implementation of land ceiling and land redistribution legislation. No reversal of ceiling will be permitted.' Meanwhile, as we shall see, land legislation across the country is being radically changed, to remove all land ceilings and make agricultural land available for industry, infrastructure, mining, Special Economic Zones (SEZs) or, quite simply, 'land banking'. 'There is real danger of reversal of the land reform agenda', admits a report of the ministry of rural development.[3]

Textbooks of development economics hardly ever acknowledge the routine uprooting of human communities and cultures, euphemistically called 'development-induced displacement'. The way industrial growth is supposed to happen by the book is something like this: mainstream development models presume that most people in a developing country are virtually living in a socio-economic vacuum—in a condition of utter destitution and barely surviving, with little access to any means of subsistence. The government of the country then opens up its markets to 'the world'. (This has happened historically in times of colonialism, under a colonial state. The process persists after independence from foreign rule, though an aggressive form of market liberalization comes to prevail only much later.) As competition arrives, investment pours in, productive jobs are generated, incomes rise, labour moves from agriculture to the cities and, ultimately, prosperity prevails everywhere. The process takes a while, and causes pain to some along the way, but is said to unfold roughly like this.[4]

We know full well—if our cognition is not tinted—that the picture of pre-development destitution and desperation is biased and distorted. Before modern development arrives, most rural families survive by living off land, water, forests, pastures, rivers, the seas or coastlines. In a country like India, every little thing— from fallen twigs and wild grasses to cow dung—finds its place in the everyday subsistence economy of the people. Before the arrival of development, they *do* have access to natural resources, often in the form of the commons, and should not even count among the 'poor' if this access provides them all their basic needs and more. In fact, rural communities even have time remaining for much else including cultural pursuits and the arts, as is clear from the incredibly sophisticated and diverse cultures prevailing in India. There are many disguised forms of deprivation today that afflict the middle classes and the elite, sometimes even more so than they affect the poor. 'Time-poverty', multiple forms of stress and the breakdown of families and communities make up only a partial list of items under what has sometimes been called 'affluenza'. These are forms of deprivation that did not exist in the earlier world order and, occasionally, one can still find poor rural communities free of these modern problems. However, when policies are made, this does not count against 'development' and in favour of the pre-existing ways of life. That is certainly not how poverty and prosperity are measured nowadays.

Insofar as the issue of land is concerned, the government recognizes land as being 'owned' if an individual has an authorized *patta*, or title. In all other cases (except major parts of north-east India) land is considered state property. However, in practice, such land may be part of the commons. It may be a common grazing area, a village forest or a coastal belt shared traditionally by fishermen. These are often areas used by communities for generations without the state providing titles or rights.

The requirements of the mainstream economy are today enormously demanding. To integrate with a globalizing world economy a domestic economy must be created that has, among many other things, smoothly functioning land and property markets. (As we will see, globally powerful firms demand this in order to have an easily transferable portfolio of assets which can be auctioned to the highest bidders at great profit.) What the vast majority of people in the country suffer is the 'collateral damage' of such imbalanced economic growth: they live in the shadow of forces and decisions taken far away from them, very often outside the country, and for considerations that do not concern them whatsoever.

It bears emphasis that the mining and mega projects intended for the 'greater good' of the nation—on account of which so much displacement has happened over the past six decades—have virtually nothing to do with the people who are forced to move. The latter are unable to partake of the benefits that accrue from the projects because, increasingly, such modernizing projects need highly qualified and skilled personnel who usually come from outside the region.

All too often land requirements are overstated and much more land is acquired than is needed for an industrial project. In the case of SEZs this is part of official policy: a very large fraction of the acquired area need not be used for (industrial) 'processing' purposes. Such 'land banking' has become typical of the way businesses now operate in the country.[5]

In places where privatization and enclosure end up depriving village communities of access to the commons, it is the marginalized groups—women and the landless classes in particular—who suffer the most. As a collective form of economic life is lost, rural society is transformed into a set of individuals competing against each other for the crumbs of development. Many of the poor, marginalized classes lose out in the race and village society gets further stratified. The well-off classes, meanwhile, are able to corner the few local gains of the development process—perhaps a few contracts or high levels of compensation with which they could start a new business. Rich landlords around Delhi, for instance, are often the new owners of cab services that have proliferated, even as Dalits who served as agricultural labour in the past go jobless or have to spend money to travel to work every day.

A line of argument often advanced in favour of land acquisition is that a change in land-use from agriculture or forestry to industry raises the value of the land dramatically, especially if the land is close to an urban area. With this greater monetary value of the land, those at the losing end can be more than adequately compensated. This argument has been used to defend land acquisition for SEZs, industry, infrastructure and mining.

This view fails to appreciate the dramatic difference in perception and perspective between the losers and the winners in the transaction. To adivasis, for instance, as for so many other social groups in the country, land is the only and the ultimate source of socio-economic support. It is a real asset which is productive in and of itself, quite independent of its exchange value. In the case of non-monetized barter economies, or those only partially in the monetized economy, it is the very basis of survival. It is also the core of a sense of place, cultural identity and social security. To the wealthy buyer, land is just another form of investment or at best a 'site' for projects whose economic value is not derived from tilling the land itself. Moreover, the people who lose their land often do not have the skill or the experience required to handle (relatively) substantial sums of cash that are offered as compensation by the corporation or the government.

The fundamental question that has to be asked of any change is whether people get to have access to the resources they have at present, or to viable alternatives; whether the change will enlarge or shrink their livelihood *options*. The experience with most displacement till now suggests that people's options shrink once they lose their access to land, water or forests.

The way land has been and is being acquired for industrial or other purposes in India exposes entrenched historical inequalities. Those who must relocate for the nation's progress and development are typically poor and powerless. (Delhi's powerful politicians and bureaucrats are after all not going to move if high-grade iron ore or gold were suddenly discovered under the city. In building the Delhi Metro, the poor were moved in large numbers and refugees were evicted from Paharganj, whereas the lines were diverted away from or taken underground in the richer parts of the city.) An anachronistic piece of legislation from colonial times (the Land Acquisition Act of 1894), meant for the extractive goals of the British empire, is invoked to enable this. In the name of 'public purpose', using the power of 'eminent domain' (the state's prerogative to acquire in 'public interest'), the land of the powerless is seized to promote 'development' projects. The latter essentially enrich an influential lobby of contractors, developers, industrialists, bureaucrats and politicians, along with the urban middle classes and the rural elite.[6]

Following an enduring colonial-era practice, the Indian state arrogates to itself a discretionary power that profoundly distorts land markets, raising asset prices for speculative ends. It is perhaps the single biggest source of corruption in the country, enabling the formation of vast fortunes. If Indian capitalism is accused of being 'crony' in nature, the land market and its sponsors have to shoulder most of the blame.[7]

As this book goes to press, the UPA government has once again postponed discussion in Parliament on what are two of the most significant pieces of proposed legislation in contemporary India, with the greatest bearing on the fate of the rural poor: the Land Acquisition Bill and the Resettlement and Rehabilitation Bill. This is understandable. All political parties, in one or the other state, are keen to keep land issues alive—it serves them well when they are in the Opposition.

Every government since 1947 has failed to notice the glaring contradiction between the forced eviction of marginalized peoples and the promises made to them in the Indian Constitution. In Article 38, to take just one instance of many, the Constitution enjoins the state to 'minimise the inequalities of income . . . and opportunities'. If there is one thing that can be accurately predicted about the use of the Land Acquisition Act in India, it is that it unambiguously increases inequalities of income and opportunities, especially in the all-too-uneven world created by rapid globalization.[8]

It is important—as the Prologue to this section of the book described—to notice the breakdown of rural society under the pressure of rapid commercialization and the accumulation of huge sums of money in the hands of the few who are able to auction out large areas of land. As the availability of guns grows (gun culture is not new to the villages), new forms of violence are emerging in the countryside and the urban centres in their vicinity, in addition to older, feudal modes of violence, especially in north India.[9]

What we are witnessing across the country today is perhaps an accelerated Indian version of the Enclosure movement which engulfed the British countryside over a period of three–four centuries stretching right across the period of the Industrial Revolution in the eighteenth century. This long and complex process entailed the forced eviction of millions of peasants from their traditional fields, commons and homesteads. The peasants of early modern Britain resisted this process, as was witnessed in the numerous insurrections. In fact, resistance continued all the way till the middle of the nineteenth century.[10]

The Enclosure movement was a violent process. Listen to British historian, Christopher Hill, writing about the enclosures in seventeenth-century Britain:

> The royal policy of disafforestation and enclosure, or of draining the Fens, as applied before 1640, involved disrupting a way of life, a brutal disregard for the rights of commoners . . . a consequence of the policy was to force men to sole dependence on wage labour, which many regarded as little better than slavery.[11]

Eric Hobsbawm writes of England a century and a half later:

> Some 5000 enclosures under the private and general Enclosure Acts broke up some six million acres of common fields and common lands from 1760 onwards, transformed them into private holdings . . . The Poor Laws of 1834 were designed to make life so intolerable for the rural paupers as to force them to migrate to any jobs offered. And indeed they soon began to do so. In the 1840s several counties were already on the verge of an absolute loss of population, and from 1850 land-flight became general.[12]

What happened in Britain—and is now being repeated in a different, far more accelerated form in India—was best summarized by the historian E.P. Thompson: 'Enclosures were a plain enough case of class robbery.'[13]

It is difficult to see how the vast majority of India's huge rural population can find a semblance of justice within the broader, aggressive dispensations of globalization without a sound, equitable, democratically developed land policy implemented by the state. A Central government report also discusses a range of measures to provide adequate security to large, threatened sections of India's rural population. Some of the more salient recommendations are:

1. The Land Acquisition Act should be amended to incorporate (Resettlement and Rehabilitation) policies.
2. Common Property Resources (CPRs) should not be acquired without providing deprived villagers with alternative sources of fodder, fuel and other necessities.
3. An independent policy needs to be drawn up to protect and develop CPRs in the interest of village communities.
4. The crucial piece of legislation for tribal (Schedule V) areas—Panchayat (Extension to the Scheduled Areas) Act (PESA)—enacted in 1996, should be implemented in these regions in order that the latter derive the full advantage of panchayat-based local governance.
5. Tribals ought to be given pattas to the land which they have been traditionally living off.
6. Legislation needs to be enacted to protect women's rights to land and homesteads.
7. Given the paucity of arable land in the country, there should be a ban on conversion of agricultural land for non-agricultural uses.
8. Much better environmental governance at the local level needs to be achieved by creating, for instance, a district regulatory authority that monitors land, water and forest issues which arise in the context of development projects. *Gram sabhas* too need to be activated for the purpose.
9. Land reforms constitute a key element in ensuring distributive justice in an agrarian society. A National

Land Reforms Policy has to be enacted to ensure the resumption of land reforms in the country.

10. There is urgent need for an active land-use plan at the local, state and national levels. While land is a state subject under the Indian Constitution, all sorts of policies (such as SEZs) have been launched by the Centre, which have actually taken land out of the access of people most in need of it. So a land-use plan needs to have concurrence and acceptance at all levels of decision-making in India's three-tier system of governance. It must address all the key concerns in relation to land: ecology, food security, livelihood and industry.[14]

Special Economic Zones (SEZs)

One way to understand the spatial impact of globalization is to recognize that we do not live in places any more. Everyone is now beginning to live in 'zones', around this or that 'hub'. Instead of rivers and meadows, lakes and mountains being the markers of our personal geographies, we now have spaces and zones, hubs and corridors. Ecology has ceased to matter, abstract economics is king. Nothing exemplifies this better than the story of SEZs, which began to unfold during the latter half of the decade gone by.

SEZs belong to a category of spatial reorganization that the globalizing world economy appears to need, in order to negotiate the political and legal challenges posed by democracies in industrializing countries. Fundamental changes to the globalizing world are being made through structural alterations in the layout and architecture of the modern industrial economy, backed by the letter of the law. Zones are probably the most elaborate method of reorganizing space for corporate interests. They insist on exclusivity and become the preferred legal home for corporations, enabling smoothness in investment and profit-making.

An SEZ is a specially demarcated area of land, typically owned and operated by a private developer in which production units are exempt from taxes, duties and tariffs. After the hasty passage of the SEZ Act by the Indian parliament in June 2005 (within a few days of the bill being tabled), the law came into effect in February 2006. A policy of immense scope, with the potential to affect tens of millions of working people in the country, was approved by our legislators as a mere formality. There was barely a murmur in the media. In contrast, Chinese policymakers, even in a totalitarian state, deliberated for years before launching their SEZs in the early 1980s.[15]

SEZs are meant primarily to promote exports and draw foreign investment, though the government claims they are also designed to generate employment, infrastructure and, of course, overall growth. The predecessors of SEZs were EPZs (Export Processing Zones), starting with the Kandla EPZ in 1965. But for EPZs, minimum export targets were set. SEZs, according to the rules issued by the Indian government, only have to earn net positive foreign exchange in order to keep their status.[16]

The policy thrust for SEZs came after former commerce minister Murasoli Maran's trip to China in 2000. Impressed by his visit to the Chinese city of Shenzhen—site of the world's largest and most successful SEZ—Maran prevailed on policymakers to get traction for SEZs as part of the Export Import or EXIM trade policy of the government.[17]

Shenzhen is the showpiece of Chinese SEZs. But what is widely hailed as a 'success' has such a fierce dark side that it led a visiting *New York Times* reporter to remark: 'Few cities anywhere have created wealth faster than Shenzhen, but the costs of its phenomenal success stare out from every corner: environmental destruction, soaring crime rates and the disillusionment and degradation of its vast force of migrant workers.' The report further points out that 'among Chinese economic planners, Shenzhen's recipe is increasingly seen as all but irrelevant: too harsh, too wasteful, too polluted, too dependent on the churning, ceaseless turnover of migrant labor. "This path is now a dead end," said Zhao Xiao, an economist and former adviser to the Chinese State Council . . . After cataloguing the city's problems, he said, "Governments can't count on the beauty of investment covering up 100 other kinds of ugliness."'[18]

This is the SEZ model that India's policymaking elite is busy trying to emulate, long after it has been rejected in China itself. The ultimate failure of Shenzhen—as well as the 'zone fever' that spawned destructive real-estate bubbles all over China—has been well-documented elsewhere.[19]

Not surprisingly, conditions in existing Indian SEZs resemble Shenzhen much more than those obtaining in other Chinese cities on the east coast. In the SEZ at Noida, near Delhi, for instance, 40 per cent of the 10,000 workers are women on casual labour who work up to ten–twelve hours a day for wages of around Rs 1800 per month, lower than the labour market outside. (Women workers are preferred because they are more 'docile'.) Their choice is between working and starving. They work and live in harsh conditions, without maternity leave, minimum wages or any other benefits like gratuity or pensions. They are issued tokens to visit the toilet. According to a maternity doctor who works in the area, the exploitation of workers is 'unimaginable'. As one can expect, the SEZ has reported high profits over the years. Similar, if marginally less worrying, conditions have been reported from recent studies of the SEZs at Santa Cruz, Mumbai, and Falta, West Bengal.[20]

The state of play

At the time of writing, the area being taken by all the SEZs with at least 'in-principle approval' is already over 200,000 ha (2000 sq km, or greater than the area of Delhi in the National Capital Region).[21]

In the name of cutting red tape, the process for approval of SEZ projects has been greatly simplified by a 'single-window clearance' procedure, making a mockery of things like environmental clearance. Ostensibly aimed at industrialization, SEZs are being created for the construction of everything from industrial and commercial complexes to residential areas, hotels, shopping malls and entertainment centres (the latter unjustly included in 'infrastructure'). In many places, a full-fledged city is being conceived, much along the lines of Shenzhen.[22]

The SEZ is to be administered by an SEZ Authority, comprising two representatives of the private developer in addition to four officials appointed by the Central government.

Recent history of the SEZ policy

The SEZ policy in India was misconceived from the start. As should have been anticipated by our policymakers, by the summer of 2006, soon after the act had taken effect, protests against SEZs took off in various parts of the country. It culminated in the massacre carried out at Nandigram by the police and CPM cadre in West Bengal on 14 March 2007. Many parts of the country—Pen, Vagholi and Alibag in Maharashtra; Barnala in Punjab; Dadri in UP; Jhajjar in Haryana; Gopalpur and Jagatsinghpur in Orissa; and Nandagudi and Mangalore in Karnataka, to name but a few—have witnessed loud and vocal protests against the SEZ policy.[23]

After the first set of protests at Nandigram in January 2007, in which half a dozen people were killed, the prime minister called a halt to SEZ construction until a 'humane' rehabilitation policy was put in place. Though the new Resettlement and Rehabilitation Bill has not been passed yet, SEZs continue to meet with formal approval every few months or less.

In the wake of Nandigram, the state was forced to amend its SEZ policy. There have been three main changes. The size of SEZs has been capped at 5000 ha for multi-product SEZs. There was no cap earlier, leaving plenty of room for speculation in real estate, apart from taking larger chunks of land from farmers. The amendment interferes with the plans of some of the larger SEZs planned by conglomerates like Reliance and DLF. It is not clear how they will acquire the size of land they desire. One way to circumvent the new law is to acquire two or more contiguous territories adding up to 8000 or 10,000 ha. The minister of commerce has indicated that the government is willing to be flexible on this score.[24]

Another change in the amended SEZ policy is potentially more important. The government will no longer be involved in acquiring the land for the developer. In other words, unlike in the past, recourse will not be taken to 'eminent domain' and the 'public purpose' clauses in the Land Acquisition Act of 1894. In a context like rural India where landholdings are small and fragmented, companies needed the state to exercise its powers of eminent domain. How they will now acquire land is an open question. In the absence of state intervention, even if one farmer refuses to sell his/her land (or demands 'exorbitant' prices), it could stall an industrial project. On the other hand, there is the very real threat of local land mafia, who can be used to coerce unwilling villagers to give up their land. The state has a constitutional duty to protect the property rights of the landowners. It is not clear whether it will meet this expectation. By now, in some cases, the land mafia have already been mobilized for their 'appointed' task.[25]

Finally, it has been promised that no irrigated land will be acquired; however, in practice this has not been implemented in most states, where both irrigated and rain-fed lands continue to be taken over.

Land acquisition and displacement

SEZs are responsible for a new round of displacement of people. Despite pronouncements to the contrary, most of the land being acquired is agricultural, some of it even multiple-cropped. In fact, a plot of planned SEZs on the Indian map suggests that these are being considered in areas of developed infrastructure clustered around twenty cities and/or ports. (Building SEZs on so-called wastelands, which constitute over 20 per cent of the land in the country, would obviously involve substantial investment in infrastructure, something no private investor wishes to do.) Not surprisingly, areas of developed infrastructure happen to be coincident with prime agricultural land. Instead of contributing to the further development of infrastructure, as per one of the official claims, SEZs will piggyback on the existing rural infrastructure—of water, roads and power—built over the decades to support rural, agricultural populations close to cities or ports.

In a few SEZ areas like Jhajjar (Haryana), some of the more affluent peasantry has not been loath to part with (at least a fraction of) their large land. The economics work in their favour in the long term. If, by selling off a quarter of their land, they raise the value of the remaining three-quarters to an amount exceeding the initial value of the entire landholding, then they strike a profitable bargain.

However, small or marginal farmers with a few acres or less are left high and dry. Their limited resources do not give them the luxury to play the market. If their land is acquired forcibly, they are typically left landless. The cash compensation, even when somewhat fair (based on the market price), does not make up for the security of owning a productive asset. Besides, for many older farmers, the shift to a non-agricultural way of life is a practical impossibility.

Loss of livelihoods

Estimates show that close to 114,000 farming households and an additional 82,000 farm worker families will be displaced by the land acquisition for SEZs. In other words, at least 1 million people who primarily depend upon agriculture for their survival will face eviction. Some experts calculate that the total loss of income to the farming and the farm worker families is at least Rs 212 crore a year. This does not include other incomes and livelihoods lost (for instance, of artisans) due to the demise of local rural economies. Many more families and communities depend on a piece of land (for work, grazing) than those who own it outright. However, compensation is discussed only for those who hold titles to land. [26]

Consequences for agriculture and food security

SEZs will affect the country's already very fragile food security. For each SEZ with an area of 5000 ha, the lost production would have been able to feed 50,000 to 100,000 people for a year. (We are assuming each hectare can produce enough cereal to feed about ten–twenty people a year.) This translates roughly to annual cereal needs of about 2–4 million people being lost across the country.[27]

The 200,000 ha being acquired may be a small proportion of the net sown area of agricultural land in the country (140,000,000 ha), but it is some of the most fertile land. Secondly, given the fact that SEZs have been assured water and power supply, the overall shortage of both in the country implies that these will be drawn from agricultural use in the surrounding countryside, adversely impacting productivity. Thirdly, the mushrooming of SEZs—should they be seen to 'work'—in the future, and thus the acquisition of more agricultural land, cannot be ruled out. What is to forestall a 'zone fever' of the kind that China experienced in the 1990s, with disastrous consequences for agriculture? Each additional hectare of agricultural land taken for industrial purposes will imply that around twenty fewer people can be fed from domestic sources. Finally, the takeover of agricultural land will have negative effects on investment in farming, especially in the vicinity of cities and SEZs. Why should farmers invest in tube wells or soil conservation if they fear losing the land in the future?[28]

It appears that the SEZ law is against agriculture only insofar as indigenous farmers practise it. Under the term 'manufacturing', the SEZ Act allows activities as variegated as industrial processes like refrigeration and engineering on the one hand, and mining, agriculture, aquaculture and horticulture on the other. If SEZs are meant to promote the industrialization of the country, how are activities like agriculture or horticulture being permitted within them? Is there some back-door provision for the future interests of national and transnational agribusiness—the lobby that drives so much of policy today? In the absence of concrete information from the state one can only wonder. [29]

SEZs: Environmental issues

The change in land-use patterns due to the transfer of land from agriculture to industry will inevitably have profound ecological consequences, both in terms of resource depletion and pollution. Units operating within SEZs are expected to abide by environmental laws and will be required to get pollution clearance from the development commissioner, the head of the SEZ Authority. Environmental clearance from the ministry of environment and forests (MoEF) is required for SEZs, much like for any development project, as per the EIA (Environment Impact Assessment) notification of 2006. [30]

However, in practice this is often just a formality, neglecting crucial clearance procedures such as public hearings. Giant SEZ projects, such as the one at Mundra in Gujarat, have typically been exempted from due process. In Mundra it has meant the loss of thousands of hectares of invaluable mangroves, as well as the livelihoods of fishers and pastoralists. [31]

Exploitation of labour in SEZs

The provisions of the SEZ Act of 2005 do not lend credibility to government claims that SEZs are in the interests of the people as a whole. It leaves little power in the hands of workers employed within them. SEZs have been declared 'public utility services' under the Industrial Disputes Act. This means that in SEZ areas workers have no right to strike or even to form unions and organize collectively to bargain for better wages or working conditions.

The SEZ policy of the government transfers all the powers of the state labour commissioner to the development commissioners of the SEZs. The development commissioner is supposed to mediate all disputes between workers and management, unlike in the case of industrial units outside SEZs, where the labour commissioner resolves them. Under such conditions the chances of the needs of workers being addressed are remote. Workers have significant concerns—protection from contract labour, child labour, sexual harassment, discrimination—to which there may be no legal recourse under the SEZ regime.[32]

In addition to the rules issued by the Central government, the state governments have been issuing their own, each one trying to outbid the other in terms of offering easier terms for investors. Some states are even allowing the use of contract labour or allowing work for 365 days per year—even for twenty-four hours a day (if overtime is paid)![33]

Revenue losses (Tax exemptions)

SEZs are leading to huge revenue losses for the public exchequer.[34] Prospective developers and entrepreneurs are being attracted to invest in SEZs through plenty of fiscal exemptions under every category of taxation. Into what sum of money do all these exemptions translate? The government's own data reveals that this was Rs 1,75,000 crore ($40 billion) between 2006 and 2010 alone, an amount equal to 6 per cent of the Central government's annual receipts in 2009–10. This huge revenue loss is why the ministry of finance had opposed SEZs from the beginning. The sum is greater than the allocation for the country's flagship employment programme, the MGNREGA, which could provide jobs to 43 million people.[35]

The SEZ, it appears, is not just about stealing land. It is about institutionalizing a subsidized way of doing business, by giving them enough state padding. Their export, employment and infrastructure potentials are hugely exaggerated. In brief, the export requirements on them are too loose and can easily lead to a drain of foreign exchange from the country. They have generated just over 250,000 jobs since 2005, compared to the 3 million which the government was expecting. And, finally, they have been 'poaching' infrastructure from agriculture, much more than generating new facilities.[36]

'Real Estate Zones'?

A walk around any large Indian city today offers a blinding spectacle of construction activity. It is aimed at making roads, flyovers, luxury residential high-rises, exclusive commercial office spaces, world-class retail spaces, glittering shopping malls, multiplexes, amusement parks, deluxe hotels and IT parks, some of these in SEZs. It is apparent that Downtown India is ready to take off from the stench of neighbouring slums, fly into a globalized stratosphere and assume its pride of place in the company of the world's most powerful nations.

In years to come it is quite possible that real estate might replace IT/BPO (business process outsourcing) as the lead growth story in the Indian economy. The reasons are many. First, there is a desperate shortage of housing and commercial space in India. Secondly, Indian developers and builders—the big names are DLF, Ansals, Unitech, Raheja, Omaxe, Hiranandani, to name but a few—have accumulated vast sums of capital in recent years. (Their owners are now some of the richest people in the world.) Thirdly, overseas investors—especially financial and real estate mega corporations in the US and the UK—are on the lookout for quick and high returns in India and China. (Most analysts expect the Indian real estate market to grow faster than the saturated Chinese one, which in any case was constrained till recently by not allowing freehold land ownership.)

In an interview, a Swiss private equity firm executive explained why he started investing in India: 'We started looking at India because the return expectations in Europe and the US were slowing down due to the huge capital overhang . . . [T]hree to four years ago, there was so much capital that investors were beginning to expect very low returns. We had to look outside because we had a target of 25–30 per cent . . . return, and we could only get that by looking at some of the more under-served markets. So, we set up operations in India.' The sentiment resonates with that of an American investor: 'We're running out of markets. Where would we go next? . . . So we're trying to invest in a platform in India that will produce profits year after year.' Really profitable investment alternatives are shrinking everywhere. The Indian sky thus shines brighter. 'In the last several decades, perhaps since World War II, there has not been this scale of opportunity anywhere in the world for the private sector to participate in upgrading a country's complete infrastructure,' says Daniel MacEachron of Hines, a large US developer invested in India.[37]

Last, and most significantly from our point of view, the SEZ policy has been designed not only to buffer the risks of industrial investment by allowing large fractions of land to be 'fallow' for real estate development but also with the thinly disguised aim of enabling developers to profit, even if industrial investors may not.[38]

As a result, SEZ developers are having a party. For example, in the huge Mundra SEZ in Kachchh, Gujarat, the developers, the Adanis, were sold 3150 ha of land at an average rate of Rs 10 per sq m by the state government. Some of this was land legally designated as 'grazing land', which should have been rightfully left in the hands of the gram sabha. The Adanis have subsequently sub-leased it for as much as Rs 1000 per sq m to private companies after basic infrastructural development. Thousands of hectares of ecologically invaluable mangrove trees have been chopped to make way for the SEZ. Similar stories of outright land-grab, which has cheated villagers of their only productive asset, are also heard from other parts of the country, such as Kalinganagar in Orissa or Dadri near Delhi.[39]

While the government has done little to preserve the land rights of farmers or to allay fears of land speculation, the real estate sector of the economy has boomed (till the recent recession). A senior executive at the investment banking firm Goldman Sachs says that 'India is the most exciting real estate market in Asia'. A 2007 ASSOCHAM report concurs.[40]

One reason why developers have shown so much interest in SEZs is because such investment—given its cheap purchase of land (and thus the potential for profit in leasing the land)—dramatically raises the share value of their firms at the stock exchange. This is what happened, for instance, when the Adanis did their Initial Public Offering for their Mundra Port SEZ a few years back: it was oversubscribed by over a hundred times and collected over Rs 2,00,000 crore. Land requirements for industrial projects are typically overstated in most cases to serve as a buffer for investors.[41]

All the big players in the Indian real estate market, including those mentioned above, are in the business of SEZs. Clearly, there is something about SEZs which is extremely attractive to a developer. In an infrastructurally inadequate country like India, even a little investment in developing the land fetches a disproportionately higher premium in the real estate market. The RBI (Reserve Bank of India) has thus, appreciating the risks of land speculation (which bankrupted so many banks in China), classified loans for SEZ investment as 'real estate lending', involving higher rates of interest.[42]

The possibility of SEZs turning into a gigantic real estate scam remains all too real—if not the most likely outcome—especially if investment in production units is not forthcoming or if exports fail to take off. The problem is that not all the area acquired for an SEZ is meant for industrial processing and manufacturing.

The processing area within an SEZ was first pegged at 25 per cent of the acquired land. It was raised to 35 per cent under pressure from critics and later, after protests, raised further to 50 per cent. The rationale for neglecting such a clause is the uncertainty surrounding the economic attractiveness (and ultimate viability) of SEZs. If adequate productive investment is not forthcoming, the SEZ developer can at least cash in on the land value.

All the problems with regard to SEZs are exacerbated by the entry of large amounts of foreign capital into the Indian real estate market. Foreign direct investment (FDI) in Indian real estate was liberalized in January 2007. This boosted the total FDI coming into India. By 2006–07 over a quarter of the overall FDI was real estate investment. Powerful global investors—from investment banks like Goldman Sachs and Morgan Stanley to private equity firms like Blackstone—have since shown significant interest in the Indian real estate market.[43]

Indian growth has a very narrow base. When investment opportunities other than in the financial and the real estate sectors begin to dry up in the future (with more saturated middle-class markets and indebted consumers), all the cash in the economy will need a place to park itself. It will either fly out of the country (particularly if the government makes the rupee 100 per cent convertible on the capital account—a proposal that is in the offing) or it will continue to feed the real estate 'boom', or bubble, to be more precise. A good proportion is likely to end up using surplus SEZ land as numbers on a roulette dial. So, in the end, the land will have been acquired from Indian farmers to allow the casino of global finance to operate more smoothly. What Wall Street invests in India may be a pittance for it. But it is enough to play with the Indian economy and turn the country into a gambling den. It would be interesting to see, after the passage of some years, what proportion of India's prime land is owned by global financial mega corporations, including the Indian counterparts.

One assessment of the situation concludes:

> The business press makes clear that the forces of globalization see the Indian real estate sector as a bonanza; land prices are by international standards low, and now is the time to make sure that the future increase in prices will benefit global capital—not the residents. Using 'development' as dress, compliant state governments are put to use, invoking colonial statutes to seize vast properties juridically. In these obscene deals, for each lakh of Reliance or Tata or Goldman Sachs' future real estate profits, a thousand or more of poor rural residents are driven from their lands into the slums.[44]

Not for nothing do our newspapers nowadays come wrapped in property market pull-outs screaming 'Venice in Greater Noida'.[45] As one analyst summarizes:

As land in India is integrated into international markets, it is being transformed into a new financial instrument: real estate. Like other financial games, real estate speculation is a form of betting based on the assumption that prices will continue to increase. Actual demand for housing does not enter the picture, as one needs little justification for short-term investing in such a hot market. However, longer term investors—large Indian developers, private equity firms, international developers, and others—require more complex justifications. Developers and private equity firms tell stories about India's growth to garner investment from abroad and guide their own investment strategies. Like the construction-site hoardings in Gurgaon, these stories describe an alternative India quite divorced from the reality on the ground; they result in buildings which cater to an imagined future and a present elite.[46]

However, the future is uncertain, as the great recession has shown recently:

As in other highly speculative enterprises, 'profit must be imagined before it can be extracted; the possibility of economic performance must be conjured like a spirit to draw an audience of potential investors.' How do Indian developers and fund managers conjure the possibility of profit? How do they attract investment to fuel the construction of Indian real estate? They do so by telling stories about growth . . . Investor presentations, industry reports, and company prospectuses—all documents used to interest potential investors—employ a rhetoric of growth to demonstrate how the demand produced by the leading edge of economic liberalization indicates plenty of future demand for real estate products like malls and office parks . . . Everything on the PowerPoint slide is rising, expanding, growing, or improving . . . These stories about growth create expectations about growth. Expectations spur investment, which in turn fuels more growth. It is an inflationary spiral . . . Real estate developers and foreign investors are building landscapes for Indian and foreign elites and becoming rich doing it . . . the gamble that many private equity firms, domestic real estate funds, real estate developers and others are taking presupposes a particular economic and social future for India . . . However far-fetched this future may seem given the present realities of poverty, underemployment, environmental abuse, and social inequality, it is guiding the transformation of India's land into a resource of capital accumulation for investors, developers, and landowners. The result is the production of elite landscapes—helipads, fancy private hospitals, golf courses, gated high-rises, and five-star hotels—which mark a gross misallocation of resources away from the infrastructure that India's people need: water, sanitation, mass transport, housing.[47]

It is not just the metropolitan cities that are being eyed with avarice. So too are smaller places (Tier II and Tier III cities). As property markets in the metros have, for the time being, peaked, land-sharks have been advising both Indian and foreign developers and investors to acquire and develop properties in younger land markets in towns and cities as far afield as Sonepat in Haryana and Siliguri in West Bengal.

The entire story of large-scale land-grab in the country, especially in the urban setting, cannot be explained satisfactorily unless one understands India as one of the chief cultivated destinations of global finance today, the IFIs having played the pivotal role in this transformation. High growth in India is needed to maximize returns from financial markets. The expansion of the real estate economy is very much part of this overall game.

The new corporate city state: A pilot experiment in private governance?

SEZs might inaugurate a fresh chapter in the privatization of governance. To serve their purpose, they will have to be run quite differently from the rest of the province in which they are geographically located. It might be a bit like the centralized rule under which Union Territories in the country function—minus the local elections. There will be no elected local government drawn from state legislatures, town councils or local panchayats. Nor will there be any labour welfare officers. What is to prevent an unaccountable corporate oligarchy from emerging from such a cabal of officials?

SEZs, having been developed by a private party, will be outside the purview of town planners and gram sabhas alike and will be run exclusively by the SEZ Authority. This, as has been noted widely, is a violation of the 73rd and 74th Amendments to the Constitution which guarantee, respectively, constitutional status to urban local governance and panchayats. It has implications for the rural poor who will stand to suffer most from regional environmental damage (such as drying up of groundwater), but will be unable to control or tax SEZs. Shenzhen is a warning poster on the wall.

Further, entry into (physically bounded) SEZs will be regulated by identity cards, making them inaccessible to people of the region. Creating an artifical 'foreign territory' within the geographical boundaries of the nation undermines constitutional rights like freedom of movement. Over time, citizens' rights are likely to be further infringed, with the state taking resort, as in South-East Asia, to concepts that can be described as 'graduated sovereignty' to legally create a citizenry of lower rank.[48]

SEZs offer us a keyhole view into the future desired by globalized corporate lobbies. They can be seen as a pilot experiment in real time and space, with real people, for a new political order: the autonomous corporate city state.[49]

SEZs may serve as just the sort of experiment corporate India wants to carry out. They may become the nucleus of newly sanitized Indian cities without the slums, *jhopadpatti*s and resettlement colonies which 'mar' the visual horizon in India's 'natural' cities.[50]

Perhaps the most heroic clause in the SEZ Act is Clause 51, which states that the provisions of the Act will 'have overriding effect' over 'anything inconsistent . . . in any other law . . . in force'. As to which laws are covered by such an overarching imposition is left happily unspecified. Jurists can perhaps comment on whether such legislation is in harmony with the required constitutionality of lawmaking. In principle, it appears to make unlawful virtually anything which runs foul of the aims of the SEZ Act.[51]

Hyper-global urbanism: Metros as financial products

We have seen how metros and cities have come to constitute the dominating space through which India has been integrating with a globalizing world. Cities are seen as engines of growth today. They compete with each other for international investment, tourism, public funds, big events like the Olympics or the Commonwealth Games. Further, to run modern industry and services, skilled and educated labour has to be attracted from around the world. Thus, there is constant discussion in India nowadays of how best to 'brand' our cities, especially since they do not have adequate infrastructure. Efficient governance and 'flexible' land and property markets are needed, as also high environmental standards and a globally competitive quality of life. So the main consequence of globalization has been that Indian cities, far from acknowledging their links with the rural hinterland on whose sufferance they are running, have been benchmarked against other 'world cities'.

As the rush to turn Indian urban spaces into 'world-class cities' grows, the patterns of urban governance are changing rapidly. Nowhere is the rise of corporate power more evident than in the way decisions concerning Indian cities are being taken and how they have come to be governed. Decision-making authority—involving large sums of money—is rapidly moving from constitutionally provided and accountable administrative boards like the urban local bodies to unelected, unaccountable platforms.[52]

The urban reform agenda has been generated by the synchronized efforts of multilateral, sometimes private, agencies such as FICCI (Federation of Indian Chambers of Commerce and Industry), CII (Confederation of Indian Industry), USAID (United States Agency for International Development), ADB (Asian Development Bank) and the World Bank in conjunction with various ministries of the Central government. Consider the government's flagship urban development programme, the JNNURM (Jawaharlal Nehru National Urban Renewal Mission). It is an incentive-driven scheme of the Central government aimed at funding state governments and urban bodies engaged in suitable urban development schemes. It involves a total investment of over Rs 1,00,000 crore over a period of seven years, the kitty within reach of only sixty-three cities in the country.

What are the main items on the urban reform agenda? It involves, among other things, *full* liberalization of the land, housing and real estate markets through such radical moves as the repeal of Urban Land Ceiling Acts (ULCAs) and the mobilization of funds for infrastructural investment through financial markets and PPPs (public–private partnerships). In the past, ULCAs have served the important purpose of protecting ordinary citizens—howsoever imperfectly—against the accumulation of exclusive land banks by powerful developers and property dealers. Crucially, funds under the JNNURM are not released by the Central government till such time as the state ULCA is repealed (land is a state subject under the Indian Constitution). Their repeal means that housing for the middle- and low-income groups and the poor (who together make up half to three-quarters of cities like Mumbai) is being neglected to make way for high-revenue-generating projects—like exclusive office blocks, luxury housing, shopping malls and multiplexes. This raises the global profile of the city in the eyes of potential investors, but makes it next to impossible for vast sections of the citizenry to inhabit it.[53]

Funds for municipalities are now contingent on performance as judged by credit-rating agencies. The former are being asked to raise their own funds from capital markets. This has consequences. Only those projects that can yield quick, high and assured returns are likely to be undertaken. Further, regional disparities may emerge as only a handful of city corporations will be in a position to raise capital. Finally, the poor, already suffering under the weight of mass evictions, are going to be priced out of the new delivery systems that are based on user charges. According to the National Urban Housing and Habitat Policy, 2007, 99 per cent of the housing shortage in India is among the economically vulnerable groups. But their needs do not find much expression in the new urban reform package.[54]

A good illustration of where the sights of policymakers are set, and how decisions are being taken about Indian metros is provided by Mumbai, which is being promoted as an international financial centre (IFC). The High-Powered Expert Committee on Urban Infrastructure (HPEC) was set up some years back by the government to recommend steps to be taken to reach such a goal. The idea is to tap into the enormous flow of money that takes place routinely nowadays through global financial hubs like London, New York and and Singapore. These cities offer a wide range of services: international consultancy, legal help, tax management and accounting, management of assets and personal wealth, and so on. Share markets in these cities have high rates of turnover of money as investors trade the shares of firms from around the world. Their foreign exchange markets also enjoy a lot of attention, and money is made through complex instruments like currency derivatives. These activities are all enormously lucrative.[55]

The HPEC pointed out in its report that India too can earn these high incomes by overhauling both Mumbai and the rest of the Indian economy in order to draw the internationally mobile financial, legal and accounting firms that control the markets. Only about a quarter of the expected employees in this sector would be Indians, the rest being expatriates.

In 2007 the HPEC laid down some forty-eight requirements for making Mumbai an IFC. Among the more radical recommendations are the following: maintain double-digit growth rates for the macroeconomy (in order to sustain the global image of India as an emerging economic giant and keep the money flowing in); drastically cut down fiscal deficits at both the Centre and the states (this was before the recession); implement full capital account convertibility; open up Indian government debt and the capital markets to funds from abroad (including the dangerous hedge funds); eliminate key taxes and duties; withdraw government from the banking sector altogether; allow unrestricted entry to global legal and accounting firms operating in IFCs, and so on. Perhaps the most striking recommendation was a political one: that a 'city manager' be appointed for purposes of urban governance!

The recommendations are sweeping. The head of the HPEC, an ex-World Bank official, told a financial daily: 'If I have to give one piece of advice to Prime Minister Manmohan Singh, I would ask him to let go of Government control over the financial sector.' Any state intervention for the purpose of developing or protecting the rest of the economy is to be avoided. The government cannot borrow to meet social priorities like health or food. It cannot prioritize credit at affordable rates for farmers, small industry or disadvantaged social groups. No revenue can be raised from the high-turnover financial and real estate markets. Government can no longer regulate international capital flows. Decision-making for virtually the entire economy is to be handed over to the whims and fancies of a cabal of globally powerful speculative investors. It is not clear how the HPEC's radical recommendations are to be implemented in a country like India. Yet, the finance minister in his 2007–08 Budget speech said, 'It is my hope that we would be able to build a consensus on the key recommendations of the Committee, promote a world class financial centre in Mumbai, and realise the objective of *making financial services the next growth engine for India.*'[56]

All urban planning and development is being geared towards transforming metropolitan India into an attractive financial product which can be hawked to globally powerful firms (and of course to the rich in India) in the expectation of drawing Downtown India even more into the mainstream circuits of global capital.

The future of Indian cities: Barricaded metropolitan republics?

Urban studies scholar Mike Davis provides a disturbing image of Third World urban futures. 'Instead of cities of light soaring toward heaven,' he writes, 'much of the twenty-first century urban world squats in squalor, surrounded by pollution, excrement, and decay.'[57]

This is an accurate picture of urban and metropolitan India. While the elite live in 'islands of cyber-modernity' and have their parties, most of a city's population is hard at work making it possible—almost all of its waking hours spent on putting together the bare means of daily survival. The rapidly rising inequalities and uncertainties of globalizing India imply that even if many urban working and serving class families are monetarily better off than half a generation ago, inflation, job insecurity, subhuman working and living conditions and everyday stress take a heavy toll on them.[58]

There is probably no arena of life in India today where socio-economic exclusion is as palpable as in the patterns of living spaces. Until now, the rich and the poor everywhere in Indian cities have lived cheek by jowl, the lives of the former inextricably dependent on the work performed by the latter. While the core of such dependency remains unchanged, there is increasingly greater physical distance between the two classes now, as the former are succeeding in creating spaces where it becomes much easier to turn one's eyes away from poverty. Urban India today offers a rapidly changing spectacle of a somewhat subtle social layering of the less privileged classes, who have been professionalized into serving the requirements of the wealthy. Many companies have come up to recruit the labour and organize the services—from security to laundry and housekeeping—which minister to the needs of the rich.

Today the wealthy can choose from a growing variety of arrangements—from secluded suburban townships and luxury high-rises with captive infrastructure to private cities, remote resorts and gated communities (the new global fashion since the 1990s)—whereby they can live, work and educate their children without having to encounter the squalor and misery in which poor and struggling India lives. Their only point of contact with people who survive the other India is that the latter are their critical service-providers. The chief selling point of these new homes for the wealthy is their exclusiveness and club-like character. Increasingly, this pattern resembles similar, long-standing arrangements in the cities of Latin America and South-East Asia, where 'apartheid' systems of segregated living, or ghettoization, have long since been institutionalized.[59]

The only significant difference between the living arrangements of colonial India and those of globalizing India is that recent economic growth has generated hopes—real or false—of the possibility of upward social mobility for *all*. The claims of the new India are universal. In a growing, globalizing economy, almost everyone who does not live in a gated community may come to aspire to live as the gated classes do.

The other difference between colonial and present-day urban living arrangements is that the segregation is more along the lines of class than of race, while in the past the two social categories were coincident to a significant degree.

There is a pattern to the visual and social transformation of the metropolitan cityscape. Utterly modest shelters of the poor—if found in the midst of otherwise posh areas—are being rapidly cleared to make way for high-value real estate projects, often with funding from multilateral institutions like the World Bank. This is happening across Indian cities. Jeremy Seabrook's term 'Infrastruction'—which in one concise word encapsulates both the destruction of the urban poor's living habitat as well as the construction of infrastructure and buildings for the wealthy—

is all too apt to describe what is happening. However, this may give the benefit of the doubt to the authorities in assuming that land is always being seized from the poor for public infrastructural development. Very often it is simply being handed over to private interests for a song.[60]

Gated living areas for the wealthy are increasingly coming to resemble well-guarded fortresses. The following description of certain neighbourhoods in Manila is increasingly familiar in Indian settings:

> An elaborate system of iron gates, roadblocks and checkpoints demarcates the boundaries of the area and cuts it off from the rest of the city, at least at night-time . . . The threats to life, limb, and property are the overwhelming common concern of the wealthy residents. Houses are turned into virtual fortresses by surrounding them with high walls topped by glass shards, barbed wire, and heavy iron bars on all windows.[61]

This 'architecture of fear', in the words of a Nigerian sociologist, is quite typical of Third World metros today.[62]

Architecture and architectural exclusion readily betray the secrets of a society. The physical spaces we create for our living and working arrangements tell us much about who we are and whom we wish to associate with and how. The fact that Indian metros are being replanned to turn Mumbai into 'Shanghai' and Delhi into 'Paris' should give us intense cause for concern. Instead, it fails to shock any more.

Living standards within gated communities are often on par with the wealthiest in the West. Complete with swimming pools, golf courses, health clubs and beauty salons, they outdo each other in matching lifestyles from Beverley Hills or Malibu Beach in California, where many of the country's tens of thousands of dollar millionaires live. People living within such arrangements are twice privileged, in that they do not have to confront the poverty all around (even as they have complete access to Indian feudal privileges, such as servants) and they get preferential access to resources and infrastructure to allow for ostentatious lifestyles.

This is how Mike Davis summarizes the urban landscape that globalization has promoted during the last two decades across the Third World:

> Fortified, fantasy-themed enclaves and edge cities, disembedded from their own social landscapes but integrated into globalization's cyber-California floating in the digital ether . . . In this 'gilded captivity,' Jeremy Seabrook adds, the third-world urban bourgeoisie 'cease to be citizens of their own country and become nomads belonging to, and owing allegiance to, a super-terrestrial topography of money; they become patriots of wealth, nationalists of an elusive and golden nowhere.'[63]

This form of nationalism has to be qualified as 'corporate'. The state that was founded in 1947 made the moral claim of representing *all* Indians—irrespective of caste, class or religion. If the duty of a state is to safeguard not merely a nation's territorial but also its moral integrity, the state in reforming, globalizing India has obviously failed to do so. With segregated living comes the decline in empathy and compassion for the condition in which one's less fortunate fellow human beings live. And if that becomes routine, violence is not too far. The 'moral commons' are fast vanishing.[64]

In addition to the evictions we have discussed, market forces play their crucial part in Indian cities. They render outright eviction of the poor redundant. Permission to a builder to make a luxury shopping plaza in some part of a city raises rents in the area, pushing the poor to localities in far-flung regions that are more affordable. This has the effect of stratifying the city laterally. The stick is not necessary when the carrot gets more expensive.

What is likely to be the long-term result of such trends? It is perhaps not too far-fetched to imagine that if globally networked, post-modern corporate city states begin to take root in the legal system of the country, and are not resisted politically, a settlement pattern might emerge in this part of the planet, which is the very obverse of the American model: there will be wealthy enclaves of privilege in the heart of the city, ringed by circles of receding affluence, the first of which will have the privilege of servicing the needs of the wealthy (and perhaps have the I-cards needed to travel inwards for the working day). But, as one moves towards the outer rings, one might encounter a massive area of the poor, low-wage informal economy, much of which is disconnected from the circuits of wealth and power that define the globally networked centre. Finally, stretching out into the rural hinterland of every major metropolitan region might be areas that would effectively be 'war zones', where conflict and insurgency against the mainstream order of things is rife. But many of these will also be regions from where the metropolises get their water, minerals, power and other resources; and such installations will be under armed guard and heavy security.

At several of these sites, radical political groups might increasingly rule the roost, as the state abdicates its balancing functions. The fringe extremism of today may no longer occupy just the fringe as it advances outward from the jungles of central and eastern India.

As globally wealthy private investors get to have more and more of a say in the arrangement of living and working spaces around urban areas, this new geography of power and resistance could come into existence. It would necessarily be unstable because of the enormous tensions and insecurities it would generate. Civil conflict is bound to grow rather fast thereafter, once the fairy tales of upward mobility have faded from the imagination of the hundreds of millions left out. It is already happening where newly kindled hopes are evaporating.[65]

If corporate cities, inspired by a global dream, become a law unto themselves and, unrestrained by any prevailing constitutional, democratic considerations, take root, they are likely to fuel ugly, destructive forms of civil conflict. P. Chidambaram's dream of making India 85 per cent urban is then more likely to mutate into an unremitting nightmare. The 'citizens of the bubble' too are unlikely to get peaceful sleep in such an atmosphere, not least because the excluded populations may simply block the service lines feeding the city with water, food, energy and minerals—even where these may be protected by the police or the military. We are likely to see further repression by the state, as protestors and dissenters are declared 'anti-national', 'Maoist' or given other such labels that make it easier to 'deal' with them. Ironically, this may ultimately prove to be the nemesis of corporate nationalism.

The consolidation of internal colonialism

As rural India continues to get stepmotherly treatment in the rush to globalize metropolitan India, the tensions between town and country surface in a dramatic fashion. The underlying causes are often well-acknowledged by leaders, who still appear to be helpless to change the course of events. Manmohan Singh, for instance, admits: 'There has been a systematic failure in giving tribals a stake in the modern economic system . . . the alienation built over decades is taking a dangerous toll . . . The systemic exploitation of our tribal communities . . . can no longer be tolerated.'[66]

The issue of land acquisition and alienation takes on particularly greater significance in the context of the adivasi areas of the country, especially nowadays when the government's Operation Green Hunt to tackle the growing Maoist insurgency is on in these regions. For these areas there is a special provision in the Constitution, under Schedule V. In these parts the sale and transfer of land are tightly regulated by law in order to protect adivasi interests—in theory. The practice has been altogether different, leading a government committee to conclude recently 'that alienation of tribal land continues unabated and . . . has actually accelerated in areas where irrigation and modernization of agriculture are making rapid strides and roadways, industrialization and urbanization [are] enveloping larger areas'.[67]

The state-backed push by powerful corporations to acquire land and resources in the adivasi areas of central and eastern India is driven by the desperate bid to win the race to lay hold of some of the finest and largest reserves of coal, iron ore, bauxite and other minerals anywhere in the world. In fact, if one places the mineral map of India on top of the areas where Maoist insurgency holds sway, the overlap is very precise.

Stories crop up every single day about the mineral rush happening across eastern and central India's adivasi belt. Consider just one of several cases: the state of Orissa. It is rich in minerals, but is also one of the poorest states in India. In addition to the massive bauxite mining—thanks to huge iron ore deposits under the forests—as many as forty-five steel plants are on the anvil in this small state alone![68]

People across Orissa have expressed their displeasure and dissent over the state government's aggressive mining and industrialization policies: places like Kashipur, Kalinganagar,

Lanjigarh, Jagatsinghpur and Gopalpur have often been under siege for months (sometimes, years) by the police and the paramilitary on account of the angry political ferment over the past decade. The war between the state and the people is on. The lands and water sources of farmers and forest-dwellers in these areas are being taken over through the powerful offices of the state government in order to make way for the steel and aluminium plants (and the associated coal, iron ore and bauxite mines) of business interests like Tatas, Jindals, POSCO, Mittal, Birlas, Alcan, Alcoa and Vedanta (Sterlite). Hundreds of thousands of acres of agricultural land have already been destroyed. Comparable areas of reserve forests have been torn out of the earth. Water sources are being polluted by mining and industrial sludge. Critical watersheds are badly threatened. The air around the mines and factories is full of cancerous gases. After all, who has time to think of clean-up measures when Chinese competition is breathing down the necks of global players?

On many occasions peasants and adivasis have been killed in police firing while resisting the takeover of their lands, forests and water resources. The defence of 'Jal, Jungle, Zameen, Zindagi' (water, forest, land, life)—and not the treacherous hope of compensation, resettlement, rehabilitation, employment and 'modernization'—is the issue as far as local populations are concerned. If 'development' implies displacement from their lands and forests, the rural communities of Orissa have declared in no uncertain terms—often through the sacrifice of human lives—that they want none of it. They are willing to discuss only those alternatives in which they get to keep at least what they have at the moment.

So, if such 'development' is not for the people of Orissa, whom is the break-neck industrialization in the state for? It is for the many companies who have been gouging the earth to extract the abundant mineral wealth from the region (most of it lying under thick forests or farmed fields) for the price of dirt and make huge profits by selling abroad. (If a company can get away by paying Rs 100–150 per tonne of iron ore to the state and fetch a price of Rs 1500–3000 abroad—depending upon the grade of the ore—it is little surprise that there is a growing queue of foreign investors.) Orissa attracted over 10 per cent of the FDI in India in 2006.

Such profits will make it a lot easier and faster for business groups like Tatas to pay off the astronomical debt (of close to $10 billion: more than half of Orissa's entire GDP) that they have taken in order to acquire the Anglo-Dutch steel major, Corus. More importantly, it will enable the rich countries to derive the benefits of cheap steel (for construction, transport and industry) and aluminium (so critical to aeroplanes and soda cans alike), while keeping 'dirty' industries and mining away from their own environmentally sanitized shores. This is the reason why companies like Corus and Novelis have been selling out so readily—and at exorbitant prices—to Tatas and Birlas. The cleaner the industry, the less likely is it to be auctioned off to bidders from countries like India or Brazil. On the other hand, service sector businesses are being taken over by multinationals from rich countries: note the acquisition of the Indian company Hutch-Essar by the British multinational Vodafone a few years back.

The injustice of such a pattern of industrialization in Orissa— fitting snugly into a socially and ecologically unfair global division of labour and pollution—is such that the beneficiaries (barring the few politicians and bureaucrats who get cuts from each business contract) are not from Orissa but are scattered around urban India and the rest of the world. It is a thinly disguised form of environmental colonialism (dovetailing with a historically entrenched internal colonialism) orchestrated by the comprador government of the state, only too happy to sell off both its people and natural wealth to outsiders.

The Patnaik government of Orissa continues on its merry path, recently inviting investment from NRIs (non-resident Indians) among many others. The Korean steel giant POSCO has planned on investing $12 billion in the state (though its tax breaks and other incentives amount, if it is possible to imagine, to an even greater sum). This is the largest ever single FDI coming to India and thus carries high prestige. The project has been resisted so fiercely (it violates the Forest Rights Act) that in August 2010, the Central government asked the Orissa government to stall it. At the time of writing, it is not clear what will happen in the future. Laxmi Mittal's ArcelorMittal group (the world's largest steel conglomerate) signed an MoU (memorandum of understanding) with the Orissa government in December 2006, agreeing to invest $9 billion in the Keonjhar district (and deriving tax benefits of comparable magnitude). Mittal has asked for 8000 acres of land (2000 acres more than POSCO) for the project. He has also asked that the land be classified as an SEZ, with all the attendant privileges.[69]

The story of Chhattisgarh is even more startling. The same social and ecological devastation witnessed in Orissa has been precipitated here by accelerated mining and industrialization during the last two decades. What is worse, the tactics adopted by the state government have involved creating (since 2005) a vigilante force (recruited from the adivasis themselves) to coerce the recalcitrant adivasis into giving up their lands. According to a draft government report, the Salwa Judum (Peace Hunt) was recruited from the local adivasi population with money handed out by Tatas and the Essar group of companies (the final version of the report deleted any reference to this). They were interested in mining some of the best iron ore in the country, which lay under lands being used by the Muria tribe. In the internecine war that ensued, more than 640 villages in Dantewada district were either burnt down or emptied, driving 350,000 adivasis away from their traditional homes. This was displacement on an almost immeasurable scale. Many were raped, maimed or killed. Those who could not escape were herded together into refugee camps managed by the Salwa Judum along the highway. This same area is now the epicentre of the battle between Maoist forces and the Central government, through its Operation Green Hunt. Too much is being written about the issue for us to need to venture into it here. Suffice it to say that the underlying causes of Maoist extremism are structural in nature and it will probably not disappear unless they are justly addressed. For the adivasis of central India, denied the benefits of development, and having had to carry all the costs, the reality is so harsh that the draft Central government ministry report described the rush for Chhattisgarh's mineral riches as 'the biggest grab of tribal lands after Columbus' (deleted from the final report).[70]

Jharkhand has so far been able to put up more of a resistance to aggressive land acquisition. Hardly any major project has taken off during the last decade despite many formal clearances by the state government. This is mainly because of the fierce resistance the people have put up, a history of adivasi rebellion and the efficacy of the Chotanagpur Land Tenancy Act (1908), which prevents transfer of land from adivasis to others. However, cases of adivasis being duped into giving up their traditional lands are growing.[71]

The Panchayat (Extension to the Scheduled Areas) Act of 1996 (or PESA) gives power to public hearings conducted by gram sabhas on the issue of land acquisition. Yet, in Jharkhand, Orissa, Chhattisgarh and elsewhere, this has either been typically ignored or the presence of the police ensures the consent of villagers who then have to surrender their lands at ridiculous rates. The public hearing, when it happens, turns into a farce. (Jharkhand has never even had panchayat elections in its decade-long existence.) It is thus no exaggeration to describe this sort of a decision-making policy regime as 'developmental terrorism'.[72]

Stories of aggressive land acquisition from adivasis and other underprivileged social groups can be multiplied from virtually every part of the country—from Kachchh on the Gujarat coast to West Bengal (Singur and Nandigram being only the most infamous examples) and from UP to AP and Tamil Nadu. If it isn't land being seized for an SEZ or a mining project, then adivasi access to lands and forests traditionally used and nurtured by them is criminalized by designating those lands as 'protected areas', or tourism projects come up on their territory. As the hunger for land and resources among the powerful urban elite classes has grown, so has the misery of the rural poor increased.[73]

Where will all this lead? We already have a good part of the answer. Civil conflict is going to grow faster and faster every time growth numbers are ratcheted up in this violent developmental process. As has been widely noted, the rise of violent left-wing extremism in recent decades coincides with the intensification of the state-backed corporate assault on central and eastern India's minerals.

We are certainly not votaries of the kinds of violence and brutalities that the Maoists have inflicted, often on defenceless innocents (who have been 'collateral damage' in some of their campaigns or have suffered on account of not taking their side). But nor is it conscionable for a state in a democratic society to unilaterally declare war on 8 to 10 per cent of its own people, perpetrating torture and other forms of brutality, often leading to custodial deaths. The home ministry's Operation Green Hunt can only make matters worse at a time when nothing is more urgent than dialogue across all the different groups and interests involved in the conflict.[74]

Fortunately, it appears that peaceful means of resolving major conflicts over land and resources are actually succeeding in a number of instances. The last few decades are replete with examples of destructive projects and processes being stopped by non-violent actions (the Koel-Karo, Bhopalpatnam, Inchampalli and Silent Valley dams are good examples). We cite here three more recent examples of huge projects—clearly damaging to the environment and local communities—being stopped through non-violent protest by adversely affected communities and/or through judicial intervention.

The first case is that of the Mahamumbai SEZ (in Raigad, Maharashtra) for which Reliance India had applied. This was intended to be India's largest (14,000 ha) SEZ. It would have swallowed up forty-five reasonably prosperous paddy-growing villages. After getting two extensions over a four-year period on the deadline for acquiring at least 70 per cent of the land on their own (the state helping them get the remaining 30 per cent), and failing to do so, Reliance was halted in its tracks by a Supreme Court order in June 2009. The court decision was considerably bolstered by the fact that in a historic referendum (the first of its kind in India for a development project) in 2008, 85 per cent of farmers voted against the project. For ordinary farmers to score such a victory through non-violent means over one of the world's wealthiest conglomerates is most significant.[75]

The case of the POSCO steel project has been mentioned earlier. Again, persistent protest, mostly non-violent, by forest-dwellers and betel nut growers in Jagatsinghpur stalled India's biggest FDI investment for over five years. A Government of India committee set up to assess the implementation of the Forest Rights Act found that state authorities had violated the act in an unseemly hurry to promote the project, compelling the MoEF to order the state government to stop land acquisition and other work related to the project. At the time of writing, the MoEF had set up an expert committee to investigate whether the project would meet the requirements of environmental and forest rights laws.[76]

Finally, there is the story of the heroic, non-violent resistance of the Dongria Kondh tribe against the depredations of the mining giant Vedanta in the Niyamgiri Hills of Orissa (see Prologue to Part II).

These are three of the largest projects in post-reform India. The fact that they have been halted or stalled in a peaceful way, howsoever long it took to do so, challenges the argument that violence is a strategic imperative for people fighting for justice.

While nothing is written in stone, and government orders can be modified or even reversed, nobody would have wagered a few years back that corporate might, backed by state power in the reform era, could be challenged in peaceful ways. Though there are enough cases (Union Carbide in Bhopal being only the best-known) where people fighting for justice are at the end of their tether in the face of stonewalling by the state, the evidence presented above suggests that things can be resolved differently from what has become customary.

Towards a rural–urban balance

In 1929 Gandhi had written in *Young India*:

> Western civilization is urban. Small countries like England and
> Italy may afford to urbanize their systems. A big country like
> America, with a very sparse population, perhaps cannot do
> otherwise. But one would think that a big country, with a teeming
> population with an ancient rural tradition which has hitherto
> answered its purpose, need not, must not, copy the Western
> model. What is good for one nation situated in one condition is
> not necessarily good enough for another, differently situated.[77]

It is being said in many quarters that the days when India
used to live in its villages are over. Now, it dies in them. Farmer
suicides are only one form in which rural distress is manifesting
itself across so many states. There are also places like Chingapur
village in Yeotmal district of Maharashtra where villagers have
gone in for a mass sale of kidneys in order to help reduce their
exorbitant debts. Yet other villages, like Shivani Rikhailapur or
Harkishenpura in the Bhatinda district of Punjab, put themselves
up for sale years ago—without finding buyers.[78]

Quite evidently, something very basic has gone wrong with
rural India. But hasn't something gone seriously wrong with
urban India too? Can the city be healthy when the countryside
is not? Let us reflect for a moment on Fritz Schumacher's words
from the 1970s:

> The all-pervading disease of the modern world is the total
> imbalance between city and countryside, an imbalance in terms
> of wealth, power, culture, attraction, and hope. The former has
> become over-extended and the latter has atrophied. The city has
> become the universal magnet, while rural life has lost its savour.
> Yet it remains an unalterable truth that, just as a sound mind

depends on a sound body so the health of the cities depends on the health of the rural areas. The cities, with all their wealth, are merely secondary producers, while primary production, the precondition of all economic life, takes place in the countryside . . . To restore a proper balance between city and rural life is perhaps the greatest task in front of modern man. It is not simply a matter of raising agricultural yields so as to avoid world hunger. There is no answer to the evils of mass unemployment and mass migration into cities, unless the whole level of rural life can be raised, and this requires the development of an agro-industrial culture, so that each district, each community, can offer a colourful variety of occupations to its members.[79]

Some of the main forces at work have been analysed earlier in this and the previous chapter. As we have seen, there are those who wish to urbanize most of India. Others—not in influential policy circles nowadays—would like to keep India primarily rural. Neither actually sees the problem for what it is: a serious souring of the *relationship* between town and country, its always fragile balance, now completely upset by the blitzkrieg of aggressive globalization. No facile dreams—whether they uphold the virtues of rural arcadia or extol the liberties of metropolitan urban life—will do under the circumstances.

The way forward may lie in the twin realization that while self-sufficient villages have perhaps always been a myth (with notable exceptions), cities too are living on a short lease if they render the countryside inhospitable through their multiple depredations. There is a necessary symbiosis between them that policies must honour if they are not to drive a further wedge in the relations between town and country—leading to the ultimate destruction of both. Hope ought not to be a monopoly of the cities, as has seemed to be the case so far. It has to be created everywhere, especially in the villages, where most of India still lives.

Perhaps it is fitting to close this chapter by recalling the ideas of one of the makers of modern India, Rabindranath Tagore. In 1924 he published an essay called 'Robbery of the Soil'.[80]

Writing as though he were expressing an all-too-contemporary concern of consumerist society, Tagore went on to castigate the greed (and its consequences) with which we have all become so familiar. Pointing to 'an epidemic of voracity that has infected the whole area of civilization', Tagore goes on:

> Civilization has turned into a vast catering establishment. It maintains constant feasts for a whole population of gluttons. The intemperance which could have been tolerated in a few has spread to the multitude. The resulting universal greed is the cause of the meanness, cruelty and lies in politics and commerce that vitiate the whole human atmosphere. A civilization with an unnatural appetite must feed on numberless victims, and these are being sought in the parts of the world where human flesh is cheap. The happiness of entire peoples in Asia and Africa is being sacrificed to provide fastidious fashion with an endless train of respectable rubbish.

Echoing Gandhi's famous thought about there not being enough in the world for everyone's greed, Tagore writes: 'Mother Earth has enough for the healthy appetites of her children and something extra for rare cases of abnormality. But she has not nearly enough for the sudden growth of a whole world of spoilt and pampered children.'

He then makes the link between this extraordinary growth of appetites and the consequences it has for the relationship between cities and the countryside. 'Such an abnormal devouring process cannot be carried on, unless certain parts of the social body conspire and organize to feed upon the whole.' This is 'manifested in the fatness of the cities and the physical and mental anaemia of the villages, almost everywhere in the world'.

Tagore was most discerning and prophetic about the importance of villages and their place in the overall scheme of things. He writes that 'the cradle of the race' is 'in their keeping':

> They are nearer to nature than towns, and in closer touch with the fountain of life. They possess a natural power of healing. It is the function of the village . . . to provide people with their elemental needs, with food and joy, with the simple poetry of life and with those ceremonies of beauty which the village spontaneously produces and in which she finds delight. But when constant strain is put upon her through the extortionate claim of ambition . . . she becomes poor in life, her mind becomes dull and uncreative.

India, with its 600,000 villages, is perhaps best placed by the facts of history and destiny to set right the centuries-old imbalance between the city and the countryside, which afflicts countries across the earth. It can pioneer a new, ecological way of life that can serve as an example for the rest of the world. In the closing section of this book, we will look at some of the concrete steps that must be taken in this direction. Some of them are already under way at the initiative of common people, mostly without the help of the state or the corporations.

8

SUICIDAL MYOPIA

THE FOLLY OF THE GROWTH IMPERATIVE

'Everything that can be counted isn't worth counting, and everything that is worth counting isn't always countable.'

—Albert Einstein

Massive resource depletion, pollution and the destabilization of ecosystems are direct consequences of unfettered, competitive economic growth in the era of globalization, though the roots of the ecological crisis are deeper and go farther back in time. The chief institutional mechanism which has been facilitating this organized predation is the market, whose liberalization in favour of the global corporate elite has been enabled by cooperative national governments the world over.

Greater volumes of (unfair) trade means that the affluent countries, by holding on to advantages they enjoy under the international division of labour (in many cases since colonial days), can readily shift environmental damage to poorer nations. Even 'green' consumers in rich nations may sometimes be ignorant of the far-flung consequences of their lifestyles.[1]

Secondly, since this phase of globalization began in the 1980s, there is far more direct investment (FDI) in physical capital across national boundaries. Corporations locate their production units across the globe according to advantages related to favourable investment opportunities, market access, availability of resources, cheap skilled labour, security, and fiscal, environmental and other incentives. This has led—from the environmental angle—to the globalization of supply chains, resulting in rising energy costs involved in the transport of components, raw materials and, of course, finished goods. The same company may be selling French water in California and Californian water in France, making handsome profits on both sets of transactions. Since the private, corporate cost of energy does not reflect all the indirect costs of generating it (from the social and environmental points of view), this environmentally destructive state of affairs can continue for a long time and lead to precipitous changes in the climate (among other effects). Such ecological and social irrationality is not a coincidental but a predictable outcome of global corporate expansion with unfettered and structurally unfair markets.

Thirdly, thanks to the deregulation of finance in Western countries since the 1970s, and to the telecommunications/Internet boom since the 1990s, there has been a dramatic explosion in purely financial transactions across the globe. This aspect of globalization has resulted in the rapid financialization of economies like India's, leading to new, more destabilizing forms of speculation with potentially deadly consequences for the real economy. From the environmental perspective: an instrumentalist, utilitarian view of nature facilitated capital accumulation and prosperity for the elites across the world for many decades and centuries; but now we have reached such a perilous stage that every patch of earth is merely a means for unbridled financial speculation, without regard for the long-run ecological, let alone the intrinsic, value of nature. For instance, increased speculation in commodities (such as metals) creates a situation in which there is a much higher turnover of money in mining. It can lead to a speeding up of mining operations (since there is suddenly much more money to be won or lost), without heeding environmental standards.

The environmental failure of the global market

In a competitive capitalist economy there are two ways to make things cheaper and enlarge your market share. You can either increase efficiency in production (by using less, or cheaper, labour and more productive machinery) or you can externalize the costs and pass them on to society, to residents of another country, to the world at large, or to future generations of humanity. Or you can do both.

Within countries there are laws and institutions to regulate (cost-cutting) environmental harm. *Across* countries there are no binding laws, only conventions, like the Biodiversity or the Toxic Trade (Basel) Convention. These, as we know, are routinely violated, since there is no global authority to enforce the agreements meaningfully. Hence it is no accident that some of the fallouts of globalization have predictably been the outsourcing of 'dirty' industries and the growth of trade in toxics. And if climate change has accelerated since the dawn of this phase of globalization, at least a part of the blame must be shouldered by transnational forces of capital which have the power to shift external costs and risks to regions with weak or non-existent environmental laws, though governments have also been lax within their own boundaries (as in the experience of both India and the US). This makes the cumulative situation of the global environment—a de facto open-access commons—ever more precarious. Nicholas Stern, author of Britain's official *Review on the Economics of Climate Change* has noted that

> the problem of climate change involves a fundamental failure of markets: those who damage others by emitting greenhouse gases generally do not pay... Climate change is a result of the greatest market failure the world has seen. The evidence on the seriousness of the risks from inaction or delayed action is now overwhelming. *We risk damages on a scale larger than the two world wars of the last century.* The problem is global and the response must be a collaboration on a global scale. [Emphasis added][2]

Some years ago, the then chief economist of the World Bank (and, at the time of writing, one of President Obama's key economic advisers) Larry Summers, in an internal memo, made a case for the export of externalities (from the affluent nations). He argued that there were at least three good reasons to believe that 'dirty' (polluting) industries should migrate to poor countries. Firstly, the forgone earnings from the greater mortality (and morbidity) that would follow in the poor countries would be lower because they are poorer. Secondly, some countries (Africa came to Summers's mind) were 'vastly under-polluted' as compared with industrialized ones. Finally, the rich were in a position to demand a cleaner environment not merely because they had more money but because of 'greater aesthetic sensitivity'. A clean and beautified environment is a cultural privilege of the elite.[3]

Summers concluded: 'I think the economic logic behind dumping a load of toxic waste in the lowest-wage country is impeccable and we should face up to that.' The poor must be poisoned in the larger interests of economic wisdom. This is the message.

Summers noted that though there were moral and technical counterarguments to his prescription, these applied equally to 'every Bank proposal for liberalization'. He left it at that, thereby implying that prevailing, even banal, flaws in the thinking and policies prescribed for poor countries by the World Bank were worth compounding in order to increase the efficiency and 'welfare' of the world economy.

The Economist, which was the first to publish Summers's memo under the mocking title 'Let them eat pollution', proceeded in its next issue to approve of Summers's approach: 'If clean growth means slower growth, as it sometimes will, its human cost will be lives blighted by a poverty that would otherwise have been mitigated.' Environmentalists who questioned Summers's logic, the magazine argued, were to be blamed for 'causing great, if well-intentioned harm to the world's poorest people'.[4]

The approach to poverty that Summers takes is not only ethically repugnant, it is also logically inadequate, empirically flawed and ecologically myopic. The poor have no health insurance and thus have nothing to fall back upon when they bear the health effects of pollution. This should—ethically speaking—provide us with good reason to locate polluting industries near the *rich* neighbourhoods of the world (since the wealthy can more readily redress the health effects of pollution). Or, best of all, not to allow such industries at all, especially since non-polluting technologies are so often available.

Summers assumes that polluting, large-scale industrialization is the only way to enhance the economic welfare of the world.

What if it turns out that such a path (especially in the era of peak oil and climate change) is simply unsustainable? What if there are very different paths—prioritizing decentralized production and consumption and emphasizing gainful employment, mindful of nature's limits and sensitive to the equal rights of each community and each individual, and not having to disprivilege some to privilege others? If so, then again Summers's argument about evening out the pollution burden of our imperilled planet holds little water.

If one follows Summers (as *The Economist* does), the life of an Orissa adivasi is worth less than that of a Wall Street financier; African countries must repeat the industrial follies and excesses of the West; and, of course, they are not in a position to care either for their health or for the environment around them as the rich are. According to this logic, the business of environmental conservation is best left in the hands of the rich. Indeed, in keeping with Summers's logic, corporations from rich countries are ever so likely to export their dirty industries to the global South—and have in fact been doing just that—to avail of cost advantages. It is such a structural defect in the price system of the market economy which had led the environmental economist K. William Kapp to remark decades ago that 'capitalism must be regarded as an economy of unpaid costs'.[5]

The deeply flawed thinking that Summers represents has actually taken hold of policymaking across the world today, shifting control over resources towards those with the capital to drive development choices and away from communities that have traditionally lived closest to them. This means that global finance, mining and industry have become lord and master of the earth, determining the pace and pattern of resource-use according to their own short-term, profit-maximizing calculus.

The earth itself has been turned into a global casino with every piece of nature having a number on the roulette wheel of investors and speculators associated with it. Not only do indigenous peoples and communities lose in the long run, such irresponsible thinking and policy choices contribute significantly to problems like the concentrated accumulation of toxic wastes, climate change and loss of biodiversity, ultimately imperilling everyone.

Tragedies of the global open-access commons are precipitated by poor overall cost-accounting, either because environmental costs are ignored altogether by the TNCs (transnational corporations), or because they are shifted and transferred to poor countries (or communities), or because of production in countries or regions far from the point of consumption, raising the energy costs of transport. If India is forced to import food from Australia, the US and Canada (thanks to the agricultural policies conceived to serve narrow corporate interests), the energy cost of shipping the food may be of short-run benefit to freight companies. But from the point of view of humanity as a whole, who can fail to see the absurdity of such a trading arrangement (which, in any case, has nothing to do with free trade)? Importing food into areas hitherto abundant and self-sufficient is not just ecologically unjustifiable, it violates the basic principles of comparative advantage on which the free trade theory rests.

The rationalizing role of mainstream economic theory becomes clearer in light of a triumphalist industrialism at war with the planet. Its well-known theorems of optimum resource allocation—if taken seriously and applied to real-world situations (as the International Monetary Fund routinely does)—are woven into a manic logic, fraught with severe environmental dangers.

The real world occupies a universe altogether alien to mainstream economic theory. If the polluting petrochemical plants that produce the polymers used in plastic products consumed by affluent residents of Greenwich, Connecticut, had to be located in their neighbourhood, urgent measures would be taken to ensure that transitional alternatives were found as consumption was reduced. But in the real world, the plant may be located on the south-east coast of China or near a poor neighbourhood in Mexico (even as it serves consumers in Connecticut), causing grave damage to air quality and public health for people who may be too poor and politically helpless to stem the rot. The products would be shipped by sea, using oil drilled from Middle Eastern lands, which are suffering from imperial wars.

When the environmental effects of industrial expansion are indirect and occur at a distance, it is easy for the people causing the problem (and benefiting from it in the short term) to turn a blind eye to it. Only those who are closer to the receiving end of the damage in the short run (rather than the long run) are in a position to know somewhat the true costs.

The market mechanism of price-signalling is *routinely* blind to tipping points—that may have already been crossed in various ecosystems—as long as those who are the first to feel the losses, costs and risks are structurally priced out of expressing their economic voice in the market. Both the producer and the consumer of paper, for instance, have an interest in ignoring the (external) environmental costs of water pollution (what economists refer to as externalities). This will keep the market price of paper low, even if the real cost is higher. Apart from specialists or experts with evidence on the matter, the only people who know the external cost of paper production are those who live in proximity to the polluted water.

Interestingly, a commonly held view, not merely among economists, is that environmental problems are best tackled by extending the domain of the market even further—by creating a market, for instance, in the right to pollute or to extract resources. An example will clarify how this only shifts and postpones the underlying problem. Consider the challenge of controlling carbon emissions. A sub-market is created to allow the polluter to carry on polluting and it appears that the problem is being tackled by the economic gains in the short term from carbon credits. Purchase of carbon credits *does* cost polluters, but not nearly as much as it should. Since the overall pollution loads are set by authorities who put their faith in cap-and-trade systems, much of the burden of such externalities falls either on the unborn, on the far-flung, economically voiceless communities, or on non-human nature. By proposing and relying on such 'solutions' like carbon credits, the day of environmental judgement is merely postponed.

Corporate market rationality is conceptually very distinct from *ecological* rationality. If relied on to tackle serious environmental challenges, it will inevitably lead to unmitigated catastrophes. Markets will fail to register approaching environmental upheavals, since they lack the appropriate depth of socio-ecological complexity—they structurally exclude the poor, the unborn and non-human natural beings. This is what has put the market economy at odds with so much of environmental and climate science today.

Economizing on environmental information?

This is an opportune moment to address one of the most influential arguments in favour of laissez-faire, given by the Nobel-winning liberal economist Friedrich Hayek. Hayek argues that no system of resource allocation (such as socialist planning) that arises from conscious human design can ever take the place of the free market, since the latter emerges from the 'spontaneous order' of civilized human societies—understood to be those founded on the institution of private property. Unlike what Karl Polanyi argued, Hayek believes that nobody ever sat down to create markets consciously.[6]

Further, for Hayek, the beauty of markets consists in the fact that they decentralize the collection and use of relevant economic information in a 'natural' way. It would be too much to expect any central planning board to have access to the range and volume of information that markets routinely use, generate and use again. Imagine how complicated, if not impossible, it would be for a central planner to know exactly how much steel or sugar should be produced in the overall economy, based on estimations of the aggregate demand for these products. Chicken-and-egg Catch-22s would reign here, since one cannot predict any single demand or supply in abstraction from all the other demands and supplies in the economy. Which particular product's demand and supply would one fix in order to know all the others, and why?

The merit in Hayek's argument is only vis-à-vis central planning. However, in an ecologically imperilled age, one has to take into account a huge range and volume of *environmental* information. As everyone knows, resources are scarce and their use leads to adverse ecological effects. We have already seen that unregulated markets are poor at utilizing such important information because of the phenomenon of externalities.

How then is relevant environmental information (especially on costs) to be obtained? We deal with this in detail in Part II of this book.

Growth forever?

For more than two centuries the system we call capitalism has been founded on the premise that financial capital can expand endlessly. But while financial capital is abstract and its growth can be reckoned in numerical monetary terms, it *represents* something which is not abstract but real. Moreover, it enables this expansion of real wealth through an intricately well-developed, sophisticated system of money and credit.

Now, here's how the growth conundrum arises. The owner of capital lends in order to maximize his returns. The borrower of capital must put it to a productive use so that he maximizes *his* profit. Actual production is carried out with real natural resources, including energy. For two centuries since the Industrial Revolution, humanity has been relying on non-renewable fossil fuels to carry out production. Such things as coal or oil are stocks, not flows. So long as a huge—and for immediate purposes, unlimited—stock of such reserves was at hand, industrial production could to a considerable degree be increased indefinitely. (This was, of course, facilitated by the temporary luxury of opting out of such limits placed by nature as the water cycle or the changing of seasons.) With rapid improvements in technology, there has indeed been a significant growth in productivity. Industry, moreover, unlike agriculture, can run three shifts to increase production.

These conditions change quite dramatically when non-renewable resource and energy stocks begin to vanish perceptibly, as is happening today. Suddenly, the concrete (production of real wealth) may not be able to keep pace with the abstract (desired growth in financial capital) when we near the bottom of the barrel. Moreover, moving to renewable energy sources will place natural limits (the rate at and the forms in which solar energy can be captured or a biomass reserve can be replenished, for instance) on the growth of capital. This gets more constrained when one realizes that the instruments and materials for capturing such forms of energy are themselves non-renewable and possibly cannot provide such efficient ways of storing energy as were available for coal and oil.[7]

It may turn out that we have been living in a more or less artificial world of credible man-made abstractions for as long as living memory goes. But they were credible only because the financial promises were usually made good by the net growth in real wealth.

This no longer seems likely, as the whole world seeks to mimic American standards of consumption in a context of rapidly depleting non-renewables. Even the flow of potentially renewable resources (such as biodiversity or fisheries) has been disrupted by the growth of the last fifty years. The UN conducted the Millennium Ecosystem Assessment, in which Delhi's Institute for Economic Growth was also involved, between 2001 and 2005. Done over a period of four years by an international team of experts, this is the world's most authoritative global environmental survey and it found that

over the past 50 years, humans have changed ecosystems more rapidly and extensively than in any comparable period of time in human history, largely to meet rapidly growing demands for food, fresh water, timber, fiber and fuel. This has resulted in a substantial and largely irreversible loss in the diversity of life on Earth. In addition, approximately 60% (15 out of 24) of the ecosystem services . . . examined are being degraded or used unsustainably, including fresh water, capture fisheries, air and water purification, and the regulation of regional and local climate, natural hazards, and pests.[8]

Since the era of deregulated finance began in the 1970s we have seen a virtually limitless explosion of money and financial instruments—all claiming to represent a parallel (or almost parallel) growth in real wealth. Compounding everything is a global race for wealth and power, which has rendered everyone impatient and thus ecologically myopic.

The current ecological and financial (as well as economic) crises are the consequences of serious market failures. What is striking is how the links between these obvious facts are barely recognized.

Relative and absolute scarcity in relation to growth

The discipline of economics presumes that endless growth is desirable, as though there are no barriers placed by nature on human activities. At the same time, economics has been understood as a science of scarcity. One of the classical definitions of economics, given by Lionel Robbins, considers it to be 'the science which studies human behaviour as a relationship between ends and scarce means which have alternative uses'.[9]

The apparent paradox is resolved when one realizes that economists are in the business of studying *relative*, not absolute, scarcities. In the above definition, it is the allocation of scarce means between alternative ends that is considered. It is the microeconomic choices—between apples and oranges or train travel and air travel—which determine the structure of relative prices that economists spend so much time studying. The overall *scale* of economic activity is not questioned, as though economic growth were an end in itself and there was no issue of the absolute scarcity of resources. The microeconomic understanding of the subject is at odds with the macroeconomic one. Ecological economist Herman Daly has pointed out that while the former has a 'when to stop' rule due to the limits on the consumer's purse, the latter does not. There seems to be a strange consensus that economic growth can and must go on indefinitely.[10]

This is making growth increasingly 'uneconomic': we are drawing more out of nature than the wealth we are able to create with it. Here is how Daly elaborates his idea. The larger the world economy grows, and the closer it gets to the scale of the whole earth, the more closely will it have to conform to the behaviour of the earth. While the subsystem of the economy is growing as an open system (drawing raw materials from the earth and pumping wastes into it endlessly), it is placed inside the closed ecosystem of the earth, which ultimately allows for qualitative change but not for infinite quantitative growth. While growth is more of 'the same stuff', development is the same quantity of superior stuff. The laws of physics—in particular the laws of thermodynamics—make the former impossible, at least when it comes to its limitlessness.

Daly underscores the fact that the remaining natural world is unable to bear the weight (supply the sources and sinks) of an already oversized economy, let alone a growing one. While economists have studied the economy's 'circulatory system' at length, they have neglected altogether to understand its 'digestive tract', with the consequences all too obvious. When the natural world was relatively 'empty' of the human economy, this was somewhat pardonable. Today, when it is quite 'full' of it, it is unconscionable.

Evidently, human survival is now contingent on the world economy's converging to a sustainable 'steady state' by reducing its physical throughput to a level in harmony with the natural limits set by the earth. As things stand, growth has turned uneconomic because the quantitative expansion of the economic subsystem is increasing environmental and social costs faster than the production benefits it is bringing, making us poorer, not richer. (Daly points out, however, that it is hard to know this for sure since we do not distinguish costs from benefits in our national accounts. Instead, they are lumped together as 'activity' in the calculation of the GDP.) It is making us live off the future. While visible market-measured production grows, the not-so-visible ecological production (and social production such as 'services rendered' to each other by family members) declines. Previously, the world was 'empty of us and our furniture and full of other things. Now, it is full of us and our stuff and relatively empty of what used to be there'.

Daly insists—standing on the terra firma of the laws of thermodynamics—that believing the earth's ecosystem to be a subset of the economy is to have an upside-down vision of reality. Economic growth necessarily makes certain invaluable things—from non-renewable resources to clean air and water—scarce. But aren't all problems easier to solve if we are richer? His response is that yes, things like poverty, unemployment, environmental degradation would be easier to tackle—in principle—if we were richer. But that is not the issue. The issue is: Does growth in the GDP any longer really make us richer? Or is it now making us poorer?

There is no simple way to know this for the reasons already mentioned. However, it would be sheer hubris to *assume* that technological improvements of the green kind are *reducing* the physical throughput of the world economy. In any case, it is unlikely to be happening at a rate fast enough to approach the sustainable steady state, which the carrying capacity of the earth will allow. We have good reason to think—given the fossil-fuel-driven growth of large countries like India and China—that the throughput is actually on the rise. We have to bear in mind that when it comes to tipping points in the natural world, it is not the per capita figures that matter but the aggregate ones: it is the total carbon emissions of China and India that affect the earth's climate, regardless of their still-low per capita emissions.

Besides, in a world of fierce social and economic competition, any resource- or energy-saving improvements readily lead to greater, not lesser, consumption of overall resources. People— both as consumers (with their income freed up) and producing firms (with their revenue released)—tend to exploit the advantage conferred by technological changes to outdo their rivals. Known to economists as the Jevons paradox, this empirical fact puts paid to all contention in favour of purely technological solutions to ecological problems. A good example of the Jevons paradox is provided by the automobile industry. New technologies and regulations around the world are cutting down exhaust pipe emissions per car. But automobile emissions worldwide continue to rise because the growth in purchase and use of cars is faster than the growth in reduction of pollution per car. No such purely supply-based solution can suffice in a context where competitive social relations are dominant. Minimally, interventions by governments and civil society will be necessary in various forms.[11]

Daly proposes that the rich countries (and, presumably, classes) should reduce their throughput growth to free up resources and ecological space for use by the poor. The former can focus on *qualitative* development via technical improvements, which can then be shared with the poor who will at last get to enjoy the benefits of economic growth that they have hitherto been denied.

There are of course economists and other experts who have no argument with the laws of physics and who insist that it is not matter or energy which is meant to grow indefinitely but that somewhat elusive unit of wealth—*value*—which is nowadays measured simply in terms of money. Daly's response to them is: 'Fine. In that case, let's restrict the throughput flow of matter and energy and you get busy with technology and let the value supported by that fixed flow grow forever and I'll applaud you and I'll be happy and you'll be happy.' In other words, economists who argue that the endless growth of value can happen without a greater throughput of matter and energy are obliged to prove that an economy can grow in value purely by recombining existing (actually, diminishing) resources in novel ways with the help of new technologies. Apart from everything else, it is unclear what 'value' becomes in such an increasingly 'knowledge-based' economy, which has ironically insulated itself from the 'knowledge' of material resource limits.

A postscript on values: The market will set you free?

This book makes an argument not just against market capitalism, in which TNCs compete for political influence and economic dominance. We stand as much against state socialism, in which nation states compete for economic influence and political dominance. Under the competitive conditions of industrial modernity, the race towards a socialist utopia paves the way to ecological dystopia no less than the paradise dreamt up by enthusiastic neo-liberals. The ecological debris left behind by the carcass of Soviet communism after its official end in 1990 stands as a testimony to this. It is all but inevitable that if societies and their leaders are devoted to maintaining or obtaining dominance, and power becomes the overarching value, justice and sustainability are the casualties. Vulnerable populations—both within and outside a country—pay for this, often with their very lives.

Yet, the dominant ideology of the day proclaims that if markets are set free, so are we. It is a claim that has to be examined. It is sometimes said that the invisible hand of the market leaves no fingerprints. In other words, the attraction of markets lies precisely in the fact that they offer a credible *appearance* of freedom and spontaneity. But contrary to appearances, markets cannot liberate people because they do not disperse power. They concentrate power in the hands of wealthy corporations and consumers. These make up one of the visible hands that guide the market, the other being the state.

The conquest of society by the market has had profound consequences for human values. In a market society, exchange-value comes to dominate all others. Fields and jungles, air and water, sceneries and experiences, love and romance, friendship and loyalty, dignity and integrity—everything tangible and intangible is converted into saleable morsels for consumerist delight by the genius of creative advertising. In such a world people are not so much free as the fact that they feel *compelled* to consume. They get *addicted* to one or another form of consumption, regardless of whether it answers their needs or not. In fact, material desires readily occlude some real needs, which could be non-material (though often, like health, they are quite material). As people widely begin to experience consumption as 'freedom', and the freedom of their vices as freedom itself, the collapse of values is inevitable. This is evidenced by the morning news, as much as by the corruption all around. If the opinion of a former Supreme Court judge is anything to go by, this may be threatening the most sacrosanct wing of a democratic state, the judiciary itself:

> High education, professional ability, advanced technology and mega-factories and wealth belong to the rich and they control the country's resources, police power and incarceratory power. If this superior class manages to gain judicial power too, Indian

law is likely to be interpreted and adjudicated in favour of the creamy layer and the robber sector. The weaker sector finds law to be its enemy if the instrument of law is in the hands of the higher class.[12]

Along the same lines, here is an opinion from the heart of the world business establishment:

> People increasingly rely on money as the criterion of value. What is more expensive is considered better . . . What used to be a medium of exchange has usurped the place of fundamental values . . . What used to be professions have turned into businesses . . . The cult of success has replaced a belief in principles. Society has lost its anchor.

Multi-billionaire finance capitalist George Soros wrote this in 1997 in an article that merits close attention, 'The Capitalist Threat'.[13]

The rise of the market privileges, above all, individual and private interests. Now, the liberties of the individual have their place in a good, civilized society. It is one of the significant achievements of modern liberal democracies to have found a measure of this political virtue. However, when individual freedom gets tied intimately, and often exclusively, to consumption, and forgets its umbilical links to human community and the environment, it deserves to be described as irresponsible, if not immature, and it will ultimately lose itself to the forces of greed and power.

The market pays no attention to collective needs, as if all human needs were solely individual. It refuses to recognize that community has both an intrinsic and an instrumental value, which can never be replaced by the market. That its conception of both society and the individual is false was brought out sharply by the collapse of financial markets at the onset of the ongoing global economic crisis. It showed that even in the sphere of global high finance, where ruthless self-seeking is the norm, there are collective (systemic) needs which a deregulated 'free' market fails to meet. The stability of the financial system itself cannot be guaranteed by the market. As trust in the system is breaking down, governments are having to step in to restore confidence.

If there is one reason why markets on their own will never be able to solve the ecological crisis, it is that they ignore communities and what they are capable of, both by way of good as well as harm. Moreover, when it comes to community, the enjoyment of human relationships is perhaps an end in itself to a much greater degree than the pursuit of endless wealth. By observing poor communities one can also learn how people support each other in material, cultural and emotional ways, which fall entirely outside the sphere of the market. Only a minority of narrow-minded economists might think that market economies exhaust the sum total of all economies possible. Relations of love, friendship, obligation, reciprocity, commitment, sympathy, compassion and solidarity—to name but a few—often form the basis of economic relations between people. Such subsistence economies may be 'bad for the industrial economy and the paper economy of financiers; it is good for the actual real-world economy by which people live and are fed, clothed, and housed', writes Wendell Berry. It is an illusion to think, as Einstein has warned us, that that which goes unmeasured (or is, perhaps, immeasurable) by national economic accounts is unimportant or irrelevant.[14]

Cars racing on a sinking ship?

After the acceleration of corporate globalization began two decades ago, all the nations of the world have been led into a race with each other—for economic dominance. This is the 'organised selfishness of nationalism' about which Tagore had written a century ago. Since this greatly facilitates, and is in turn facilitated by, political dominance, militarism has been added to economic growth as one of the key mantras of our bedevilled age. A strong nation today is not just one with a large GDP. It must also have the military power to defend it and to expand it endlessly. This is why GDP is actually a much better measure of the economic strength of a state than of the welfare of a human society.[15]

Today, the real situation is such that countries the size of China or India cannot industrialize and reach anywhere close to the living standards of the Western world without threatening the carrying capacity of the planet in a suicidal way. Each of them alone has more people than the entire industrialized world—the US, the EU, Japan, Australia and New Zealand—taken together. Most of these countries achieved those standards through prolonged exploitation of the rich resources of their colonies. To repeat that blunder would not only be imprudent but impossible, since those resources will not last too long. 'God forbid that India should ever take to industrialization after the manner of the West,' Gandhi had said. 'The economic imperialism of a single tiny island kingdom [the UK] is today keeping the world in chains. If an entire nation of 300 million took to similar economic exploitation, it would strip the world bare like locusts.'[16]

The First World lifestyles that are enjoyed by the minority elites in India and China simply cannot be generalized for the whole population. Every Indian (or Chinese) cannot own a car, a mansion and a swimming pool—and perhaps does not *need* to. Beyond a certain point, freedom has nothing to do with consumption. What we perhaps need is to democratically redefine minimum acceptable standards of living and publicly discuss in an honest way what it means to be free. Rabindranath Tagore had written: 'An automobile does not create freedom of movement, because it is a mere machine. When I am myself free I can use the automobile for the purposes of my freedom.'[17]

Externalities are bound to grow as long as the policy elite think like most economists and maximize a few variables of interest to the exclusion of all else. It is such reductionist thought which has brought us to the precipice in the first place. It has given birth to a fragmentary perception of social and ecological reality. Ponds, rivers and watersheds will continue to dry up so long as the exclusive goal remains the maximization of profit or the production of steel or aluminium. And such a goal will be in place till we are in competition with other countries and their corporations.

What we need to tackle the ecological challenges of today is to set aside competition and initiate an imaginative cooperation on a scale perhaps unprecedented in history. We discuss such values in Part II of this book.

PART II

DAWN

There *Is* an Alternative

Prologue II

THE ECOLOGICAL SIGNIFICANCE
OF PLACE

'A BIG VICTORY FOR LITTLE PEOPLE?'[1]

'In their dealings with the countryside and its people, the promoters of the so-called global economy are following a set of principles that can be stated as follows. They believe that a farm or a forest is or ought to be the same as a factory; that care is only minimally necessary in the use of the land; that affection is not necessary at all; that for all practical purposes a machine is as good as a human; that the industrial standards of production, efficiency, and profitability are the only standards that are necessary; that the topsoil is lifeless and inert; that soil biology is safely replaceable by soil chemistry; that the nature or ecology of any given place is irrelevant to the use of it; that there is no value in human community and neighbourhood; and that technological innovation will produce only benign results.'

—Wendell Berry[2]

'We, the forest people of the world—living in the woods, surviving on the fruits and crops, farming on the jhoom land, re-cultivating the forest land, roaming around with our herds—have occupied this land since ages. We announce loudly, in unity and solidarity, that let there be no doubt on the future: we are the forests, and the forests are us, and our existence is mutually dependent. The crisis faced by our forests and environment today will only intensify without us.'

—From the Dehradun Declaration of June 2009 by the National Forum for Forest Peoples and Forest Workers[3]

'The mere degree of a society's industrialisation and mechanisation will be less significant than the measure of its success in providing solutions to the problems of pollution, of resource exhaustion, and of social tension, that are at present the unexorcised concomitants of the industrial system. The future may reveal a non-Western answer to a problem that was originally presented to the world by the West.'

—Arnold Toynbee, *A Study of History*[4]

The battle over the Niyamgiri mountain range in Orissa, from where the mining giant Vedanta wanted to extract bauxite, has finally been won by the Dongria Kondh tribe, the original inheritors and stewards of the land. While the battle was still on, and it looked virtually impossible for something as unexpected as this to happen, a member of the tribe said about their predicament:

We are used to the Indian government here. But the Vedanta government has come and devastated so many people. They won't let us live in peace. They want to take these rocks from the mountain. But if they take away these rocks, how will we survive? Because of these the rain comes. The winter comes, the wind blows, the mountain brings all the water. If they take away these rocks, we'll all die. We'll lose our soul. Niyamgiri is our soul.[5]

The poignancy and sense of devastation in this cry of despair provides a glimpse of how sacred a place nature occupies in a cosmology strikingly alien to the utilitarian calculations of industrial modernity. To many cultivated, rational and urbane minds this cosmology may merely suggest a deep but childish superstition that rain comes from rocks. But that may precisely be the problem with the urbane mind—the tendency to misread the metaphor and miss the deep causalities inscribed in a life-affirming cosmology. Instead, in the interstices of its foundations we find a sophisticated ecological premise that may escape even those schooled formally in the ecological disciplines.

The rocks the Dongria Kondh man is talking about happen to be bauxite. The layer of bauxite near the top of these mountains holds monsoon water throughout the year. It is released gradually in the form of perennial streams, which would dry up if the bauxite is mined. Moreover, if the 'rocks' are taken out, erosion will take place in short order, leading to deforestation, with possible effects on local precipitation, compounding the water crisis created by the mining. That is why the bauxite has to be left in the mountain. That is why the mountain is 'sacred' to the Dongria Kondh. It is, in fact, the impatient, technocratic superstitions of modern engineering that ignore such facts of ecology to lay waste a mountain for monetary gain. And what is ignorant, and childish, is to imagine that any sum of money could ever 'compensate' for the ecological and cultural losses entailed by the mining.

The hundreds of Indian communities fighting for their land and resources today have traditionally obeyed simple principles of ecological balance. These principles have allowed a way of life in which the question of sustainability rarely arises, unless artificial increases in population or modern habits of consumption take root in the community. Such forces disrupt not only world views, but also ecological practices, often leading a community very far from the conditions under which it could survive. This has happened to places as far-flung as Ladakh and the north-east.[6]

Indigenous peoples around the world have mostly lived by an instinctive sense of ecological integrity because they have stayed true to the *place* of their birth. This is true even for nomads, who obey the rhythms of the ecosystems they use and inhabit. Such peoples have also had a marginally adverse impact on the environment, but nowhere near as irreversible and on the scale which modern industrial economies have. It is no coincidence that most of the so-called 'wilderness' areas that modern societies want to protect as 'national parks' or other 'protected areas' are those inhabited by such peoples. Had they been as destructive as us, their habitats would have little wildlife or biodiversity.

All human cultures change and transform nature in order to make her habitable. But the extent of such intervention varies. The modern world has taken it to such dizzy heights that a large number of people have come to believe that continuing technological improvements in the global, human-made hardware (and software) of industrial modernity will finally free humanity from the necessities dictated by nature, rendering human culture altogether autonomous of the biosphere. It sometimes seems as though the ultimate goal of the modern enterprise is to make nature redundant. Many people today measure 'progress' in terms of the distance from nature—as though the human condition could ever be free of her.

Such an outlook not only profanes the residual wisdom of indigenous cultures, but often finds itself seriously at odds with the facts of natural science, as the climate crisis shows us every day. Most readers of this book will be accustomed to living in highly processed human-made environments, from where it may *appear* as though humanity is living outside nature. A moment's reflection is enough to indicate how deceptive such an inference is.

As modern media, technology, industry, trade and finance increasingly penetrate the more remote corners of the globe, more and more parts of the world become captive to monocultures, ignoring all the preconditions of biodiversity, which have hitherto made multiple forms of life possible on earth.

The experience of the last few centuries, however, leaves little doubt as to the power of abstractions. It is no exaggeration to say that utilitarian abstractions—from those of science and mathematics to economics and finance—continue to shape the modern human experience. This is particularly so in a digital age, cluttered with the temptations of cyberspace.

Equally, however, we know that human sensuous experience is most palpable only in the concrete realities of specific *places*, which serve to create the context in which human cultures live and thrive. Natural places have a power that human-made spaces can never have. A truly ecological culture recognizes this, almost by instinct.

In a global age like ours, there is an urgent need to ground our visions and aspirations, to constantly subject them to natural, earthly realities. As we have seen, size and scale are germane to the modern developmental vision. While it may be true that certain projects and processes are conceivable only on a large scale, all available assessments suggest that they have already taken humanity beyond the limits of what the earth can absorb and provide for.

On the other hand, we are learning that small is not just beautiful, it may be the only thing sustainable and ecological, and may be more consistent with the requirements of human freedom. If one thinks of the viability of democracy, for instance, face-to-face neighbourhood assemblies are far more conducive to it than huge societies living off a technologically overdeveloped edifice of unsustainable mass production. And regionally and locally grounded economies—as opposed to globally networked ones—may be both the precondition and the result of such a grass-roots democracy.

In the end, human economies will once again have to accommodate themselves to natural ones. Today, a minority of the world is able to draw on the resources and energy reserves of the entire planet with the help of powerful technologies, thereby jeopardizing the life-chances of billions of people (today and tomorrow), in addition to endangering so many species and ecosystems. Such a way of life is made possible because it masks our enormous dependence on fragile, dying ecosystems and human communities in areas that appear remote from wherever we live and work.

A new commitment to *place* is required in the alternatives that we conceive. Only such a commitment, which will bring the mounting ecological costs of our lifestyles closer home, can help address the challenges we face. For this, a long overdue 'naturalization' of humanity is necessary. Without befriending the purling brook and the gazing mountain, not to forget the people who still live by them, we will continue to repeat the growing follies amidst which we live, encouraging millions of others to mimic our absurdly unsustainable lifestyles. By allowing the last remaining communities on earth who know how to live at peace with nature to disappear, we may enjoy the freedom of our excesses for a while. But in the end such myopia can only pave the steep downward slope towards an incredibly tragic ecocide, engulfing us all.

STORIES FROM TOMORROW

FROM DEVELOPMENTALITY TO
ECOLOGICALITY

'The village produces a few things, and tries to sell them . . . Most of the things we sell are "unfinished products", such as harvested crops, unpasteurized milk, nuts for oil . . . We send these off someplace else . . . to be processed, packaged, and transported back to us. Typically, there is a 100% markup in price in that process. We think of ourselves as consumers only of finished goods, but there is no reason why we cannot be the buyers of the unfinished goods as well as the processors who make the finished goods. In the same move, you can eliminate all the middleman costs, and also find employment through new economic activity. From this there is self-reliance, a sense of pride and independence. You can call that gram swaraj.'

—Ramasamy Elango, panchayat head,
Kuthambakkam village, Tamil Nadu[1]

In the low-rainfall region of Zaheerabad, Andhra Pradesh, Dalit women have brought about an agricultural revolution in seventy-five villages. Mobilized under the banner of Deccan

Development Society (DDS), an organization started with the purpose of promoting sustainable agriculture, women's *sangha*s (assemblies) have used a mix of strategies to achieve food security, economic independence and social transformation. Organic farming and pastoralism, with a diversity of seeds and livestock, is one fulcrum of their work. Other focus areas include economical water use, community grain reserves, celebration of biodiversity as part of cultural events and festivals, and outreach through locally generated media.

One of the most innovative moves is the creation of an alternative public distribution system (PDS), freeing consumers and farmers from the clutches of the official PDS. This alternative PDS brings in organic, diverse local foodgrains from local farmers, offering consumers a healthy choice. An organic food restaurant, Café Ethnic, caters to urban consumers in Zaheerabad. All this has helped transform a situation of chronic food shortage, unemployment and dependence on the government—particularly among Dalit women and other disprivileged sections—into one of self-sufficiency and self-reliance, dignity and control over their own lives. But the DDS has not restricted itself to local transformation; it has connected the women farmers to regional, national and international networks of solidarity and resistance, challenging several elements of globalization.[2]

The DDS story is remarkable, but it is not the only such initiative in India. Indeed, the country is brimming with stories of alternative experiments, many wildly successful, others struggling, but all pointing to the immense possibility of a world that is more ecologically sustainable and socially equitable than what globalized growth has given us.

The bricks of the future: Experiments in ecological democracy

The all-pervasive nature of the 'development' ideology makes any presentation of an alternative vision rather difficult. People look at one askance, as if one were suggesting an alternative to food or oxygen. Yet, as we have tried to show in Part I, 'development' is a failing god, its globalized version already collapsing under the weight of its own contradictions; and, as we will attempt to show here, if the real aim of human society is happiness, freedom and prosperity, there are indeed many alternative ways to achieve this without endangering the earth and ourselves, and without excluding more than half of humanity.

We make no pretence of presenting a comprehensive blueprint for an alternative India. It is of course not within the power of two individuals to do so; such a blueprint, or rather blueprints as we will argue below, must emerge from the collective voices of various sections of India and global society. We only present the bare outline of what we think are some key ingredients of a more sustainable, equitable and just India, within a framework we call *radical ecological democracy* (RED).

Most crucially, we require a radical form of democracy in which each citizen and community has a responsible voice in decision-making—very different from the current representative forms of democracy where we vote once in five years and leave all major decisions to those who come to power.[3] There is nothing necessarily new in this concept. It has been advocated by many. Indeed, various rudimentary or radical forms of democracy or decentralized governance appear to have existed from ancient times in India, e.g. in the clan *samiti*s and sabhas of the period 1200–600 BC; the *gana-sangha*s (assemblies of people claiming equal status) that existed from at least 600 BC to around AD 500; village assemblies in the Chola period (AD 900–1300); the Buddhist sanghas or the *sreni-praya* (economic guild communities) in various regions and ages.[4] But, of course, new forms of radical democracy will have to contend with the vastly different world in which we live now.

An additional element in the political aspects of such a democracy is the need for each citizen to be aware of, and responsible towards, the imperatives of ecological sustainability, including the survival of the natural world.

Thus, RED can be conceived of as a framework of social, political and economic arrangements in which all citizens have the right and full opportunity to participate in decisions impacting their lives; and where such decision-making is based on the twin principles of ecological sustainability and human equity. The terms 'ecological sustainability' and 'human equity' and the values linked to them are discussed in the next section.

Before we explore the various dimensions of RED, let us look at some initiatives (other than that of Deccan Development Society presented above) which are already pointing to alternative visions of relating to nature and each other.

- Kuthambakkam village, Tiruvallur district, Tamil Nadu, was, till a decade ago, a typical settlement with its share of poverty and hunger, caste inequities and absence of appropriate development. Then a young Dalit panchayat head, Ramasamy Elango, mobilized the community to take up a number of activities including water management for agriculture; local processing of agricultural produce; drains for sewage; women's collective enterprises; and housing for the poor as also new housing that integrates people from various castes within one colony. In most of these, local employment and involvement were stressed, sometimes encountering resistance and attempts by outside vested interests to undermine the panchayat. Inspired by the Gandhian economics of J.C. Kumarappa (referred to later in this chapter), Elango is now organizing a cluster of seven to eight villages to form a 'free trade zone', in which they will trade goods and services with each other (on mutually beneficial terms) to reduce dependence on the outside market and the government. This way, the money stays back in the area for reinvestment in local development, and relations among villages get stronger.

This example shows that while the idea of every village being entirely self-sufficient is perhaps illusionary, the idea of self-sufficient or self-reliant regions (village clusters, settlements within an ecoregion, and so on) is not. Encouraged by his success, Elango has been in dialogue with hundreds of other panchayat heads to persuade them to take up similar models of economic swaraj. Continuing challenges include caste biases (partly resolved through the integrated housing project) and moving towards a more holistic ecological vision for the village or village cluster. Elango's village has also set up a panchayat academy, which provides instruction in the processes of local self-government to villages in the vicinity of Kuthambakkam.[5]

- Irrigation projects in India have often been beset with problems of inequity in the access to water, unresponsive or corrupt project authorities, and so on. There are several people's initiatives for achieving equity and transparency in community-based irrigation efforts, such as some of the examples of sustainable agriculture and decentralized water-harvesting given in this chapter or other well-known ones like the Pani Panchayat in Maharashtra.[6] However, one of the few initiatives at democratizing a state-run project is that of the Ozar Water User Associations (WUAs) in the command area of the Waghad Irrigation Project in Nashik district, Maharashtra. Three WUAs were started in 1990–91 by the Samaj Parivarthan Kendra (a local people's organization) with technical support from the Society for Promoting Participative Ecosystem Management (SOPPECOM). The initiative was built on the work of R.K. Patil and S.N. Lele of the Centre for Applied Systems Analysis in Development (CASAD), who had initiated participatory irrigation management in Maharashtra. Over a few years, farmers learnt various aspects of managing an irrigation system, including the conjunctive use of surface- and ground-water; resolved issues of distribution, seasonal quotas and irrigation scheduling; and, in other ways, showed themselves capable of taking control. A number of other WUAs were started, till the entire command was covered and the government was convinced to hand over its management to a federation of these WUAs. This is the first instance in India of an entire command area being handed over to farmer beneficiaries. The impacts have included a significant increase in crop production and value. Continuing concerns include the shift from subsistence to cash crops—reducing self-reliance for food and increasing risky dependence on outside markets—

and inequities in the distribution of benefits from the project.[7]

• Moving away from the classic model of a city parasitically dependent on the countryside for all its needs, and unable to provide even basic amenities for a substantial number of its residents, is a huge challenge in India. Yet, this is precisely what Bhuj, the district headquarters of Kachchh (Gujarat), is aiming for. Civil society and consultancy groups like Hunnarshala, Sahjeevan, Kutch Mahila Vikas Sangathan and ACT (Arid Communities and Technologies) have teamed up to mobilize slum-dwellers, women's groups and other citizens into reviving watersheds and creating a decentralized water storage and management system; managing solid wastes; generating livelihood for poor women; creating adequate sanitation; and providing dignified housing for all. Going beyond providing the basics of material living, the process is also re-establishing common spaces for all to use, and seeking informed citizens' involvement in the full planning process to realize the vision of the 74th Amendment of the Indian Constitution (which provides for urban decentralization).[8]

• The Students' Educational and Cultural Movement of Ladakh (SECMOL) has brought about a quiet revolution in school education in India's northernmost region. Till 1988, education here was locally irrelevant and culturally inappropriate (mostly in Urdu, displacing Ladakhi) and trivialized the traditional learning environment of family, village and monasteries. Starting in 1991 in one village (Saspol), SECMOL pushed for the use of localized materials and the involvement of villagers as parents. Using a provision of the 1986 National Educational Policy, it helped establish Village Education Committees for local democratic management. Ladakhi (and its written form, Bodyik) was given prominence in teaching and some educational material was developed. Textbooks up to class five were rewritten to have greater local relevance. The work families do during the planting and harvesting season (and the use of solar technologies to heat the school in winter) was incorporated into formal subjects like the sciences and mathematics. Several of these innovations have been picked up by the Ladakh Hill Council to spread to other schools. According to SECMOL, such education is a way to 'preserve and strengthen the wisdom, cultural heritage, and unique identity of Ladakh'.[9]

- The National Biodiversity Strategy and Action Plan (NBSAP) process facilitated by the Indian government's ministry of environment and forests (MoEF) attempted to broad-base and deepen levels of participation for a national-level exercise. Sponsored by the Global Environment Facility through the United Nations Development Programme (UNDP), the process was coordinated by a civil society organization with the help of a fifteen-member core group from diverse backgrounds, over the period 2000–03. Well over 50,000 farmers, fishers, adivasis, students, teachers, academics, government officials, armed forces personnel, journalists, activists, politicians and others took part in a series of exercises including cultural festivals, workshops, public hearings, educational events, media outreach and art events. About seventy local, state, ecoregional and thematic action plans were prepared, based on which a national-level draft action plan was finalized by the core group. Unfortunately, at this final stage, faced with a set of recommendations that pointed to the need for radical reforms in governance and planning in all sectors of the economy and polity, the government backed out. One weakness that emerged was the relative lack of political stake, which could possibly have forced the government to accept the draft plan. Nevertheless, the process had a number of benefits including ongoing awareness programmes and networking, inclusion of certain recommendations in local, state and national plans and setting an example for other such exercises.[10]

- Thousands of community-led efforts to protect and regenerate forests, wetlands, grasslands and coastal/ marine areas, as also wildlife populations and species, dot the country. Such 'community conserved areas' are a crucial reason for the continued presence of natural ecosystems and wildlife even amidst dense human populations. An important component of these initiatives is the enormous diversity of rules and institutions that communities have developed for governance and management. These institutions range from a small youth committee to the full gram sabha, and the rules may be oral or written, traditional or new, usually accompanied by varied sanctions and penalties for violation. Increasingly, communities are demanding legal backing for their efforts, but on their own terms and not under top-down, uniform prescriptions. As in many other initiatives, there remain challenges such as caste, class and gender inequities and the inadequacy of livelihood options related to conservation.[11]

Key principles and values

Two fundamental principles underlie such alternatives. One is *ecological sustainability*, or the continuing integrity of the ecosystems and ecological functions on which all life depends (including all hydrological, chemical and physical processes that give us the air, water and soil without which we cannot live). This encompasses the continuation of biological diversity as the very basis of life, ensuring the protection of species from human-caused extinction. The other is *human equity*, comprising a mix of features: equality of opportunity; full access to decision-making forums for all (which would include the principles of decentralization and participation); equity in the distribution and enjoyment of the benefits of human endeavour (across class, caste, age, gender, race and other divisions); justice; and cultural security.

Needless to add, these are complex requirements and very rarely met in actual practice in entirety anywhere. Yet, they must serve as guiding principles, as bulwarks against the worsening of existing realities, and as yardsticks of positive change from the present.

Linked to the above is a set of basic values, which are at the heart of RED: respect for cultural diversity and pluralism; cooperation rather than competition as the basis of human relations; respect for all life forms including other species and fellow human beings; dignity of labour; defining the 'good life' as the pursuit of knowledge, happiness and satisfaction through cultural and social interactions (rather than only material accumulation); maintaining strong links with nature; simple lifestyles; prioritizing the commons over the private; and valuing non-violence.

Taking the above principles together, we see RED as a continuously evolving and mutually respectful dialogue among human beings and between humanity and the rest of nature. It is a path, not a fixed destination. It is in complete contrast to the world view in which one or some sections of human beings determine the way ahead for, and dominate, other sections and in which humanity as a whole treats nature as external to itself, present only for 'conquest' and exploitation.

Diversity, localization and landscapes

Moving towards sustainable and equitable alternatives is not only about recycling and reuse, clean technologies and waste reduction, but also about fundamental changes in the way we relate to nature and to each other. This involves changes in governance, economics, technology, social relations, ethics and a host of other aspects of human life. We elaborate on some key elements of RED here.

A diversity of alternatives

A big mistake which will have to be addressed everywhere in the country in the future is the imposition of one economic model or indeed one model of governance, education, health and environmental management on the enormous diversity of ecological and cultural situations that defines India.

Moving away from such uniformity and the domination of one world view would enable respect and recognition for many ecologies (where different ecosystems and species have varying needs) and the myriad human ways of living. These include systems once considered valuable but now seen as outdated and/ or 'primitive': subsistence economies; barter; local market-based trade; oral knowledge; work–leisure combines; dignity of labour;

the machine as a tool and not a master; local health traditions; handicrafts; 'learning by doing' with parents and elders; encouraging simplicity, and so on. This does not mean an unconditional acceptance of traditions—indeed there is much in traditional India that needs to be left behind, like women's subjugation and the exploitation of Dalits and the 'lower' castes—rather, a reconsidered engagement with the past and the rediscovery of many valuable practices that seem to have been forgotten. The baby of the future, so to speak, has to be recovered from the bathwater of the past. Traditions also need to be rescued from those who use them in a bigoted way.[12]

Localization

A key plank of the alternative futures will be localization—a trend diametrically opposed to globalization. This is based on the simple but powerful belief that those living closest to the resource to be managed (the forest, the sea, the coast, the farm, the urban facility, etc.) would have the greatest stake, and often the best knowledge, to manage it. Of course, this is not always the case and in India many communities have lost the ability and often even the zeal to manage their surrounds because of two and a half centuries of government-dominated policies, which have effectively crippled their own institutional structures, customary rules and other capacities.

Nevertheless, a move towards the localization of essential production, consumption, trade, health, education and other services is eminently possible if communities are sensitively assisted by civil society organizations and the government. The few examples given in this chapter are among the thousands of Indian initiatives of decentralized water harvesting, biodiversity conservation, education, governance, food and materials production, energy generation, waste management and others (in both villages and cities).[13]

Nor are these only initiated by civil society groups. Indeed, the 73rd and 74th Amendments to the Indian Constitution (mandating decentralization to rural and urban communities), taken to their logical conclusion, are essentially about localization. 'Communitization' (providing for greater local collective control) of education, health and other aspects has been successfully attempted by the state of Nagaland. These are ready testimonies to the power of localization and, though still drops in the ocean, serve as forerunners to a growing trend that will emerge as the globalized sections of national and regional economies collapse.[14]

If one advocates localization, it is important to deal squarely and justly with the very real issue of socio-economic exploitation that is embedded in India's caste system, in the dynamics between religious majorities and minorities, and in the relations between men and women. Rural oppression is often cited as an argument against localization. Dr B.R. Ambedkar (one of India's pioneering advocates of the rights of Dalits and other oppressed sections), for instance, described villages as 'the ruination of India . . . a sink of localism, a den of ignorance, narrow-mindedness and communalism'. This has led a number of his followers to embrace capitalist globalization and its apparent opportunities for the social mobility of Dalits, especially in the 'anonymity' of the city.[15] Yet, as we have seen in chapter 4 and elsewhere in this book, the Indian city is no utopia. Urbanization may have contributed to the empowerment and emergence of Dalit politics, but if rural life is going to be denounced in all respects, we run the real risk of distancing and alienating whole generations from nature (as most people begin to grow up in cities). And we will also persist in the age-old error of allowing the policy and business elite in city-centres to make decisions about natural resources that lie at a great distance from them, resources in which they have little direct stake, unlike those who do but have been disenfranchised. In any case, as we see in the examples given here, empowerment of Dalits and other oppressed and poor sections can and has taken place through many alternative, ecologically sensitive ways.

The fact remains that 800 million people still live in India's 600,000 villages. This is not something which will change too dramatically, even if 10–20 per cent of this population moves to the cities in the future. So the issue of local forms of oppression will remain and will have to be addressed through struggle, education, reform, the legal system, the three-tiered system of governance and all other means that can be imagined.

Subjugation, not only of Dalits but also of those belonging to the minority faiths by those of the dominant ones, of adivasis by non-adivasis, and of women by men, remains all too commonplace. But many of the initiatives described in this chapter show that there is nothing permanent about such inequities, that they can be tackled, that those once oppressed can come up to terms of equality with their oppressors and that this can happen without causing irreversible ecological damage. Social, economic and ecological transformations often go hand in hand (though there is no necessary correlation here), as witnessed in the case of Dalit women gaining dignity and pride through the activities of Deccan Development Society in Andhra; Dalits and 'upper' castes interacting with much greater equality in Kuthambakkam village of Tamil Nadu; and adivasi children being empowered through the Narmada Bachao Andolan's *jeevan* *shala*s (described elsewhere in this chapter). None of these is as yet a full transformation to a socially equitable order, but they are inspiring signs of future possibilities.

Moreover, for every equitable opportunity that Indian cities may have provided, they have also brought in new forms of inequality and created new forms of oppression for the same classes, including exploitation in the workplace (see chapters 4 and 6). Nobody should be under any illusion that the struggle against millennia-old forms of discrimination and exploitation will end successfully tomorrow. We will need to keep the struggle alive as part of the search for alternative, saner futures that have localization as one of their planks. In this sense, Indian villages of the future may be diverse combinations of Gandhian, Nehruvian, Marxist and Ambedkarite visions (a mix of tradition and modernity, ethics and technology, social equity and political struggle).[16]

A number of other elements of RED, laid out below, will help in this. India will not be alone if it moves towards localization: it is happening in various measures even in the most globalized economies of the world. The localization of production, consumption and finances, or the slow food movements in the USA and Europe are examples.[17] This trend will increase as communities realize that the roots of the economic crisis starting in 2007–08 (see chapter 1) lie in the globalization of economic and financial systems, contrary to the vision of Keynes.

Working at the landscape level: Initiating bioregionalism

The local and the small-scale, however crucial as fulcrums of RED, are not by themselves adequate to achieve it. For many of the problems we now face are on a much larger scale, emanating from and affecting entire landscapes (and seascapes), countries, regions and, indeed, the earth itself. Climate change is an obvious example, but there were many well before it: the spread of toxics and desertification, to name two.[18]

Landscape and trans-boundary planning and governance (also called 'bioregionalism' or 'ecoregionalism', among other things) are now exciting new approaches being applied in several countries and regions.[19] These are as yet fledglings in India, but some are worth learning from. The Arvari Sansad (parliament) in Rajasthan (see box on 'Water democracy and a people's parliament' below) is aimed at managing a 400-sq-km river basin

---

Water democracy and a people's parliament

The semi-arid region of the Alwar district, Rajasthan, has for several decades faced severe water and food shortages, due partly to the breakdown of village institutions and technologies related to water storage and use. But in the last two decades the civil society organization (CSO) Tarun Bharat Sangh, comprised mostly of local villagers, has transformed this situation through the use of decentralized, small-scale *johad*s (check dams) and other water-storage techniques, combined with a regeneration of catchment forests and the creation of village-level institutions to regulate water, forest and land use. Agricultural productivity has jumped, in some villages threefold, within the space of a decade. In 1999, at a mass public meeting held to discuss continuing problems (policy and administrative hurdles from government agencies, inter-village conflicts, etc.), settlements in the Arvari river basin (spread over about 400 sq km) decided to form a people's parliament (Arvari Sansad) to regularly discuss and resolve issues.

Perhaps the first such institution in India, the Arvari Sansad comprises 242 members chosen from seventy-two villages, who meet twice a year. It regulates inter-village water flows and use; allows cropping primarily for local use; discourages growing water-intensive crops for sale; ensures protection of fish and all other wildlife; restricts the felling of trees; enables the regeneration and conservation of catchments; prohibits sale of land to outsiders; prevents mining; and facilitates restoration of previously mined areas. In the early 2000s the Arvari Sansad participated in the creation of a biodiversity action plan for the entire basin. Problems of caste divisions, lack of women's participation and others remain, but the Sansad is increasingly bringing these under its purview.

Importantly, the presence of a democratic local political institution provides a forum and a framework within which a whole set of issues can be raised and discussed to reach consensus for collective action—just how a good democracy ought to work.[22]

through inter-village coordination, making integrated plans and programmes for land, agriculture, water, wildlife and development.[20] In Orissa the state government has made a bold effort to bring several thousand square kilometres of the Chilika lagoon and catchment hills under integrated and participatory planning through the creation of a Chilika Development Authority with membership of all the relevant departments. Reports are mixed about the success of this initiative. Some sources claim it has helped reduce the shrinking of the lake, increase fish stocks and improve the lake's health. Others say that siltation, encroachment by commercial shrimp aquaculture, lack of tenurial security for traditional fishers, and poaching remain problems. But even as a partial success, it has important lessons to impart, especially with regard to the potential of various departments, disciplines and knowledge systems being able to work together.[21]

Unlike some other parts of the world, the South Asian subcontinent should actually be an ideal place for effective experimentation with bioregionalism, given the staggering diversity of agro-climatic zones that define this part of the world. A necessity may often be virtue in disguise. We should recognize and respond to the unique ecological opportunities that our natural settings offer.

In some parts of the country, traditional practices of local environmental governance are still present; for instance, several 'particularly vulnerable tribal groups' (PTGs) of central and eastern India (such as Abhuj Maria, Baiga, Birhor, Maria Gond, Hill Kharia, Dongria Kondh, Chukti Bhunjia) retain their tribe-wide system of decision-making that cuts across the more recent panchayat system.[23]

Working at the landscape necessarily envisages thinking across political and cultural boundaries. In a detailed exercise conducted as part of the National Biodiversity Strategy and Action Plan process,[24] this kind of planning was envisaged for ten such landscapes across India.

As an example, the Western Ghats ecoregion stretches across the coast of western India, from southern Gujarat to Kerala. Known as one of the world's biodiversity 'hotspots', this ecoregion has suffered from the uncoordinated policies and practices of five different states, as also from the lack of participatory forums for its various communities (including many of India's oldest adivasi communities and nomadic pastoralists). The action plan envisaged coordinated planning, based on an enhanced understanding of the ecological dynamics of the region, vested in a Western Ghats Conservation Planning and Development Board. Such a board would be constituted of government agencies from the five states and of civil society and local community members.[25]

Interestingly, precursors to such an approach are already present in the case of the Western Ghats, with the Planning Commission funding a special scheme for ecologically sensitive development here since the Fifth Five-Year Plan (mid-1970s).[26] The concept behind this scheme was ecoregional in the above sense and stressed that all development must be in tune with the ecologically sensitive nature of the region. But in practice, the scheme does not empower local communities or encourage independent citizens to oversee the process, and does little to change the overall (unsustainable) 'development' mindset of the respective state governments.

Crucial components of the bioregional or landscape approach are *resilience* and *adaptability*—the capacity of ecosystems and human communities to absorb disturbances (up to reasonable limits) and achieve restoration in original or modified forms in order to sustain ecological and livelihood security. In the case of human communities, this would also entail the ability to continuously learn from experience and enhance or improve governance and management.

Building on decentralized and landscape-level governance and management, and in turn providing it with a solid backing, would be a land-use plan for each bioregion and state, and the country as a whole. This plan would permanently put the country's ecologically and socially most fragile or important lands into some form of conservation status (mindful of local rights and tenure) including biodiversity hotspots; sacred sites (especially of traditional communities); territories of vulnerable adivasis and fisherfolk; community-conserved and government-managed protected areas; catchment forests, and so on. Mining, ports, industries, etc., could simply not come up here. In 2010 India's minister for environment and forests began to list such 'no-go' areas for coal mining (following up on a specific component on this in the National Environment Policy 2006), but immediately encountered resistance from fellow ministers and even the prime minister's office, prompting a rethink.[27]

Such a land-use plan would also enjoin upon towns and cities to build as much of their resources within their boundaries as possible, through water harvesting, rooftop and vacant-plot farming, decentralized energy generation, etc.; and to build mutually beneficial rather than parasitic relations with rural areas from where they will still need to take resources. The greater the say of rural communities in deciding what happens to their resources, and the greater the awareness of city-dwellers about the impact of their lifestyles, the more this will happen. The city as envisaged by Tagore—as one of the centres of innovation, giving as much to the village as taking from it—could become a reality through such a process.[28]

Ultimately, as villages get revitalized through locally appropriate development initiatives, migration—which today seems inexorable—would also slow down and may even get reversed, as has happened with villages like Ralegan Siddhi and Hivare Bazaar (Maharashtra); villages in Dewas district (Madhya Pradesh) where Samaj Pragati Sahayog is active (see chapter 10); and some villages in Alwar district (Rajasthan) where Tarun Bharat Sangh is active.[29]

Governance, local to national

Central to the notion of RED is the practice of democratic governance that starts from the smallest, most local unit, to ever-expanding spatial units. A number of theories of democracy or governance have expounded on this, across the broad spectrum of political ideologies. Markovic brings in a neo-Marxist perspective when he advocates 'council democracy', with all citizens involved in decision-making at the level of their basic work unit or community, building into expanding 'self-governing' bodies at various levels from local to global.[30] Gandhi spoke in terms of 'oceanic circles' of decision-making, starting from the individual and building up to a federal structure, complementing his views on *gram swaraj*.[31] Morrison talks of 'a series of nested and overlapping social and economic commons, ranging from the local to the global', and planning by 'confederations and associations of community enterprises, institutions and local government' at 'state, national, regional and international levels'.[32] Ostrom's seminal work on the commons, which won her the Nobel Prize in Economics in 2009, focuses on the idea of nested institutions or enterprises.[33]

In each of these—and crucial to the concept of RED—is the right of every individual to take part in the affairs of his/her community or work unit (though they may choose not to exercise this right), and to have or acquire the capacity to do so. But such a right is also tempered by responsibilities towards fellow human beings, foremost among them being to honour the same rights they have. Additionally, RED requires that there be a responsibility towards the environment, including the natural world. A number of examples of alternative paths given in this chapter, or available to observers across India, display such a balance of universal rights and responsibilities at the local level. From this basic level emanate federations, platforms or institutions of decision-making at expanding geographical or thematic levels: clusters of communities, federations of worker organizations, and so on. Clearly, all citizens cannot take part in daily decision-making at all levels up to the national and the global, so there has to be delegation of powers *upward*. What is crucial is that such delegation be the prerogative of the smaller unit (starting from the smallest), that it have the full right of recalling non-performing delegates and that delegates be mandated to be fully accountable to the people, their decisions being transparent *from below*.

In India, at the village-level, panchayats are already mandated by the Constitution, in particular its 73rd Amendment and the related legislation. However, these are representative bodies, subject to the same pitfalls that currently plague representative democracy at the higher levels (albeit on a much smaller scale): destructively competitive politics to get elected (compounded by the exclusion of many individuals due to caste and gender discrimination), a tendency to ignore the interests of large sections of the community, and so on. This is particularly true where panchayats are spread over several villages and cover a substantial geographical area, and where the communities are of multiple ethnicities (e.g. adivasi and non-adivasi). Moreover, they do not have the power to make laws for the local region, which are binding at other levels of the polity.

There is therefore the need to focus more on empowering the gram sabha, adivasi council or other equivalent body (here referred to as *village assembly*) that consists of all the adults of the individual hamlet or village. This should be the functional decision-making unit, where all adult women and men are conveniently able to participate in decision-making using the basic principles of participatory democracy, and where rights and responsibilities are clearly established and transparent (see the example of Mendha-Lekha in the box below). All critical

Local self-governance: The case of Mendha-Lekha, Maharashtra

Something close to full local empowerment in governance has been achieved by the Gond adivasi village of Mendha-Lekha, in Gadchiroli district, Maharashtra. This village was mobilized in the 1980s in the struggle against two mega dams planned in the area, which were successfully stopped. It was also part of the strong but only partially successful push towards adivasi self-rule across central India. It successfully fought against large-scale bamboo extraction by a paper mill. Gradually, it built up a system of full gram sabha gatherings to take all the decisions, using information generated by *abhyas gat*s (study circles involving villagers and, where necessary, external experts). Decisions are taken only by consensus, creating a high stake in their implementation. All government departments have to seek the consent of the gram sabha for their activities and the village is able to influence what these activities are.

In the last three decades the village has moved towards fulfilment of all basic requirements of food, water, energy and local livelihoods. It has also conserved 1800 ha of forest. In 2009 Mendha-Lekha became one of the first villages in India to obtain the community right to manage their forests under the Scheduled Tribes and Other Traditional Forest Dwellers (Recognition of Forest Rights) Act 2006, thereby reversing the act of the colonial government in taking over their control under the Indian Forest Act 1927.

However, challenges of transferring the values of collective decision-making, conservation and the primacy of the community to new generations are emerging. There is also a continuing weakness in the policy environment to support such initiatives, limiting their spread to other villages.[35]

decisions relating to local natural resources should be taken by the village assembly. Decisions at larger (district, state, national) levels that involve local resources should be taken only with the consent of the relevant village assemblies—who might exercise veto powers in certain extreme situations (of the kind that happened in Niyamgiri, Orissa, recently). Special provision needs to be made to facilitate the equal participation of women and other underprivileged sections including the landless[34] and to revive and strengthen the spirit of collective actions that characterizes traditional relations.

In the case of towns and cities, the basic decision-making unit has been mandated in the 74th Constitutional Amendment (and related legislation) to be the *urban ward*. A further refinement is the concept of *area sabhas*—smaller, more manageable units within wards (but larger than the resident welfare associations or colony associations that exist in many cities). These sabhas, where all citizens of the locality can participate, are the basic decision-making units for all matters related to their territorial jurisdiction; they would need to coordinate with each other on common property resources cutting across sabha and ward boundaries, such as larger urban green areas and wetlands. Of course, creating a sense of 'community' in urban areas would be especially challenging, given the much greater divergence of interests and backgrounds than is typically found in a rural settlement. Facilitation for such coordination, and for sabhas/wards to be able to perform conservation and sustainable-use functions, should be the responsibility of municipal corporations or equivalent city management bodies, with the role of mediation being played by CSOs and independent experts where necessary. Each town/city could also have an overall environment management committee, comprising officials from relevant line departments, CSOs, independent experts and representatives of sabhas and wards on a rotational basis. Some examples of initiatives at achieving deeper urban democracy are given below.

These people's forums or associations could be linked to *micro-landscape-level bodies*, which also have representation of the relevant government line departments. Existing initiatives towards this kind of a structure—such as the district planning committees, district rural development agencies and forest development agencies—need to be reviewed and reoriented with respect to local community empowerment, the sharing of decision-making powers and ecological principles of the entire micro-landscape. These bodies should include, on a rotational basis, representatives of village clusters and urban committees. The same would apply in the case of autonomous district councils or other such larger landscape agencies.

One critical gap in current governance structures relating to environment and development is to do with *inter-state* issues. Since ecoregions often cut across state boundaries, governance mechanisms that involve multiple states, including communities on both sides, are required. There is not much in the form of successful experience on this in India. Starting with the Damodar Valley Corporation (DVC) in the 1940s, the Government of India has set up a series of river valley boards, authorities and committees. Even though some of these landscape-level institutions, like the DVC, have had the explicit function of planning for integrated, ecologically sensitive development, the stress has remained on power, irrigation and other ways to exploit the river or share its benefits amongst riparian states. Thus, for the most part, they have failed in integrated planning of basins.[36]

Ecological and social considerations and participatory principles must be at the core of any new institutions for landscape governance and planning. The movement towards bioregional planning in some countries also includes discussions on political realignments; it would be worth observing the results to learn lessons relevant for India's unique conditions. It seems inevitable that in the long run, if ecological soundness and the landscape approach have to become the basis of economic and political life, some realignment of political and administrative boundaries will be necessary.

The role of knowledge and education

The realization of RED is contingent on the availability and use of good environmental and social knowledge. The idea is to not privilege modern scientific knowledge over other forms or systems of knowledge, as has happened for too long a time. Rather, it will strive for a synergistic combination of all such systems.

Traditional or local knowledge systems, continuously evolving from ancient to modern times, retain considerable contemporary relevance. This is true not only for the several hundred million people who continue to depend on natural ecosystems and agricultural/pastoral lifestyles but also for sectors of the modern economy including pharmaceuticals, health, education, and so on. [37]

A range of industrial products are dependent on or use traditional knowledge in different ways. This is true, for example, for sectors like textiles, pharmaceuticals and household goods. Health care, through all systems of medicine, is to varying degrees dependent on traditional knowledge alone or in combination with modern knowledge. According to the World Health Organization (WHO), about 80 per cent of the world's population is dependent, in some form or another, on medicinal plants known through traditional health-care systems. Numerous studies have demonstrated the contribution that traditional knowledge also makes to the modern pharmaceutical industry and modern health care, a contribution that may only increase as people in the Western world (including westernized people in the 'developing' countries) become more conscious of plant-based cures.[38]

Services like food distribution, education, climate forecasting and warning, and community care also continue to be performed through institutions using traditional means. In some cases, modern institutions of the government or the corporate sector are discovering the value of this. For instance, in parts of Africa, rates of maternal mortality at childbirth were reduced significantly when traditional institutions (including the traditional birth attendant) were used in combination with modern ones.[39]

Such adaptability could be a key factor in the response that we offer to the challenge of climate change. The use of traditional knowledge in all the sectors named above could provide the alternatives needed to build towards a more sustainable way of dealing with our changing atmosphere. Combining the knowledge of indigenous peoples such as the Inuvialuit, with modern scientific understanding, was crucial to the ambitious Arctic Climate Impact Assessment (ACIA) brought out in 2004.[40] Indigenous peoples are now conducting their own assessments in several regions of the world under the Indigenous Peoples' Assessment of Climate Change process.[41] In initiating this process, the United Nations University noted that:

Observations of ecosystem change by indigenous peoples are acting as a sentinel-like warning system for climate change.

More importantly, the long-term place-based adaptation approaches developed by indigenous peoples provide valuable examples for the global community of low-carbon sustainable lifestyle, critical to developing local adaptations strategies in the face of climate instability.

A crucial scientific question that faces us today is: how does one assess unsustainability? What indicators, criteria and methods can be used for this? Here, too, traditional knowledge plays a vital role, for indigenous peoples and local communities have used a wide range of their own indicators and methods to ascertain sustainability. Water flows; the presence/absence or appearance/disappearance of certain species; the behaviour of domestic or wild animals; and other kinds of changes in their natural settings are observed and used in myriad sophisticated ways to learn about ecological changes. Synergizing these with the best of what modern technologies and insights make available is the key to envisioning a more sustainable future.

Most relevant knowledge for RED will also disregard the artificial boundaries between the 'physical', the 'natural' and the 'social' sciences, and between these sciences and the 'arts'. The more we can learn and teach and transmit knowledge in holistic ways, the better will we understand nature and our own place in it.

A number of innovative experiments in alternative learning, which combine modern and traditional methods and focus on locally relevant learning, have come up in India (other than the Ladakh initiative described on page 259):

- The *pachasaale* school of Deccan Development Society (DDS), at Pastapur in Andhra Pradesh, focuses on disprivileged children from a dozen villages. It combines literacy and other standard skills with vocational capacities, using as teachers both trained professionals and village experts. Textbooks have been prepared (some by or with the children) to reflect on and learn from local reality, and substantial interdisciplinary teaching takes place through involvement in festivals, agricultural activities and other practical events. Respect for all religions and knowledge systems is encouraged. A team of *vidya karyakarta*s, trained youth from the villages, has been employed to persuade and help households reluctant to send their children to school. Children's committees have been established to promote democracy in the functioning of the school.[42]

- The Narmada Bachao Andolan, struggling to save the Narmada Valley and its inhabitants from mega dams, has set up a number of jeevan shalas, or life schools, to provide meaningful education to adivasi children who are otherwise deprived of any educational opportunities. The aim of these shalas is 'to provide education that is rooted in tribal culture and knowledge base, while exploring the horizon of the new and the unknown'. The teachers are local adivasi youth, who with the students have produced textbooks in local adivasi languages, used oral folklore and knowledge as a base to devise lessons, and employed products from the surrounds to enable literacy and teach other skills. The shalas are also frequently visited by the Andolan's partners and well-wishers from outside the valley and students travel to other parts of India, both providing them regular exposure to the outside world.[43]

- The Adharshila Learning Centre in Sakad village, Badwani district, Madhya Pradesh, has a curriculum that 'combines academics, world issues, practical skills, and cultural heritage with a lot of fun'. Learning has a particular focus on continuing oral traditions, documenting local knowledge and history by talking to village elders and imbibing new ideas related to the environment, human rights and development. The children have even written their own books, collecting local folk tales, writing them up in the local dialect Bareli and illustrating them. In the midst of all this, regular lessons continue and most children have been able to pass the state board exams.[44]

- The Adivasi Academy at Tejgadh, Gujarat, aims to train adivasi youth at the college level, in various subjects of relevance to them. It offers a two-year diploma in tribal studies, as also certificate courses in subjects as diverse as adivasi arts and culture, computers, rural health, organic agriculture and forest management. Teaching methods include standard classroom exercises with interactions and learning from adivasi experts and field visits. Instead of examinations, students conduct seminars and write dissertations. All students are encouraged to go back to their villages to work on tribal welfare and development issues; most have been absorbed into either the activities of the parent organization, Bhasha Trust, its various affiliated organizations or other similar institutions.[45]

Employment and livelihood

The combination of localization and landscape approaches also provides massive opportunities for livelihood generation, thus tackling one of India's (and the world's) biggest ongoing problems: unemployment due to redundancy. For many years now, CSOs in India have been saying that land and water regeneration, and the resulting increase in productivity, could provide one of the country's biggest sources of employment and create permanent assets for sustainable livelihoods. The Mahatma Gandhi National Rural Employment Guarantee Act (MGNREGA) 2005,[46] one of the Indian government's flagship programmes of the new millennium, as also other schemes such as the Jawaharlal Nehru National Urban Renewal Mission (JNNURM),[47] could well be oriented towards such environment–employment combinations. Also important in the new 'green job' deal would be a renewed emphasis on labour-intensive rural industries and infrastructure, including handloom and handicrafts, local energy projects, rural roads and others that people can be in control of, building on their own traditional knowledge or with easily acquired new skills.

The United Nations Environment Programme (UNEP) and the International Labour Organization (ILO) estimate that there is considerable employment opportunity in 'green jobs', defined as 'decent work',[48] which could help tackle the ecological crises we face. For instance, organic, small-scale farming can employ more people than conventional chemical-based agriculture: 'More labour-intensive than industrialized agriculture, the conversion of farmland for organic production could provide a good source of green employment in the future.'[49]

This is beginning to be realized in India too. The Andhra Pradesh government in its draft policy on organic farming (see more on this below) states: 'Organic agriculture requires significantly greater labour input than conventional farms thereby increasing employment opportunities and reverse migration to urban areas.'[50]

The drive towards renewable energy generation (see the section on Energy below), still in its infancy, could provide jobs to tens of millions. Already, though such energy is only 2 per cent of the total energy produced in the world, it employs at least 2.3 million people, a figure obtained from only a handful of countries.[51] Similarly, energy efficiency, e.g. in buildings and construction, has enormous potential, with over 4 million jobs already in the USA and some European countries.[52]

For both farming and energy (generation and efficiency), as also several other sectors that the UNEP–ILO study discusses— such as public transportation, energy-efficient building, decentralized manufacture, recycling, forestry and others—the potential in India must be truly astounding. Yet, no comprehensive study has ever been carried out on this potential. This is the kind of task that the Planning Commission and relevant ministries should be undertaking and budgeting for, if they are serious about moving the country towards sustainability and 'inclusiveness' (the slogan for the current, Eleventh Five-Year Plan).

A significant contribution to models of livelihood security based on ecologically sustainable practices comes from the work of K.R. Datye. He placed a strong emphasis on biomass-based renewal of rural areas. He showed empirically that every family can generate three tonnes of biomass every year after meeting the basic needs (food, fuel, fodder), and that could be the basis of energy security and enhanced livelihoods through rural industry. Technological and design innovations were also at the core of his ideas, combining the strength of both traditional and modern knowledge and science, for instance, in construction practices. A number of groups and individuals are trying out his ideas on the ground.[53]

Agricultural swaraj

What would be the elements of a more ecologically sustainable and socially equitable framework for agriculture? Clues for this come from the very many grass-roots initiatives at organic, biologically diverse, holistic farming that dot various regions of India (including the examples cited elsewhere in this chapter, such as the Deccan Development Society).

- In Karnataka, the NGO Green Foundation works with dry-land farmers in over sixty villages to sustain or revive organic practices that maintain soil fertility while producing healthy crops.[54] It too reports a range of positive impacts in situations where farmers who were once convinced of the use of chemicals are switching to organic cultivation.

- About 4000 villages are reported to be taking part in the Jaiv Panchayat initiative of Navdanya, pledging to conserve their traditional seed diversity; promote organic farming and local water management; and participate in larger movements against biopiracy.[55]

- In Andhra Pradesh, the state government, having developed a draft policy on organic farming, is supporting possibly the country's biggest sustainable agriculture programme. Under the sponsorship of the rural development department's Society for Elimination of Rural Poverty, the Sustainable Agriculture Network of NGOs is spreading community-based sustainable agriculture (CMSA). Between 2004 and 2009, over 318,000 farmers have adopted these practices, covering 1.36 million acres of farmland (5.1 per cent of the net cropped area in the state). The reduction in pesticide and fertilizer use has so far led to a cost saving of over US$38 million. Also in Andhra

Pradesh, the Watershed Support Services and Activities Network (WASSAN) is working towards 'a new paradigm for the development of rain-fed areas that is founded on the principles of diversity of livelihoods, secure farming systems, low-external inputs and inclusive growth'.[56]

- Sikkim and Kerala have announced aims to convert totally to organic farming by about 2015.[57]

Some key elements of sustainable and equitable farming—many of which would also be relevant for fisheries, animal husbandry and forestry—are the following:[58]

1. Localized production or availability of the basic inputs, including seeds/livestock/fingerlings, manure, water, fodder, technologies, knowledge and affordable credit from institutional sources.

2. Integration of crop, livestock, fodder and/or fish production and of forest conservation and use.

3. Assistance to farmers to switch from chemical-dependent to organic farming, including the conversion of current fertilizer subsidies.

4. Linking the public distribution system and other food security schemes such as midday meals and food for work to locally produced food.

5. Building on local agricultural, forestry and aquatic produce to generate additional livelihoods through village-based industry.

6. Feeding agriculture's energy needs through decentralized, renewable-energy sources.

7. Ensuring equitable access to water.

8. Facilitating the empowerment of the most marginalized, including landless and marginal farmers, and women.

9. Encouraging urban agriculture to meet basic household needs.
10. Decentralized R&D (research and development) in the form of joint, on-field programmes by farmers and modern agricultural scientists.
11. Facilitating direct producer–consumer links, using local 'certification' of organic, healthy produce (through, for instance, the Participatory Guarantee System).[59]

Sustainable and democratic cities

There are relatively few initiatives towards radical alternatives for urban sustainability (such as the one for Bhuj described on page 258), but the few that do exist point to the potential.

An attempt to bring citizens into the planning process is the participatory budgeting exercise in a number of cities in India (and many other countries). Among the first to initiate this process was Bengaluru, followed by Hubli-Dharwad and Pune. In Pune, the process has enabled even poor ragpicker women to participate in the city's planning,[60] while in Bengaluru, a model Nagara Raj Bill has been formulated for empowering area sabha–level democratic processes.[61] And in Delhi, the NGO Parivartan forced the government to abandon a proposed World Bank–funded project that would have hiked up water costs.[62]

In these and other ways, India's urban areas could potentially start moving towards the ideal of an 'ecopolis', characterized by zero-energy buildings (generating all the energy they use), zero-waste colonies, local water havesting, non-polluting public transport, encouragement to cycling and walking, localized markets and producer–consumer links, and radical forms of democracy.[63]

Decentralized, renewable energy

Mainstream energy generation and its distribution through a centralized grid system has not reached more than 40 per cent of India's population. The reasons are the poor and wasteful distribution networks and lack of financial resources for the poor to buy connections or even bulbs. The ambitious attempt to generate 20,000 MW of solar power under the National Action Plan on Climate Change (NAPCC) may be a positive development for those advocating substantial increases in renewable energy, but it is unlikely to achieve the objective of providing energy security to the poor because of a predominant focus on supplying the grid. What is needed is *decentralized*, renewable energy.[64]

Some initiatives are oriented precisely towards this:

- The company SELCO India has, over a period of fifteen years, reached out to poor households in rural and urban areas (mostly in Karnataka, Tamil Nadu and Maharashtra), providing solar energy solutions by tying up with third-party financiers. Over 115,000 households (weavers, street vendors, farmers, beedi workers, nomadic pastoralists and others) and institutions (rural hospitals and schools) are now being reached, with direct, tailor-made, door-step servicing and financing. This has helped quietly revolutionize the lives of these families, enabling longer and more efficient work hours, creating new jobs, reducing pollution from cooking stoves or kerosene lamps, and allowing children to study at night.[65]
- Delhi-based Yogeshwar Kumar, IIT engineer-turned-activist, has been instrumental in the construction of community-led micro-hydel power plants, including a

30 KW power station for eighty households in Kargil, near the Line of Control in Kashmir. He transforms small power stations into producer companies by creating village enterprises. Successful micro-hydel units have been set up in Uttarakhand and Meghalaya as well.[66]

- In 2003 the world's first biomass-based power plant, with a capacity of 4.5 MW, fired with low-density crop residues, was set up in Karnataka under the leadership of K. Krishan. He has been involved since then in the construction of similar units in Punjab, ultimately capable of delivering 156 MW of power.[67]

- Mini grids—which serve local areas—are also being experimented with. In the Sunderbans in West Bengal, for instance, mini grids with peak power ratings of 55–110 KW have been constructed, based on a supply from solar photovoltaic cells. One possible danger to these interesting experiments is the entry of big players—such as the NTPC—in the renewable energy sector. If grid-based power supply, using renewable energy, takes off in a big way, chances are that local needs will get neglected once again even as resources for power generation are supplied by the villages. In other words, many of the problems of today will reappear.[68]

Economic democracy

RED requires not only a fundamental change in political governance but also in economic relations of production and consumption. Globalized economies tend to emphasize the democratization of consumption (with the consumer as 'king', though in many cases there is only a mirage of choice) but not the democratization of production. Production is more and more concentrated in the hands of a few. This can only change with a fundamental reversal, towards decentralized production (at least of the basic needs of life and conceivably of much else) in the control of primary producers rather than corporations. This would in turn be linked predominantly (but not exclusively) to local consumption, which would be in the control of consumers rather than of retailers and advertisers.

Village-based or 'cottage' industry would be oriented to meeting, first and foremost, local needs, and then national or international needs. Since this would be part of a localized economy in which producer–consumer links are primarily (though not only) local, the crucial difference between such production and the current capitalist production is that it would exist chiefly as a service and not for profits.[69] Production becomes as much a means of self-expression, in which the worker finds meaning and satisfaction, as a means for material fulfilment. In his *Paris Manuscripts* Marx spoke about the creative activity of the worker as a vehicle for meaningful self-expression, something that could end his/her alienation within the assembly-line production systems of modern industrial society. A huge variety of such 'social enterprises' are springing up in India and the rest of the world, offering the promise of productive and socially meaningful livelihoods for hundreds of millions of people; these are part of a more general move towards a 'social economy', providing an alternative, community-driven model to the one led by the state or the private corporate sector (see box on 'Social enterprise and the social economy' below).

Under RED, money may remain an important medium of exchange, but it would be much more locally controlled and managed rather than being controlled anonymously by international financial institutions and the abstract forces of

Social enterprise and the social economy

Businesses that are driven by social goals rather than private profits can be termed 'social enterprise'. There is no universally accepted definition for this phenomenon, which takes different forms in different countries. The network Social Enterprise London describes it thus: 'A social enterprise is a business with primarily social objectives whose surpluses are principally reinvested for that purpose in the business or in the community, rather than being driven by the need to maximise profit for shareholders and owners.'[70]

What is important is that while such businesses may make profits, these are used for furthering social goals. Governance and ownership is based on the participation of those who are the primary stakeholders (users, consumers, producers, community groups), and ethical concerns such as environmental sustainability, equity, fulfilling livelihoods and community benefits direct the way the business is done. Such businesses are also fully accountable to the public regarding their environmental, social, economic and political impacts. They seek to give priority to the *local* (in terms of resources used, needs met and benefits generated), while not excluding the possibility of catering to larger (regional, national, global) needs.[71]

global capital. Considerable local trade could revert to locally designed currencies or barter; and the prices of products and services, even when expressed in monetary terms, could be decided as locally relevant, between producers and consumers rather than by an impersonal, non-controllable distant 'market' dominated by remote players. Such local decision-making regarding prices or exchange values has been a phenomenon of local markets since ancient times. (Though there have often been inequities in these, reflecting the relative power of those involved in the exchange, which would need to be dealt with in the modern avatar of local markets.) A huge diversity of local currencies and non-monetary ways of trading and providing/ obtaining services are being employed around the world.[72] Just one worldwide database which registers such initiatives recorded a rise from forty initiatives in nineteen countries with 93,304 members in 2005 to 165 initiatives in twenty-eight countries with 336,928 members in 2007.[73]

With the old traditions of local *haat*s, barter and community-supported activities, as also the new experiments in direct producer–consumer links, many areas of India appear suitable for the adoption of such systems. And so, markets may cease to be distant, abstract forces. They will be more in the nature of *bazaar*s or *mandi*s. They will once again be, at their core, local, emphasizing trade among people who can relate to each other face-to-face. The central place of *conversations*, rather than abstract faceless transactions, can then be re-established.[74] National and international trade will be built on this core and be subject to local ecological and social considerations, never undermining local needs and sustainability; examples of this already exist in some fair trade practices.[75]

The village cluster 'free trade zone' being attempted by Panchayat President Elango in Tamil Nadu (described on page 257) is one example of what locally democratic trade relations could look like. Another is the concept of an adivasi-led 'green economic zone' (GEZ), in Gujarat. The NGO Bhasha, which has been working with adivasis in the Tejgadh area of south-east Gujarat, has proposed this idea as an alternative to the official SEZ (Special Economic Zone) concept (see chapter 7 on SEZs), which will give priority to private corporations. Based on the 'concepts of sustainability, ecological sensitivity, and an ingrained understanding of the cultural roots of a people', the GEZ is meant to optimize organic agricultural output and promote local industry and market links, without disrupting the biodiversity and local livelihoods.

Initiated by a march through about 120 villages in June 2009, its proponents hope to eventually cover 2200 villages. All funds are to be generated locally and all development based on local skills and resources, with the aim of 100 per cent employment. Several hundred self-help groups have been initiated over the last decade, helping to considerably reduce the severe debts into which adivasis have been trapped by moneylenders, and enabling farmers to get much better prices in the market. Cultural events such as festivals, fairs, yatras and drama are used to promote the ideas of ecologically sustainable livelihoods. The GEZ concept is still in its infancy, with a large number of pieces of the jigsaw to be put into place.[76]

A number of new initiatives have tried to bring markets under the control of producers, some of them emphasizing the role of women.

- The Nowgong Agriculture Producer Company Ltd (NAPCL), started in 2006, has enabled over 1100 farmers to control the entire process of production as well be involved in the trading of their produce in the drought-hit Bundelkhand region of Madhya Pradesh.[77]
- The Dharani Farming and Marketing Mutually Aided Cooperative Society Ltd in the Anantpur district of Andhra Pradesh originally comprised 350 organic farmers. The collective has grown and facilitated value addition to crops,

providing rural and urban marketing linkages, building capacity, and enabling certification through the Participatory Guarantee System. From a sales figure of Rs 70,000 in 2006–07, the cooperative reached Rs 30 lakh in 2009–10.[78]

- The Aharam Traditional Crop Producer Company (ATCPC), initiated by the NGO Covenant Centre for Development, has similar aims and activities, reaching over fifty villages around Madurai city in Tamil Nadu.[79]

- The Amar Bazaar in Assam is a marketing mechanism controlled by women producers and traders from the local area, facilitated by the NGO Rural Volunteers Centre. Over fifty Amar Bazaars are federated as the Matri Amar Bazaar Kendriya Samiti, eliminating the exploitative middleman in several villages.[80] From 1997 to 2006, the Tawa Matsya Sangh (Fishers' Cooperative) mobilized small-scale fishers to obtain a fishing licence in the Tawa Reservoir (Madhya Pradesh) and ensure responsible fishing (e.g. no use of explosives or catching of young fish), equitable distribution of benefits and fair price in the market. Unfortunately, a mix of government policies and vested interests led to non-renewal of the Sangh's lease in 2006.[81]

Financial management itself needs to be radically decentralized, away from the mega concentrations that today's banks and financial institutions represent. Across the world, a host of localized, community-based banking and financing systems have cropped up over the last couple of decades, e.g. the Spanish credit union Caja Laboral Popular of the Mondragon cooperatives.[82] Controlled and run by community cooperatives or collectives, these are a crucial part of future economic democracy, with financial inclusion as one of its core principles.

We will need a new notion of efficiency, which would be more focused on ecology than the present one. The current idea of efficiency is driven by business motives, emphasizing technical or allocative efficiency, and does not consider ecological and other external costs. The new notion of ecological efficiency will take a public, rather than a private, view of costs and benefits.

Whatever the scale of production chosen by future societies, economic democracy (and more generally, RED) necessitates the demise of large-scale capitalist enterprises and the capitalist relations of production, for these are by their very nature undemocratic and iniquitous. Businesses will be owned by those who work in them, through various forms of cooperative arrangements (learning from the shortcomings and strengths of cooperatives in various fields that currently exist), such as the examples described above.

Industry and infrastructure

The low-employment (or even job-destructive) and ecologically damaging nature of modern industrialization (with consequences described earlier in this book) has driven the search for another vision of industry.

- While handicrafts are often not seen as 'industry' in the modern sense of the word, they certainly offer productive, non-farm employment in rural and urban areas. In Jharkhand, the state handloom and handicraft department has initiated a successful scheme for employment generation and for the revival of traditional handicrafts among the adivasi population. Their products are sold under the name of Jharcraft. They have marketing outlets in many of the country's big cities where the market for such products is 'booming'. Their revenues are more than doubling every year and are targeted to cross Rs 100 crore in the next few years. The range of products produced and offered includes tussar silk, saris, shawls, terracotta artefacts, jewellery and much else that is typical of the tribal heartland of the state. Self-help groups have been roped in and tens of thousands of adivasi women, hitherto below the poverty line, have got work.[83]

- Another instance of low-impact light industry are the more than 100 business and manufacturing units in Auroville, Tamil Nadu. They produce textiles, processed food, leather goods, incense, furniture, paper products, metal-work, pottery and other items. They are all labour-intensive, hand-based crafts and most of the requirements of raw material are met locally. The scale of industries is small, not allowing extensive backward and forward linkages. Most of the units do their own production, assembly, finishing and packaging of products, often for export.[84]

- A most interesting and important experiment in low-impact labour-absorbing industry is happening in rural Andhra. The organization Deccan Cotton Yarn Trust (DCYT) has been working on reviving pre-colonial methods of cotton production for handloom weaving. They discovered that baling and un-baling—central to cotton processing for mill production today—was a nineteenth-century innovation brought in for the purposes of speedy mass production of mill cloth from long-staple cotton. This is damaging to the cotton fibre, apart from being energy- and capital-intensive. With the help of some engineers of the Indian Institute of Technology (IIT) and of Anna University in Chennai, DCYT has pioneered machines that have succeeded in making weavers produce a brand of fabric they call *malkha* (*malmal*-cum-khadi). It is made directly from raw cotton through gentle processing and avoids unnecessary damage to the fabric.

In the nineteenth century the East India Company had also succeeded in cutting off cotton-growing farmers from weavers, in order to make room for the Lancashire mills. DCYT has been working on renewing the direct link between the farmers and the weavers, in order to establish an entirely rural production-and-supply chain. Starting from the town of Chirala in the Praksam district of Andhra Pradesh, the Handloom Weavers' Cooperative has now spread its initiative to many more districts, giving respectable employment to hundreds of weaver families working out of small units. It has brought a semblance of hope to a region where handloom weavers thrown out of work by the forces of globalization have been committing suicide in recent times. This is also a good example of the power of combining traditional Indian principles of cotton-cloth-making with modern small-scale technology.

Our emphasis on small-scale production should not lead the reader to think that we imagine a future world where no large-scale investments, production or infrastructure will exist. In advocating a 'small is strong' or 'small is sustainable' view, we seek to correct the excessive focus on big industry. We do argue that 'eco-facture' must gradually take the mainstream spot that energy and resource-intensive 'machino-facture' occupies today. Large investments and production must become peripheral in the overall scheme of things.

Will big industry still have a place? Very likely, yes, though this will depend on what future societies—far more conscious of the ecological and social impacts of production and consumption—will want to produce and how they wish to do so. Moreover, the choice of technologies will be a matter of open public discussion and argument, rather than being unilaterally decided by powerful corporations or government bodies. But even if big industrial units are necessary, they will only be the last resort for products that small-scale industry simply cannot make. Any big industry that remains necessary must be subject to the social requirement of being 'service-oriented' rather than profit-oriented,[85] or it must fit into the concept of 'social enterprise' described above (see box on page 282). The role of an accountable, democratic state in the regulation or management of such necessary big industries would be important.

Will profits and private property (the means of production) have a place at all? From the vantage point of today, it is hard to imagine how they will not! Both may survive in limited spheres if they serve to supplement the collective good as an incentive, but they must be subject to the principles of RED. They would not be allowed to dominate human relations and economic activity and would need to be subservient to collective and community interests.

All industrial production will need to conform to the basic principles of what has been called 'industrial ecology':

- The elimination of products and production processes that are destructive, poisonous and unsustainable, and their replacement with sustainable and beneficial processes and products.
- The ongoing pursuit of efficiency, and the elimination of waste in resource- and energy-use.
- The development of production and consumption patterns based on reuse and recycling, where 'waste'

products are reclaimed and used as inputs for further productive processes.[86]

There is also large-scale infrastructure—especially in areas like transport and some forms of energy production—which we envisage as surviving into the future, well beyond the present age of high industrialization. Railways and international air travel, for instance, will and must survive into the future. However, there are two caveats to this. Firstly, the *full* cost of production of such items and services should be reckoned with, inclusive of all major social and environmental externalities (for example, the ecological damage caused by new airport terminals or the climate cost of plane emissions). Secondly, given the scale of investments involved (and their social and ecological consequences), such things ought to be subject to democratic scrutiny and reviews—even if they are sometimes, as might happen, in private hands. Society risks more serious disasters like the BP oil spill of mid-2010, if such accountability is absent.

The role of the state

If communities (rural and urban) are to be the fulcrum of the alternative futures, there still remains a role for the state. The state will need to retain, or rather strengthen, its welfare role for the vulnerable, facilitating their participation in decision-making (see box on 'Participatory planning' below). It will assist communities in situations where local capacity is weak, such as in generating resources; providing MGNREGA kind of schemes that guarantee minimum livelihood security, especially to vulnerable groups; and ensuring tenurial security. It will facilitate the larger, landscape-level linkages that communities require. It will rein in business elements or others who act irresponsibly towards the environment or people (rather than disrupt protests of the takeover of land and resources by industry, as it is doing currently!). It will have to be held accountable in its role as guarantor of the various fundamental rights that each citizen should enjoy under the Constitution of India.

There is considerable cynicism among the public about whether the state would ever be able to play such a role, given its rather poor track record (see chapter 3) and its propensity to side with (or even become) the exploitative sections of society. But one must remember that the state itself is not a monolith and that time and again positive steps have been taken by it. In recent times, much against the grain of globalization, the state produced progressive legislations like the Right to Information Act, the MGNREGA and the Scheduled Tribes and Other Traditional Forest Dwellers (Recognition of Forest Rights) Act. The experience of a number of CSOs struggling on the ground (such as the examples given in this chapter) is that such policy tools, and the constitutional responsibilities the state is supposed to perform, can often be called upon to transform exploitative situations.

Participatory planning by the government

A truly democratic state would facilitate planning processes that maximize public participation. An instance where this was partially achieved is the Peoples' Plan Campaign (PPC) of Kerala. Begun two years after the 1994 Kerala Panchayat Raj Municipal Act (based on the 73rd and 74th Amendments to the Indian Constitution), the PPC was a bold initiative by the state government to decentralize a variety of functions and powers to the village and district levels. Panchayat bodies were empowered to take over planning for development;

natural resource management; schools and *anganwadis*; public health clinics; veterinary services; *krishi bhavans* (agricultural training and research centres), and so on. Like any ambitious programme that is implemented without adequate capacity and process, the PPC too suffered a number of setbacks, including continued resistance from government departments to the sharing of power, lack of coordination among the various panchayat levels (village to district), inadequate empowerment of women, and difficulties in addressing local inequities. Nevertheless, the decentralization was more successful than in most other parts of India and had several positive impacts: better and more housing; improved sanitation; greater access to drinking water and power; enhanced rural connectivity; initiation of group farming; and even reduced corruption. A comprehensive review commissioned by the state government in 2009 exposed the shortcomings and recommended various steps to overcome these, which have been considered for a renewed thrust during the Eleventh Five-Year Plan.[87]

International relations and governance

The reversal of economic globalization does not imply the end of global relations. It should open a fresh chapter in international understanding and cooperation. There has always been a flow of ideas, people, services and materials across the world, and this has often enriched human societies. Radical ecological democracy, with its focus on localized economies, ethical lifestyles, a renewal of freedom, and new forms of knowledge and exploration, would actually facilitate the *meaningful* flow of ideas and innovations at global levels, as against a world of ostensibly 'open' economies that require increasingly barricaded societies and unidirectional cultural flows in order to keep them going.

The rationale for an internationally acceptable radical ecological democracy is the same as the one for RED within a country. It has to be based on the twin principles of ecological sustainability and social equity, encompassing the ideals of cooperation between and within nations and peoples, respect for diversity, and so on.

This book is not intended to go into the contours of international economic and ecological crises and how we could come out of them (within the prevailing framework). We would not even feel qualified to take on such a task and there are already a number of others who have attempted this. However, idealistic and far-fetched as it may seem, we lay down below a few thoughts towards a global RED, which would be necessary as concomitant to what is being tried out in India.[88]

We would have to start with a very different framework (compared to the one prevailing) to tackle the challenges we face. A global RED will obviously require a huge change in governance and economic paradigms at every level. It must challenge militarism and conflict; prevalent models of development and growth; unequal and unsustainable trade and investment regimes; the might of global capital and markets; the insatiable demands of the rich consumer classes; and other forces that are at present so powerful that they overwhelm and paralyse us. Yet, these forces are not insurmountable. Just as thousands of successful alternatives are manifesting themselves in India, worldwide too there is a growing body of initiatives showing how it is possible to do things differently.

Most importantly, there needs to be a radical redistribution of power, emanating from the churning that is taking place at the grass roots around the world. People's forums between countries and regions, sprouting up all over the place, are one manifestation. There has been much talk of a global parliament, but it is worth emphasizing that any such global body must comprise not so much nation states, as peoples. This may call, for instance, for a major change in the United Nations, converting it into a United Peoples of the World, where indigenous peoples and other citizens' groupings would be able to make their voices heard as much as nation states. In the interim there could be renewed attempts by countries of the global South to regroup at such forums as ILO, UNICEF (United Nations Children's Fund), UNCTAD (United Nations Conference on Trade and Development), UNDP, UNEP and WHO, while facilitating the full participation of their diverse peoples in these forums. International forums dealing with environmental and human rights agreements also need more teeth. Most of these are today unable to enforce any decisions because the power for sanctions and global action lies largely with security establishments or with the economic and trade agreements.

There is a need to transcend even the system of nation states if ecological challenges are to be addressed. The concept of bioregional or ecoregional governance and management, mentioned in the Indian context earlier, is applicable across national boundaries too. Fledgling efforts at trans-boundary protected areas in the South Asian region (e.g. in the Manas area between Bhutan and India or the terai area between India and Nepal) are one small step in that direction, though nowhere near as democratic in their conceptualization and implementation as needed (since they lack local community involvement). More robust bioregional approaches in this part of the world would mean, as example, joint governance and planning of the Indus, Brahmaputra and Ganga river basins; the Himalayan ranges; or the Bay of Bengal, the Gulf of Mannar and the Gulf of Khambat.[89] Not just South Asian countries, others like China and Myanmar would also need to be involved.

To escape the consequences of conforming to the dictates of the system of trade, investment and finance that undergirds the current pattern of globalization, countries of the global South must first withdraw from the agreements that sustain it. This may mean walking out of bilateral free trade agreements and the so-called multilateral agencies like the World Trade Organization (WTO), the International Monetary Fund (IMF) and the World Bank, as (given their track records) these operate fundamentally against the norms of democracy, equity and ecological sustainability. From the ruins of such institutions can be built radically democratic economic forums that encompass the principles of RED, respecting local needs and rights, with an overarching respect for cultural and ecological diversity.

Countries of the South must also cooperate and reach collective agreements among themselves to ensure that the rich nations and the TNCs (transnational corporations) do not continue to play one of them against another, signing bilateral deals that hurt the interests of the poor or of the environment. South–South cooperation prevailed to a degree in the decades after decolonization and manifested in groupings like the Bandung Conference, the Group of 77 or the South Commission (of which India's present prime minister, Dr Manmohan Singh, was once a part). This kind of cooperation has to be revived, but with far greater levels of participation by the citizens in decision-making forums. The experience of Latin America during the past few decades—with its attempts to form regional trade groupings through such arrangements as Mercosur—can be instructive, though even these are in dire need of greater democratization and ecological sensitivity. There are also experiments of alternative monetary arrangements, which escape the net of the uncertain, dying dollar.

Demilitarization is as crucial to the global alternatives agenda as anything else. A number of actions already under way, or proposed above, could seriously challenge the current systems that promote militarization and conflict (and thus, ecological waste). These include: more people-to-people forums; access of citizens in global decision-making; gradually decoupling the economy from fossil fuels (the hunger for which is a major source of international conflict); more responsible use of land and water (other major current and future sources of conflict); the push for denuclearization and reduction of conventional arms stockpiles; and the conversion of international conflict borders into peace parks (also a great way to conserve nature, as evidenced in the zone between the two Koreas, and possible in the Siachen area between Pakistan and India).

These are just a few of the ideas and actions necessary for a global 'order' that can support local, national and regional initiatives towards RED-like alternatives; but equally, these alternatives, already in motion, will push for the realization of such a global change. We have no doubt that such a process will take time, but there is no alternative for humanity but to work towards this even if it takes a few generations.

10

VENTURING INTO 'NEWHERE'

THE PATH TO RADICAL ECOLOGICAL
DEMOCRACY

'Wanderer, there is no way. The way is made by walking.'

—Antonio Machado, Spanish poet

'Asking, We walk.'

—Zapatista peasants of the Chiapas, Mexico[1]

The stories of people's resistance to destructive projects and their search for alternatives, described in earlier chapters, continue to inspire peoples' struggles in defence of their land and livelihood everywhere in the country. They prove that if people are willing to sacrifice, even a corrupt and criminalized state ultimately has to retreat instead of forcing 'development' projects through. They show that even small communities, if united, can match the influence of some of the world's most powerful corporations and chart their own paths to well-being.[2]

'Newhere' refers to unknown places in the future which may be reached through the route of a radical ecological democracy.

Although these successes do not signal a fundamental shift in the way India treats its environment and the people who depend directly on natural ecosystems, they are significant milestones towards a world saner than the one deregulated globalization has unleashed. In their own small way, they point to some of the possible paths to radical ecological democracy.

Is such a profound transformation possible?

Radical ecological democracy (RED) entails huge shifts in governance and will encounter considerable resistance from today's political and corporate power centres. But in India there are many signs that a transformation to RED is possible over the next few decades.

Following are some key elements that will help in the transition towards a sustainable, equitable society. All these need to be based on, and in turn promote, the principles and values laid out in the previous chapter. Most crucially, the journey towards RED is itself important, for, like the Zapatistas quoted above, we do not believe there are any rigid rules or premeditated pathways to reach it.

Growing civil society mobilization to resist elements of the dominant economic growth model

People's resistance to destructive 'development' projects and processes has been significant throughout independent India's history and has gained ground in the globalization phase. Such resistance, even where not always successful, helps to buy time and space for genuine alternatives to emerge. To give just a few examples other than those related to Vedanta, POSCO, etc., cited earlier:[3]

- One of the most widespread agitations over the last three decades is that of 7 to 8 million fisherfolk against the deep-sea fishing policies of the government. Apart from achieving an impressive following among fishing communities, the agitation, supported by a cross section of intellectuals, scientists and politicians, led the Government of India to appoint a committee to review the policy on deep-sea fishing. After a year of consideration, the committee recommended that all permits for joint venture or charter vessels for deep-sea fishing should be cancelled (subject to legal processes) and that no such permits should be given in future. The fisherfolk have had to repeatedly bring up violations of this decision and other policy distortions that affect their lives.

- The proposal of the ministry of environment and forests (MoEF)—once in the 1980s, again in the 1990s—to lease forest lands to industry for growing commercial plantations was quietly buried both times after intense opposition from environmental and social action groups. These groups are keeping a close tab on events, as proposals such as this have a habit of resurfacing time and again.

- In 2008 the government of Andhra Pradesh issued an order to develop a coastal stretch of 972 km into a Coastal Industrial Corridor. This would contain industrial and theme parks, chemical complexes, amusement parks, pharma parks, tourism resorts, and so on. A lot of land was acquired and MoUs (memorandums of understanding) signed with several industries. However, strong local community opposition forced the government to announce, later that year, that it would withdraw the order. Local people remain alert to the possibility of it resurfacing.

- A proposal to convert an 11-km stretch of beach at Bekal, Kerala, into a special tourism area, with an investment of Rs 1000 crore, would have affected 30,000 fishing and farming families. Sustained opposition and a writ petition forced the government to scrap the plan. Legal action has been successful in several other tourism cases also, e.g. the demolition of a resort in Karwar (Karnataka), amusement parks in the Vizag–Bheemunipatnam coastal belt (Andhra Pradesh) and hotels and resorts on the Midnapore coast (West Bengal), all ordered by courts on petitions filed by citizens' groups.

- Action by alert citizens' groups, networking with international groups, blew the whistle on two toxics-laden ships that were sent illegally to India for disposal and recycling. The French ship *Clemenceau* became an international embarrassment for the French government, which had to give in to intense pressure by civil society organizations (CSOs) and recall the ship, in 2006. In 2008 the US ship *Platinum II*, attempting to sneak in with forged papers, was detected by CSOs that alerted the Indian government, which refused it permission to dock in 2009.

- Several regions have mobilized against the bottling plants of Coca-Cola. Most well-known is the struggle of Plachimada village of Palakkad district in Kerala. In 2003, utilizing its powers under the Kerala Panchayat Raj Act 1994, Perumatty panchayat (to which Plachimada belongs) refused to renew the bottling plant's licence. The plant has not been allowed to resume operations since 2004 by the Kerala Pollution Control Board. In 2007 civil society exposés of water pollution and over-extraction, and protests by villagers gathered under the Coca-Cola Bhagao, Krishi

Bachao Sangharsh Samiti (Get Rid of Coke, Save Farming Struggle Committee) led the company to shut down its plant at Sinhachawar in Ballia district, Uttar Pradesh.

- Special Economic Zones (SEZs) are facing opposition across the country. Several SEZs have had to be scrapped as it has been impossible to acquire the land needed, with farmers putting up stiff resistance. Nandigram happened in 2007. Goa's SEZs were cancelled in December 2008. As this manuscript goes to press, a proposed SEZ by Mahindra & Mahindra, in the Pune district of Maharashtra, had to be abandoned as farmers refused to give the 1188 ha needed.

The above is just an indication of the growing ecological and political consciousness in India that has intensified since the start of the reform era.

Civil society replacing some government functions

The repeated failure of the state to deliver on many counts has prompted CSOs (community-based or others) to take on the role of providing basic amenities and facilitating local empowerment. Increasingly, such initiatives are displacing the state in its role as the facilitator of the essential conditions of life. But it is important that they do not free the state from its role as the guarantor of rights and welfare, as facilitator and regulator (including of the CSOs themselves), and its role of formulating policy (even with public pressure and expert inputs). In many areas there can be no replacement for the state, at least in the foreseeable future, so it must be held to its responsibilities. It is also important that CSOs from the relatively well-off sections of society do not corner the democratic space and public resources or pretend to speak on behalf of the poor and the disprivileged. In many urban areas, for instance, CSO coalitions have taken on the role of liaising with the administration, bypassing not only councillors but also the mass of poor slum-dwellers, labourers, hawkers, etc. Their vision and advocacy can also at times arise from an elite form of civic and environmental sensibility (e.g. in arguing for the removal of slums and hawkers for a 'cleaner' city), leaving out the needs and rights of the poor.[4] Civil society groups also tend to become unresponsive like the state, especially when they assume very large dimensions; such tendencies will be discouraged the more aware and active the general public is.

A good example of how rural transformation can take place through civil society interventions is the Samaj Pragati Sahayog (SPS). SPS started with one tribal village in Dewas district in Madhya Pradesh, during which villagers became equal decision-makers in the initiative. After almost two decades of work, SPS was able to cover over 45,000 acres in thirty-four villages under watershed management, providing drinking water and irrigation, and increasing the *rabi* crop production by 50–60 per cent. SPS's work in about 220 villages and towns now covers sustainable agriculture (using no chemical fertilizers, moving towards the phasing out of pesticides); livestock improvement; panchayat and women's empowerment; microfinance; renewable energy; low-cost shelter; and sanitation. Overall, outgoing migration has reduced by 80 per cent and many families have even returned to their villages. The experience has been used to influence state and national policies, including advocacy for the right to food, a better public distribution system and inputs to the framing of guidelines for watershed management.[5]

Policy shifts and reforms

Civil society advocacy and initiatives by individuals interested in social change from within the state itself have led to some policy shifts and reforms that are moving Indian society more in the direction of RED. Three recent legislative measures are examples of this: the Right to Information Act 2005; the National Rural Employment Guarantee Act 2006; and the Scheduled Tribes and Other Traditional Forest Dwellers (Recognition of Forest Rights) Act 2006. At the time of writing, some others under consideration are laws providing the right to education and the right to food, as also welfare of the unorganized sector, land acquisition, and resettlement and rehabilitation. Depending on how they are framed, they could have the same potential that the earlier three laws have, granting the currently disprivileged and weak sections of society a greater voice, more livelihood opportunities and a dignified life. (Though in their current form the Land Acquisition and the Resettlement and Rehabilitation bills could also lead to greater displacement through 'soft' measures, and the proposed bills on right to education and food are seriously flawed.) Several states are also announcing policy shifts of a radical nature, with Kerala and Sikkim deciding to go fully organic by 2015 (see previous chapter). And yet these are only the tip of the iceberg, for policy changes are needed in a range of sectors including macroeconomics, governance, trade, land- and water-use, agriculture, industry, infrastructure, health, knowledge and environment. These are likely to become possible not only due to grass-roots pressure but also India's ratification of a number of progressive international policy agreements, especially on issues like human rights, indigenous rights and the environment.[6]

A remarkable tale of a very localized, village-based initiative leading to one of India's most progressive national legislations is that of the Mazdoor Kisan Shakti Sangathan (MKSS). Formed in 1990 in central Rajasthan as an attempt to ensure the payment of minimum wages and to redistribute excess land to the landless, MKSS realized early on that the struggle would not succeed unless villagers had access to government records. But such records had been kept away by citing the colonial Official Secrets Act. Through a diversity of pressure and advocacy tactics MKSS was able to obtain the relevant records and make these openly available to villagers at *jan sunwais* (public hearings). This evolved into the practice of 'social audits' by which the public could hold government agencies accountable. Pressure built on the state government to make policy changes. Rajasthan became one of the first states to initiate legislation granting public access to government information. Eventually MKSS's struggle (along with some similar ones such as by the Delhi-based group Parivartan in an urban context) formed the basis of the National Campaign on the People's Right to Information (NCPRI), which spearheaded the move to convince and pressurize the Indian government to enact the national Right to Information Act 2005.[7]

Learning from this, there are many policy shifts that could, in a relatively short period, lead to a much greater creation of ecologically sensitive livelihoods and employment opportunities. The MGNREGA should be reworked to focus on the creation and regeneration of rural assets, which in the long run help make communities self-sufficient in basic needs. Activities could include reviving degraded lands, water harvesting, agricultural land productivity, infrastructure for rural industry, and so on. A similar National Urban Employment Guarantee Scheme (NUEGS) ought to be considered, keeping in view the dramatic need for jobs in the burgeoning cities of the country. Some states, like Tripura, have already launched such a scheme in 2009. In all such cases where the state is deploying a welfare policy, it is crucial that the employment programme does not lead either to labour shortages in agriculture (which have been reported from several places) or result in the decline of traditional skills and crafts as people get used to a dole system—especially in areas where corruption is rife. To address labour shortages in agriculture it may be worth experimenting with a government-backed employment scheme that centrally involves local farmers in need of labour.[8]

Fiscal autonomy ought to be given to village panchayats and urban municipalities to fund or manage such programmes wherever possible. There is a provision in the Constitution (Article 243) to this effect. These bodies have to become financially viable on their own over time and it can happen if good local and regional business models are generated.

Also, as the economist Amit Bhaduri has proposed, in order to render them financially independent and responsible, panchayats and municipalities could have their own accounts and a credit line with nationalized banks.

> This would avoid duplication of institutions, while a system of mutual check and balance between the *panchayats* and the local branch of nationalized banks can be devised based on their performance as borrowers and lenders. Banks would lend the next round only if the previous project succeeds, and *panchayats* can borrow the next round only if the money is well-spent.[9]

Over time, mutuality of interest between the banks and the panchayats/municipalities would sustain this novel form of financing for development.[10]

A major macroeconomic policy priority is the hitherto neglected home market. Under globalization, policies have been centred on cheapening the cost of *supply* of goods from India to the West (in order to meet the competition from countries like China and Brazil). Policies must now shift towards the strengthening of domestic *demand*. As we have seen, in a world where capital is so mobile it is highly doubtful that deregulated international commerce ('free trade') would increase output and welfare all around. The lesson for India here is that easing the path for foreign investment is rather a roundabout way to enhance the welfare of working people (if it does that at all). There are far simpler and more obvious ways of achieving the latter. The first is for policies to focus more on the home market, rather than being designed for TNC investment.

In a new transitional strategy, the state must have a far bigger role in the economy, if Indian polity is to become genuinely sensitive to social and ecological considerations. Public institutions and corporations are not *inherently* inefficient and corrupt, as so much of the corporate media appears to allege. Whether we consider reputed institutions like the Reserve Bank of India or the Central Election Commission, or we look at public sector firms like Maruti, BHEL (Bharat Heavy Electricals) and the four largest oil corporations, or banks like SBI (State Bank of India) or Corporation Bank, there are plenty of success stories. The issue is more a matter of work culture and clean, accountable management, rather than about private or public ownership. Whenever bureaucracies get too big—under either system— possibilities of corruption increase. But, in a good system, there are democratic checks and balances against this, especially through genuine decentralization of decision-making to rural and urban communities.

In the long run, as we have laid out in the previous chapter, a crucial policy shift is the return of custodianship and control over local resources to local communities. In India, *direct* control of natural resources was mostly with local communities (even if 'owned' by rulers), till the colonial rule brought them under actual state control. The situation now calls for a reversal. Such a form of *sansadhan swaraj* (resource sovereignty) is very much in the spirit of Gandhi's village republics, as also the community forest governance provisions of the recent Forest Rights Act (2006). RED can ultimately find a home in this part of the world only if sovereignty over land, water and forests returns to the people who live by them in a proximate day-to-day sense, coupled with partnerships that allow transfer of some resources to non-local populations who need them. Of course the modern context is vastly different from that of the past, so local controls need to go hand in hand with mechanisms of monitoring and regulation that do not allow any section of society to misuse rights and powers.[11]

Technological shifts

Some of the most amazing changes are taking place in the technological world, many of them towards making human life not only less dreary but also more ecologically sensitive.

A very significant one is in the field of energy. As the age of fossil fuels may mercifully be drawing to a close—hastened by the alarm over climate change—a range of renewable, clean and efficient energy options has emerged. India is rapidly emerging as a hub of renewable energy initiatives. These include an ambitious goal to produce 22,000 MW of solar power by 2022 under the Jawaharlal Nehru National Solar Mission of the National Action Plan on Climate Change (NAPCC). However, a radical policy overhaul is needed in this to focus on decentralized generation that will be within the reach of the poor. [12]

Similarly, innovative technologies in industrial and agricultural production, housing and construction, transportation, household equipment and a number of other fields are moving towards greater efficiency, less waste generation and more recycling. Nor are all of these modern inventions. There is also a growing appreciation of the continued relevance of many traditional technologies, e.g. in agriculture, textiles and manufacturing, and other fields. Countries in a 'developing' stage have the unprecedented opportunity to leapfrog directly from some of the most wasteful industrial, energy and transportation technologies, into super-efficient ones. But they need to be given the opportunity and support to do so by the industrialized world, which currently puts all kinds of obstructions in their way, including high costs, intellectual property rights monopolies, and so on. This support has been the promise of 'sustainable development' agreements the world has reached for the last three decades—a promise never really fulfilled.

Growing civil society mobilization, especially around climate change, may well be the factor that will force the promised technological paradigm shifts with the 'three pillars of efficient use, renewable resources and industrial ecology . . . recycling, re-use, re-manufacturing, and product life extension'[13] or into the even more radical 'cradle to cradle' designs that emulate nature, treat 'wastes' as 'food', use various forms of energy from the sun and respect diversity.[14] Companies too will drive such change, as they smell business opportunities in it; indicative of this is an article in the Indian edition of the popular magazine *Entrepreneur*, which listed sixteen 'most promising sectors of today and the future', of which eleven were related to environmental and social goals like water, organic food, green transport, low-cost housing, alternative energy and e-waste.[15] It will of course be a challenge to convert the profit motive behind this interest into a more socially oriented goal, which can happen only when businesses themselves become more public-owned or controlled (see box on 'Social enterprise' in the previous chapter).

Financial and fiscal measures

A number of reforms in macroeconomic and fiscal policies have been suggested for moving towards greater sustainability. Shifting subsidies from ecologically destructive practices such as chemical-heavy agriculture to truly sustainable ones like organic farming is one of them. Bringing in a range of taxes that reflect something of the true value of the natural resources being used by urban and industrial-scale consumers—which will discourage ecologically destructive practices (including excessive consumerism)—and taxes that reduce income disparities would also contribute to a large extent. Making substantially larger public funds available to alternative technologies and processes would also be important, though citizens would need to be alert to false solutions. For instance, the 'clean development mechanism' promoted under climate change agreements is in theory supposed to help 'developing' countries make the transition to sustainable technologies. But in practice it has been more of a greenwash, at least in India.[16]

As indicated earlier, the democratization of credit and finance has to become a priority of the government. The ending of priority sector lending for agriculture and small industry after the economic reforms began has played havoc; it is one of the main reasons for not only farmers but also handloom weavers and others committing suicide in large numbers. Nor has microfinance been much of a solution, given, in many cases, the high rates of interest charged and the conditions under which the loans are given (see chapter 3). Financial inclusion has to be more radical to be real.

In the arena of international policies, India could pioneer a global proposal for what economists know as the Tobin Tax, which regulates international financial speculation by imposing a small levy on such transactions. It lends greater stability to the global financial system (by inhibiting such investments) and mobilizes the necessary public funds for social purposes, besides indirectly slowing down the rate of environmental destruction.

Indicators of well-being

A number of exciting new ways to measure real human progress are being developed to replace the primitive, dangerously misleading ones that most countries still use. The move from a GDP and per capita income kind of model to the Human Development Index (led by the United Nations Development Programme) was progressive, but even this has remained limited. A number of countries now also use 'sustainable development' indicators, which include aspects like resource use, health, energy, transportation, waste, housing, crime, community participation, education, social justice and others.[17]

Even more radical alternatives have been proposed by groups like the New Economics Foundation (NEF, famous for its Happy Planet Index), which combine objective and subjective factors. For instance, the National Accounts of Well-Being of the NEF includes measures of personal well-being (emotionally positive state; satisfaction; vitality; resilience and self-esteem; autonomy; competence; engagement; meaning and purpose), social well-being (supportive relationships, trust and belonging) and well-being at work (job satisfaction; satisfaction with work–life balance; emotional experience of work; and work conditions). The NEF has already tested these measures on European countries, with interesting results. Public debate is ongoing in many countries on how 'happiness' measures can be added to other measures of progress. Bhutan already uses a Gross National Happiness index based on nine core dimensions: psychological well-being, time use, community vitality, culture, health, education, environmental diversity, living standard and governance.[18]

Awareness, education, capacity

Ecological and social awareness and the capacity to deal with associated problems have risen exponentially in the last two to three decades and seem to be skyrocketing with the onset of climate change. Nevertheless, and in particular for countries undergoing major transitions like India, the awareness and capacity are often half-baked and incomplete. For instance, most people are aware that deforestation is a problem, but do not necessarily know the complex factors behind it or the fundamental changes needed to address it. Ecological literacy among decision-makers and the business elite is particularly poor. On the other hand, ordinary citizens, such as in India's villages, do not always have the capacity to deal with a host of relatively new problems, like the chemicalization of their fields and the hydrological/biological impacts of climate change. A transition to RED will require a massive campaign to spread awareness about the multiple crises we face and their root causes, building capacity to spread meaningful solutions.

What is in store for the transition period?

If the above changes in policies and practices can be brought about over, let's say, a period of a decade, India could reach many desirable goals. First, mass unemployment and poverty could be eliminated in the foreseeable future. Secondly, by putting purchasing power into the hands of the hitherto poor the domestic market for industrial products (increasingly made through an ecologically sensitive process) and basic needs will grow, giving an impetus to the macroeconomy. Thirdly, through the public works programmes that the poor execute, infrastructure (like roads, irrigation, etc.) can be strengthened and expanded. Fourthly, priority environmental projects (such as watershed development and soil conservation) can be undertaken to reverse the worsening ecological crisis. And finally, by generating jobs in the countryside the policy changes will begin to reverse the flow of distress migrants to the cities.

One crucial question is: what will be the agency for such a transformation? It is clearly not going to be the state, given its current character as an agency geared, for the most part, to the interests of the elite. It has to be from within civil society, but who and how?

It is not easy to answer this, for there have been numerous 'revolutions' of various hues in Indian history, many of them promising a more equitable future, yet most have ultimately failed to achieve their goals. Many have got bogged down in the same issues against which they rose in protest: internal inequities and hierarchies; leadership tussles; inability to empower and build capacity of the 'masses'; failure of the imagination with respect to 'development' paradigms, and so on.

However, these movements have also helped create wider and deeper awareness, provided learnings on what *not* to do on gaining power, brought up innovations in governance and, through all this, advanced the cause of a more just and sane future. Each people's movement—whether successful as in the case of the Dongria Kondhs versus the Vedanta corporation or unsuccessful in their immediate aims as in the anti–Sardar Sarovar (Narmada) struggle—has pushed the boundaries of public consciousness and increased the pressure for change. As civil society matures in India and elsewhere, it will hopefully be able to build on these gains and overcome the shortcomings of past movements. This will be aided by the new contexts in which we are living, such as a greater push towards decentralized decision-making; transparency relating to information; the ability to communicate more effectively; the availability of new ecologically sensitive technologies—all of this combined with the continuation of the elements of sustainability, equity and collective action from our traditions.

While we are not bright-eyed and romantic about the capacity of civil society to rise above earlier shortcomings, we do think that all these elements of the emerging context, and the increasing realization that we *have to* forge new paths to human welfare, provide hope. Necessity may be a blessing in disguise.

In this sense, India is perhaps *uniquely placed* to achieve the transformation to RED. This is for a variety of reasons: its thousands of years of learning and adaptation (including ancient democratic practices that perhaps predate even the famed Greek republics); its ecological and cultural diversity; its resilience in the face of multiple crises; the continued existence of a myriad lifestyles and world views, including of people who still tread the most lightly on earth; the powerful legacy of Buddha, Gandhi and other radical thinkers; the adoption of revolutionary ideas from thinkers like Marx; zealously guarded practices of democracy and civil society activism; and the very many peoples' movements of resistance and reconstruction. But, of course, it cannot do this alone; it will need to continue to convince, teach and learn from other countries and peoples, which it has done for many centuries. We return to this issue—of India's place in the global movement towards sustainability—in the concluding chapter.

Possible future scenarios

What does the future hold for us? Prediction is a hazardous task for several reasons. We are not fully knowledgeable about the complex ecological, social, economic and political dynamics and trends that are manifest today or how they will play out tomorrow. Nor do ecological and human systems always behave predictably; there can always be a sudden, surprising change of events. In addition, tomorrow's human choices may be different from the ones being made today and we cannot read into the minds of future generations.

It is, nevertheless, possible to come up with a range of future scenarios and suggest which of these seems most likely, given the current dynamics and trends. A number of attempts have been made along these lines for the earth as a whole. For instance, the Global Scenario Group of the Stockholm Environmental Institute has drawn up three broad scenarios for the future: Conventional Worlds, Barbarization and Great Transitions.[19]

The first of these envisages the increasing use of market and/ or policy instruments to deal with ecological and other crises, with some degree of success but ultimate failure. The second is a situation where such instruments do not work even in the short run, the current crises continue to get compounded till there is mass collapse, conflict and a 'descent into anarchy or tyranny'. The third is a bold new vision with fundamental changes in values, social organization and development paradigms, leading humanity to achieving lasting sustainability and equity.

In the case of India, we envisage similar (though not quite the same) scenarios for the future. The next few decades will see an increasing trend towards one of the following:

1. Business as usual and descent into visible insanity: Continuation of today's dominant economic growth paradigm, with increasing ecological damage and socio-economic inequity. Alternative visions and experiments remain marginal and scattered. Conflict inevitably increases as masses of deprived people retaliate and the privileged try to keep their privileges with whatever force they can muster. Some form of corporate totalitarianism is attempted in a formal way. Biological extinction reaches its peak. Eventually, ecological collapse drives humanity itself into either extinction or a constant, desperate struggle for survival.

2. Slow transition to sanity: Continuation of today's dominant models for some time, leading to partial ecological collapse and an increase in social conflict in the near future. From this, however, emerge alternatives (many of them already seeded in today's world), which slowly become dominant, perhaps with a series of ups and downs or zigzags rather than a straight progression. In the short run, this means moderate to heavy suffering (especially for the poor and for non-human beings), but in the long run it leads to the sort of sustainability and equity envisioned in Radical Ecological Democracy.

3. Rapid transition to sanity: Humanity quickly realizes the folly of today's dominant models (perhaps with the alarm over climate change as a catalyst), people's mobilizations are rapid, and governments and civil society invest quickly in a range of alternatives. This scenario involves the least suffering and biological extinction, and a quick transition to Radical Ecological Democracy.

Our limited understanding of current dynamics and trends leads us to imagine that the most likely scenario is the second one. This is because, even though there is a visible growth in alternatives, it is still too slow to *quickly* arrest the ecological and social decline we see today. Moreover, those who benefit most from today's economic and political models will undoubtedly resist fundamental change and they cannot be overcome (or convinced) in the space of a few years.

There are also a number of false or unsustainable starts we have already embarked upon: trying to solve problems of social origin through technological or financial interventions (like hunger through genetically modified crops, and climate change through carbon trading and engineering the atmosphere or the oceans); elite environmentalism that ignores equity, such as exclusionary conservation that attempts to separate humans from non-human nature; handing over environmental decisions to 'experts' of the formal sciences with no involvement of traditional knowledge experts or of ordinary people with the relevant experience; and other such. These will lead us on to paths with dead ends (or difficult terrain), but we may not necessarily realize this till we have already walked a considerable distance down the slope. And, finally, while today's and tomorrow's youth are likely to be the major catalysts of fundamental change, they too will take time to realize and bring into effect collective alternative visions in the midst of the multiple distractions of today's consumerist society.

For all these and other reasons, alternative visions will grow and consolidate slowly. They will be beaten down and will rise again, much like the ecological resistance movements around the world. But grow they will, till they reach critical mass. This cautious optimism is justified, we feel, observing the way in which ecological and social awareness, experimentation of alternatives and policy shifts are today much more visible than they were even a couple of decades back. It is also justified because, for perhaps the first time in history, there is both a *local* and a *global* mindset, a sense that we are both individual human beings and communities, as also one humanity—and one with other life on earth. There is a growing sense that we are a part of our local ecosystem as well as of one global ecological system. Multiple global crises have made an increasing number of us acutely aware that we depend on each other and on our biological and physical surrounds, wherever we are in the world. Such an understanding may still be limited to a minority, but it is rapidly growing to become much more commonplace.

Many people will label the ideas laid out in this chapter as utopian dreams. Most certainly, to any of us immersed in today's depressing world, where the slightest positive change seems such a struggle, radical ecological democracy would seem like a manifesto without a future. But we submit that the many real alternatives already being practised show how the 'impossible' *is* possible. It is the promises made by the mandarins of today's economic growth and globalization paradigm—of a world in which no one will go to bed hungry, where the next generation will have as many (or more) options as we do now, and where everyone will be 'educated' (on the Western model) and 'healthy and happy'—that will prove to be pipe dreams rather than the visions we have sketched here. All trends point to the utter unsustainability and horrifying inequities of the current paradigm. We have no choice but to embark on the pathways to RED, however difficult, distant and unlikely they may seem from our present vantage point.

Between the seemingly 'impossible' path and the manifestly insane one, we prefer the former.

II

ANOTHER INDIA, ANOTHER WORLD

'I sympathize therefore, with those who would minimize rather than those who would maximize, economic entanglement between nations. Ideas, knowledge, art, hospitality, travel—these are the things which should of their nature be international. But let goods be homespun whenever it is reasonably and conveniently possible; and, above all, let finance be primarily national.'

—John Maynard Keynes, 1933[1]

Tying up the threads

Given the staggering complexity of the socio-economic, political, cultural and ecological processes that have been unleashed by deregulated globalization, it is necessary, by way of conclusion, to tie at least some of the threads together, as best we can.

We have tried to say in this book that globalizing India is in a state of rapidly deteriorating ecological and social health. Economic reforms were hurriedly and stealthily pushed through under extraordinary conditions at the start of the 1990s. They have since had a dramatic effect on the life of the country. While raw economic growth rates, especially since 2003, have been impressive, they have been driven by a structural change in which the country's metropolitan areas have been integrated into the global economy on terms suitable to the global and Indian elites, leaving behind the rest of India.

This has given more power to metropolitan India to preside over the destinies of people in the countryside, even as it has become culturally more distant from it. Large numbers of people stand excluded from, or rejected by, this process. Inequalities have touched new heights as opportunities for quick money—such as in finance—have grown for a tiny minority, even as inflation, joblessness and development-induced displacement steal the life-chances of the majority of people. India's integration into long global supply chains controlled from the top by the TNCs (foreign and Indian) has only worsened the levels of exploitation and over-exploitation of working people around the country who continue to work for very low wages.

We continue to be faced with many of the old problems—chronic hunger and malnutrition; entrenched poverty and unemployment; class, caste, and gender inequities; loss of land and livelihood—and, of course, a whole host of social and political tensions and conflicts that we have not had the time or the expertise to analyse in this book. To these have been added worsening ecological woes. Due to the globalization of supply chains (and demand-chains!), more and more decisions involving resource-use are now being taken at ever greater distances from the 'hinterlands'.

The pressure to industrialize, urbanize and modernize rapidly—catch up with the West and race with countries like China—is so strong that states like Orissa have signed MoUs for as many as forty-five new steel plants, even as it pushes its agricultural sector into rapid decline. States like Chhattisgarh are following suit with a whole slew of industrial and mining projects. Hundreds of dams are being planned in seismically sensitive regions of the country like Uttarakhand and Arunachal. Indiscriminate and illegal mining, pushed by a powerful corporate–political nexus, continues to destroy the environment and erode the base for millions of livelihoods.[2]

We have tried to draw some of the possible links between these problems and the policies of globalized growth that have been launched during the past two decades. To address these challenges, small piecemeal efforts undertaken by individuals and civil society groups will prove to be quite inadequate. Because they are hegemonic, the destructive forces at work are enormously stronger. We will find ourselves quite badly stranded—ecologically and socially—unless *state policies* undergo a radical shift and the powerful elites make themselves available for democratic dialogue, consensus and compromise (or are compelled to do so by events).

This point needs further clarification. Prior to the reforms, the resources (material, institutional, human) in this country were allocated by remote bureaucracies ruled by sometimes ignorant, often indifferent, politicians. This had to go. After the reforms, they are being allocated to a greater degree by market processes dominated by powerful corporations abetted by a willing state (still steeped in corruption), though state bureaucracies and development authorities have hardly taken a back seat. We have seen not only the serious limitations of both these approaches, especially when adopted in an exclusive fashion, we have also seen the new problems they are creating.

We now need to focus our collective energies on building and mobilizing *communities and their institutions* to ensure for the first time a *democratic* allocation of resources. In every case, markets will be part of the allocation of resources (much like policies are). The only question is who or what will regulate them in a just and sustainable way. State bureaucracies and corporations have both failed to do this. It is time communities took on the task themselves and compelled the state to facilitate them. This is consistent (if not required) in both letter and spirit with the Indian Constitution (see, for instance, Articles 38 and 243 and especially the Directive Principles of State Policy under Part IV) and recent amendments to it, such as those mandating rural and urban decentralization.

There are very strong reasons to believe that the expected outcomes (by way of elimination of poverty, for instance) that have been promised from the present growth process in the Indian economy will never be realized. Firstly, when the West was industrializing rapidly in the nineteenth and early twentieth centuries, resources (including those accessible from the colonies) were plentiful, and pollution and climate change had not become serious regional and global threats. Today's ecological crisis is critical and will put definite limits on the extent of modern energy-intensive industrialization still possible for the late industrializers. In a desperate bid to overcome these limitations, industrializing countries (like India and China) are often seen these days trying to gain control of resources in the less powerful nations, like those of Africa.

Secondly, when the West industrialized, markets—both within and outside the rich countries—had, for all practical purposes, unlimited scope. Today, markets are saturated in the West, and developing countries no longer have colonies over which they can impose 'imperial preference' to sell their products. In terms of both the requirements—of markets as well as resources—

today's developing countries will have to 'cut into their own stomachs' to grow quickly. However, as incomes in the bottom three-quarters of the population in countries like India have stagnated in real terms, markets for the goods and services produced by the modern economy are limited to the top quarter. Resources, as we have seen, are severely limited.

Thirdly, when the peasantry and farm labour were forcibly evicted from the countryside in the presently industrialized nations, they could be absorbed in mines, in industries in the cities, or sent to the colonies as settlers. The industrial technology of the day was labour-intensive and could thus employ the labour displaced from the countryside. During the past century the trajectory of technology has evolved in a much more capital-intensive direction. With mechanization and automation, the capacity of modern industry and services to absorb displaced labour from the countryside has dropped sharply. Labour redundancy is a growing crisis everywhere. Jobless—even job-destroying—growth is a reality today, and often the norm, giving rise to plenty of 'structural unemployment'.

Fourthly, modern industry and service sectors today need very precise skills among the workforce. These are not readily available among the displaced (usually farming and often illiterate) populations and even when retraining is possible, only a minority of those displaced can find jobs in the industries that develop on their land. This is one reason why resistance to land acquisition in places like India is more acute.

Finally, when the West, as also Japan, Russia and, later, South Korea and China, industrialized, they were not adequately democratic. Some of those countries were (and still are) totalitarian systems. Certainly, none of the presently industrialized countries had, like India today, universal adult franchise *while* industrializing and urbanizing. This made it easier to forcibly move millions of peasants out of rural areas. For better or for worse, India is today a vocal, restless democracy with a large rural population. The latter is refusing to blindly follow state diktat when it comes to vacating the land for industry, mining or infrastructure—because they cannot see any benefit for themselves through the change, either in the short or in the long run. This resistance is evident in the difficulties faced nowadays in the process of land acquisition. It is also manifest in the Maoist and other movements in central India's mining belt, though it is not their only cause.

For all the above reasons, the expected large-scale shift of labour from rural agriculture and related activities to the industrial or service sectors in urban areas is unlikely to take place. This means that livelihoods have to be sustained and jobs have to be created in the countryside where more than two-thirds of India still lives. If agriculture and allied activities (such as forestry, fisheries and pastoralism) get the kind of attention they deserve, they will be able to support a substantial part of the working population. At the same time, jobs have also to be created in industry and services, ideally in rural areas.

Large-scale, capital- and resource-intensive industrialization is not the way out of the growing crisis of unemployment. We have drawn attention, instead, to small-scale industrial initiatives in different parts of the country—whether in textiles, crafts or renewable energy—to demonstrate their sustainability as well as their capacity for offering people dignified livelihoods. The question of 'scaling up' these initiatives is besides the point, given that they are meant for a very different purpose from catering to large markets; however, if scaling up means the ability to absorb large sections of our population in such employment, that potential is very much alive.

India, indeed any country, must have a set of policies (and alternatives for prevailing ones), which would be effective even if the global economy were to capsize. As the consequences of the global financial crisis and the desire for 'decoupling' revealed, it is plain that India is not insulated today from the fortunes of the rest of the world. If it has remained somewhat shielded from the reversal of fortunes abroad (compared to, say, countries of the EU), it is on account of financial conservatism—increasingly passé in policy circles, despite the risks involved—and the large home market. However, Indian economic policies presume the continuation of business-as-usual integration with the global economy into the indefinite future. All growth and other projections for future decades rest on this assumption.

So far, India, like most other industrializing countries (with some notable exceptions in Latin America), has fallen in line with the IMF–World Bank–WTO diktat of opening up its economy to powerful transnationals, at the cost of its own people and environment. A country like India needs to embrace a far more discriminating and selective approach to globalization.

Moreover, the state needs to step up programmes and enact laws like the MGNREGA and adapt them better to local conditions to generate further employment, without creating artificial labour shortages in areas like agriculture. Making room for small-scale rural entrepreneurship—involving the local peasantry—is crucial to this. Operations under the MGNREGA have to become self-sustaining in the future, rather than having to rely on state funding every year. Marrying the goal of employment with the preservation and improvement of the environment is an eminently feasible proposition, and is actually bearing fruit in some areas of the country. An urban employment programme along the lines of the rural one is also needed to absorb the growing ranks of the jobless in the cities.

Part II of the book has argued that there *is* an overall framework of policymaking which can and must serve as an alternative to the infamous market-led TINA (There Is No Alternative) model. We call it 'radical ecological democracy' (RED). If policy space can be freed up for it over time, by cutting loose from the hegemonic framework created by the WTO and the international financial institutions, it can pave the way to a sustainable future.

RED is founded on principles of bioregional governance which, in turn, honour ground realities of cultural and ecological diversity. Not only is it consistent with the letter and spirit of the Indian Constitution, it is the only framework which can take the place of the misleading market economy, when it comes to an accurate assessment of the unpaid ecological and social costs of modern economic growth. An adivasi woman on the planning board of a district can tell us more about the real costs of our urban lifestyles than perhaps anyone else. Because she is the one who will have to walk that extra mile to fetch water year after year if, for instance, water is diverted for or polluted by mining or mega projects.

We get indignant when we see our country, among other industrializing nations, receiving shoddy treatment at the hands of the affluent countries in international forums like the WTO, the IMF or the UN Security Council. But we fail to notice how those of us living in metropolitan India treat small-town or rural India and slum-dwellers in our own city. For instance, we want the rich countries to reduce their ecological footprint since it hurts us, but we do not wish to reduce our own, even though we know it hurts people living in the countryside or those living next to radioactive nuclear reactors and other such high-risk plants.

If we want the affluent countries to treat us fairly when it comes to the distribution of the costs of adjustment to a sustainable world, should we not apply the same criterion when it comes to treating our own population? This is expected especially because our government repeatedly claims in international forums that India ought not to be held back in its economic growth as we have to bring so many millions above the poverty line. It is a strange way to 'hide behind the poor' when the ones who are enlarging India's footprint feel personally entitled to all sorts of ecological luxuries in the name of 'development'. Lasting feudal and growing capitalist privileges quietly conspire to allow us to live off the ecological budget of the Indian poor. If we were more just towards our poor, there would be a far greater chance for the industrialized world to be just towards 'us'—the wealthy of this country. We would also be on a far higher moral ground to make the same arguments we make today, which are otherwise visibly hypocritical.

The poorest 20–40 per cent Indians are bearing a remarkably disproportionate burden of the costs of climate change, especially since they inhabit ecologically vulnerable habitats. Just as our government morally demands the rich countries to exempt India from emissions reductions, do the Indian poor not have a similar right to ask the government to place a carbon tax on (or in other ways limit the consumption by) the super-rich? Certain items of consumption have to be clubbed under a quota system, or even banned outright if their ecological costs are prohibitive (certain kinds of plastic, or minerals for luxury uses, are examples). Yet, hardly anyone in the policymaking circles gives pause to these issues. We remember ethics only when it comes to dealing with those more powerful than ourselves.

If the terribly strained relationship between town (where most of the rich live) and country (where most of the poor reside) is to have a chance to heal, the city must not only reduce the demands it makes on the countryside, but find ways to give back to it and add to rural India's appeal as a place to live and work in. This will ultimately be of great value to city-dwellers themselves. Part of the way this can be done is by listening much more to people who live in the villages and in the slums in cities.

Only a radical ecological democracy can ensure that the processes of growth and development are decentralized, sustainable and create employment, instead of being driven by globally powerful corporations to meet their goals at the cost of the country's future. If a growth strategy does not create livelihoods quickly, it is likely to be derailed by social unrest and political protests. Only if the political and economic initiative and participation of the ordinary citizenry of the country are harnessed are there any chances that employment will be created, growth will be democratized, and the wealth generated by it widely shared. So far, no political party of any hue has seen things this way and risen to the challenge.

The true merits of a radical ecological democracy can only emerge when artificial political boundaries are transcended and there is greater respect for bioregional connections cutting across such boundaries. This would also entail questioning the dominance, and the merits, of the current nation-state system which the world has been living under for a long, long time. Ecological problems do not obey national territorial boundaries. The climate crisis is only the most obvious example. Only an effective, decentralized model of global and regional governance, befitting a truly globalized world, can tackle it—a structure of downwardly accountable authority which can prevail over the power of giant corporations. Nation states on their own are quite impotent, since they are easily played off against one another.

In the long and difficult transition to a sustainable world, India—with its unique cultural and ecological diversity—has the historic opportunity of playing the part of the world's ecological pioneer. 'India's problem is the problem of the world in miniature,' Tagore had written. If we can get our act together, India's solutions can set an example for the world. Given the hurdles involved in such a transition, this is probably the hardest of all political tasks that confront us.[3]

Moreover, India and the rest of the so-called developing world are strangely better off in one sense, compared to the West. The latter is deeply vested in the unsustainable modern industrial system, whereas countries of the global South are less entrenched. This will make the ecological and energy transition much easier for us than for the West. We can also leapfrog through the adoption of green technologies.

Finally, India (and South Asia in general) is among the few places in the world (Africa and parts of Asia and Latin America being the others) where indigenous peoples and other traditional or small-scale communities have survived the onslaught of industrial modernity to this day. Elsewhere, such as in the West (as also in our own metropolitan areas), societies have been fragmented into atomized individuals ruled by powerful states; though in these too, indigenous peoples are gathering force to reclaim their space and identity. It is easier to obtain the cooperation needed to tackle environmental challenges when a collective ethos is already present. If policy and legislation can be created to defend collective rights, as distinct from the individual rights normally defended in modern law everywhere, it would contribute significantly to the creation of an ecological democracy.

Has globalization really happened?

We live in a time that abounds in misnomers. One of them is 'globalization'. This book is *not* against globalization. On the contrary, it argues that true globalization—in the sense of a mature cultural understanding between the peoples of the earth, which would render the arms industry obsolete and allow free movement of people across borders—has yet to happen.

We argue, instead, against the deregulated international commerce and investment that goes by the name of 'globalization' today. What we see is actually a well-disguised form of imperialism, sophisticated enough to leave room for the national (if not truly nationalist) elite to share the spoils of exploitation with the dominant classes in industrialized nations. This has the most destructive ecological and social consequences and is clearly unsustainable.

The prevailing form of globalization has created a weird world. It is a world for international business, not for people. As capital moves freely across the world, global supply chains are stretched longer across the earth and have thus grown more energy- and resource-intensive. Transnationals and powerful governments have ensured that much of the brick-and-mortar dirty work of industrial society (resource extraction and manual labour in the early stages of the value chain) has been exported from the affluent countries to those now industrializing, while the bulk of the markets for these products is still in the 'industrialized' world (now including the richer parts of the industrializing countries). The same is done by the elite and governments within countries: ecological costs are shifted to poorer areas, while markets are mostly in the cities. There is, thus, a successful separation between those who pay the costs (especially manual labour and environmental costs) and those who derive the benefits of economic growth. This means that corporations or their subcontractors do not necessarily have to pay workers in the developing world well in order to create markets for their products. The emerging economy and the global elite and those who occupy high-end service sector jobs in the rich countries are still their main customers.

This makes blue-collar workers in the West understandably upset as jobs vanish from their shores even as the welfare state is on the decline. (This is especially the case now that government budgets have been strained by the multiple bailouts in the wake of the financial crisis.) Employed workers in industrializing countries, though poorly paid, might still see the bright side of things in such jobs. This is so not just because of the vast unemployed labour pool that is behind them in the queue. It is also because their fallback options from the past rarely exist, since state policies of 'development' in Third World countries have neglected agriculture and often brought about permanent displacement. All this is true despite the fact that such employment, as we have seen, has never been more insecure and devoid of benefits as it is today.

From an ecological standpoint, such a world could not be worse off. Those who derive the benefits of environmentally destructive growth live at a safe distance from the sites of current devastation—or can withstand damage by the occasional disaster that may visit them (think of the rich households affected by the Mumbai floods in 2005). They have little interest in paying for the externalities involved in their consumption. Those who suffer the externalities in the poor countries (or in the rural areas of the latter) have little market muscle or political power to get fair bargains from the governments, corporations and consumers responsible for the damage. The net result is that the environment inevitably suffers.

This 'weird world' that globalization has created involves consumption with shadows that stretch across the oceans and the continents. The resource base for First World lifestyles—whether they are enjoyed within the geographical territories of the rich or the poor nations—is the entire planet. Shifting ecological and social costs has become a facile affair—to the detriment of the poor, the unborn and the voiceless non-human species. In the end, as the planet becomes less and less hospitable, there will be no winners from such an arrangement, even if it seems otherwise to the myopic eye of privilege today.[4]

How inexorable is deregulated corporate globalization?

Great power invites interpretations of inevitability. Driven by powerful technologies, the expansion of globalization over the past few decades has been so fast, and its penetration into far-flung corners of the earth so close to completion, that it has come to be seen as inexorable, like gravity, according to some savants. And yet, we have seen that there is nothing 'natural' about this kind of globalization, that it has been planned and executed by the powerful after the end of the Cold War to meet the special interests of elite minorities around the world.

Given the rapidly closing pincers of vanishing resources and climate change in which humanity is slowly but surely being trapped, it would be naïve to assume that deregulated globalization is a permanent phenomenon. Even before serious environmental alarms began to go off, the first two experiments with globalization (1870–1914 and 1945–73) failed, ended by war and stagflation respectively.[5] The latest project of globalization is up against much more formidable limits, both those imposed by nature and those by human society.

Financially, in keeping with John Maynard Keynes's warnings three-quarters of a century ago, globalization of markets has led the world into multiple catastrophes. The present global crisis may have started in the US, but its reverberations have been felt throughout the world, from the eurozone nations to Japan, China and other 'emerging' economies, including India. In virtually every country, the tail of finance has been wagging the dog of the real economy for a long time now. It is as though these tails have been ever more intricately tied together since the 1970s. And now, as the knotted tails go berserk with the tensions they have generated among themselves, each real economy feels the tugs and pressures largely in a helpless, relentless way. As financial markets gyrate and collapse, there are debt defaults which have consequences for every society's real economy that suffers from rising unemployment and/or inflation.

Nowadays, in the US and the EU, the state repeatedly has to intervene on a historically unprecedented scale to bail out sinking banks, financial institutions and even car manufacturers. Free markets have failed in the most emphatic manner possible. State-managed capitalism has emerged as a necessary step to 'save the system'.

As if all this were not enough, political protests against unemployment, inflation, poor working conditions and land-grabbing, not to forget oil spills, have been on the rise around the world during the last several years. Even nations like China are facing social and political turmoil (such as strikes) like never before, though they are not formal democracies.[6]

We have to prepare for the end of the prevailing form of globalization. It is far easier to foresee its end than to imagine how the almost insurmountable ecological, financial and social problems that it is generating with each passing day will ever be tackled successfully, especially given the inertia of powerful governments who should be most responsible for taking timely action. The question is whether we will be ready for a crisis of unimaginable proportions when it reaches the surface of human events. In the absence of alert, ecologically responsible collective action, we are likely to fall victim to the possibly still preventable events which may unfold in the future. We may well suffer the consequences of several 'inconvenient' truths, only one of which is catastrophic climate change.

Can this be avoided? The primary challenge that has to be met everywhere is re-establishing cooperation founded on collective action—not just where governments, businesses and civil society are concerned. Such a mobilization is even more urgent for the multitudes of working people bearing the brunt of ecological disasters. But the difficulties here—from the local to the global level—are formidable. What the French sociologist Pierre Bourdieu has written about his own country is valid everywhere:

> The dominant in our society travel; *they have money*; *they are polyglot*; and they are linked together by affinities of culture and lifestyle. Ranged against them are people who are dispersed geographically and separated by linguistic or social barriers. Bringing all these people together is at once very necessary and very difficult.[7]

Meanwhile, despite overwhelming financial and ecological crises, the juggernaut of elite ambitions rolls on.

The perilous illusions of competitive corporate nationalism

It may appear to some readers that this book is principally a critique of the free market. However, it is not the market economy per se which is at the root of our difficulties. In fact, there are plus points to properly functioning markets, which have been analysed at length by economists. A bazaar or a farmer's market with lots of buyers and sellers is not only a visual delight, it also has economic virtues. But what we have in fact been observing in India, as also in China and the world at large, is not the operation of free markets at all, as much as active state intervention on behalf of powerful corporations—at the cost of the poor, the environment and the future.[8]

What is utterly destructive from an ecological and social standpoint is the *competitive nationalism* that motivates the corporate oligarchies of today, especially in 'emerging economies' like India and China. This is as destructive in the case of a capitalist society as for a socialist one—as the collapse of the Soviet Union and the growing problems of today's China demonstrate. There is not much hope from either economic system, so long as the logic of competition drives national economic ambitions.

Nationalism has been the guiding force in human affairs for some time now. Even the adjective 'competitive' sounds redundant before it. Most of the major wars of the past 100 years can be explained by it. Nationalism is the political lubricant for the modern militarism which feeds and is, in turn, fed by economic growth. This is as true of capitalist societies as of socialist ones.

Yet, what is happening today is somewhat different from the past. Before 1990, when official communism was alive, there was a balance of power in the world. As the world became unipolar under US dominance since the early 1990s, there has emerged, as we have seen, a global market for the very first time. Even as laws restricting the free movement of people grow everywhere, capital moves freely across the world today, seeking the best opportunities from its exclusivist point of view. The tightening controls on the free movement of people around the earth, even as money and capital enjoy such freedom, is an anomaly that fills the term 'globalization' with inescapable irony.

The rise of global corporate power has had a profound consequence on the behaviour of states. Every state—and within every state, each provincial government—has offered more and more attractive concessions to corporations to invest within their borders. In the bidding processes, corporations have been able to play off one state or province against another. Besides offering access to markets and tax incentives, governments have relaxed labour and environmental laws and offered corporations cheap resources, infrastructure and, importantly, security. In such a race-to-the-bottom corporations naturally gravitate towards places (such as China or, within India, to states which offer maximum sops, such as Orissa) that are able to offer the most attractive terms to them.

The obvious corollary of all this is that states have begun to see their interests as virtually identical to those of globally mobile corporations. To survive as credible political entities in a globalized world they must continually keep the corporations interested. Their revenues and fiscal strength follow from the economic growth ushered in by corporate investment. In turn, they ensure the 'right climate' for investment that corporations need. Little wonder then that growth in GDP is of overriding importance not just to investors but to governments too.

The competition for power has perhaps always been a hallmark of human affairs. In a globalized world, it takes the shape of a convergence between state power and corporate influence. This is already proving very destructive. As the French thinker Simone Weil once observed with an ecologically-aware prescience, 'the necessarily limited character of the material bases of power and the necessarily unlimited character of the race for power' means that every 'oppressive system carries within itself like a seed of death' a violent internal contradiction. The social miseries and ecological devastation we witness today are perhaps the early warning signs of bigger catastrophes that lie in wait.[9]

India, like so much of our world today, is arranged for the expansion of power, not for the delivery of socio-economic justice. We are ruled by a widely shared materialistic ideology (common to business lobbies no less than political parties of all persuasions, cutting across all sections of society), which we have described as 'developmentality'. Its political analogue for the hegemonic policy elite is what we call corporate nationalism, whose hallmark is the search for power through economic growth and militarization. Nationalism is usually associated with the state rather than with a business interest. But so peculiar are India's current political dynamics that the term 'corporate nationalism' is appropriate. In fact, even the chief economist of the IMF has pointed out the 'privatization by stealth of the state in India'.[10]

After independence from British rule in 1947, India was a civilization trying to be a nation. Today it is a nation trying to become a corporation, India Inc.

The difference is vast. As long as Mrs Gandhi was alive, India was ruled by an elite who could still be considered somewhat nationalistic (as the elite still stressed on self-reliance). Some of the legacy of the freedom struggle was still at work. However, since the days of Rajiv Gandhi, and especially after the inception of the economic reforms in 1991, the effective political leadership of India has been technocratic and corporatized. The old vision of the freedom fighters is entirely lost. Today's nationalism has nothing to do with the anti-colonial nationalism of the past. Many of today's members of Parliament and ministers are businessmen, and the class of non-resident Indians (NRIs) has become so influential that there is a separate ministry for NRI affairs. Top executive positions in the government are often occupied today by dollar millionaires, some of whom have never fought or won an election in the country.

As the economy clocks high growth rates and the state militarizes—both internally and externally—there is much talk of India becoming a superpower in the coming decades. The dream is fed by the fact that India has been in favour with the world's richest investors for some years now. This has given the country a high profile (compared to in the past) in world media.

India is important to TNCs today because even if only 20–25 per cent of the country can be roped into the global consumer economy, it amounts to over 250 million people, which is more than the size of the populations of the UK, France and Germany taken together, and almost the size of the US. In absolute terms, the consuming classes of India are large enough to interest the TNCs, thousands of whom are today invested in India. But if a substantial portion of the country is left out of the process of rapid growth and consumption, and often suffers actual declines in their living standards, new inequalities are generated which will prove to be socially destabilizing. We are already seeing signs of this in the violent insurgencies, mass protests and bandhs mushrooming in various parts of the country.

The class of 'global Indians' has been making its presence felt around the world. We have been buying mines in Australia and Latin America; producing and selling software and cars in the EU; buying cheap land for exporting roses from Africa;

generating jobs in the deflating US economy. We have, not to forget India's cultural presence, begun appearing alongside Hollywood stars. And so on.

The real question pertaining to all this goes unasked: how does any of this serve the needs and interests of ordinary people back home? The links to their socio-economic destinies are missing. We are talking of the success of a limited class of people when it comes to finding a measure of recognition by the affluent world. It also indicates that we have refused the challenge of decolonizing our minds, as we still care more about approbation and plaudits from the West than from our own people.

By any reasonable yardstick there are almost *twice* as many poor people in India today as the entire population of the country at the time of Independence. This is a fact that would have given nightmares to the millions of men and women who fought so valiantly for freedom from colonial rule. Men like Tagore had warned that 'it does India no good to compete with Western civilisation in its own field'. And yet, that is the path we have been led to take by our leaders in collaboration with powerful international institutions.[11]

The real question that has been asked in this book is why and when did India's national goals shift from bringing a measure of social and economic justice for its people—as promised under the Constitution—to mimicking the reigning superpower. Is it not obvious that becoming a superpower through such means, even if it were possible, would be tantamount to a betrayal of Constitutional promises? And, being a superpower, as tens of millions of unemployed, homeless Americans can testify today, does not guarantee that poverty will be eradicated or that justice will be delivered. Britain was a superpower in the nineteenth century when it was sending little children and women deep under the ground to fetch coal. The experience of other 'great' nations—Russia and China—has not been so different.

To applaud India's achievements in the field of technological modernization—as evidenced, for instance, in its successful satellite launches; its state-of-the-art oil refineries; its increasingly impressive airports; its glass-and-chrome business buildings; its luxury hotels—is one thing. To suggest that the process which has brought forth this kind of energetic enterprise will somehow magically deliver the vast poor population of the country from malnutrition and age-old forms of deprivation is at best an elite delusion. At worst, it justifies a historic fraud on the people, most of whom do not stand the ghost of a chance, under the present dispensation of policies, to share in the prosperity being enjoyed by the country's assorted elite minority. And to assert that such a process can be ecologically sustainable is sheer tomfoolery and a grand deception.

Academic economists celebrating India's recent economic successes as a triumph of the market seem to be ignorant or are in deliberate denial of the role of state power in economic change. They are also being disingenuous about the manner in which the so-called 'free market' plays out in actual Indian realities, dominated as it continues to be by industrial and mining barons, not to omit the myriad land mafia and operatives of hawala, or informal, markets who keep the system well-greased for the functioning of more powerful economic actors.

What is all the industrialization and economic growth worth if it is founded on the blood and bones of the very people in whose name such great ambitions are being launched? The rising stock market index cannot give us the health of an economy like India's: according to the ministry of finance, only 2 per cent of the country is invested in it. We are being fraudulent in selling the dream of a First World consumer lifestyle to the vast majority of our people.[12]

We know in advance that this is ecologically impossible. Not only do the numbers not add up, *we* are not ultimately the people who have the prerogative to do the math, when it comes to numbers of the magnitude we are talking about. (India has not been able to make a significant dent in climate negotiations so far, nor has it been able to secure even modest justice for the hundreds of thousands of victims of Union Carbide. We should have a clearer, humbler appreciation of the limits of our power as a nation in today's world.)[13]

Therefore, we should be honest and upfront with our people. The vast majority of them will never come even close to having lifestyles of the sort that most readers of a book like this enjoy. For instance, most of them (and their children) will never sit in an aeroplane or have a family member who gets a foreign education. This is not to perpetuate our well-entrenched feudal–capitalist club system, so much as to underscore our wilful hypocrisy in advertising our way of life as a generalized possibility for the majority of our people to achieve.

What is worse is that so many communities are being tempted (or tortured) out of sustainable ways of living to comply with the psychological compulsion to modernize the way our elites have. We in the rich urban classes so readily assume that our ambitions for ourselves and our children coincide with the hopes of the communities we allow to get uprooted.

Unfortunately, this may have become true for a significant number of poor rural and urban youth who have been influenced by the barrage of commercial propaganda through mass media today. But most people past a certain adult age harbour no illusions about what they can reasonably expect: it is not much more than what they already have. In fact, they want less of certain things, like the unemployment, inflation, pollution and traffic congestion that have been eating away at their lives and livelihoods.

We must be wary of assuming and acting as though the future is inevitably urban for every Indian. It is particularly tragic when primary education instils these thoughts in little children. Before long, they despise their language, their food, their traditional attire, their music and dance and, often, their own less-fortunate cousins and families, learning to desire and respect *only* the foreign—Western—forms of these things.

But this subconscious inculcation of inferiority towards one's own culture and civilization is almost the hegemonic definition of patriotism today. How many chief ministers have we heard over the past several years wanting to turn their capitals into London, Paris, Singapore or Shanghai? Could we ever imagine a Gandhi or an Ambedkar express such rash desires? Are we so bankrupt in our vision and devoid of cultural self-confidence that we cannot summon an independent vision and imagination to measure our own steps? Are we not forever condemning ourselves to playing an unwinnable 'catch-up' game with the West, Japan and China? The shadow of Western colonialism on Indian cultures is proving to be the longest, long after the sun of colonialism has formally set.

With integration into the global economy—especially with global finance—has also come, as we have seen, considerable loss of sovereignty over our policies. This has led to a striking political anomaly. While every ruling coalition—whether led by the BJP or the Congress—may have received high marks by its policy-masters (the IMF, the World Bank, the ADB and various corporate bodies like the CII), it has been defeated at the polls. 'Shining India' slogans have been ground into the dust. The notable exception is the present UPA coalition which still holds office (in 2012) mainly because of 'against-the-tide', pro-people legislations like the MGNREGA, the Forest Rights Act and the Right to Information Act. The present coalition is the first in many decades to retain office because it has had the political shrewdness to enact and implement (to varying degrees) such popular laws. However, even in its dominant mindset, these have been anomalies.

Nothing is more dangerous today for India's educated classes than to imagine turning India into a great superpower by 2020. When such visions are laid out, it feeds our nationalistic egos as we imagine our 'best and brightest' vaulting to the top of the globe, whatever that may mean. We do not pause to think that there are other peoples on this planet. We do not mind doing to people in Africa what our colonizers did to us. We do not think about our own working people and uprooted cultures either. We take the beneficent abundance of nature—both within India and abroad—for granted, as though all of it were there precisely to minister to our demands and 'entitlements'. We repeat all the terrible blunders of our imperial colonizers.

The urge for external domination can only be met through internal repression. This becomes clear when one takes into account incidents ranging from the police firings in Kashipur and Kalinganagar in Orissa to the more recent ones in Lalgarh in Bengal and Srikakulam in Andhra Pradesh, and the thousands of resisting men and women, adivasis and Dalits, farmers and fishermen who have died in the cause of the nation's 'advancement'.[14]

It is no coincidence then that the Indian state is becoming increasingly intolerant of public criticism. In an imitative domestic version of 'either you are with us or against us' statecraft, it is beginning to categorize as 'Maoist', 'Naxalite', 'extremist' or 'terrorist' anyone who dissents from its unjust economic policies. Since they are structurally exclusive, due to the way market forces function, policies aimed at a neo-liberal market utopia *necessitate* authoritarian politics. Development under globalization in its present incarnation will be inevitably rapacious and thus routinely violate human rights. Never have 'free' markets and democratic rights stood farther apart.

Nor is it a coincidence that the oxygen for democracy in India is provided not by the privileged classes but by the collective political muscle of excluded and rejected majorities and an active civil society. The interests of the former, unlike those of the latter, are served well by the system in place. It is in fact India's unique achievement to have ensured for so long political democracy in a country financially so poor and culturally so diverse. The affluent countries were a lot wealthier than India is today, at the time they created universal suffrage for their people. And if we observe the experiences of South Korea, Taiwan and now, China, authoritarianism has marked the early stages of development in each case. This is one of the reasons we are optimistic about India being at the forefront in finding alternative futures for human welfare (discussed in chapters 9 and 10).

The consequences of globalized growth for the environment are as telling as they have been for political democracy (as we saw in chapters 4 and 5). There are growing threats to water and food security no less than the ecological devastation of coastlines and rainforests in places as far afield as Kachchh in Gujarat and Khandadhar in Orissa. It thus becomes necessary to say that deregulated corporate globalization is today toying with the agro-ecological foundations of the civilization that the people of the subcontinent have known for millennia. In the standard analyses of development, the impositions the mainstream economy makes on the natural environment and the resources of the poor are ignored—because they are taken for granted as inevitable or acceptable 'by-products'.

Almost none of the external social and ecological costs of such 'development' are factored in. This is one of the covert ways in which policies have been made in India all along. The consequences are there for all to see.

At some point in our future, as the sociopolitical fabric of the country comes under increasing pressure, thanks to the fault lines already growing around us, we will have to make up our minds as to whether we wish to remain a civilization or are willing to risk becoming a full-fledged corporation. There is a real public choice to be made. If we allow corporate nationalism to continue to influence us, it will mean the steady erosion of any hope for a radical ecological democracy. Again, we might heed Tagore's words: 'It is my conviction that my countrymen will truly gain their India by fighting against the education which teaches them that a country is greater than the ideals of humanity.'[15]

The cultivated failure of cognition

Nowadays we consume within a few years what it took the earth millions of years to create. Surviving the loss of the planet—in other words, the hospitability of the earth to human civilization—will not be possible for anyone. The failure of 'development' ought to have rendered developmentality obsolete by now. But myths do not rise or fall with facts. They obey passions born of hope and despair. When it comes to the future, we do not have to be either optimists or pessimists but, as the philosopher William James once put it, 'possibilists' or perhaps 'circumstantialists'. In this book, we have chosen two-eyed realism and 'possibilism' over blind optimism. What we can no longer afford is opportunism—that is, seeking one's own short-term material interests at the cost of others. Bold hopes are certainly in order, but exactly where we place them is all-important. If we buy our hopes at a discount today, we and our descendants will be paying back the ecological and social debt at a very high rate of interest tomorrow. Let us not forget that both nature and history are most cruel just when they are forgotten. Inescapable facts are trying to speak to us. Are we listening?

Most 'educated' people, including the 'experts', are so caught up in executing the commands of the globalized market economy or the state power structure that they fail to see the significance and scope of the gathering crises. It also seems that they are unable to make the necessary connection between the worsening environmental situation and the global economic expansion, of which India is now an integral part.

Perhaps there is no greater obstacle to facing the crises around us today than the propaganda-driven beliefs that dominate the consciousness of the educated public, not merely in India but around the world. Propaganda moves more smoothly on the trained, reliable rails of formal schooling and education. Thomas Babington Macaulay, responsible for much of the education that still goes on in the Queen's Commonwealth, knew this two centuries ago, when he designed India's modern factories for the mind. Much of the media—owned by large corporations—manages to hide the burning end of the noose, while it shines the bright lights on impressive statistics like growth rates and stock market booms. More than anything else, by presenting a fragmented picture of the world, it anaesthetizes the public to human suffering and the structural causes behind it. In the process, the media controls the climate of opinion to such a degree that widespread self-censorship ensures the perpetuation of the status quo. Critical faculties are thus suspended because nothing 'negative' can be raised and discussed. Such a media is more interested in recording and photographing disasters (as the movie *Peepli Live* showed so vividly) than in ensuring their prevention or recurrence. There are, of course, notable and praiseworthy exceptions, which keep alive the hope of the survival of an independent media.

The Indian *economy* may be in good statistical health. But, as we have seen, it is by no means in good social or ecological health. While growth rates break the old speed limits, the connection between growth and development becomes ever more tenuous. Trickle-down hopes evaporate and social frustration and anger grow with rising prices, unemployment and inequalities.

Corporate think-tanks, government intellectuals and mainstream economists, keen to justify what they do not readily acknowledge as a predatory style of growth, typically ignore such indicative vital facts as dying species, cultures and languages. In this day and age of information, ignorance of environmental crises cannot be used as a plea. The Rio conference on the environment in 1992 had proposed the Precautionary Principle, which advises governments not to use the absence of scientific certainty as an excuse to plunder resources or reduce biodiversity, whenever there is a perceived threat to them. Currently, our economic decision-makers seem to have consigned this wise principle to the dustbin of history and it is only being revived because of citizens' struggles.[16]

In closing: Another world is necessary

In a time of restless despair, one looks for signs of hope. For our purposes, the many struggles for socio-economic and ecological justice and the thousands of real-life experiments in sustainable living around the country and the world offer just that (as we have attempted to show in chapters 9 and 10).

They all make one thing clear. The way to the economic future for the vast majority of people is ecological, is rooted in the local and the regional, and is built on the past. It depends crucially on the recovery of the best traditions of Indian cultures, even while rejecting the worst, and combining these with the best of modernity. Only on the basis of such a revival can a sustainable future be imagined and built from the point in the historical trajectory we have collectively reached, both as a civilization and as a species. This is not a 'back to nature' approach so much as one of a 'return to nature' in the best sense of the expression—something we are compelled to embrace in the face of the ecological crisis. It does not mean giving up so much of what is of value in modern life, such as its capacity for technological innovation. It *does* mean turning our back towards its absurd and dangerous excesses (especially the technological ones) and avoiding the hubris that comes with it.

Moreover, it is these struggles that hold the future of democracy in their hands. Democracy is not a mere system of decision-making that has reached some final stage of development. Political complacency at this stage will mean compliance with corporate plans and ambitions for everybody, not just the readers of a book like this. It would mean the tacit acceptance of the structural exclusion and rejection we have analysed in this book. It may lead to a situation in which, after a generation or less, 'democracy' will begin to appear as a strange twentieth-century aberration in human affairs.

Democracy is nothing, if not an ongoing *movement*, a way of social, political and economic life which involves *practices* that take into their vision the concerns of the underprivileged. Nothing assures this better than the direct participation of the underprivileged in the decisions concerning their lives. Listening to those at the receiving end of the environmental excesses and economic exclusion is necessary if we are to avoid the fatal structural defects of the deregulated market economy. Any institutional process that enables this change is welcome. It is unlikely that democracy will survive in the future unless it is deepened in this fashion.

We are rapidly approaching the moment when the choices before us would be stark: an institutionalized, hazardous corporate totalitarianism at indefinite war with the people and the earth, or the consensual emergence of a radical ecological democracy which will leave everyone with a semblance of hope. The middle ground between these two choices is already beginning to vanish.

We have not attempted to provide a comprehensive blueprint for a new world. We have only offered a few ideas, examples and principles along the lines of which a new world can be conceived and birthed. These, and those offered by myriad other thinkers and activists, must be publicly discussed at length for clearer answers to emerge. We trust in the imagination and wisdom of citizens in India and elsewhere to take this process further in the direction of a saner world.

NOTES

PART I: TWILIGHT

Prologue I

1. Karl Polanyi, *The Great Transformation* (Boston: Beacon Press, 1957).
2. Ashis Nandy, *The Romance of the State and the Fate of Dissent in the Tropics* (New Delhi: Oxford University Press, 2003).
3. Ruzbeh Bharucha, *Yamuna Gently Weeps: A Journey into the Yamuna Pushta Demolitions* (New Delhi: Sainathann Communication, 2006), pp. 24–28.
4. *Abandoned: Development and Displacement* (Delhi: The Perspectives Group, 2008), p. 111.
5. Action Aid, *Shadow Report*; and 'Role of non-state players in slum evictions worries rights activists', *The Hindu*, 12 July 2009, http://www.thehindu.com/2009/06/12/stories/2009061253270300 .htm. Menon-Sen's figures are based on 'Testimonies and evidence on JNNURM' presented at the Independent People's Tribunal on the World Bank, September 2007, New Delhi. Documents and reports available at www.worldbanktribunal.org.
6. Belinda Yuen, 'Squatters no more: Singapore social housing', *Global Urban Development Magazine*, Vol. 3, No. 1, November 2007, http://www.globalurban.org/GUDMag07Vol3Iss1/Yuen.htm.

Chapter 1: Globalization?

1. Quoted in Christian Comeliau, *The Impasse of Modernity* (London: Zed Books, 2002), p. 96.
2. See, for instance, Amartya Sen, *The Argumentative Indian* (London: Penguin Books, 2005), p. 345.
3. John Maynard Keynes, 'National Self-sufficiency', *Yale Review*, Summer 1933.
4. Aid figures are from OECD, http://www.oecd.org/document/17/ 0,3343,en_2649_33721_38341265_1_1_1_1,00&&en-USS

_01DBC. html. Data on debt-servicing is from James Henry, 'The mirage of debt relief', in Steven Hiatt (ed.), *A Game As Old As Empire* (San Francisco: Berret-Koehler, 2007), p. 222.

5.   Margaret Thatcher's interview for *Woman's Own*, 23 September 1987, Margaret Thatcher Foundation, http://www.margaretthatcher.org/document/106689; and Susan George, 'A Short History of Neoliberalism', Transnational Institute, March 1999, http://www.tni.org/article/short-history-neoliberalism.

6.   The term 'Washington Consensus' was coined by the economist John Williamson in 1989.

7.   Amit Bhaduri, 'The imperative as alternative', *Seminar*, February 2008.

8.   *Triennial Central Bank Survey*, Bank for International Settlements, Basel, April 2007, http://www.bis.org/publ/rpfxf07t.pdf. D. Felix, 'Asia and the Crisis of Financial Globalization', in D. Baker, G. Epstein and P. Pollin (eds), *Globalization and Progressive Economic Policy* (Cambridge: Cambridge University Press, 1998).

9.   Alfred Chandler et al. (ed.), *Big Business and the Wealth of Nations* (Cambridge: Cambridge University Press, 2000); and Alice Amsden, *Asia's Next Giant: South Korea and Late Industrialization* (New York: Oxford University Press, 1989).

10. Peter Linebaugh, *The London Hanged: Crime and Civil Society in the Eighteenth Century* (Cambridge: Cambridge University Press, 1993), p. 272.

11. See Ha-Joon Chang, *Kicking Away the Ladder* (London: Anthem Press, 2003), Chapter 4; Ha-Joon Chang, *Bad Samaritans* (New York: Bloomsbury Press, 2008), Chapter 1; and Mark Weisbrot, 'The "Washington Consensus" and Development Economics', paper prepared for UNRISD Meeting, Cape Town, South Africa, September 2001.

12. Amiya Bagchi, *Perilous Passage: Mankind and the Global Ascendancy of Capital* (New Delhi: Oxford University Press, 2005).

13. Deepak Nayyar, 'Globalization and Development', in Ha-Joon Chang (ed.), *Rethinking Development Economics* (London: Anthem Press, 2006).

14. Adam Smith, *The Wealth of Nations* (London: Penguin Books, 1983), Book I, Chapter X.

15. To sample the vast literature on neo-colonialism, see, for instance, Hiatt (ed.), *A Game As Old As Empire*; Kwame Nkrumah, *Neo-Colonialism: The Last Stage of Imperialism* (Humanities Press International, 1965); Jean-Paul Sartre, *Colonialism and Neo-colonialism* (London: Routledge, 2001); Immanuel Wallerstein, *The Modern World System: Capitalist Agriculture and the Origins of the European World Economy in the Sixteenth Century* (New York: Academic Press, 1974); and Ankie M.M. Hoogvelt, *Globalisation and the Postcolonial World: The New Political Economy of Development* (Baltimore: Johns Hopkins University Press, 2001).

16. While the word globalization seems to have entered the Webster dictionary in the 1950s, having been used on a few occasions in non-economic contexts, its first use in an economic context appears to have been in 1959 in *The Economist* (http://www.wordorigins.org/index.php/site/comments/globalization/). The phrase 'globalization of markets' appears to have been used for the first time in 1983 by Theodore Levitt of Harvard Business School (http://hbr.org/product/globalization-of-markets/an/83308-PDF-ENG).

17. For useful reviews of this important period of recent economic history from different perspectives, see Thomas Friedman, *The Lexus and the Olive Tree* (New York: Anchor Books, 2000); Jerry Mander and Edward Goldsmith (eds), *The Case Against the Global Economy* (San Francisco: Sierra Club Books, 1996); Nayyar, 'Globalization and Development'; Comeliau, *The Impasse of Modernity*; and Pierre Bourdieu, *Firing Back* (New York: Verso Books, 2003).

18. See Bagchi, *Perilous Passage*, Chapter 22, for a brief history of the fall of Bretton Woods and the rise of the Dollar Standard. A more elaborate history of the Bretton Woods system is given in Benjamin Cohen, 'The Bretton-Woods System', prepared for the *Routledge Encyclopedia of Political Economy*, available at http://www.polsci.ucsb.edu/faculty/cohen/inpress/bretton.html.

19. Thomas Friedman, 'A manifesto for the fast world', *The New York Times*, 28 March 1999.

20. For a clear statement of imperial strategy see Ralph Peters, 'Constant Conflict', *US Army War College Quarterly*, Summer 1997.

21. Arun Kumar, 'India's Growth Target', *The Tribune*, 3 February 2009, http://www.tribuneindia.com/2009/20090203/edit.htm#4.

22. Dr Manmohan Singh, quoted in *Financial Express*, 27 October 2008.
23. Alan Greenspan, former chairman of the US Federal Reserve, commenting on the financial crisis in testimony to Congress, 23 October 2008.
24. 'Seeking job quota, Jats threaten to disrupt Commonwealth Games', *The Times of India*, 28 July 2010, http://timesofindia.indiatimes.com/india/Seeking-job-quota-Jats-threaten-to-disrupt-Commonwealth-Games/articleshow/6228686.cms.

Chapter 2: The Drunken Stunted Dog

1. As stated by Chakravarty, one of India's foremost economists, at a lecture at the Delhi School of Economics in the mid-1980s, attended by one of the authors of this book.
2. Sri Aurobindo, *Out of the Ruins of the West . . . India's Rebirth* (Paris: Institut de Recherches Evolutives, 1994), p. 85.
3. *The 'Bird of Gold': The Rise of India's Consumer Market*, McKinsey Global Institute, 2007, http://www.mckinsey.com/mgi/reports/pdfs/india_consumer_market/MGI_india_consumer_executive_summary.pdf; the NCAER estimate is from Rajesh Shukla, 'Why does the middle class matter?', *The Economic Times*, 27 April 2009, http://www.ncaer.org/downloads/MediaClips/Press/RajeshShukla-Why%20does%20the%20middle%20class%20matter.pdf.

   See, for instance, the estimates of NCAER, which claims that by 2010 there were more 'high-income' households in India (46.7 million) than 'low-income' ones (41 million), http://timesofindia.indiatimes.com/india/India-has-more-rich-people-than-poor-now/articleshow/6242324.cms
4. 'Factsheet on FDI', GoI, http://dipp.nic.in/fdi_statistics/india_FDI_April2010.pdf. China and Hong Kong data is from UNCTAD, *World Investment Report*, Annex, Table 3, http://www.unctad.org/Templates/Page.asp?intItemID=5545&lang=1.
5. 'Number of taxpayers growing at 2.4% CAGR', *Financial Express*, 12 March 2008, http://www.financialexpress.com/news/number-of-taxpayers-growing-at-2.4-cagr/283153/.

6. *The Challenge of Employment: An Informal Economy Perspective,* NCEUS, GoI, New Delhi, 2009, http://nceuis.nic.in/The _Challenge_of_Employment_in_India.pdf; *Economic Survey 2007–08*, GoI, New Delhi, http://indiabudget.nic.in/.

7. GoI, Ministry of Finance, Department of Economic Affairs, 'Economic Reforms: Two Years After and the Task Ahead', Discussion Paper, New Delhi, July 1993, pp. 1–2.

8. For a view in defence of the reforms on grounds that the government was stifling entrepreneurship before 1991, see Gurcharan Das, *India Unbound* (New Delhi: Penguin Books, 2000).

9. Amit Bhaduri and Deepak Nayyar, *The Intelligent Person's Guide to Liberalization* (New Delhi: Penguin Books, 1996).

10. Charan Wadhwa, 'India trying to liberalise: Economic reforms since 1991', in Vijay Joshi and I.M.D. Little (eds), *India's Economic Reforms: 1991–2001* (New Delhi: Oxford University Press, 1996).

11. See Meghnad Desai, 'Economic Reform by Stealth', *Tehelka,* 4 July 2009, http://www.tehelka.com/story_main41.asp?filename =Ne040409economic_reform.asp.

12. Ashis Nandy, *Time Treks: The Uncertain Future of Old and New Despotisms* (New Delhi: Permanent Black, 2007), p. 98.

13. *Directive Principles of State Policy,* available at http://www .constitution.org/cons/india/p04.html.

14. This section relies on Bhaduri and Nayyar, *The Intelligent Person's Guide to Liberalization*; Jayati Ghosh and C.P. Chandrashekhar, *The Market That Failed* (New Delhi: Leftword Books, 2004); and Dolly Arora, 'Structural Adjustment Program and Gender Concerns in India', *Journal of Contemporary Asia*, Vol. 29, No. 3, 1999.

15. For a detailed survey of the set of policy changes brought about after 1991, see Bhaduri and Nayyar, *The Intelligent Person's Guide to Liberalization*; and Ghosh and Chandrashekhar, *The Market That Failed*.

16. Constitution of India, accessed at http://lawmin.nic.in/coi/ coiason29july08.pdf.

17. Joseph Stiglitz, 'Do as the US says, not as it does', *The Guardian*, 29 October 2003.

18. 'Favourite lobby horses', *Outlook*, 17 May 2010, http://www.outlook india.com/article.aspx?265345.

19. For a small sample of human rights violations, see *'Being Neutral Is Our Biggest Crime': Governments, Vigilante, and Naxalite Abuses in India's Chhattisgarh State*, Human Rights Watch, New York, 2008. 'India—Amnesty International Report 2008', available at http:// www.amnesty.org/en/region/india/report-2008.

20. *Economic Survey 2007–08*, p. A-4; *Economic Survey 2009–10*, GoI, New Delhi, http://indiabudget.nic.in/es2009-10/chapt2010/ chapter01.pdf.

21. Ha-Joon Chang, *Bad Samaritans* (New York: Bloomsbury, 2008), pp. 28–29.

22. *Economic Survey 2007–08*, p. A-10; *RBI Annual Report 2008–09*, p. 80, http://rbidocs.rbi.org.in/rdocs/AnnualReport/PDFs/ IRAR200809_Full.pdf. To say that the national savings rate has kept pace with investment is not to negate the Keynesian logic that investment can sometimes spur growth of incomes and hence, savings. It is only to discern the role of foreign capital inflows to India.

23. EAC, *Review of the Economy 2007–08*, January 2008, cited in 'India's Runaway Growth: Distortion, Disarticulation, and Exclusion', *Aspects of Political Economy*, No. 44–46 (April 2008), Research Unit in Political Economy (RUPE), p. 52.

24. Amit Bhaduri, 'A Failed World View', Foundation Day Lecture, IUCAA, Pune, 29 December 2008. On job losses, see http:// indianaviationnews.net/careers/2009/05/more-job-losses-in-air-as -domestic.html; *Economic Survey 2008–09*, GoI, New Delhi, p. 265, http://indiabudget.nic.in/es2008-09/chapt2009/chap105.pdf and http://www.business-standard.com/india/news/exports-may-fall-to -155-bn-in-2009-10-says-fieo/369871/.

25. The International Energy Agency data is from Trevor Morgan, 'Energy Subsidies', UNFCC Secretariat, 2007, http://unfccc.int/files/ cooperation_and_support/financial_mechanism/application/pdf/ morgan_pdf.pdf.

26. John Madeley, *Big Business: Poor Peoples* (London and New York: Zed Books, 2008), p. 43; and I. Angus, 'Food Crisis: "The Greatest

Demonstration of the Historical Failure of the Capitalist Model"', *Global Research* (28 April 2008).

27. Chapter A-100, *Economic Survey 2009–10*, http://indiabudget.nic.in/ es2009-10/chapt2010/tab75.pdf; Manmohan Agarwal, 'The China and India Factor: Implications for Developing Countries in the Asia and Pacific Region', Presentation to UNIDO, 4 December 2007, http://www.unido.org/fileadmin/media/documents/pdf/ UNIDO_Worldwide/Asia/09-Presentation_by_Panelist__Agarwal _-_IND_.pdf.

28. See Kasturi Das, 'GATS negotiations and India: Evolution and state of play', CENTAD, November 2006, http://www.centad.org/cwp _09.asp.

29. *India's External Debt: A Status Report*, GoI, New Delhi, 2006, available at http://finmin.nic.in/the_ministry/dept_eco_affairs/economic_div/ Indian%20External%20Debt06E.pdf.

30. 'India is world's best performing stock market', *The Economic Times*, 21 November 2007, http://economictimes.indiatimes.com/Markets/ Analysis/India-is-worlds-best-performing-stock-market/articleshow/ 2559788.cms.

31. *Economic Survey 2007–08*, p. A-81; *Economic Survey 2008–09*, pp. 129, 148; World Bank Country Data: India, http://ddp-ext .worldbank.org/ext/ddpreports/ViewShared Report?&CF=1 &REPORT_ID=9147&REQUEST_TYP=VIEWADVANCED &HF=N&WSP=N; and Sunanda Sen, 'State, Society and the Market: Indian Economy under Economic Reforms', Paper presented at the Italian Institute of Political Economy, Rome, 2008.

32. D'Street Community, Thread: Sensex Timeline: 1000 to 20000, a 17-year-old journey, http://www.dstreetdirect.com/stock-discussion -market-buzz/1823-sensex-timeline-1000-20000-17-year-old -journey.html.

33. '2009 Stock Market Returns – Emerging Markets in Triple Digits', Darwin'sFinance.com, 20 September 2009, http://www .darwinsfinance.com/2009-stock-market-returns/.

34. 'World Stock Markets: Best Performing Markets of 2009', EconomyWatch.com, 25 May 2009, http://www.economywatch .com/stock-markets-in-world/world-stock-markets-best-performing -markets-2009.html; and 'India ranks 75th among world's best nations for business', *The Economic Times*, 20 March 2009, http://

economictimes.indiatimes.com/News/Economy/Indicators/India
-ranks-75th-in-worlds-best-nations-for-business-Forbes/articleshow/
4287419.cms.

35. 'Triennial Central Bank Survey of Foreign Exchange and Derivatives
    Market Activity in 2007 – Final Results', Bank for International
    Settlements, 19 December 2007, http://www.bis.org/press/
    p071219.htm; *World Economic Situation and Prospects 2009* (New
    York: United Nations, 2009), http://www.un.org/esa/policy/wess/
    wesp2009files/wesp2009.pdf; and World Bank, http://ddp-ext
    .worldbank.org/ext/ddpreports/ViewSharedReport?&CF=1
    &REPORT_ID=9147&REQUEST_TYPE=VIEWADVANCED
    &HF=N&WSP=N.

36. Sunanda Sen, *Globalisation and Development* (New Delhi: NBT,
    2007), pp. 60, 103.

37. 'India's Runaway Growth'.

38. Ibid.

39. *Economic Survey 2007–08*, pp. 7, 123.

40. 'Dizzy in Boomtown', *The Economist*, 17 November 2007.

41. 'India's Runaway Growth'.

42. Sen, *Globalisation and Development*, pp. 103–04.

43. Ibid., p. 108.

44. 'India's Runaway Growth', pp. 57–58; and Pragya Singh and Arti
    Sharma, 'A Shot in the Dark', *Outlook*, 5 December 2011, http://
    www.outlookindia.com/article.aspx?279090.

45. The literature on these crises is vast. For a specialist's overview, see
    Charles P. Kindleberger and Robert Aliber, *Manias, Panics, and
    Crashes: A History of Financial Crises*, 5th ed. (New Jersey: John Wiley
    & Sons, 2005); and for a journalistic overview, see John Lee, 'Dollar's
    fate written in history', *Asia Times*, 4 June 2009, http://www
    .atimes.com/atimes/Global_Economy/KF04Dj03.html.

46. *Economic Survey 2009–10*, http://indiabudget.nic.in/es2009-10/
    chapt2010/chapter06.pdf.

47. Asit Ranjan Mishra, 'Tax–GDP ratio slated to drop to 10.94% in
    2008–09', *LiveMint.com*, 7 July 2009, http://www.livemint.com/
    2009/07/07002528/TaxGDP-ratio-slated-to-drop-t.html; and
    G. Srinivasan, 'Low tax-GDP ratio daunts India's quest to join
    the developed world', *The Hindu Business Line*, 13 October 2005,

http://www.thehindubusinessline.com/2005/10/13/stories/2005101
301531200.htm.

48. 'Indian Investments Abroad', http://www.ibef.org/artdispview
.aspx?art_id=23469&cat_id=599&in=37; *Economic Survey 2008–09*,
p. 133; and 'India's Runaway Growth'.

49. Anand Sharma, 'India Inc contributes $105 bn to US economy', *The
Economic Times*, 18 June 2009, http://www.thaindian.com/
newsportal/business/india-inc-has-contributed-105-bn-to-us
-economy-anand-sharma_100206602.html.

50. 'Land Grab: The Race for the World's Farmland', *The Independent*,
3 May 2009, http://www.independent.co.uk/news/business/
analysis-and-features/land-grab-the-race-for-the-worlds-farmland-
1677852.html, 'India Cultivates Africa', http://farmlandgrab.org/
5819.

51. Various issues of *Economic Survey 2002–09*, GoI, New Delhi, http://
indiabudget.nic.in/.

52. *Economic Survey 2008–09*, http://indiabudget.nic.in/es2008-09/
chapt2009/tab31.pdf; and *The Challenge of Employment*, p. 14.

53. *The Challenge of Employment*, pp. 2, 14.

54. Edward Luce, *In Spite of the Gods* (London: Little Brown, 2006),
p. 51.

55. Stephen Roach (chief economist, Morgan Stanley), 'Dateline India:
From Mumbai to Pune', *The Globalist*, 25 October 2004, http://
www.theglobalist.com/StoryId.aspx?StoryId=4226.

56. D.K. Das and Gunajit Kalita, 'Do labour-intensive industries generate
employment?', ICRIER Working Paper 237, New Delhi, June 2009.

57. Quoted in Luce, *In Spite of the Gods*, p. 54.

58. Judith Banister, 'Manufacturing Employment in China', *Monthly
Labor Review*, July 2005, http://www.bls.gov/opub/mlr/2005/07/
art2full.pdf; '"Jobless growth" in Asia fails to tackle poverty – UN
Report', ILO, 20 February 2007, http://www.ilo.org/asia/info/public/
pr/lang—en/WCMS_BK_PR_171_EN/index.htm.

59. Quoted in Samuel Bowles and Herbert Gintis, 'The Revenge of Homo
Economicus', *Journal of Economic Perspectives*, Vol. 7, No. 1, Winter
1993.

60. NSS (National Sample Survey) data (from Report #525) and results
of OECD study, quoted in 'India's Runaway Growth'; and Alok Sheel

and Sean Dougherty, 'Constraining labour gains', *Business Standard*, 28 October 2007.

61. 'India's Runaway Growth'.

62. 'A Ten Foot Trench, Rs. 14.50', *Outlook*, 9 April 2007. Also see Praveen Jha, 'Employment in the time of liberalisation', in M. Kelley and D. D'Souza (eds), *The World Bank in India: Undermining Sovereignty, Distorting Development* (New Delhi: Orient Blackswan, 2010).

63. CSO (Central Statistical Organization) data cited in 'India's Runaway Growth'.

64. 'Missing Links', Chapter IV.1, in 'India's Runaway Growth', http://rupe-india.org/44/links.html.

65. Ajit Singh and S. Dasgupta, 'Will services be the new engine of growth for India?', Working Paper, Centre for Business Research, University of Cambridge, http://www.cbr.cam.ac.uk/pdf/WP310.pdf.

66. *Report of the Steering Committee on Agriculture and Allied Sectors for Formulation of the 11th Five-Year Plan (2007–12)*, Planning Commission, New Delhi, 2007; Kaustava Barik, 'Industry', in *AES India 2007–08* (New Delhi: Daanish Books, 2008); and 'India's service sector will prop growth rate', *Financial Express*, 29 December 2008, http://www.thefinancialexpress-bd.com/2008/12/29/54416.html.

67. *The Challenge of Employment*, pp. 13–23.

68. C.M. Wilkinson-Weber, 'Skill, Dependency and Differentiation: Artisans and Agents in the Lucknow Embroidery Industry', *Ethnology*, Vol. 36, No. 1, 1997.

69. Padma Deosthali, 'Sick and Tired', *Agenda*, No. 9, September 2007, http://infochangeindia.org/200709036508/Agenda/Women-At-Work/Sick-and-tired.html; and Susan Abraham, 'A Lawless Sector', *Agenda*, No. 9, September 2007, http://infochangeindia.org/200709186493/Agenda/Women-At-Work/A-lawless-sector.html.

70. Aparna Pallavi, 'We pay for the work with our dignity', *Agenda*, No. 9, September 2007, http://infochangeindia.org/200709166495/Agenda/Women-At-Work/We-pay-for-the-work-with-our-dignity.html.

71. Freny Manecksha, 'Carriers of the dregs of humanity', *Agenda*, No. 9, September 2007, http://infochangeindia.org/200709156496/Agenda/Women-At-Work/Carriers-of-the-dregs-of-humanity.html.

72. Quoted in UNICEF's *State of the World's Children 1997*, Oxford 1998, p. 35. The data on domestic workers is from UNICEF: Press Release, 'Efforts against child labour often overlook domestic workers', http://www.unicef.org/media/media_21576.html.

73. *Report of the ILO Forum on Decent Work and a Fair Globalization*, ILO, Geneva, 2008, http://www.ilo.org/wcmsp5/groups/public/—ed_norm/—relconf/documents/meetingdocument/wcms _090953.pdf; Ronaldo Munck, *Globalisation and Labour* (New Delhi: Madhyam Books, 2002), Chapter 5; and Satyaki Roy, 'Employment and Labour Market: The Myth of "Rigidity"', in *AES 2007–08*.

74. 'Gap, Next and M&S in new sweatshop scandal', *The Observer*, 8 August 2010, http://www.guardian.co.uk/world/2010/aug/08/gap -next-marks-spencer-sweatshops.

75. Calculated from data given in the *Economic Survey 2007–08*; 'Indian "slave" children found making low-cost clothes destined for Gap', *The Guardian*, 28 October 2007, http://www.guardian.co.uk/world/2007/oct/28/ethicalbusiness.retail.

76. Rahul Varman and Manali Chakrabarti, 'Labour in Global Value-Chains: A Study of the Leather and Footwear Manufacturing Sector of Kanpur', *Aspects of India's Economy*, No. 47, March 2009, http://www.rupe-india.org/47/leather.html.

77. *The Challenge of Employment*, pp. 13–14; E.T. Mathew, *Employment and Unemployment in India: Emerging Tendencies during the Post-Reform Period* (New Delhi: Sage, 2006), p. 137; and 'India's Runaway Growth'.

78. *The Challenge of Employment*, p. 254; *Informal Employment curbs trade benefits for developing countries*, ILO, 2009, http://www.ilo.org/global/About_the_ILO/Media_and_public_information/Press_releases/lang—en/WCMS_115083/index.htm.

79. Teodor Shanin, 'What is the informal economy?', *New Scientist*, August 2002.

80. Fifth Economic Census, GoI, 2005, p. 19, http://www.mospi.gov.in/index_6june08.htm, http://www.mospi.gov.in/economic_census_prov _results_2005.pdf.

81. 'India's Runaway Growth'.

82. Jan Breman, *The Poverty Regime of Village India* (New Delhi: Oxford, 2007), p. 412.

83. John Harris, 'Globalization(s) in China and India: Introductory Reflections', *Global Labour Journal*, Vol. 1, No. 1, 2010, http://digitalcommons.mcmaster.ca/cgi/viewcontent.cgi?article=1018 &context=globallabour.

84. Breman, *The Poverty Regime*, p. 418.

Chapter 3: Trickle-Down?

1. James B. Davies, Susanna Sandstrom, Anthony Shorrocks and Edward N. Wolff, *The World Distribution of Household Wealth* (UNU-WIDER, 2007).

2. Chetan Ahya, 'Globalisation, Capitalism and Inequality', *The Economic Times*, 9 July 2007.

3. Estimated by the authors using World Bank data. The data on billionaires is from *Forbes* magazine: http://www.forbes.com/2009/03/11/india-financial-loss-billionaires-2009-billionaires-india.html.

4. D. Tripathi and J. Jumani, *The Concise Oxford History of Indian Business* (Delhi: Oxford, 2007); Arun Kumar, 'Macro Overview', *AES India 2006–07* (New Delhi: Daanish Books, 2007), pp. 40–41; *RBI Annual Report 2007–08*, Table 2.18, http://rbidocs.rbi.org.in/rdocs/AnnualReport/PDFs/86531.pdf; 'Marauding Maharajahs', *The Economist*, 29 March 2007; 'Rich Man, Poor Man', *The Economist*, 20 January 2007; and 'India's Runaway Growth: Distortion, Disarticulation, and Exclusion', *Aspects of Political Economy*, No. 44–46 (April 2008), Research Unit in Political Economy (RUPE), pp. 42–45.

5. P. Sainath, 'CEOs and the wealth of notions', *The Hindu*, 12 June 2007, http://www.hindu.com/2007/06/12/stories/2007061201821000.htm; data from *Business World*, 5 February 2007, cited in K.N. Kabra, 'Poverty, Inequalities and the Neo-liberal Policy Regime', in *AES India 2006–07*.

6. A. Deaton and V. Kozel (eds), *The Great Indian Poverty Debate* (Delhi: MacMillan, 2005); and Breman, *The Poverty Regime*.

7. Breman, *The Poverty Regime*, p. 6.

8. '55% of India's population poor: Report', *The Times of India*, 15 July 2010. See also the UN website http://www.un.org/apps/news/story.asp?NewsID=35323&Cr=undp&Cr1=.

9. C.P. Chandrasekhar, 'New light on global poverty', *The Hindu*, 2 September 2008, http://www.thehindu.com/2008/09/02/stories/2008090256571000.htm.

10. *Human Development Report 2009*, UNDP, http://hdr.undp.org/en/statistics/, http://hdr.undp.org/en/media/HDR_2009_EN_Table_G.pdf.

11. Jeremy Seabrook, *In the Cities of the South* (London: Verso, 1996), p. 63.

12. NCEUS data, quoted in Satyaki Roy, 'Employment and Labour Market: The Myth of "Rigidity"', in *AES 2007–08* (New Delhi: Daanish Books, 2008).

13. 'The moon and 26 pence', *Outlook Business*, 29 November 2008, http://business.outlookindia.com/article.aspx?101689.

14. Utsa Patnaik, 'Neo-liberalism and Rural Poverty in India', *Economic and Political Weekly* (*EPW*), 28 July 2007.

15. FAO, 'Food and Agriculture Statistics Global Outlook', 2006, http://faostat.fao.org/Portals/_Faostat/documents/pdf/world.pdf; other data on calorie intake is from Shahla Shapouri and Stacey Rosen, 'Global diet composition: Factors behind the changes and implications of the new trend', in *Food Security Assessment* (USDA, 2007).

16. NSS Reports No. 405 and No. 513, cited in 'India's Runaway Growth'.

17. Ibid.

18. Patnaik, 'Neo-liberalism and Rural Poverty in India'.

19. S.K. Bhasin, 'New poverty line and growth chart bring forth sharp inequalities in the Indian population', *Indian Journal of Community Medicine*, Vol. 34, No. 3, July 2009, http://www.ijcm.org.in/temp/IndianJCommunityMed343171-7205109_200051.pdf.

20. National Family Health Survey, GoI, 2005–06, http://www.rchiips.org/nfhs/factsheet.shtml and http://www.rchiips.org/nfhs/nfhs3_national_report.shtml.

21. *Global Hunger Index*, IFPRI, Washington DC, 2009, http://www.ifpri.org/sites/default/files/publications/ghi09.pdf; Rahul Goswami, 'The Hunger Index', http://infochangeindia.org/200901097562/Agriculture/Analysis/The-hunger-index.html.

22. *Economic Survey 2007–08* (New Delhi: Department of Economic Affairs, Ministry of Finance, GoI), p. A-18, http://indiabudget.nic.in/.

23. Independent Commission on Banking and Financial Policy (ICBFP), Interim Report, April 2005, p. 30, available at http://www.macroscan

.com/pol/may05/pdf/ICBP_Interim_Report.pdf; 'India's Runaway Growth'; and 'In the shadow of India's loan boom', *The Wall Street Journal*, 8 January 2008.

24. RBI data cited in 'India's Runaway Growth'.

25. Sunanda Sen, *Globalisation and Development* (New Delhi: NBT, 2007), pp. 63–71; P. Sainath, '4750 Bank branches closed down in 15 years', *The Hindu*, 28 March 2008, http://www.thehindu.com/2008/03/28/stories/2008032857540100.htm; 'India's Runaway Growth'; and Mihir Shah, Rangu Rao and P.S. Vijay Shankar, 'Rural Credit in 20th Century India', *EPW*, 14 April 2007.

26. 'India's Runaway Growth'.

27. ICBFP, Interim Report, April 2005, p. 30; *The Challenge of Employment: An Informal Economy Perspective*, NCEUS, GoI, New Delhi, 2009, http://nceuis.nic.in/The_Challenge_of_Employment_in_India.pdf, p. 261; and RBI statements, quoted in 'India's Runaway Growth'.

28. ICBFP, Interim Report, p. 30; Breman, *The Poverty Regime*, p. 418.

29. M. George, 'A Primer on Microfinance in India', Microfinance Gateway, 4 June 2008, http://www.microfinancegateway.org/p/site/m/template.rc/1.26.9150/.

30. 'Microfinance Fever', *Forbes*, 7 January 2008, http://www.forbes.com/forbes/2008/0107/050.html, http://www.microfinancegateway.org/p/site/m/template.rc/1.26.9150/; and 'India's Runaway Growth'.

31. Laxmi Murthy, 'Micro Gains, Mega Hypes', *Agenda*, No. 9, 2007, http://infochangeindia.org/200709056506/Agenda/Women-At-Work/Micro-gain-mega-hype.html.

32. Shah, Rao and Vijay Shankar, 'Rural Credit'. The AP story was told to us by members of an NGO in Kakinada district. They wish to retain confidentiality.

33. Cited data is from Prabhu Ghate, *Microfinance in India: A state of the sector report, 2006*, CARE, SDC and Ford Foundation, New Delhi.

34. 'India's Runaway Growth'.

35. See chapter 8, especially the section on SEZs.

36. Lester Brown, 'Biofuels Blunder: Massive Diversion of U.S. Grain to Fuel Cars is Raising World Food Prices, Risking Political Instability',

testimony before the US Senate Committee on Environment and Public Works, Earth Policy Institute, 13 June 2007, http://www.earth -policy.org/index.php?/press_room/C68/SenateEPW07.

37. *Economic Survey 2007–08*, p. 155.

38. V. Upadhyay and Shakti Kak, 'Prices, Food Security and PDS', in *AES India 2004–05* (New Delhi: Daanish Books, 2005); Madhura Swaminathan and Neeta Mishra, 'Errors of Targeting: Public Distribution of Food in a Maharashtra Village 1995–2000', *EPW*, 30 June 2001.

39. Erika Kinetz, 'Wheat rots in India as world prices at two-year high', CNBC, 6 August 2010, http://www.msnbc.msn.com/id/38591224/ ns/world_news-south_and_central_asia.

40. Inflation rate data from *RBI Annual Report 2008–09*, Table 2.33, http://rbidocs.rbi.org.in/rdocs/AnnualReport/PDFs/IRAR200809 _Full.pdf; data on retail prices from Ministry of Consumer Affairs is quoted in C.P. Chandrasekhar, 'Gone with winds of liberalisation', *Frontline*, 25 April 2008.

41. Aseem Shrivastava, 'The Failed Harvest of Food Policy', *Himal*, June 2008.

42. 'Tur dal prices up on fear of low outputs, imports', PTI, 16 July 2009, http://www.financialexpress.com/news/tur-dal-prices-up-on -fears-of-low-output-imports/489907/; Devinder Sharma, 'Yet to learn drought lessons', *Hardnews*, September 2009, http://www.hardnews media.com/2009/09/3204.

43. Ravinder Bawa, 'Pawar's rice shortage warning may lead to hoarding', IndiaToday.in, 24 September 2009, http://indiatoday.intoday.in/site/ Story/63483/LATEST%20NEWS/Pawar%C3%A2%E2%82%AC %E2%84%A2s+rice+shortage+warning+may+lead+to+hoarding.html.

44. 'A nation forced to go on distress diet', *The Times of India*, 27 July 2010, http://timesofindia.indiatimes.com/india/Inflation-A-nation -forced-to-go-on-distress-diet/articleshow/6235046.cms.

45. *Economic Survey 2008–09* (New Delhi: Department of Economic Affairs, Ministry of Finance, GoI), p. 79, http://indiabudget. nic.in/.

46. Varun Soni, 'Slumming it', *Hindustan Times*, 24 October 2003, quoted in Mike Davis, *Planet of Slums* (New York: Verso, 2007), p. 100.

47. 'Towards Faster and Inclusive Growth', An Approach to the 11th Five-Year Plan, Planning Commission, New Delhi, 2006, http://planningcommission.gov.in/plans/planrel/app11_16jan.pdf.

48. RBI Price data cited at http://www.hsph.harvard.edu/research/takemi/files/RP256.pdf; NSS data quoted in Dipankar Gupta, *The Caged Phoenix: Can India Fly?* (New Delhi: Penguin-Viking, 2009), p. 250; and 'DuPont targets $1 billion revenue from India', *Financial Express*, 14 May 2008, http://www.financialexpress.com/news/dupont-targets-1-bn-revenues-from-india/309502/.

49. WHO data from '16% of Indians pushed into poverty by rising health costs', *Hindustan Times*, 5 February 2007.

50. Sivaprasad Madduri, 'The ills of corporate medicine in India', *The Hindu*, 10 September, 2006, http://www.hindu.com/op/2006/09/10/stories/2006091000061400.htm.

51. Cited in 'India's Runaway Growth'.

52. Healthcare, IBEF.org, http://www.ibef.org/industry/healthcare.aspx.

53. Arun Kumar Singh, '30 litres for some, 1600 for others', *Agenda*, October 2005.

54. 'Migrant influx not an issue for Delhi: Maken', ExpressIndia.com, 9 January 2008, http://www.expressindia.com/latest-news/migrant-influx-not-an-issue-for-delhi-maken/259411/.

55. 'Delhi Water Privatization Plan', Independent People's Tribunal on the World Bank, New Delhi, September 2007, http://www.worldbanktribunal.org/Delhi_privatisation.html.

56. Karen Coelho, 'The political economy of public sector utilities reform', *Agenda*, October 2005.

57. Ibid.

58. 'Manila water system shows failure of privatisation', *The Times of India*, 26 November 2002, http://timesofindia.indiatimes.com/news/city/mumbai/Manila-water-system-shows-failure-of-privatisation/articleshow/29494324.cms.

59. 'The Poor Pay More', Human Settlements, UN ESCAP, http://www.unescap.org/huset/urban_poverty/poorpaymore.htm; and 'The price the poor pay in Mumbai', *Agenda*, October 2005.

60. R. Mumtaz, M. Asher and A. Behar, 'Rivers for sale: The privatisation of common property resources', *Agenda*, October 2005; Rukmini Shrinivasan, 'Sold to the bidder: A river', *The Times of India*,

14 August 2010, http://timesofindia.indiatimes.com/india/Sold-to -the-bidder-a-river/articleshow/6309983.cms.

61. Saikat Datta, 'Everyone's Nira', OutlookIndia.com, 16 February 2009, http://www.outlookindia.com/article.aspx?239727.

62. 'Campaign to Hold Coca-Cola Accountable', India Resource Center, http://www.indiaresource.org/campaigns/coke/.

63. 'Growth Forecast for Indian Bottled Water Market', FineWaters.com, 1 October 2009, http://www.finewaters.com/Newsletter/The_Water _Connoisseur/Growth_Forecasted_for_Indian_Bottled_Water _ Market.asp; Emily Arnold and Janet Larsen, 'Bottled Water: Pouring Resources Down the Drain', Earth Policy Institute, 2 February 2006, http://www.earth-policy.org/index.php?/plan_b_updates/2006/ update51; Laxmi Murthy, 'Boond-boond mein paisa: Bottled water is big business', *Agenda*, October 2005; Chandra Bhushan, 'Bottled Loot', *Frontline*, 8–21 April 2006, http://www.hinduonnet.com/fline/ fl2307/stories/20060421006702300.htm; and 'Indian bottled water industry', http://www.scribd.com/doc/14143227/indian-bottled -water-industry.

64. Bhushan, 'Bottled Loot'.

65. P.H. Gleick and H.S. Cooley, 'Energy implications of bottled water', *Environmental Research Letters*, No. 4, 2009.

66. Walter Fernandes, 'Rehabilitation policy for the displaced', *EPW*, 20 March 2004 and 'Singur and the displacement scenario', *EPW*, 20 January 2007. See also H.M. Mathur (ed.), *India: Social Development Report 2008*, Council for Social Development, New Delhi, 2008, http://www.csdindia.org/social-development-report/india-social -development-report-2008.

67. Fernandes, 'Rehabilitation policy for the displaced'; and Kanchi Kohli and Manju Menon with Sanchari Das and Divya Badami, *Calling the Bluff: Revealing the State of Monitoring and Compliance of Environmental Clearance Conditions* (New Delhi: Kalpavriksh, 2009), p. 4.

68. This refers to the Supreme Court judgement in the famous 1985 case *Olga Tellis versus BMC*, cited in Action Aid, *Shadow Report* on GoI's Combined Report on ICESCR, April 2008, http://www2 .ohchr.org/english/bodies/cescr/docs/cescr40/ActionAid_India.pdf; see also Jayna Kothari, 'A Right to Housing?', *India Together*, April

2002, http://www.indiatogether.org/opinions/rhousing02.htm, and Prashant Bhushan, 'Supreme Court and PIL: Changing perspectives under liberalisation', *EPW*, 1 May 2004.

69. 'UN flays India for slum demolition', Rediff.com, 30 March 2005, http://www.rediff.com/news/2005/mar/30un.htm; Housing and Land Rights Network, 2005, http://www.hlrn.org/img/cases/IND -FE%20110105.pdf; and 'Will Mumbai's Shanghai dreams be hit?', *Indian Express*, 2 August 2005, http://www.expressindia.com/news/fullstory.php?newsid=51930.

70. Kalyani Menon-Sen and Gautam Bhan, *Swept off the Map* (Delhi: Yoda Press, 2008); *Abandoned: Development and Displacement* (Delhi: The Perspectives Group, 2008); and Action Aid, 'Homeless in Delhi', 2009, http://www.merinews.com/article/homeless-in -delhi/155591.shtml.

71. Gautam Bhan, 'Whose Delhi is it anyway?', *Tehelka*, 7 October 2006.

72. Sushil George and Suresh Nautiyal (eds), *Eviction Watch India–II* (New Delhi: HRLN, 2006), pp. 55–58.

73. Ibid., p. 53.

74. Action Aid, *Shadow Report*; and 'Role of non-state players in slum evictions worries rights activists', *The Hindu*, 12 July 2009, http://www.thehindu.com/2009/06/12/stories/2009061253270300.htm. Menon-Sen's figures are based on 'Testimonies and evidence on JNNURM presented at the Independent People's Tribunal on the World Bank, September 2007, New Delhi. Documents and reports available at www.worldbanktribunal.org.

75. Belinda Yuen, 'Squatters no more: Singapore social housing', *Global Urban Development Magazine*, Vol. 3, No. 1, November 2007, http://www.globalurban.org/GUDMag07Vol3Iss1/Yuen.htm.

76. '49,000 slums in India: NSSO', *The Times of India*, 27 May 2010. UN data cited in Davis, *Planet of Slums*, p. 25.

77. *Economic Survey 2007–08*, p. 243. See World Bank data on poverty in India at http://www-wds.worldbank.org/external/default/WDS ContentServer/IW3P/IB/2004/06/08/000160016_20040608153 404/Rendered/PDF/289690PAPER0WDI02004.pdf.

78. Priyadarshi Siddhanta, 'Poverty line fluctuates with conflicting data', 20 August 2009, ExpressIndia.com, http://www.expressindia.com/

latest-news/Poverty-line-fluctuates-with-conflicting-data/504141/; and NFHS data.

79. Cited in 'India's Runaway Growth', p. 46.

80. 'Inclusive Growth', *India: Selected Issues*, IMF, February 2008, http://www.imf.org/external/pubs/ft/scr/2008/cr0852.pdf.

81. Amit Bhaduri, 'Predatory Growth', *EPW*, 19 April 2008.

82. *Asian Experience on Growth, Employment and Poverty*, ILO, Geneva, 2007, http://www.ilo.org/wcmsp5/groups/public/—asia/—ro -bangkok/documents/publication/wcms_bk_pb_142_en.pdf.

83. *Economic Survey 2008–09*.

84. Ashis Nandy, *Time Treks: The Uncertain Future of Old and New Despotisms* (New Delhi: Permanent Black, 2007), pp. 95, 110.

85. *Growth Isn't Working*, New Economics Foundation, London, 2006, http://www.neweconomics.org/sites/neweconomics.org/files/ Growth_Isnt_Working_1.pdf.

86. Rabindranath Tagore, 'The Robbery of the Soil', in *Tagore on Books* (New Delhi: Rupa & Co., 2007).

Chapter 4: A House on Fire

1. The speech is available at http://pmindia.nic.in/speech/content .asp?id=811.

2. Manmohan Singh, 'Environment and the new economic policies', Foundation Day Lecture, Society for Promotion of Wastelands Development, Delhi, 17 June 1992.

3. Madhav Gadgil and Ramachandra Guha, *This Fissured Land: An Ecological History of India* (Delhi: Oxford University Press, 1992); Ranabir Chakravarti, 'The Creation and Expansion of Settlements and Management of Hydraulic Resources in Ancient India', in Richard H. Grove, Vinita Damodaran and Satpal Sangwan (eds), *Nature and the Orient* (Delhi: Oxford University Press, 1998); E.P. Flint, 'Deforestation and Land Use in Northern India with a Focus on Sal Forests 1880–1980', in Grove et al., *Nature and the Orient*; C.S. Rangachari and S.D. Mukherji, *Old Roots, New Shoots: A Study of Joint Forest Management in Andhra Pradesh, India* (Delhi: Winrock-Ford Book Series, 2000); and *Securing India's Future: Final Technical Report of the National Biodiversity Strategy and Action Plan Process*

(Delhi/Pune: TPCG [Technical and Policy Core Group] and Kalpavriksh, 2005).

4. Forest Survey of India, 1988.

5. Data obtained from the MoEF, in response to RTI applications filed by Kalpavriksh. There are, however, discrepancies in the data thus obtained (see analysis of this in Kanchi Kohli, Manju Menon and Vikal Samdariya, 'Crouching data, hidden forest', d-sector.org, 6 August 2010, http://d-sector.org/article-det.asp?id=1331).

6. Data from the MoEF, obtained through RTI applications.

7. Neeraj Vagholikar and Kaustubh A. Moghe, *Undermining India: Impacts of Mining on Ecologically Sensitive Areas* (Pune: Kalpavriksh, 2003); Chandra Bhushan, Monali Zeya Hazra and Souparno Banerjee, *Rich Lands Poor People: Is Sustainable Mining Possible?*, State of Environment, 6th Citizens' Report (Delhi: Centre for Science and Environment, 2008); and see also, Mines, Minerals and People, http://www.mmpindia.org/.

8. Vagholikar and Moghe, *Undermining India*.

9. Banikanta Mishra, 'Agriculture, Industry and Mining in Orissa in the Post-Liberalisation Era: An Inter-District and Inter-State Panel Analysis', *EPW*, Vol. XLV, No. 20, 15 May 2010, pp. 49–68.

10. See http://www.mmpindia.org/Multinationals.htm.

11. Annual Reports 1999–2000 to 2008–09, Ministry of Mines and Minerals, GoI; National Mineral Policy: Report of the High-Level Committee, Planning Commission 2006, GoI, Delhi; Shelley Saha-Sinha, 'India's new mineral policy will usher in gloom for adivasis', InfoChange News & Features, January 2009, http://infochangeindia.org/200901077561/Environment/Analysis/India's-new-mineral-policy-will-usher-in-gloom-for-adivasis.html; 'Aerial survey for exploration of minerals', Press Information Bureau, GoI, Ministry of Mines, 19 January 2010, http://www.pib.nic.in/release/rel_print_page1.asp?relid=57039; and Vagholikar and Moghe, *Undermining India*.

12. Annual Reports 2005–06 and 2007–08, Ministry of Mines and Minerals, GoI; Nagesh Prabhu, '11,896 cases of illegal mining detected', *The Hindu*, 10 December 2009, http://www.hindu.com/2009/12/10/stories/2009121058660800.htm; and Priyadarshi

Siddhanta, 'CBI to probe illegal mining', Expressindia, 7 December 2009, http://www.expressindia.com/latest-news/CBI-to-probe-illegal -mining/550850/.

13. Annual Report 2008–09, Ministry of Mines and Minerals, GoI.

14. 'Bauxite Deposits of India', Geologydata.info, http://www.geology data.info/bauxite_deposits.htm.

15. Sahib Singh, 'Third Five-Year EXIM Policy (2002–07): A Free Trade Regime', Indian Institute of Foreign Trade (IIFT), http://www .iift.edu/iift/papers/faculty/exim_ss.pdf; Chapter 4 on Foreign Trade Policy, in Annual Report 2008–09, Department of Commerce, Ministry of Commerce and Industry, GoI, http://commerce.nic.in/ publications/anualreport_chapter4-2008-09.asp; and 'Maran Launches FOCUS: AFRICA Programme', EXIM Policy 2002–07, PIB, GoI, http://pib.nic.in/archieve/eximpol/eximpolicy2002/ eximpolicy2002_rel.html.

16. The Marine Products Export Development Authority (MPEDA), Ministry of Commerce and Industry, GoI, www.mpeda.com. All pages in the MPEDA site open with the same URL; readers would need to search for the relevant data by accessing the links on the home page.

17. Ibid.

18. 'Impacts of aquaculture farming and remedial measures in ecologically fragile coastal areas of India', investigation report submitted to the Supreme Court (Nagpur: NEERI, 1995); 'Impacts of aquaculture farming and remedial measures in ecologically fragile coastal areas in the states of Andhra Pradesh and Tamil Nadu', investigation report submitted to the Supreme Court (Nagpur: NEERI, 1995); and John Kurien, 'State and shrimp: A preliminary analysis of economic and ecological consequence of India's fishery policies', papers presented at the Bangkok FAO Technical Consultation on Policies for Sustainable Shrimp Culture, Bangkok, Thailand, 8–11 December 1997 (FAO, Rome, 1999).

19. Ramachandra Bhatta, 'Impact of globalization on the marine exports of India', Foreign Trade Review, IIFT, New Delhi, 2002.

20. B. Vishnu Bhat and P.N. Vinod, 'Development of seafarming in India – An export perspective', in A. Lovatelli, M.J. Phillips, J.R. Arthur and K. Yamamoto (eds), FAO/NACA Regional Workshop on the Future of Mariculture: A Regional Approach for Responsible

Development in the Asia-Pacific Region, Guangzhou, China, 7–11 March 2006 (FAO Fisheries Proceedings, No. 11, Rome, 2008), pp. 301–06, ftp://ftp.fao.org/docrep/fao/011/i0202e/i0202e15.pdf.

21. Sebastian Matthew, 'Trade in fisheries and human development: Country case study India', Asia-Pacific Regional Initiative on Trade, Economic Governance and Human Development (Asia Trade Initiative), UNDP, 2003.

22. *S. Jagannath v. Union of India*, WP 561/1994, 11 December 1996, http://www.elaw.org/node/1974.

23. 'Guidelines for Sustainable Aquaculture', MPEDA, http://www.mpeda.com/AquaCulture/guidelin.htm; 'Standards for Coastal Aquaculture', CAA, http://www.caa.gov.in/standards_caa.htm.

24. C.M. James and M.R. Kitto, 'Marine fish farming in India – Failed expectations?', *Current Science*, Vol. 94, No. 12, 25 June 2008.

25. Matthew, 'Trade in fisheries and human development'.

26. John Kurien, 'Impact of joint ventures on fish economy', *EPW*, Vol. 30, No. 6, 11 February 1995, pp. 300–02.

27. Annual Reports, Ministry of Minerals.

28. Export Import Data Bank, Department of Commerce, GoI, http://commerce.nic.in/eidb/Default.asp; Department of Commercial Intelligence and Statistics, Ministry of Commerce and Industry, data supplied on RTI application by Kalpavriksh, February 2010.

29. Kishore Wankhade, 'Is India becoming dumping ground for British e-waste?', Toxics Link, Delhi, 24 September 2004, http://www.toxicslink.org/mediapr-view.php?pressrelnum=5.

30. Office Memorandum, No. 23-9/2009-HSMD, MoEF, 2 July 2009.

31. 'Mercury in our Backyard', The South Asian, 10 December 2004, http://www.thesouthasian.org/archives/2004/mercury_in_our_backyard.html; and Murali Krishnan and Sandeep Unnithan, 'Ticking Time Bombs', *India Today* (online), 25 October 2004, http://www.india-today.com/itoday/20041025/nation2.html.

32. Ravi Agarwal and Papiya Sarkar, 'The globalisation of waste', Toxics Link Position Paper, December 2002; and Krishnan and Unnithan, 'Ticking Time Bombs'.

33. Paul J. Bailey, 'Is there a decent way to break ships', International Labour Organization (ILO), Geneva, 2000, interview of 2006 available at http://www.ilo.org/global/about-the-ilo/press-and-media

-centre/insight/WCMS_076903/lang—es/index.htm; and search results for 'Alang' on Greenpeace: http://www.greenpeace.org/india/en/System-templates/Search-results/?all=alang and on Toxics Link: http://toxicslink.org/search/?cx=011346277552360787107%3A7wtozl9bnka&q=alang&sa=Search&cof=FORID%3A11&siteurl=www.toxicslink.org%2F.

34. Naomi Lubick, 'Drug companies accused of polluting water in India', OneWorld South Asia, 5 February 2009, http://southasia.oneworld.net/todaysheadlines/drug-companies-accused-of-polluting-water-in-india.

35. 'Bioinvasions: Stemming the Tide of Invasive Species', World Resources Institute, 1998–99, http://www.wri.org/publication/content/7956; 'Biological globalisation a major threat to biodiversity', *The New Zealand Herald*, 28 January 2006, http://www.nzherald.co.nz/world/news/article.cfm?c_id=2&objectid=10365728&pnum=1; 'Causes and impacts of invasive alien species', Convention on Biological Diversity, 2009, http://www.cbd.int/idb/2009/about/causes/; R.S. Rana, 'Invasive alien species and biodiversity', subthematic paper for the National Biodiversity Strategy and Action Plan process, MoEF, GoI, 2002, in *Securing India's Future*; A.S. Raghubanshi, L.C. Rai, J.P. Gaur and J.S. Singh, 'Invasive alien species and biodiversity in India', *Current Science*, Vol. 88, No. 4, 25 February 2005; and T.N. Ananthakrishnan, 'Invasive insects in agriculture, medicine and forestry' (a report on the Ninth Annual Discussion Meeting in Entomology on 'Invasive Insects in Agriculture, Medicine and Forestry' held on 13 December 2008 at Centre for Advanced Studies (C.A.S.) in Botany, University of Madras, Guindy Campus, Chennai), *Current Science*, Vol. 97, No. 3, 10 August 2009.

36. R.K. Pachauri and P.V. Shridharan, *Looking Back to Think Ahead: GREEN India 2047* (New Dehli: Tata Energy Research Institute [TERI], 1998); *State of Environment Report India 2009* (Delhi: Ministry of Environment and Forests, GoI, 2009), http://moef.nic.in/downloads/home/home-SoE-Report-2009.pdf.

37. *Hiding behind the Poor* (Bengaluru: Greenpeace India Society, October 2007), http://www.greenpeace.org/india/Global/india/report/2007/11/hiding-behind-the-poor.pdf.

38. *Hiding behind the Poor*; Praful Bidwai, *An India That Can Say Yes: A Climate-Responsible Development Agenda for Copenhagen and Beyond* (Delhi: Heinrich Boll Foundation, 2009).

39. The numbers have been estimated using World Bank data on income distribution.

40. Ruhi Kandhari, 'Plastic Shakeout', *Down to Earth*, Vol. 18, No. 15, 14 December 2009, http://www.downtoearth.org.in/node/2542; and State of Environment Report India 2009, MoEF.

41. Ibid.

42. 'India's Demand on Nature Approaching Critical Limits, Report Finds', Global Footprint Network, 13 October 2008, http://www.footprintnetwork.org/en/index.php/GFN/blog/indias_demand_on_nature_approaching_critical_limits; and 'India's Ecological Footprint: A business perspective', Global Footprint Network and CII, 2008, http://www.footprintnetwork.org/en/index.php/GFN/page/indias_ecological_footprint_a_business_perspective.

43. *India's Environment Pollution and Protection*, Report No. 97ED57 submitted to Central Research Institute of Electric Power Industry (CRIEPI), Japan (New Delhi: TERI, 1998); Pachauri and Shridharan, *Looking Back to Think Ahead*.

44. Partha Dasgupta, 'Measuring sustainable development: Theory and application', *Asian Development Review*, Vol. 24, No. 1, June 2007, pp. 1–10.

45. Unless otherwise mentioned, this full section is based on the following sources: *National Action Plan on Climate Change* (Delhi: Prime Minister's Council on Climate Change, GoI, 2009), http://pmindia.nic.in/Pg01-52.pdf; Bidwai, *An India That Can Say Yes*; Himanshu Thakkar, *There is Little Hope Here* (Delhi: South Asia Network on Dams, Rivers, and People, February 2009), http://sandrp.in/CRTITUQE_ON_INDIAs_CLIMATE_PLAN-There_is_Little_Hope_Here_Feb_2009.pdf; *Still Waiting: A report on energy injustice* (Bengaluru: Greenpeace India Society, October 2009), http://www.greenpeace.org/india/Global/india/report/2009/11/stillwaiting.pdf; a series of articles at http://www.dionnebunsha.com/; and *Case Studies on Climate Change and World Heritage* (Paris: UNESCO World Heritage Centre, 2007).

46. *The State of Food Insecurity in the World* (Rome: FAO, 2009), ftp://ftp.fao.org/docrep/fao/012/i0876e/i0876e.pdf; *State of Environment*

Report India 2009, MoEF; and *Economic Survey 2008–09* (New Delhi: Department of Economic Affairs, Ministry of Finance, GoI).

47. *Securing India's Future*; *State of Environment Report India 2009*, MoEF; D. Kozhiserry, 'Farming sand', *Down to Earth*, 14 November 2008, http://www.indiaenvironmentportal.org.in/node/267019.

48. *State of Environment Report India 2009*, MoEF.

49. *India Assessment 2002: Water Supply and Sanitation*, a WHO-UNICEF sponsored study (Delhi: Planning Commission, 2002), http://planningcommission.nic.in/reports/genrep/wtrsani.pdf; and *India's Water Economy: Bracing for a turbulent future*, Report No. 34750-IN (World Bank, 2005), http://www-wds.worldbank.org/external/default/WDSContentServer/WDSP/IB/2006/ 01/24/ 000090341_20060124094858/Rendered/PDF/34750.pdf.

50. *State of Environment Report India 2009*, MoEF; Bidwai, *An India That Can Say Yes*; and 'Groundwater in 33% of India undrinkable', *The Times of India*, Pune, 13 March 2010.

51. *India Assessment 2002: Water Supply and Sanitation*; *India's Water Economy*; and 'River Water Disputes' under Water Resources Management, Water Resources, GoI, http://india.gov.in/sectors/water _resources/index.php?id=14.

52. M. Raju with H. Babu, N. Banerjee, G. Bandopadhyay, N. Barot, C. Bedi, A. Chowdary, T. Kocherry, S. Lele, H. Rawat and E. Theophilus, 'Livelihoods and Biodiversity', thematic action plan for the National Biodiversity Strategy and Action Plan process (MoEF, GoI, 2003) in *Securing India's Future*; and *Securing India's Future*.

53. P.K. Misra and N. Prabhakar, 'Non-pastoral nomads and biodiversity', subthematic paper for the National Biodiversity Strategy and Action Plan process (MoEF, GoI, 2002) in *Securing India's Future*; P. Vivekanandan, 'Pastoral communities and biodiversity conservation', subthematic paper for the National Biodiversity Strategy and Action Plan process (MoEF, GoI) in *Securing India's Future*; and V.P. Sharma, I. Kohler-Rollefson and J. Morton, *Pastoralism in India: A scoping study* (Ahmedabad: Centre for Management in Agriculture [IIM Ahmedabad], League of Pastoral Peoples, and Natural Resources Institute), http://www.research4development.info/PDF/outputs/ ZC0181b.pdf.

54. *Securing India's Future*.

55. 'PAC Calls for Cancellation of Privatisation Contract of Sheonath Project', Manthan Adhyan Kendra, 3 April 2007, http://www .manthan-india.org/spip.php?article25.

Chapter 5: Adding Fuel to Fire

1. *Report on Reforming Investment Approval and Implementation Procedures* (Delhi: Cabinet Secretariat, GoI, May 2002), http://dipp .nic.in/implrepo/implrepo1.pdf.

2. K. Kohli and M. Menon, *Eleven Years of the Environment Impact Assessment Notification, 1994: How Effective Has It Been?* (Delhi: Kalpavriksh, Just Environment Trust and Environment Justice Initiative, 2005); L. Saldanha, A. Naik, A. Joshi and S. Sastry, *Green Tapism: A review of the environmental impact assessment notification 2006* (Bengaluru: Environment Support Group, 2007); M. Menon and K. Kohli, '"Re-Engineering" the Legal and Policy Regimes on Environment', *Economic and Political Weekly (EPW)*, Vol. 43, No. 23, 7–13 June 2008, pp. 14–17; and M. Menon and K. Kohli, *'Re-engineering' of India's Legal and Policy Regime on Environment: The Influence of the World Bank*, Deposition made to the Independent People's Tribunal on the World Bank, New Delhi, 21–24 September 2007 (Delhi/Pune: Kalpavriksh, 2007).

3. K. Kohli and M. Menon, with S. Das and D. Badami, *Calling the Bluff: Revealing the State of Monitoring and Compliance of Environmental Clearance Conditions* (Delhi/Pune: Kalpavriksh, 2009).

4. Data supplied by the ministry of environment and forests (MoEF), in response to Right to Information applications filed by Kalpavriksh.

5. See, for instance, the speech of the chief minister of Maharashtra, Vilasrao Deshmukh, at the Fiftieth National Development Council Meeting on 21 December 2002 at New Delhi, http:// planningcommission.nic.in/plans/planrel/pl50ndc/maha.pdf; and Ravinder Makhaik, 'Forest Conservation Act Hindering Himachal Road Projects—Dhumal', 5 March 2008, http://himachal.us/2008/ 03/05/forest-conservation-act-hindering-himachal-road-projects —dhumal/4723/general/ravinder.

6. M. Menon, S. Rodriguez and A. Sridhar, *Coastal Zone Management Notification '07: Better or Bitter Fare?* produced for the Post-Tsunami

Environment Initiative Project (Bengaluru: ATREE, 2007); K. Kasturi, 'Coastal regulations flip-flop', *Infochange Agenda*, No. 18, 2010, www .infochangeindia.org; and Machhimar Adhikar Rashtriya Abhiyan, National Fishworkers' Forum, Kolkata, http://www.coastalcampaign .page.tl/Home.htm.

7. N. Biswas, *The Gulf of Kutch Marine National Park and Sanctuary: A Case Study* (Chennai: International Collective in Support of Fishworkers); and Port Policy, Department of Commerce and Transport, Government of Orissa, http://www.orissa.gov.in/commerce &transport/portpolicy.pdf.

8. This section is based on A. Malekar, 'Tradition vs. Tourism', *Infochange Agenda*, No. 18, 2010, www.infochangeindia.org; Ministry of Tourism Annual Report 2008–09 (Delhi: GoI), http://www.scribd.com/doc/ 18027757/Annual-Report-Tourism-MinistryIndia; and the following reports by EQUATIONS, Bengaluru:

    a) *SE(i)Zing India through Tourism* (November 2007).
    b) 'Not in my backyard! How governments and industry have washed their hands off responsibility in tourism: Exploring Indian realities', paper presented at the Second International Responsible Tourism Conference, 21–23 March 2008, Kochi.
    c) 'No more holidays from accountability! We need stronger environmental regulation for tourism', statement on World Tourism Day, 27 September 2008.
    d) 'The "Privatization of Governance": Natural resources, peoples' rights and tourism in India', November 2008.
    e) *Tourism, trade and globalization: Impacts on biodiversity—A one act play* (2009).
    f) *Scott free! Protecting children against sexual exploitation in tourism: Challenges and imperatives in the Indian situation* (March 2009).

9. This is not to uncritically valorize local ways of life, but simply to raise the issue of the pace and scale of influence by outsiders that give little choice to local people to understand and adopt or reject the cultural changes being imposed.

10. Ashish Kothari, 'To Save the Sanctuaries', *Frontline*, 30 July 1999.

11. M. Menon, K. Kohli and V. Samdariya, 'Diversion of Protected Areas: Role of the Wildlife Board', *EPW*, Vol. XLV, No. 26–27, 2010, pp. 18–21.

12. ELDF and WWF, *Conserving Protected Areas and Wildlife: A Judicial Journey* (Delhi: WWF-India, 2009).

13. S. Koonan, 'Legal Implications of Plachimada: A Case Study', Working Paper 2007 – 05, International Environmental Law Research Centre, Geneva, http://www.ielrc.org/content/w0705.pdf; several articles at India Resource Center, http://www.indiaresource.org/issues/water/index.html, accessed 27 February 2010; and 'Coke Rejects Panel Report, Rs 216 crore Fine Likely', *Rediff News*, 22 March 2010, http://www.indiaresource.org/news/2010/1008.html.

14. Several articles by Suman Sahai at Gene Campaign, www.gene campaign.org; A.B. Sharma, 'New Amendments to Patents Act, 1970, to Affect Farm Sector', *Financial Express*, 3 January 2005, New Delhi, http://www.financialexpress.com/fe_full_story.php?content_id =78652, cited in T. Apte, *Simple Guide to Intellectual Property Rights, Biodiversity and Traditional Knowledge* (Delhi/Pune: Kalpavriksh, GRAIN and IIED, 2006); V. Shiva, 'The Indian Seed Act and Patent Act: Sowing the seeds of dictatorship', *Z* magazine, 14 February 2005, http://www.zmag.org/content/showarticle.cfm?ItemID=7249; Apte, *A Simple Guide to Intellectual Property Rights*; and Monsanto vs Schmeiser at http://www.percyschmeiser.com/.

15. Apte, *A Simple Guide to Intellectual Property Rights* and cited from the book: J.R. Ghose, 'The right to save seed', SUB Working Paper 2003, International Development Research Centre, Ottawa, http://www.idrc.ca/en/ev-84559-201-1-DO_TOPIC.html; and S. Sahai, 'India's Protection of Plant Varieties and Farmers' Rights Act', in U. Kumar and S. Sahai (eds), *Status of the Rights of Farmers and Plant Breeders in Asia* (New Delhi: Gene Campaign, 2003).

16. *Six Years of the Biological Diversity Act in India* (Delhi/Pune: Kalpavriksh and GRAIN, 2009).

17. Open Letters at Kalpavriksh, http://www.kalpavriksh.org/petitions -letters-action-alerts/open-letters?layout=default; and A. Sridhar, *Environmental Governance Reforms: Rephrasing the Reform Process* (Bengaluru: Ashoka Trust for Research in Ecology and the Environment), http://www.dakshin.org/DOWNLOADS/Rephrasing %20Environmental%20Reforms.pdf.

18. Agarwal et al., 'Will The Draft National Environment Policy Really Safeguard India's Environment?', open letter to the MoEF, 29 October

2004, signed by eighty-nine organizations and individuals, http://www.kalpavriksh.org/petitions-letters-action-alerts/open-letters?layout=default; A. Kothari et al., 'Please Make the National Environment Policy Public Before Finalisation', open letter to the prime minister of India, 26 August 2005, signed by over seventy organizations and individuals, http://www.kalpavriksh.org/petitions-letters-action-alerts/open-letters?layout=default; S. Lele and A. Menon, *Draft NEP: A Flawed Vision* (Bengaluru: Centre for Interdisciplinary Studies in Environment and Development, 2004); and A. Kothari, 'Draft National Environment Policy 2004: A Critique', *EPW*, 23–29 October 2004, Vol. 39, No. 43, pp. 4723–27.

19. K. Kohli et al., 'Why Are the Expert Committees of Ministry of Environment and Forests Dominated by Ex-Bureaucrats, Politicians and Engineers?', fourth open letter to the MoEF, 8 April 2005, signed by sixty-two organizations and individuals, http://www.kalpavriksh.org/petitions-letters-action-alerts/open-letters?layout=default.

20. MoEF Circular No. 20011/3/2003-GC, 1 April 2004.

21. H. Thakkar et al., 'Conflict of Interest for EAC Chair for River Valley Projects', letter to Jairam Ramesh, Minister of State for Environment and Forests, 12 June 2009, South Asia Network on Dams, Rivers & People, Kalpavriksh Environmental Action Group, Affected Citizens of Teesta, All Idu Mishmi Students Union, Peoples Movement for Subansiri-Brahmaputra Valley and Waterwatch Alliance, http://www.sandrp.in/hydropower/PR-Project_Promoter_is_chairing_Environment_Clearance_Committee_15June2009.pdf; Campaign for Conservation and Community Control of Biodiversity, 'Issues of legal violations, bias, conflict of interest and lack of independent decision making relating to the Expert Committee for Evaluation of Applications for Access, Seeking Patent, Transfer of Research Results and Third Party Transfer of Bioresources', letter to P.L. Gautam, Chairman, National Biodiversity Authority, 24 April 2009, signed by fifty-three organizations and individuals, under the CCCCB, http://www.kalpavriksh.org/images/CCCBD/LettertoNBAonAccess Committeecomposition decisions_April2009.pdf; 'Move to Increase Transparency in Environmental Clearance: Jairam Ramesh', PIB, GoI, http://pib.nic.in/release/release.asp?relid=49431; and Bahar Dutt, 'Mining Watchdog on Board of Mining Firms', IBNLive, 20 August

2009, http://ibnlive.in.com/news/double-role-mining-watchdog-on-board-of-mining-firms/99597-3.html.

22. M. Menon and K. Kohli, 'Environmental confessions', *Mint*, 17 November 2009, http://www.livemint.com/2009/11/16230530/Environmental-confessions.html; TAI-India *How Green Will Be the Green Tribunal? Concerns and Suggestions on the National Green Tribunal Bill 2009* (Delhi: Legal Initiative for Forest and Environment, The Access Initiative and Environics Trust, 2010); and S. Lele, N. Dubash and S. Dixit, 'A Structure for Environmental Governance: A Perspective', *EPW*, Vol. XLV, No. 6, pp. 13–16, 6 February 2010.

23. Personal communication with Bhaskar Goswami, April 2009; S. Upadhyay and B. Raman, *Land Acquisition and Public Purpose* (Delhi: The Other Media, 1998); P. Parker and S. Vanka, 'New Rules for Seizing Land', PRS legislative brief, *India Together*, 19 May 2008, http://www.indiatogether.org/2008/may/law-land.htm; and M. Asher, 'The Inheritors of Loss', *Tehelka*, 28 August 2009, www.tehelka.com/story_main42.asp?filename=Ws050909The_Inheritors.asp.

24. 'Pilfering Citizens' Rights', *Down to Earth*, Vol. 5, No. 20, 14 March 1997.

25. 'National Litigation Policy', Law-in-perspective, 7 July 2010, http://legalperspectives.blogspot.com/2010/07/national-litigation-policy.html.

26. *Task Force Report on National Security and Terrorism* (Delhi: Federation of Indian Chambers of Commerce and Industry, 2009), http://www.ficci.com/SPdocument/20032/terrorism-report.pdf.

27. Ibid.

28. *Economic Survey 2008–09*, GoI, New Delhi.

29. N. Rao, G. Sant and S.C. Rajan, *An Overview of Indian Energy Trends: Low Carbon Growth and Development Challenges* (Pune: Prayas, 2009).

Chapter 6: Town and Country

1. Chidambaram's Interview to *Tehelka*, 31 May 2008; *India: Vision 2020*, Planning Commission, December 2002, http://planningcommission.gov.in/reports/genrep/pl_vsn2020.pdf; 'No Villages in Gujarat, Declares CM Modi', *The Times of India*, 28 September 2009, http://timesofindia.indiatimes.com/news/

india/No-villages-in-Gujarat-declares-CM-Modi/articleshow/ 5063530.cms; and S. Faizi, 'Gujarat: An Ecological Nightmare', *Countercurrents*, 2 May 2009, http://www.countercurrents.org/ faizi020509.htm. Rural pollution in Gujarat is reported at great length in 'Industry at any cost', *Down to Earth*, 15 April 2000, http:// www.rainwaterharvesting.org/crisis/Industrial-pollution.htm. For details of pollution in Gujarat's famed Golden Corridor, see Michael Mazgaonkar, 'Detoxify the Corridor', *India Together*, September 2001, http://www.indiatogether.org/petitions/hchem.htm. More stories of health-impairing levels of pollution in rural Gujarat are available in *Down to Earth* issues of 15 November 2004; 15 March 2007; 15 January 2008; and 16 February 2009.

2.   Rabindranath Tagore, 'Robbery of the Soil', in *Tagore on Books* (Delhi: Rupa & Co., 2006), p. 37.

3.   Amit Bhaduri, 'Predatory Growth', *Economic and Political Weekly* (*EPW*), 19 April 2008.

4.   See *Financial Times*, weekend magazine, 5/6 August 2006. Also see, Aseem Shrivastava, 'Pushing India towards a Dollar Democracy', *Counterpunch*, 27 October 2006, http://www.counterpunch.org/ shrivastava10272006.html.

5.   Mike Davis, *Planet of Slums* (New York: Verso, 2007), p. 2.

6.   Patricia Nunan, 'Megacities Must Urgently Address the Needs of Slum Dwellers to Prevent Human Disaster', *City Mayors*, 8 March 2006, http://www.citymayors.com/society/megacities_mumbai.html.

7.   Census of India, 2001, http://censusindia.gov.in/Census_Data_2001/ Census_Newsletters/Newsletter_Links/eci_3.htm; and http:// censusindia.gov.in/Data_Products/Library/Post_Enumeration_link/ eci6_page1.html.

8.   Davis, *Planet of Slums*, p. 6.

9.   Numbers cited from *The Economist* in Herbet Werlin, 'The Case for Democracy: Remaining Questions', *Journal of Developing Societies*, Volume 25, No. 9, July 2009. Also, see Asit Ranjan Mishra, 'Tax-GDP ratio slated to drop to 10.94% in 2008–09', *Mint*, 7 July 2009, http://www.livemint.com/2009/07/07002528/TaxGDP-ratio -slated-to-drop-t.html; and G. Srinivasan, 'Low Tax-GDP Ratio Daunts India's Quest To Join The Developed World', *The Hindu Business Line*, 13 October 2005, http://www.thehindubusiness line.com/2005/10/13/stories/2005101301531200.htm.

10. Census of India, 2001.

11. Quoted in Subrata Dutta, 'Urbanisation and Development of Rural Small Enterprises', *EPW*, Vol. 37, No. 30, 27 July 2002.

12. Davis, *Planet of Slums*, p. 52. Gooptu's seminal work is cited by Davis. JNNURM data is from its Mission Overview, Ministry of Urban Development, New Delhi, http://jnnurm.nic.in/nurmudweb/toolkit/Overview.pdf.

13. Davis, *Planet of Slums*.

14. Ibid., Chapters 1–3; and Sandeep Ashar, 'Mumbai Is India's City with the Greatest Inequalities', *DNA*, 3 November 2009, http://www.dnaindia.com/mumbai/report_mumbai-is-india-s-city-with-the-greatest-inequalities_1306460.

15. Davis, *Planet of Slums*, p. 18.

16. Quoted by M.S. Swaminathan, 'The Crisis of Indian Agriculture', *The Hindu*, 15 August 2007.

17. Data is quoted in 'India's Runaway Growth: Distortion, Disarticulation, and Exclusion', *Aspects of India's Economy*, Nos. 44–46, April 2008, Research Unit in Political Economy (RUPE), http://rupe-india.org/44/links.html, p. 38.

18. Ibid., p. 128.

19. These are government Central Statistical Organization figures cited by agricultural economist and Planning Commission member Mihir Shah in 'NREGA: A Historic Opportunity', *EPW*, 11 December 2004. See also Mihir Shah, 'Killing Fields of 21st Century India', *The Hindu*, 18 December 2006. The data on plan expenses is given by Amit Bhaduri, 'The Imperative as Alternative', *Seminar*, February 2008.

20. Swaminathan, 'The Crisis of Indian Agriculture'; 'India's Runaway Growth', p. 130; B.C. Roy, C.N. Chattopadhyay and Reyes Tirado, 'Subsidising Food Crisis: Synthetic Fertilisers Lead to Poor Soil and Less Food', Greenpeace India Society, 2009, http://www.greenpeace.org/raw/content/india/press/reports/subsidising-food-crisis.pdf; and Reyes Tirado, 'Chemical Fertilisers in Our Water', Greenpeace India Society, 2009, http://www.greenpeace.org/raw/content/india/press/reports/chemical-fertilisers-in-our-wa-2.pdf. The quotation about food is from Dipankar Gupta, *The Caged Phoenix: Can India Fly?* (New Delhi: Penguin-Viking, 2009), p. 103.

21. *Economic Survey 2009–10*, GoI, New Delhi, p. A15.
22. P. Sainath has assiduously documented farmer suicides in India. See 'Farm Suicides: A 12-Year Saga', *The Hindu*, 25 January 2010, http://beta.thehindu.com/opinion/columns/sainath/article94324.ece. Also see '1.5 Lakh Farmer Suicides in 1997–2005', *The Hindu*, 14 November 2007; and 'The Largest Wave of Suicides in History', *The Hindu*, 16 February 2009. Information about the rest of the world can be obtained from UN reports. See *International Farmer Suicide Crisis*, UNCSD Report, http://www.un.org/esa/sustdev/csd/csd16/PF/presentations/farmers_relief.pdf.
23. M.S. Swaminathan, 'India on the Verge of Disaster on Farm Front', *Deccan Herald*, 6 January 2010. See also Swaminathan, 'The Crisis of Indian Agriculture'.
24. 'Farming in Punjab at Crossroads', *The Times of India*, 10 February 2010. The quote from the National Agricultural Policy is taken from Gupta, *The Caged Phoenix*, p. 108.
25. Raj Chengappa with Ramesh Vinayak, 'Grain Drain', *India Today*, 11 June 2007, http://www.india-today.com/itoday/20070611/cover1.html.
26. 'India's Runaway Growth', p. 135.
27. See for instance, *World Development Report 2008* (Washington DC: World Bank, 2008).
28. James K. Boyce and Peter Rosset, 'Land reform and sustainable development', in James Boyce, Elizabeth Stanton and Sunita Narain (eds), *Reclaiming Nature: Environmental Justice and Ecological Restoration* (Anthem Press, 2007), p. 136. See also Peter Rosset, 'Small is bountiful', *The Ecologist*, Vol. 29, Issue 8, December 1999, http://www.mindfully.org/Farm/Small-Farm-Benefits-Rosset.htm; and Miguel Altieri, 'Agroecology, Small Farms and Food Sovereignty', *Monthly Review*, July–August 2009, http://monthlyreview.org/090810altieri.php.
29. P. Sainath, 'And Yet Another Pro-Farmer Budget', *The Hindu*, 1 March 2010.
30. Ibid.
31. E. Wesley F. Peterson, *A Billion Dollars a Day: The Economics and Politics of Agricultural Subsidies* (London: Wiley-Blackwell, 2009).
32. Adam Smith, *The Wealth of Nations* (Modern Library, 1994), Book 4, Chapter 2.

33. Quoted by Raj Patel, *Stuffed and Starved* (London: Portobello Books, 2007), p. 316.

34. Mathew Aerthayil, *Impact of Globalization on Tribals* (Jaipur: Rawat Publications, 2008).

35. Sainath, 'And Yet Another Pro-Farmer Budget'; and 'The Largest Wave of Suicides in History'.

36. P. Sainath, '4750 Rural Bank Branches Closed Down in 15 Years', *The Hindu*, 28 March 2008. Data on falling proportions of marginal groups with bank accounts is from V.L. Antowein (president, AIBEA), Deposition to the People's Tribunal on the World Bank, Jawaharlal Nehru University, New Delhi, 2007. Data on shares of agriculture and personal loans is from *Harvesting Despair* (New Delhi: The Perspectives Group, 2009), p. 83.

37. Sainath, 'And Yet Another Pro-Farmer Budget'. See also R. Ramakumar and Pallavi Chavan, 'Revival of Agricultural Credit in the 2000s: An Explanation', *EPW*, 29 December 2007.

38. Sainath, 'And Yet Another Pro-Farmer Budget'.

39. The account of the KIA offered here is taken from Kavitha Kuruganti, 'Targeting Regulation in Indian Agriculture', *EPW*, 29 November 2008.

40. Kuruganti, 'Targeting Regulation'.

41. K.P. Prabhakaran Nair, 'Corporatising Agriculture', *Indian Express*, 8 March 2010.

42. Gagandeep Kaur, 'New Terms of Harvest', *India Together*, 20 February 2007, http://www.indiatogether.org/2007/feb/agr-contract.htm.

43. Kuruganti, 'Targeting Regulation', p. 21.

44. A Karnataka Rajya Raitha Sangha farmer, quoted in Patel, *Stuffed and Starved*, p. 42.

45. Dipankar Gupta, 'Whither the Indian Village', *EPW*, 19 February 2005.

46. Davis, *Planet of Slums*, p. 9.

47. Jan Breman, *The Poverty Regime of Village India* (New Delhi: Oxford, 2007), p. 413.

48. Farshad Araghi, 'The Great Global Enclosure of Our Times: Peasants and the Agrarian Question at the End of the Twentieth Century', in F. Magdoff, J.B. Foster and F.H. Buttel (eds), *Hungry for Profit* (New York: Monthly Review Press, 2000).

Chapter 7: Crony Capitalism, Land Wars and Internal Colonialism

1. 'Many of India's billionaires have made money by their proximity to government', *The Times of India*, 31 July 2010, http://timesofindia .indiatimes.com/business/india-business/Many-of-Indias-billionaires -have-made-money-by-their-proximity-to-govt/articleshow/6239 385.cms.

2. Krittivas Mukherjee, 'Farmers' Protest in Delhi Underscores India's Land Woes', *Reuters*, 26 August 2010, http://in.reuters.com/article/ idINIndia-51080720100826; and 'Mayawati Govt Bans Forced Acquisition of Farmers' Land', *The Times of India*, 4 September 2010.

3. Quotations from the Committee on State Agrarian Relations and Unfinished Tasks of Land Reform, Ministry of Rural Development, GoI, New Delhi, 2009, pp. i and ii available at http://www.rd.ap.gov .in/IKPLand/MRD_Committee_Report_V_01_Mar_09.pdf.

4. While this may be seen by some as a rude caricature of the complexity of developmental processes, the popular meaning, if not the essence, of the latter is certainly captured by this description. This popular meaning has such persuasive force today that even as sophisticated a writer as Amartya Sen, for instance, omits any discussion of the loss of land and livelihood, human community and culture that is invariably involved in the displacement induced by development. See his much lauded book *Development as Freedom* (New Delhi: Oxford, 2000).

5. *Analytical Monthly Review*, September 2006, available at http://mrzine .monthlyreview.org/amr210906.html.

6. For detailed critical scrutinies of the act, see Usha Ramanathan, 'Displacement and the Law', *Economic and Political Weekly* (*EPW*), Vol. XXXI, No. 24, 15 June 1996 and Colin Gonsalves, 'Judicial Failure on Land Acquisition for Corporations', *EPW*, Vol. XLV, No. 32, 7 August 2010. On eviction of poor families due to the Delhi Metro, see Dunu Roy, '"World Class": The Arrogance of the Ignorant', *Hardnews*, August 2009, http://www.hardnewsmedia.com/2009/08/ 3133. Also see 'The City and the Metro', National Roundtable, *Parisar*, Pune, 2012, http://www.indiaenvironmentportal.org.in/ files/Metro_and_the_City.pdf.

7. For detailed critical scrutinies of the Land Acquisition Act, see Ramanathan, 'Displacement and the Law' and Gonsalves, 'Judicial Failure'.

8. *The Constitution of India*, Part IV, Article 38.

9. 'Indian School Shooting Sparks US Gun Crime Fears', *The Telegraph*, 12 December 2007, http://www.telegraph.co.uk/news/worldnews/1572359/Indian-school-shooting-sparks-US-gun-crime-fears.html; 'Vedic Village Land-Grab Goon Nabbed', *The Times of India*, 9 September 2009, http://timesofindia.indiatimes.com/city/kolkata/Vedic-Village-land-grab-goon-nabbed/articleshow/4988654.cms; and Shoma Chaudhury, 'Weapons of Mass Desperation', *Tehelka*, Vol. 6, No. 39, 3 October 2009, http://www. tehelka.com/story_main42.asp?filename=Ne031009coverstory.asp. For an extended critique of the growth of organized, so-called 'Far Left' rural violence, see Sailendra Nath Ghosh, 'Lalgarh and Junglemahal: Where Are We Heading', *Mainstream Weekly*, Vol. XLVII, No. 50, 28 November 2009, http://www.mainstreamweekly.net/article1801.html.

10. Eric Hobsbawm, *The Age of Revolution* (London: Abacus Books, 1980), p. 65.

11. Christopher Hill, *The World Turned Upside Down* (London: Penguin Books, 1975), p. 53.

12. Hobsbawm, *Age of Revolution*, p. 188.

13. E.P. Thompson, *The Making of the English Working Class* (London: Penguin Books, 1991), pp. 217 and 237.

14. Report of the Ministry of Rural Development (Delhi: MoRD, GoI, 2009), p. vii.

15. Shankar Gopalakrishnan, 'Negative Aspects of Special Economic Zones in China', *EPW*, 28 April 2007.

16. The SEZ Act 2005, *The Gazette of India* (New Delhi: Ministry of Law and Justice), 23 June 2005, http://sezindia.nic.in/writereaddata/pdf/SEZ%20Act,%202005.pdf.

17. Press Information Bureau, Press Release, 1 April 2000, http://pib.nic.in/archieve/eximpol/eximpol00-01/eximpolrl1.html.

18. 'Chinese Success Story Chokes on Its Own Growth', *The New York Times*, 19 December 2006.

19. The interested reader can see Weiping Wu, 'Proximity and Complementarity in Hong Kong—Shenzhen Industrialization', *Asian*

Survey, 1997, Vol. 37, No. 8; Ashok Upadhyay, 'SEZ Idea Must Be Revisited', *The Hindu Business Line*, 4 October 2006; 'Shenzhen Becomes "World's Factory"', *China People's Daily*, 19 February 2002; 'S China's Shenzhen Leads Nation in External Trade', *China News*, 19 January 2007; 'Mao's Promised Land Ends in Sweated Labor', *The Guardian*, 9 May 2004; 'Chinese Success Story Chokes'; Gopalakrishnan, 'Negative Aspects'; and *Corporate Hijack of Land* (New Delhi: Navdanya, 2007).

20. T.K. Rajalakshmi, 'Sita and Her Daughters', article reproduced by *Third World Network*, http://www.twnside.org.sg/title/sita-cn.htm; Sunanda Sen and Byasdeb Dasgupta, *Unfreedom and Waged Work* (New Delhi: Sage, 2009), Chapters 3 and 4; and Sunanda Sen and Byasdeb Dasgupta, 'SEZs: Modern Enclaves to Reward Capital by Exploiting Labour and Displacing Livelihoods in the Agrarian Economy', *Mainstream*, 4 May 2007.

21. 'New Factsheet on SEZs', Ministry of Commerce, GoI, available at http://sezindia.nic.in/writereaddata/updates/FACT%20sheet.pdf.

22. The information in this section is based on the SEZ Act 2005; also, on *A Citizens' Report Card on Special Economic Zones* (New Delhi: Intercultural Resources, 2010).

23. See Sampat Kale, *The Anti-SEZ Movement in India: An Account of the Struggle in Maharashtra* (Pune: NCAS, 2010). See also Citizens Research Collective, *SEZs and Land Acquisition: Factsheet for an Unconstitutional Economic Policy* (New Delhi, 2007), available at http://www.sacw.net/Nation/sezland_eng.pdf.

24. Aseem Shrivastava, '*Adjust Kar Lenge*: The New SEZ Policy?', *Infochange News & Features*, April 2007, http://infochangeindia.org/200704126056/Trade-Development/Analysis/Adjust-kar-lenge-The-new-SEZ-policy.html.

25. Aseem Shrivastava, 'The Growing Revolt against Disposability', *Radical Notes*, 3 May 2007, http://radicalnotes.com/content/view/46/39/. The Orissa government used police and paramilitary to acquire land from farmers in Jagatsinghpur for the POSCO project; see 'Officials Close Ranks to Push POSCO Project', in *Hindustan Times*, 19 April 2007, http://www. hindustantimes.com/StoryPage/StoryPage.aspx?id=277e86bc-c624-4a05-80f7-75d8e6d08c85; 'Smaller SEZs, No Snatching of Land', *Hindustan Times*, 6 April

2007, http://www.hindustantimes.com/StoryPage/StoryPage.aspx?id
=fd91f26e-8e43-4ca7-bdf2-e1e830f40dd8.

26. Devinder Sharma and Bhaskar Goswami, 'The New Maharajahs of
India', *Countercurrents*, 17 December 2006, http://www.counter
currents.org/gl-sharma171206.htm; computed from government data
by Jaya Mehta, 'Globalisation and Crisis in Indian Agriculture', in
Ecological Democracy: Land, Water, Food, Environment and Agriculture
(New Delhi: Citizens' Global Platform India, 2005).

27. The calculation has been done using data available from FAO and
GoI's *Economic Survey*. All-India wheat yields in 2008–09 were
2890 kg per ha on average (including both dry and irrigated areas).
The desirable annual consumption of wheat per capita can be
calculated by using the FAO recommendation that 75 per cent of
daily calories come from consumption of cereals, with the daily
requirement being 2400 kcal. Again, using FAO data on the calorific
content of a kilo of wheat (3200 kcal per kilo), this works out to
562.5 grams a day or 205 kilos per capita per year. An area of 200,000
ha can produce 578,000,000 kilos of wheat, and is thus able to feed
2.8 million people. See *Economic Survey 2009–10* (New Delhi: GoI),
Chapter 8, http://indiabudget.nic.in/es2009-10/chapt2010/
chapter08.pdf; FAO data sources are 'Nutritional Requirements in
India', http://www.fao.org/docrep/x0172e/x0172e02.htm; and 'Food
Composition Tables', http://www.fao.org/docrep/w0073e/w0073e06
.htm#P5431_644864. The higher figure is computed under the
assumption that if, perchance, government policies were to be
redirected to focus on agriculture, with greater investment in irrigation
and dry-land farming, for instance, yields could approach Chinese
levels, which were 4590 kilos per ha in 2007–08, much higher than
India's (US Department of Agriculture data, http://www.pecad.fas
.usda.gov/wap_current.cfm#).

28. Data on sown area is from *Agricultural Statistics at a Glance* (New
Delhi: Ministry of Agriculture, 2004), http://agricoop.nic.in/
statatglance2004/AtGlance.pdf.

29. The SEZ Act 2005, Clause 2 (r), p. 3.

30. EIA Notification (New Delhi: Ministry of Environment and Forests,
GoI, 2006), http://www.ecacwb.org/editor_upload/files/Gazette%20
Excerpt.pdf.

31. Kanchi Kohli, 'Exempt, but Not Exempt', *India Together*, 31 August 2009, http://www.indiatogether.org/2009/aug/env-exempt.htm; M.S. Swaminathan et al., *Final Frontier: Agenda to Protect the Ecosystem and Habitat on India's Coast for Conservation and Livelihood Security*, Report of the Expert Committee on CMZ Notification constituted by the ministry of environment and forests, 16 July 2009, http://envfor.nic.in/mef/cmz_report.pdf; Manshi Asher and Patrik Oskarsson, 'Se(i)zing the Coast and the Countryside', *Seminar*, February 2008.

32. The information in this section is based on the report *Abandoned: Development and Displacement* (Delhi: The Perspectives Group, 2008).

33. Ibid., p. 88.

34. The information in this section has been drawn from the SEZ Act 2005, Chapter VI, p. 24 and 'The Battle Most Hard: SEZ Facts' (Pune: NCAS, 2006).

35. 'Government's Net Gain from SEZs Is Rs. 62,907 crores', *The Hindu Business Line*, 4 February 2010, http://www.thehindubusinessline.com/2010/02/04/stories/2010020452791500.htm.

36. Vinod Matthew, 'Infrastructure or SEZ Investment?', http://www.thehindubusinessline.com/2005/03/31/stories/2005033100380800.htm. The investment cost per job has been computed from data available from the ministry of commerce at http://sezindia.nic.in/writereaddata/updates/New%20Fact%20Sheet%20on%20SEZs%20as%2018.3.2010.pdf. Data on jobs is from the ministry of commerce, http://sezindia.nic.in/writereaddata/updates/FACT%20sheet.pdf.

37. The first two quotations in the paragraph are from investors quoted in Seminarist, 'Betting on Growth', *Seminar*, February 2008. The last quote in the paragraph is from an investor quoted in Piya Singh, 'The Great Indian Land Rush', *Businessworld*, http://www.businessworld.in/index.php/The-Great-Indian-Land-Rush.html.

38. Yasser Pitalwalla, 'Indian Real Estate: Boom or Bubble?', http://money.cnn.com/magazines/fortune/fortune_archive/2006/07/10/8380919/index.htm.

39. 'Mahesh Langa, 'The Gujarat Government Doesn't Care', *Tehelka*, 6 August 2005, http://www.tehelka.com/story_main13.asp?filename=ts080605The_Gujarat.asp; Asher and Oskarsson, 'Se(i)zing

the Coast'; Sreelatha Menon, 'Kalinga Cries and Whispers', *Business Standard*, 28 March 2010; and *Corporate Hijack of Land*, pp. 64–67.

40. Quoted in *Analytical Monthly Review*, September 2006, http://mrzine.monthlyreview.org/amr210906.html; ASSOCHAM Report, *Study on Future of Real Estate Investment in India*, New Delhi, 2007, http://www.domain-b.com/industry/associations/assocham/20061120_estate.html.

41. Gopal Modi, 'Adani IPO Collects Rs 60,000 crore; Public Issue Subscribed 21 Times', *DNA*, 1 August 2009, http://www.dnaindia.com/money/report_adani-ipo-collects-rs60000-cr-public-issue-subscribed-21-times_1278897.

42. 'Cash Cows', *The Economist*, 12 October 2006.

43. *Study on Future of Real Estate Investment*.

44. *Analytical Monthly Review*, September 2006, http://mrzine.monthly review.org/amr210906.html.

45. Headline in 'Times Property', a pull-out in *The Times of India*, 7 April 2007.

46. Seminarist, 'Betting on Growth'.

47. Ibid.

48. See the ministry of commerce description given here: http://india.gov.in/sectors/commerce/sezs.php. The notion of graduated sovereignty is developed by Aihwa Ong, in 'Graduated Sovereignty in South East Asia', *Theory, Culture and Society*, August 2000, Vol. 17.

49. 'Draft Law Gives SEZs Powers of a Local Body', ExpressIndia.com, http://www.expressindia.com/latest-news/draft-law-gives-sezs-powers-of-a-local-body/642302/.

50. Ibid.

51. The SEZ Act 2005, Clause 51, p. 34.

52. Much of the analysis presented here is based on Lalit Batra, 'Deconstructing the World-class City', *Seminar*, February 2008.

53. On the conditions laid down for JNNURM funds, vis-à-vis the ULCA, see 'Maharashtra Gets Warning from Centre on Repeal of ULCA', *Business Standard*, 11 September 2007.

54. Batra, 'Deconstructing the World-class City'.

55. This section is based on the discussion of HPEC in 'India's Runaway Growth: Distortion, Disarticulation, and Exclusion', *Aspects of Political*

Economy, No. 44–46 (April 2008), Research Unit in Political Economy (RUPE), pp. 98–100.

56. The quotation is cited in 'India's Runaway Growth', p. 100.

57. Mike Davis, *Planet of Slums* (New York: Verso, 2007), p. 19.

58. The phrase in quotation is from Mike Davis, 'Hausmann in the Tropics', World-Information.org, 7 August 2006, http://world -information.org/wio/readme/992003309/1154965269.

59. See Ong, 'Graduated Sovereignty'.

60. Quoted in Davis, 'Hausmann in the Tropics'.

61. The long quotation is from Erhard Berner, *Defending a Place in the City* (Manila: Ateneo de Manila University Press, 1997), in Davis, 'Hausmann in the Tropics'.

62. Tunde Agbola's phrase in Davis, 'Hausmann in the Tropics'.

63. Davis, 'Hausmann in the Tropics'.

64. Rajesh Kasturirangan, 'Keep Off the Grass', *Outlook*, 18 August 2008.

65. '3 killed in West UP's farmers' land protest', *Hindustan Times*, 16 August 2010, http://www.hindustantimes.com/3-killed-as -farmers-go-on-rampage-near-Aligarh/Article1-587270.aspx.

66. 'Biggest Grab of Tribal Lands after Columbus', *Mint*, 13 November 2009, http://www.livemint.com/2009/11/13230356/8216Biggest -land-grab-after.html.

67. Report of MoRD (2009), Chapter 4.

68. The account of Orissa's industrialization and its consequences is drawn from Aseem Shrivastava, 'Industrialization or Environmental Colonialism', *Infochange News & Features*, March 2007, http:// infochangeindia.org/200702276053/Trade-Development/Analysis/ Industrialisation-or-environmental-colonialism.html.

69. Shrivastava, 'Industrialization or Environmental Colonialism'; 'Stop POSCO Project, Centre Tells Orissa', *The Hindu*, 7 August 2010, http://www.hindu.com/2010/08/07/stories/201008076409 1200.htm.

70. Report of MoRD (2009), Chapter 4. Both this phrase and references to specific corporate houses were removed from the final report (http://www.dolr.nic.in/).

71. Gladson Dungdung, 'Breach of Land Laws in Jharkhand', *Infochange News & Features*, December 2008, http://infochangeindia.org/

200812267553/Livelihoods/Features/Breach-of-land-laws-in
-Jharkhand.html.

72. 'Public Hearings on Tipaimukh Project a Farce', *Down to Earth*,
31 December 2006. The term 'developmental terrorism' was first
used by the macroeconomist Amit Bhaduri. See 'Development or
Developmental Terrorism?', *Countercurrents*, 7 January 2007,
http://www.countercurrents.org/ind-bhaduri070107.htm.

73. Marie Marcel Thekaekara, 'Disquiet in Gudalur Valley', *Infochange
News & Features*, September 2007, http://infochangeindia.org/
200709146497/Agenda/Women-At-Work/Disquiet-in-Gudalur
-valley.html.

74. On state torture see, for example, this press release by the Asian Centre
for Human Rights, 13 April 2010: http://www.achrweb.org/press/
2010/IND08-2010.html. There are many other reports on this topic
by human rights groups. ,

75. Lyla Bavadam, 'Farmers' Victory', *Frontline*, 3 July 2009,
http://www.hinduonnet.com/fline/fl2613/stories/200907032613
11900.htm.

76. Letter No. 8-63/2007-FC, dated 5 August 2010, from the ministry
of environment and forests, GoI, to Principal Secretary, Government
of Orissa (http://moef.nic.in/downloads/public-information/
POSCO.pdf); MoEF/MoTA Committee on Forest Rights Act,
Report of Visit to Jagatsinghpur (site of proposed POSCO project),
Orissa, 23–24 July 2010, http://fracommittee.icfre.org/TripReports/
Orissa/POSCO%20visit %20report,%20final,%204.8.2010[1].pdf.

77. M.K. Gandhi, 'The Curse of Industrialism', *Young India*, 25 July
1929, available at http://bapu.wordpress.com/.

78. Devinder Sharma, 'Indian Villages for Sale', *Countercurrents*,
13 February 2006, http://www.countercurrents.org/gl-sharma130
206.htm.

79. E.F. Schumacher, *Small Is Beautiful* (London: Vintage, 1993),
p. 169.

80. All the quotations are from the version of the Tagore essay published
as 'City and Village' in S.K. Das (ed.), *The English Writings of
Rabindranath Tagore* (New Delhi: Sahitya Kala Akademi, 1999).

Chapter 8: Suicidal Myopia

1. Peter Dauvergne, *The Shadows of Consumption* (Cambridge: MIT Press, 2008).
2. Quoted in *The Guardian*, 29 November 2007.
3. 'Let Them Eat Pollution', *The Economist*, 8 February 1992, http://www.okcu.edu/economics/ASSIGN/JWILLNER/4013/2002Spring/LetThemEatPollution.PDF.
4. Ibid.
5. K. William Kapp, *The Social Costs of Private Enterprise* (Cambridge: Harvard University Press, 1950).
6. Friedrich Hayek, *The Fatal Conceit* (London: Routledge Press, 1988).
7. David Owen, Annals of Design, 'The Inventor's Dilemma,' *The New Yorker*, 17 May 2010, p. 42.
8. 'Current State & Trends Assessment', *Ecosystems and Human Well-Being*, Millennium Ecosystem Assessment, 2005, http://www.millenniumassessment.org/en/Condition.aspx.
9. Lionel Robbins, *Essay on the Nature and Significance of Economic Science* (London: Macmillan, 1932).
10. The discussion of Daly's work here is taken from his Feasta Lecture, 'Uneconomic Growth in Theory and in Fact', 26 April 1999, available at http://www.feasta.org/documents/feastareview/daly.htm.
11. Dauvergne, *Shadows of Consumption*, p. 228.
12. V.R. Krishna Iyer, 'Majesty of the Judiciary', *The Asian Age*, New Delhi, 17 February 2007.
13. George Soros, 'The Capitalist Threat', *The Atlantic Monthly*, February 1997, http://www.theatlantic.com/past/docs/issues/97feb/capital/capital.htm.
14. Wendell Berry, *Homo Economicus* (Berkeley: Counterpoint Press, 1987), p. 185.
15. Rabindranath Tagore, *Nationalism* (New Delhi: Rupa & Co., 1991), p. 93.
16. Quoted by Ramachandra Guha, 'A Father Betrayed', *The Guardian*, 14 August 2007, http://www.guardian.co.uk/world/2007/aug/14/india.features111.
17. Tagore, *Nationalism*, p. 71.

PART II: DAWN

Prologue II

1. Monty Python star, Michael Palin, who has been active on the Niyamgiri issue, said this in 'Vedanata Mine Halted by Indian Government', *The Guardian*, 24 August 2010, http://www.guardian.co.uk/business/2010/aug/24/vedanta-mine-plan-halted-indian-government.
2. Wendell Berry, *Another Turn of the Crank* (Washington DC: Counterpoint, 1995), p. 13.
3. Dehradun Declaration of forest people, World Rainforest Movement, http://www.wrm.org.uy/bulletin/144/India.html.
4. Quoted in Christian Comeliau, *The Impasse of Modernity* (London: Zed Books, 2002), p. 163.
5. Sikaka Lodu, a Dongria Kondh, says this in a 2008 film, *Mine*, on Niyamgiri, made by Survival International, http://indigenouspeoples issues.com/index.php?option=com_content&view=article&id=412:mine-story-of-a-sacred-mountain&catid=68:videos-and-movies&Itemid=96.
6. See, for instance, the work of Helena Norberg-Hodge: *Ancient Futures: Learning from Ladakh* (New Delhi: Oxford University Press, 1991).

Chapter 9: Stories from Tomorrow

1. Interview with Rangasamy Elango, *India Together*, August 2002, http://www.indiatogether.org/govt/local/interviews/elango.htm.
2. DDS, www.ddsindia.com; A. Kumbamu, 'Subaltern Strategies and Autonomous Community Building: A Critical Analysis of the Network Organization of Sustainable Agriculture Initiatives in Andhra Pradesh', *Community Development Journal*, Vol. 44, No. 3, July 2009, pp. 336–50, http://www.ddsindia.com/www/pdf/Buildingsocial.pdf.
3. Lappe calls this 'thin democracy', characterized by inequities of various kinds, including concentration of economic power. In this, democratic opportunities are predominantly restricted to elections and supposed choice in the market. Many countries today, including India, can perhaps be classified as 'thin' democracies slowly moving towards

more radical forms, as citizens become increasingly organized and vocal, winning the right to participate in decision-making of various kinds. F.M. Lappe, 'The Promise of Living Democracy', in H. Girardet (ed.), *Surviving the Century: Facing Climate Chaos and Other Global Challenges* (London: World Future Council and Earthscan, 2007).

4.   For elaborate expositions of more participatory forms of democracy, see the concept of 'radical democracy' in M. Markovic, 'Radical Democracy', in L.H. Legters, J.P. Burke and A. DiQuattro (eds), *Critical Perspectives in Democracy* (Lanham MD: Rowman and Littlefield, 1994), pp. 131–45; and 'associative democracy' in P. Hirst, *Associative Democracy: New Forms of Economic and Social Governance* (Amherst: University of Massachusetts Press, 1994), cited in Roy Morrison, *Ecological Democracy* (Boston: South End Press, 1995). For glimpses into ancient Indian democratic or republic-like practices, see S. Muhlberger, 'Democracy in Ancient India', World History of Democracy site, 1998, http://www.nipissingu.ca/department/history/muhlberger/histdem/indiadem.htm (accessed 5 October 2009); on clan assemblies, village assemblies, and gana-sanghas, see R. Thapar, *Early India: From the Origins to AD 1300* (Berkeley: University of California Press, 2002). The environmental angle to radical democracy has been brought out by many, including by Morrison in *Ecological Democracy*; R.E. Mitchell in 'Building an Empirical Case for Ecological Democracy', *Nature and Culture*, Vol. 1, No. 2, Autumn 2006, pp. 149–56; and Lappe, 'The Promise of Living Democracy'. An earlier and shorter exposition of RED occurs in A. Kothari, 'Radical Ecological Democracy: Escaping India's Globalization Trap', *Development*, Vol. 52, No. 3, September 2009, pp. 401–09.

5.   Jamuna Rangachari, 'Community–Village Governance: The Only Way Forward', *LifePositive*, http://www.lifepositive.com/Mind/Community/Village_Governance_The_Only_Way_Forward32009.asp; 'Ethical Economics, Endless Enthusiasm', *India Together*, http://www.indiatogether.org/govt/local/interviews/elango.htm, August 2002; and 'The Importance of Rangasamy Elango', *GoodNewsIndia*, www.goodnewsindia.com/index.php/Magazine/story/elango-kuthambakkam/.

6.   Pani Panchayat, http://panipanchayat.org/.

7. S. Paranjape and K.J. Joy, *The Ozar Water User Societies: Impact of Society Formation and Co-management of Surface Water and Groundwater* (Pune: SOPPECOM), http://www.soppecom.org/pdf/DownloadablePapers/OzarStudyReport.pdf.

8. Hunnarshaala Foundation, www.hunnar.org.

9. J. Mingle, 'Rewriting the Books in Ladakh', *Cultural Survival Quarterly*, No. 27.4, 15 December 2003.

10. *Securing India's Future: Final Technical Report of the National Biodiversity Strategy and Action Plan Process* (Pune/Delhi: NBSAP Technical and Policy Core Group [TPCG] and Kalpavriksh, 2005); and T. Apte, *An Activist Approach to Biodiversity Planning: A Handbook of Participatory Tools Used to Prepare India's National Biodiversity Strategy and Action Plan* (London: International Institute of Environment and Development, 2005).

11. N. Pathak (ed), *Community Conserved Areas in India: A Directory* (Pune/Delhi: Kalpavriksh, 2009); and 'Community Conserved Areas', Kalpavriksh, http://www.kalpavriksh.org/community-conserved-areas.

12. On this, see an incisive essay by M. Sharma, 'Passages from Nature to Nationalism: Sunderlal Bahuguna and Tehri Dam Opposition in Garhwal', *Economic and Political Weekly (EPW)*, Vol. 44, 21–27 February 2009, http://epw.in/epw/user/viewAbstract.jsp.

13. A. Agarwal and S. Narain, *Dying Wisdom: Rise, Fall and Potential of India's Traditional Water Harvesting Systems*, 4th State of India's Environment Report (Delhi: Centre for Science and Environment, 1997); *Towards Sustainability: Learnings from the Past, Innovating for the Future: Stories from India* (Ahmedabad: Centre for Environment Education and Ministry of Environment and Forests, GoI, 2002); P.V. Satheesh, *Crops of Truth: Farmers' Perception of the Agrobiodiversity in the Deccan Region of South India* (Hyderabad: Deccan Development Society, 2002); and Pathak, *Community Conserved Areas*. For several dozen case studies, see Planning Commission reports, http://planningcommission.nic.in/reports/sereport/ser/seeds/stdy_seed.htm; see also *Down to Earth* Special Issue 'Good News', at http://www.downtoearth.org.in/default20090115.htm.

14. Decentralization has so far had very mixed results in India. Widespread bureaucratic resistance, local power play and lack of capacity among

communities to handle decentralized functions have undermined implementation across much of the country. But in many states, organized communities, civil society groups and sensitive officials have also managed to utilize localization for people's benefit. For a detailed review see various essays in N.G. Jayal, A. Prakash, and P.K. Sharma (eds), *Local Governance in India: Decentralisation and Beyond* (New Delhi: Oxford University Press, 2006). For more on Nagaland's initiatives, see 'The Communitisation in Nagaland', *NENA*, Vol. 3, No. 28, http://www.nenanews.com/ANE%20June %201-15,%2007/special%20report1.htm.

15. C.B. Prasad, 'Markets and Manu: Economic Reforms and Its Impact on Caste in India', CASI Working Paper Series No. 08-01, Philadelphia: Center for the Advanced Study of India, University of Pennsylvania, 2008.

16. For a useful account of how Gandhi, Nehru and Ambedkar viewed the village, see S.S. Jodhka, 'Nation and Village: Images of Rural India in Gandhi, Nehru and Ambedkar', *EPW*, 10 August 2002, pp. 3343–53.

17. See for instance, C. Hines, *Localization: A Global Manifesto* (London: Earthscan, and Slow Food, 2000), http://www.slowfood.com/.

18. Virginia Institute of Marine Science, http://www.vims.edu/features/ people/geisz_h.php.

19. T. Sandwith, C. Shine, L. Hamilton and D. Sheppard, *Transboundary Protected Areas for Peace and Co-operation*, World Protected Areas Commission Best Practice Guidelines Series No. 7 (Gland, Switzerland and Cambridge, UK: IUCN, 2001); A. Phillips, *Management Guidelines for IUCN Category V Protected Areas: Protected Landscapes/ Seascapes* (Gland, Switzerland and Cambridge, UK: IUCN, 2002); Global Transboundary Conservation Network, http://www.tbpa.net/; and 'Protected Landscapes Task Force', International Union for Conservation of Nature, http://www.iucn.org/about/union/ commissions/wcpa/wcpa_what/wcpa_science/wcpa_protectedland scapes/.

20. S.M. Hasnat, 'Arvari Sansad: The Farmers' Parliament', *LEISA India*, December 2005, pp. 16–17, http://india.leisa.info/index.php?url =getblob.php&o_id=82240&a_id=211&a_seq=0; and 'Arvari Sansad (Parliament): The Voice of Common People', Tarun Bharat Sangh,

       http://www.tarunbharatsangh.org/programs/water/arvariparliament
.htm (accessed 1 June 2009).

21.   Chilika Development Authority, www.chilika.com; A. Kothari and
N. Pathak, *Protected Areas, Community Based Conservation, and
Decentralization: Lessons from India*, a report prepared for the
Ecosystems, Protected Areas and People (EPP) Project of the IUCN
World Commission on Protected Areas (through the IUCN Regional
Protected Areas Programme, Asia), 2006; A. Malaviya, 'Fighting for
Chilika', *Infochange News and Features*, January 2009, http://
infochangeindia.org/200901057559/Livelihoods/Changemaker/
Fighting-for-Chilika.html; and R. Satapathy, 'Hunters, Prawn Gheries
Threaten Chilika's Winter Guests', *The Times of India*, Bhubaneshwar,
16 January 2010.

22.   Tarun Bharat Sangh, www.tarunbharatsangh.org; Hasnat, 'Arvari
Sansad', pp. 16–17; Tarun Bharat Sangh, *Arvari Catchment, A Sub-
State Site In Rajasthan: Biodiversity Strategy And Action Plan*,
coordinated by O.P. Kulhari, prepared for National Biodiversity
Strategy and Action Plan process, Ministry of Environment and
Forests, 2003, in *Securing India's Future*; 'Arvari Sansad' (Parliament)',
Tarun Bharat Sangh; and discussions with Tarun Bharat Sangh and
Arvari Sansad members.

23.   FAO, *Overview of Socio-Economic Situation of the Tribal Communities
and Livelihoods in Madhya Pradesh and Bihar*, a Socio-economic and
Production Systems Study – 1998, FAO Investment Centre Studies
and Reports, India: Bihar–Madhya Pradesh Tribal Development
Programme.

24.   *Securing India's Future.*

25.   R.J. Ranjit Daniel, *Western Ghats Ecoregion*, prepared for the National
Biodiversity Strategy and Action Plan process, MoEF, 2003, in
Securing India's Future (subsequently adapted into R.J. Ranjit Daniel
and J. Vencatesan, *Western Ghats: Biodiversity, People, Conservation*
[Delhi: Rupa & Co., 2008]).

26.   Planning Commission, *Eleventh Five-Year Plan 2007–12*, Vol. 1:
Inclusive Growth (Delhi: Oxford University Press, 2008).

27.   Press Release, MoEF, 8 July 2010, http://moef.nic.in/downloads/
public -information/prima-facie.pdf; N. Thakur, 'No-Go Area Rules
Altered; Move to Help Coal India IPO', *DNA*, 9 July 2010.

28. R. Tagore, 'City and Village (*Palli-prakriti*)', in *Towards Universal Man* (London: Asia Publishing House, 1961), http://www.homeand localfood.org.uk/tagorecityandvillage.htm.

29. G. Pangare and V. Pangare, *From Poverty to Plenty: The Story of Ralegan Siddhi* (Delhi: INTACH, 1992); N. Sakhuja, 'A Village with 54 Millionaires', *Down to Earth*, 31 January 2008; B. Mishra, 'A Successful Case of Participatory Watershed Management at Ralegan Siddhi Village in Ahmadnagar, Maharashtra, India', FAO Corporate Document Repository, http://www.fao.org/docrep/x5669e/ x5669e06.htm; N. Anand, 'Hivare Bazaar: Community Stewardship of Water Resources', in Planning Commission and Lokayan, *Seeds of Hope*, http://planningcommission.nic.in/reports/sereport/ser/seeds/ seed_watr.pdf; Tarun Bharat Sangh, www.tarunbharatsangh.org; and Samaj Pragati Sahayog, www.samprag.org.

30. Markovic, 'Radical Democracy', pp. 134–38.

31. Sarva Seva Sangh Prakashan, *A New Social Order: The Gandhian Alternative* (Varanasi, 1991), pp. 30–35.

32. Morrison, *Ecological Democracy*, pp. 13–14 and 174.

33. Elinor Ostrom, *Governing the Commons: The Evolution of Institutions for Collective Action* (New York: Cambridge University Press, 1990); E. Ostrom, 'The Rudiments of a Theory of the Origins, Survival, and Performance of Common-Property Institutions', in D.W. Bromley (ed.), *Making the Commons Work: Theory, Practice and Policy* (San Francisco: ICS Press, 1992).

34. *Securing India's Future*.

35. N. Pathak and V. Gour-Broome, *Tribal Self-Rule and Natural Resource Management: Community Based Conservation at Mendha-Lekha, Maharashtra, India* (Pune/Delhi: Kalpavriksh and International Institute of Environment and Development, 2001); N. Pathak and E. Taraporewala, *Towards Self-Rule and Forest Conservation in Mendha-Lekha Village, Gadchiroli, India*, report of a consultation for an ICCA Consortium and IUCN TILCEPA-TGER project sponsored by GTZ (Pune/Delhi: Kalpavriksh, 2008), http://www.iccaforum.org/images/ media/grd/mendha_india_report_icca_grassroots_discussions.pdf; Vivek Deshpande, 'Gadchiroli Villages Get Rights to Forests', *The Indian Express*, 16 December 2009, http://www.indianexpress.com/ news/gadchiroli-villages-get-rights-to-forests/554714/.

36. H. Thakkar, 'The Zero Success of the State in River Basin Management in India' *Dams, Rivers & People*, Vol. 6, No. 12 and Vol. 7, No. 1–2, January –March 2009, http://www.sandrp.in/drp/Jan_March_2009.pdf.

37. We recognize that the terms 'traditional' and 'local' have limitations, but use them here to encompass the range of knowledge systems that are generated and continue to be evolved by indigenous peoples and other local communities.

38. ICSU, *Science and Traditional Knowledge*, report from the ICSU study group, International Council of Science, 2002, http://www.icsu.org/publications/reports-and-reviews/science-traditional-knowledge/Science-traditional-knowledge.pdf; WHO, IUCN, and WWF (World Wildlife Fund), *Guidelines on the Conservation of Medicinal Plants* (Gland, Switzerland: IUCN, 1993); 'Traditional Medicine', WHO Media Centre, December 2008, www.who.int/mediacentre/factsheets/fs134/en/.

39. M. Musake, 'The Challenge and Opportunities of Information and Communication Technologies in the Health Sector', paper prepared for the African Development Forum 1999, Makerere University, Kampala, cited in N. Gorjestani, 'Indigenous Knowledge for Development: Opportunities and Challenges', in S. Twarog and P. Kapoor (eds), *Protecting and Promoting Traditional Knowledge: Systems, National Experiences and International Dimensions*, Document No. UNCTAD/DITC/TED/10 (Geneva: United Nations Conference on Trade and Development, 2004).

40. ACIA, *Impacts of a Warming Arctic: Arctic Climate Impact Assessment* (Cambridge: Cambridge University Press, 2004), www.acia.uaf.edu.

41. 'Indigenous Peoples' Climate Change Assessment', United Nations University, http://www.unutki.org/default.php?doc_id=96.

42. 'Pachasaale—The Green School', DDS, http://www.ddsindia.com/www/psaale.htm; personal communication with Suresh Kumar Challa, DDS, December 2009; and http://www.ddsindia.com/www/Education.htm.

43. 'Narmada Jeevan Shalas: Reconstruction through Tribal Education', Friends of River Narmada, http://www.narmada.org/ALTERNATIVES/jeevanshalas. html; and 'Three Day BAL MELA of Thousands of Children Culminates in the Narmada Valley', Friends

of River Narmada, 17 February 2009, http://www.narmada.org/nba-press-releases/february-2009/17Feb.html.

44. Adharshila Learning Centre, http://adharshilask.tripod.com/aboutadh.html.

45. Adivasi Academy, http://www.Adivasiacademy.org.in.

46. Mahatma Gandhi National Rural Employment Guarantee Act 2005, http://nrega.nic.in.

47. Jawaharlal Nehru National Urban Renewal Mission, http://jnnurm.nic.in/.

48. Decent work is defined by the International Labour Organization (ILO) as opportunities for women and men to obtain dignified and productive work in conditions of freedom, equity, security and human dignity, http://www.ilo.org/global/About_the_ILO/Mainpillars/WhatisDecentWork/index.htm.

49. United Nations Environment Programme, International Labour Organization, International Union of Employers and International Trade Union Confederation, *Green Jobs: Towards Decent Work in a Sustainable, Low-Carbon World* (Nairobi: UNEP, 2008), www.unep.org/civil_society/Publications/index.asp, pp. 11–12.

50. Andhra Pradesh State Policy on Organic Farming, Government of Andhra Pradesh, http://www.indiaenvironmentportal.org.in/content/andhra-pradesh-state-policy-organic-farming.

51. *Green Jobs*, p. 5.

52. Ibid., p. 8.

53. S. Paranjape, K.J. Joy and S. Kulkarni, 'K.R. Datye: Visionary of a Sustainable and Equitable Future', *EPW*, Vol. XLIV, No. 39, 2009, pp. 8–12; and K.R. Datye, *Banking on Biomass: A New Strategy for Sustainable Prosperity Based on Renewable Energy and Dispersed Industrialization* (Ahmedabad: Centre for Environment Education, 1997).

54. Green Foundation, http://www.greenconserve.com/.

55. 'Jaiv Panchayat', Navdanya, http://www.navdanya.org/campaigns/jaiv-panchayat/.

56. Wassan, http://www.wassan.org/; Centre for Sustainable Agriculture, http://www.csa-india.org/; Community Managed Sustainable Agriculture, http://www.serp.ap.gov.in/CMSA; draft of Andhra

Pradesh Organic Farming Policy, http://el.doccentre.info/eldoc1/k33_/KICS1_080505zzz1B.pdf; and T. Vijay Kumar, D.V. Raidu, J. Killi, M. Pillai, P. Shah, V. Kalavadonda and S. Lakhey, *Ecologically Sound, Economically Viable: Community Managed Sustainable Agriculture in Andhra Pradesh, India* (Washington DC: The World Bank, 2009).

57. 'Organic Farming Policy Announced', *The Hindu*, 18 May 2010, http://www.thehindu.com/2010/05/18/stories/2010051853630400.htm; K.S. Yangzom, 'Sikkim "Livelihood Schools" to Promote Organic Farming', *The Hindu Business Line*, 7 August 2010; and Report of the Committee for Evaluation of Decentralised Planning and Development, Government of Kerala, 2009, http://www.lsg.kerala.gov.in/htm/PDF/report_decentralised_planning.pdf.

58. Adapted from D. Sharma, 'Reviving Agriculture', *Seminar* 595, March 2009; and A. Kothari, 'Agro-biodiversity: The Future of India's Agriculture', in G.M. Pillai, *Challenges of Agriculture in the 21st Century* (Pune: Maharashtra Council of Agricultural Education and Research, 1999). See also, memorandum of Agri-Vision Coalition of several dozen civil society organizations to the prime minister of India, on 'Holistic Ecological Agriculture Agenda for India's Eleventh Plan and the National Development Council Meeting on Agriculture', 28 May 2007, http://www.petitiononline.com/agvision/petition.html.

59. See Participatory Guarantee System India, http://www.pgsorganic.in/.

60. S. Menon, 'Participatory Budgeting', Decade of Education for Sustainable Development, 2009, http://www.desd.org/efc/Participatory%20Budgeting.htm.

61. Janaagraha, www.janaagraha.org; A. Rao, 'Janaagraha: Harnessing the Force of the People', *Infochange*, January 2006, http://infochangeindia.org/200601276557/Other/Changemaker/Janaagraha-Harnessing-the-force-of-the-people.html.

62. Sustainable Transport Award, Institute for Transportation & Development Policy, www.st-award.org; A. Baviskar, 'Winning the Right to Information in India: Is Knowledge Power?', in John Gaventa and R. McGee, *Citizen Action and National Policy: Making Change Happen* (London/New York: Zed Books, 2010), pp. 129–51.

63. H. Girardet, 'Creating Sustainable and Liveable Cities', in H. Girardet (ed.), *Surviving the Century: Facing Climate Chaos and Other Global Challenges* (London: World Future Council and Earthscan, 2007).

64. R. Deshmukh, A. Gambhir and G. Sant, 'Need to Realign India's National Solar Mission', *EPW*, Vol. XLV, No. 12, 20 March 2010, pp. 41–50.

65. *Access to Sustainable Energy Services via Innovative Financing: 7 Case Studies* (Bengaluru: SELCO); personal communication with H. Harish Hande, SELCO, June 2010; and P. Bidwai, *An India That Can Say Yes: A Climate-Responsible Development Agenda for Copenhagen and Beyond* (Delhi: Heinrich Böll Stiftung, 2009).

66. Karunakaran, 'Light from Small Power', *Outlook Business*, 20 October 2007, http://business.outlookindia.com/printarticle.aspx?100275; personal communication with authors.

67. Karunakaran, 'Light from Small Power'.

68. Ibid. NTPC: National Thermal Power Corporation.

69. J.C. Kumarappa, *Gandhian Economic Thought* (Varanasi: Sarva Seva Sangh Prakashan, 1962).

70. Social Enterprise London, www.sel.org.uk.

71. N. Johanisova, *Living in the Cracks: A Look at Rural Social Enterprises in Britain and the Czech Republic* (Dublin: Foundation for the Economics of Sustainability, 2005); L. Cox and C. Mullan, 'Social Movements Never Died: Community Politics and the Social Economy in the Irish Republic', in International Sociological Association/British Sociological Association special movements conference, November 2001, Manchester, http://eprints.nuim.ie/1529/1/LCSocial_movements_never_died.pdf; and website of the Social Economy Student Network, http://socialeconomy.info/en/overview.

72. T. Cohen-Mitchell, 'Community Currencies at a Crossroads: New Ways Forward', *New Village*, Issue 2: Community Scale Economics, 2005, http://www.newvillage.net/journal/issue2/2commcurrencies.html (accessed 28 September 2009); R. Bakshi, *Bazaars, Conversations and Freedom: For a Market Culture beyond Greed and Fear* (Delhi: Penguin, 2009); see also, *International Journal of Complementary Currency Systems* at http://www.uea.ac.uk/env/ijccr/index.html.

73. Stephen DeMeulenaere, '2007 Yearly Report of the Worldwide Database of Complementary Currency Systems', *International Journal*

of Currency Community Research, Vol. 12, No. 1, 2008, pp. 2–19, http://www.ijccr.net/IJCCR/IJCCR_Home.html.

74. Bakshi, *Bazaars, Conversations and Freedom*.

75. See Fairtrade International, http://www.fairtrade.net/, for activities globally, and Fair Trade Forum India, http://www.fairtradeforum.org/, for some activities in India.

76. H. Siganporia, 'The Green World Order', *Tehelka*, Vol. 6, Issue 25, 25 June 2009, www.tehelka.com/story_main42.asp?filename=cr270609the_green.asp; Bhasha, http://www.bhasharesearch.org/Site.html; and personal observations of one of the authors, November 2009.

77. Avani Mohan Singh, NAPCL Board, personal communication, 2009.

78. 'Enhancing sustainable livelihoods – in a different way – Report to investors', Dharani FaM Cooperative Ltd and The Timbaktu Collective, CK Palli Village, Anantpur, 2010, Andhra Pradesh, http://www.timbaktu-organic.org/aboutdharani.html; and Participatory Guarantee System India, http://www.pgsorganic.in/.

79. U. Ghate, *Prosumer Model and 'Glocalisation' in Tamil Nadu and Orissa* (Durg, Chhattisgarh: Covenant Centre for Development, 2009 unpublished).

80. Ravindranath, 'Amar Bazaar', unpublished note, Akajan, Assam: Rural Volunteers Centre, 2010.

81. *Social Science: Social and Political Life II*, textbook for class VII (NCERT, 2007), pp. 116–19, http://www.ncert.nic.in; S. Kumar, 'Tawa Matsya Sangh, Fishing Co-operative in Madhya Pradesh, Loses Licence', *Down to Earth*, Vol. 15, No. 20, 15 March 2007, http://www.downtoearth.org.in/full6.asp?foldername=20070315&filename=news&sid=6&page=1&sec_id=4; and Sunil, Kisan Adivasi Sangathan, personal communication, 14 April 2010.

82. Morrison, *Ecological Democracy*, pp. 195–97.

83. 'Buoyed Jharcraft to Spread Wings', *The Telegraph*, 30 January 2010; and personal communication with Dhirendra Kumar, handloom commissioner in Ranchi, May 2009.

84. 'Study of Industries in Auroville', available at http://www.auroville.org/economy/Study%20of%20Industries%20in%20Auroville.pdf.

85. Kumarappa, *Gandhian Economic Thought*.

86. Morrison, *Ecological Democracy*, p. 219.

87. Report of the Committee for Evaluation of Decentralised Planning and Development, http://www.lsg.kerala.gov.in/htm/PDF/ report_decentralised_planning.pdf; G. Sebastian, 'Kerala People's Plan Revisited', *Mainstream*, Vol. XLVI, No. 12, 2008, http://www .mainstreamweekly.net/article568.html; R.M. Thomas, 'Kerala's Silent Revolution', *Countercurrents*, 18 March 2005, http://www .countercurrents.org/eco-thomas180305.htm; and Local Self Government Department, Government of Kerala, http://www .lsg.kerala.gov.in/htm/main.php.

88. See, for instance, the excellent compilation of articles in Girardet, *Surviving the Century*, especially those by Lappe, Wallis and Girardet. See also, the special issue on 'Beyond Economics' of the journal *Development*, Vol. 52, No. 3, September 2009; and the section on 'civilizing globalization' in *National Accounts of Well-being: Bringing Real Wealth onto the Balance Sheet* (London: New Economics Foundation, 2009), www.nationalaccountsofwellbeing.org. Other relevant writings are Bakshi, *Bazaars, Conversations and Freedom* and J. Mander and E. Goldsmith (eds), *The Case Against the Global Economy* (San Francisco: Sierra Club Books, 1996).

89. Note that we are here using the dominant Indian names for these areas, with apologies to our neighbouring countries and to peoples within India who may have other names.

Chapter 10: Venturing into 'Newhere'

1. Cited in Corinne Kumar (ed.), *Asking, We Walk: The South as Political Imaginary* (Bengaluru: Streelekha Publications, 2007).

2. Lyla Bavadam, 'Farmers' Victory', *Frontline*, 3 July 2009, http://www.hinduonnet.com/fline/fl2613/stories/2009070326 1311900.htm.

3. These examples are from various references cited in this and other chapters; additionally, 'DuPont (E.I. Dupont De Nemours And Company): A Corporate Profile', Corporate Watch, 2002, http:// www.corporatewatch.org/?lid=205 (accessed 8 April 2010).

4. See a case study of advanced locality management groups and the NGO Council in Mumbai, in B. Singh and D. Parthasarathy, 'Civil Society Organisation Partnerships in Urban Governance: An Appraisal

of the Mumbai Experience', *Sociological Bulletin*, Vol. 59, No. 1, January–April 2010, pp. 92–110.

5. SPS profile, Sir Dorabji Tata Trust and Other Allied Trusts, www.dorabjitatatrust.org/NGO_profiles/pdf/18%20SPS.pdf; Samaj Pragati Sahayog, www.samprag.org; V. Chhotray, 'How *Samaj Pragati Sahayog* Works the State and Why It Succeeds', School of Development Studies, University of East Anglia, Norwich, www.uea.ac.uk/polopoly_fs/1.54220!how%20samaj%20pragati%20sahyog%20works%20the%20state.pdf.

6. See United Nations Treaty Collection, http://treaties.un.org; United Nations Declaration on the Rights of Indigenous Peoples, http://www.un.org/esa/socdev/unpfii/en/declaration.html; and the Universal Declaration of Human Rights, http://www.un.org/en/documents/udhr/index.shtml.

7. S. Kidambi, 'Mazdoor Kisan Shakti Sangathan: Championing the Right to Information in Rural India', *SAMAR* (*South Asia Magazine for Action and Reflection*), No. 16, www.samarmagazine.org/archive/article.php?id=128; A. Baviskar, 'Winning the Right to Information in India: Is Knowledge Power?', in John Gaventa and R. McGee, *Citizen Action and National Policy: Making Change Happen* (London/New York: Zed Books, 2010), pp. 129 –51; Mazdoor Kisan Shakti Sangathan, http://www.mkssindia.org/; and 'Right to Information', *InfoChange News & Features*, http://infochangeindia.org/right-to-information/.

8. 'Tripura Move for Urban Poor', *The Telegraph*, 21 May 2009, http://www.telegraphindia.com/1090521/jsp/northeast/story_10995445.jsp.

9. Amit Bhaduri, 'The Imperative as Alternative', *Seminar*, February 2008.

10. Ibid.

11. *Agenda Unlimited*, collection of articles published in *Down to Earth* (New Delhi: Centre for Science and Environment, 2005), p. 270.

12. See the previous chapter; Jawaharlal Nehru National Solar Mission, 'Towards Building Solar India', http://mnre.gov.in/pdf/mission-document-JNNSM.pdf; *Still Waiting: A Report on Energy Injustice* (Bengaluru: Greenpeace India Society, 2009); and R. Deshmukh, A. Gambhir and G. Sant, 'Need to Realign India's National Solar

Mission', *Economic and Political Weekly* (*EPW*), Vol. XLV, No. 12, pp. 41–50, 20 March 2010.

13. P. Raskin, P. Banuri, G. Gallopin, P. Gutman, A. Hammond, R. Kates and R. Swart, *Great Transition: The Promise and Lure of the Times Ahead* (Boston: Stockholm Environment Institute, 2002), http://tellus.org/documents/Great_Transition.pdf.

14. M. Braungart, 'Cradle to Cradle Production', in H. Girardet (ed.), *Surviving the Century: Facing Climate Chaos and Other Global Challenges* (London: World Future Council and Earthscan, 2007).

15. 'Billions Beckon', *Entrepreneur*, Vol. 1, No. 1, September 2009.

16. R. Fisher, *Carbon Offsets and Climate Finance in India: The Corporate-driven Climate 'Solutions' of the World Bank, Asian Development Bank and United Nations*, Occasional Paper 7 (Bangkok: Focus on the Global South, 2010).

17. See the indicators used by the Department for Environment, Food and Rural Affairs, the United Kingdom, http://www.archive.defra.gov.uk/sustainable/government/progress/national/index.htm.

18. *National Accounts of Well-being: Bringing Real Wealth onto the Balance Sheet* (London: New Economics Foundation, 2009), www.national accountsofwellbeing.org; and Gross National Happiness, http://www.grossnationalhappiness.com/.

19. Raskin et al., *Great Transition*.

Chapter 11: Another India, Another World

1. John Maynard Keynes, 'National Self-sufficiency', *Yale Review*, Vol. 22, No. 4, 1933.

2. 'Plunder and Profit', *Frontline*, 16 July 2010, 'Blockade', *Down to Earth*, 16–31 July 2008.

3. Rabindranath Tagore, *Nationalism* (Delhi: Rupa & Co., 1991), p. 88.

4. Peter Dauvergne, *The Shadows of Consumption* (Cambridge: MIT Press, 2008).

5. See Amiya Bagchi, *Perilous Passage: Mankind and the Global Ascendancy of Capital* (New Delhi: Oxford University Press, 2005) and Deepak Nayyar, 'Globalization and Development', in Ha-Joon Chang (ed.), *Rethinking Development Economics* (London: Anthem Press, 2006).

6. 'Strikes in China Halt Toyota, Honda Factories', *USA Today*, 23 June 2010, http://www.usatoday.com/money/world/2010-06-23-honda-toyota-strikes_N.htm.

7. Pierre Bourdieu, *Firing Back* (New York: Verso, 2003), p. 43.

8. Rajni Bakshi, *Bazaars, Conversations and Freedom: For a Market Culture beyond Greed and Fear* (Delhi: Penguin, 2009).

9. Simone Weil, *Oppression and Liberty* (London: RKP, 1958), p. 76.

10. 'Many of India's Billionaires Have Made Money by Their Proximity to Govt', *The Times of India*, 31 July 2010, http://timesofindia.indiatimes.com/business/india-business/Many-of-Indias-billionaires-have-made-money-by-their-proximity-to-govt-/articleshow/6239385.cms.

11. Tagore, *Nationalism*, p. 94.

12. 'Only Two Percent of Indians Invest in Stocks', IBN Live, 22 October 2008, http://ibnlive.in.com/news/only-two-percent-of-indians-invest-in-stocks/76419-16.html.

13. Ibid.

14. 'Uneasy Calm in Lalgarh Villages after Killings', *Outlook*, 8 January 2011, http://news.outlookindia.com/items.aspx?artid=707681; and 'Two Killed in Police Firing in Srikakulam District', *The Hindu*, 15 July 2010, http://www.hindu.com/2010/07/15/stories/2010071556330100.htm.

15. Tagore, *Nationalism*, p. 83.

16. 'The Tragedy of Dying Languages', *BBC News*, 5 February 2010, http://news.bbc.co.uk/2/hi/in_depth/8500108.stm.

INDEX